DELICATE
DANCES

The Public Policy and the Third Sector Series

DELICATE DANCES

PUBLIC POLICY AND THE NONPROFIT SECTOR

Edited by
Kathy L. Brock

Published for the School of Policy Studies,
Queen's University
by McGill-Queen's University Press
Montreal & Kingston • London • Ithaca

National Library of Canada Cataloguing in Publication

Delicate dances : public policy and the nonprofit sector / edited by Kathy L. Brock.
(The public policy and the third sector series ; 4)
Includes some text in French.
Includes bibliographical references.
ISBN 0-88911-955-4 (bound).—ISBN 0-88911-953-8 (pbk.)

1. Nonprofit organizations—Government policy—Canada.
2. Nonprofit organizations—Canada. I. Brock, Kathy Lenore, 1958-
II. Queen's University (Kingston, Ont.). School of Policy Studies
III. Series: Public policy and the third sector series ; 4.

HD2769.2.C3D33 2003   361.7'63'0971   C2003-904827-6

Contents

vi / DELICATE DANCES

7. La liberté d'association : réalité juridique évanescente et
   contrainte
   Georges leBel   221

8. The Third Sector Meets the National Security State:
   The Anti-Globalization Movement in Canada after 9/11
   Ann Capling and Kim Richard Nossal   275

9. NGOs, Technology and the Changing Face of Trade Politics
   Elizabeth Smythe and Peter J. Smith   297

Contributors   341

Tables and Figures

Tables

Figures

Preface

This book is the fourth and final volume in the Public Policy and the Third Sector Series published by the School of Policy Studies and McGill-Queen's University Press. In the preface to the first volume in this series of books on the nonprofit sector in Canada, Keith Banting observed that "in comparison with the massive research efforts that have been devoted to the roles of the state and the market in Canadian life, we have only a partial understanding of the nature of the nonprofit sector, its capacities and limitations, the roles that it plays, and its relations with governments and private corporations." While our understanding remains partial, research on the nonprofit sector in Canada has grown exponentially and new researchers are entering the policy field on a regular basis.

The papers from both established and new academics in this volume strive to illuminate our appreciation of the nature and prospects of the Canadian nonprofit sector. In this endeavour, they capture the shifting character of the sector and its intricate dance with the Canadian state as nonprofit and voluntary organizations influence and implement policy in key areas of economic, social, and political life. The authors raise some important questions about the history, desirability, and extent of this activity.

The Public Policy and Third Sector series was made possible by the generous support of the Nonprofit Sector Research Initiative established by the Kahanoff Foundation to promote research and scholarship on nonprofit sector issues and to broaden the formal body of knowledge on the nonprofit sector. This support has stimulated new and exciting research into various facets of the nonprofit sector from a wide variety of disciplines. In the process, it has encouraged a cross-discipline dialogue to the benefit of all.

With financial support from the foundation, the School of Policy Studies at Queen's University sponsored a national research grants program. Applications for research funding were invited from researchers across the country, and a peer-review panel organized by the School awarded the grants. This book incorporates papers issuing from the fourth wave of funded projects. All of the papers were discussed in detail at a workshop administered by the School and were then subject to a final peer-review process before being included in this volume.

Given the competitive nature of the research grants program, the papers in this volume cover a diverse range of topics. No one theme governed the selection of successful research projects. However, in this volume the papers do speak to the common concern with governance and the relationship between the third sector and the state. By covering these issues from different points of interest and disciplinary lenses, they convey a sense of the complexity of the role and nature of the sector.

This book is the result of a collaborative undertaking that reflects the work of many people. First, I would like to acknowledge the encouraging support of Shira Herzog of the Kahanoff Foundation for this series of works. The firm commitment of the foundation to enhancing research on the nonprofit sector has stimulated new and important lines of research that will influence researchers for many years to come. I also appreciate the work of Michael Hall in his role as coordinator of the various components of the foundation's Nonprofit Sector Research Initiative.

The authors must be thanked for their enthusiasm, dedication to their projects, and their patience with all the demands of an extended editorial process. Rebecca Miller and Julie Birch were helpful in attending to the administrative minutiae of the project. The papers benefited from the constructive and perceptive comments offered by Gordon Floyd, David Good, Femida Handy, Luc Juillet, Tish O'Reilly, Alasdair Roberts and Robert Young. The consummate professionalism of Mark Howes, Valerie Jarus and colleagues in the Publications Unit of the School of Policy Studies was critical in transforming these papers into a book. The commitment of McGill-Queen's University Press to the *Queen's Policy Studies Series* has ensured a solid corpus of work on the nonprofit sector.

Finally, a special thank you must go to Keith Banting whose energy, drive and foresight underlie this series of works. Keith was the editor of the first volume and provided sage guidance and direction as co-editor of the second and third books. He remained an intelligent commentator and friendly counsellor on this volume. His support to me both as editor of this book and in my capacity as Head of the Public Policy and Third Sector Initiative has benefited many scholars, researchers, and students of the sector. His legacy in this area cannot be underestimated.

While the strengths of the book are the results of this cooperative and dedicated team, the remaining flaws are mine. Enjoy!

Kathy L. Brock

1

Delicate Dances: New Moves and Old Steps

Kathy L. Brock

Much has changed in the world of state and voluntary sector relations since this series of books commenced over four years ago. And yet, many refrains in the relationship seem to be playing over again, albeit with variations. The federal government and Voluntary Sector Initiative (VSI) designed to redefine their relationship has largely wrapped up with the VSI morphing into a new structure. And yet the issues of regulatory reform including financing and advocacy, awareness, and capacity linger on. The Banff research initiative has progressed through two structures and is now struggling with issues first raised in Banff as the initiative expanded to include new people. Research on the voluntary and nonprofit sector has significantly increased through the national surveys and through the writings of academic and sector researchers, but knowledge on the sector remains limited with large gaps. Strong ties and working relationships have been forged, both within the sector and across government, third sector, and academic communities; but changes in leadership in the sector and government mean relationships and ties must be forged anew. Coalitions and alliances are forming at the national, provincial, and local levels but much is still to be done to strengthen government and sector relations. As this series of books draws to a close, the voluntary sector is fighting to keep itself on the federal government dance card and to ensure that it is on the cards of other governments.

The chapters in this book deal largely with the relationship between the state and the sector, capturing both the new and old tensions as they survey the relationship from various perspectives and points in time. It is useful to introduce the chapters through a review of the current state of the relationship between the state and sector in real time and in research, and then to offer a brief summary of each chapter and its contribution to our knowledge of the state and sector.

THE VSI: ACHIEVEMENTS, CONTINUING WORRIES, NEW STRUCTURES, FUTURE PROMISE

As a reminder, the VSI was born out of the Joint Tables Report which was a cooperative undertaking by the federal government and selected leaders from the voluntary sector. In the 1999 report, the Joint Tables recommended that the federal government and leaders from the voluntary sector participate in a series of seven joint tables to redefine and strengthen the relationship between the government and sector. The federal government committed $94.6 million over five years to the work to be carried out by the seven Joint Tables, accordingly named the Joint Coordinating Committee (the central body known as the JCC), the Accord Table, the Awareness Table, the Capacity Table, the Information Management and Technology Table, the Regulatory Table, and the National Volunteerism Initiative Table. In addition, the sector created two working groups to address the issues of funding and advocacy while the federal government kept their participation on these topics in-house.

The VSI was managed to specific outcomes and outputs or deliverables.[1] A cursory review of the JCC vision for the initiative reveals five major outcomes with specific deliverables (outputs). First, the VSI was intended to improve and sustain a dialogue or collaboration between the federal government and the voluntary sector in areas of mutual interest with the broader goal of improving quality of life for Canadians. The specific deliverable was an accord signed by representatives of both sectors on 5

December 2001 with subsidiary implementation agreements in the form of codes of good practice in the areas of policy dialogue and funding, annual reporting requirements, and ongoing mechanisms to ensure a continued relationship. Second, the VSI was intended to strengthen the capacity of the voluntary sector to serve Canadians well. This was reified in the development of strategic approaches to building human resources, financial management, and information technology and management capacities with the necessary resources, and in the experimental Sectoral Involvement in Departmental Policy Development (SIDPD) aimed at building policy and research capacity. The latter, the joint voluntary organization and departmental proposals for policy development collaboration, are expected to yield significant models of best practices and serve as a basis for future cooperation. Third, the VSI was intended to increase awareness of the contributions made by volunteers and role of the voluntary sector in Canadian society. The VSI was much more successful in the former through activities conducted during the International Year of the Volunteer but should do more on the latter with a media and public awareness campaign in the later phase of the VSI. Fourth, an important outcome of the VSI has been the increased knowledge about the sector and its role in all facets of Canadian life achieved through ongoing mechanisms such as the Canadian Survey on Giving, Volunteering and Participating, the Statistics Canada Satellite Account to the System of National Accounts, and the National Survey of Voluntary and Nonprofit Organizations. The target of a joint research agenda was not pursued. Finally, the JCC envisioned a streamlined regulatory framework, revised tax form with clarified definitions of allowable activities for charities, and a review of the director's liability. A further objective of achieving clarity, consistency and transparency in the funding relationship between the sector and state was undertaken through the federal funding review, the code of funding practice and a strategic funding approach but was not joint in the sense of the other five outcomes. Despite the difficulties of coordinating two sectors across a broad array of issues affecting the whole relationship, the VSI was remarkably successful. Leadership on both sides kept the VSI on track to achieve these products.

Were these achievements sufficient to provide assurance to the sector and the Canadian public that the $94.6 million was spent wisely? One of the greatest challenges facing the VSI is the intangible nature of many of the benefits of the process. Although the tax forms, new definitions, and revised monitoring and registration mechanisms for charities are more tangible results, even they will affect different charities to different extents and most nonprofits will not be directly affected in daily operations. Little if any progress was made in harmonizing regulatory systems across the country for nonprofits. The Accord has received criticism for being more about process than substance as Susan Phillips observes in her chapter in this volume. A recurring observation is that the Accord has been signed signalling a new era in relations and yet departments like Human Resources Development Canada are still imposing unreasonable monitoring burdens on organizations and often acting in the command and control model rather than as a collaborator or partner in the goal of serving Canadians better. In fact, the effects of the Accord will only be felt in the future as the commitment of both sides to the principles established in the Accord are put to the test. The implementation of the Codes on Policy and Funding and the compliance of both sides to their terms will provide a basis for assessing the state of the future relationship. However, given that the prescribed scope for joint action is limited, the future partnership may resemble a modern dance with each moving as it desires rather than a waltz with each responding to the other's movements.

Similarly, knowledge on the sector is being collected now and its impact on relations with the corporate and government sector are yet to be realized. The Capacity Table is engaged in ongoing production of work on the sector. The awareness campaign is only gaining steam. SIDPD is more promising than felt. And so, criticisms of the VSI as using valuable resources needed for direct provision of services are understandable in the short term but are perhaps premature. The longer term will prove a more accurate basis for evaluating the effectiveness of the VSI.

The VSI has assumed a new structure as the work of the tables winds down and implementation of the principles established in the Accord and codes continues. The Voluntary Sector Roundtable, which was the primogenitor of the movement to reform the relationship, quietly faded into the background during the life of the VSI, allocating more responsibility for directing the VSI to the Voluntary Sector Steering Group (VSSG) comprising leaders of national organizations and the VSI chairs from the sector. In turn, the VSSG has now been replaced by the Voluntary Sector Forum, composed of nine leaders from the VSSG and ten new leaders from the voluntary sector who had not served on any of the VSI tables and who were chosen by an independent selection committee of five individuals from across the country.[2] The new steering body has been chosen by an independent, semi-open, and fairly transparent process with the explicit intention of ensuring representation from the major regions, national, and regional organizations, large and small organizations, different ethnic and racial backgrounds, various subsectors in the voluntary field among other things.

The new structure put in place by the federal government to deal with the voluntary sector and its issues on an ongoing basis has seven layers. First, the federal component of the joint structure will be housed in a regular department, Heritage Canada, with its minister assuming the responsibility. Second, the work of the Voluntary Sector Task Force (VSF) also moves to Heritage Canada, with key responsibilities of promoting the Accord across government and advising the coordinating mechanisms. This structure was heavily criticized when first proposed. Many voices from the sector and academic community argued that the initiative should remain housed in a central agency with sufficient clout to ensure that the sector remained on the Cabinet agenda and that line departments complied with the spirit and principles of the new relationship as laid out in the Accord. However, government and academic representatives familiar with the internal machinations of the federal policy process responded that the initiative would benefit if leadership and resources were concentrated within one department provided that mechanisms were put in place to enforce compliance across departments. The other five layers of the initiative were devised with this objective in mind. These spokespersons also cautioned that the Voluntary Sector Initiative could not realistically be expected to have as high a profile as in the first phase given that key changes in the relationship had been achieved. It was only natural that the structure would be less visible, although not less effective.

So what were the five layers designed to ensure further effectiveness? The third layer involved a ministerial committee representing 12 departments to replace the Reference Group of Ministers, and to be consultative to the minister. The minister for human resources will act as vice-chair of the committee. The ministerial committee will meet with the sector at least once a year to review progress on the implementation of the Accord and the two codes, and report to Cabinet annually. Thus, two departments with the heaviest involvement with the sector shepherd the initiative. The fourth layer is a joint steering committee with the voluntary sector and including the assistant deputy minister of heritage to ensure continued collaboration and coordination. Fifth, the assistant deputy minister committee mirroring the ministerial committee will do the horizontal work. Both the chair and the vice-chair from Human Resources and Heritage respectively are well known and respected within the voluntary sector for their commitment to the new relationship. The sixth layer is a critical component of the new plan. The accountability of the ministers and deputy ministers to the principles of the new relationship is secured through explicit requirements in their mandate letters. The evaluation requirement is a powerful tool of ensuring compliance. Finally, the Privy Council Office will continue its involvement in the VSI through the assistant deputy minister responsible for the machinery of government (currently the former JCC co-chair, Kathy O'Hara). This will be more or less the government counterpart to the VSF and ensure that policy is viewed through a voluntary sector lens to operationalize the VSI.

Will the new structures be sufficient to achieve the vision and mission of the VSI? While it is too early to tell, there is a sense that the initiative is in danger of falling off the government agenda without having significantly altered the relationship between the state and sector or having penetrated either the sector or government departments deeply. In her account of the life of the Accord, Susan Phillips sketches some of the obstacles both on the way to achieving the Accord and the lingering doubts today. Similarly, Paul Pross and Kernaghan Webb provide a concrete understanding of how far regulatory reform still needs to reach. And Capling and Nossal, in contrast to Smith and Smythe, paint a dark picture of the influence of civil society organizations on the development of government policy in the area of foreign relations. These authors capture points of tension in the relationship and whether the reforms begun by the VSI, Accord, and codes will remedy them remains to be seen. In particular, issues of funding, advocacy, and policy involvement require some sort of resolution whether through positive action or neglect, before the extent to which the relationship has been altered can be gauged.

Will the commitment of both sides to the principles and spirit of the Accord and codes be sustained as both sectors face significant changes in personnel? Not only has the leadership of the VSI within the federal government and voluntary sector changed, both sectors are facing major changes in personnel that might affect the future of the relationship. On the federal government side, a new leader of the Liberal Party will be elected in the fall to replace the current prime minister who has announced his intention of stepping down in February 2004. Expectations are that a federal election will soon follow with the new Liberal leader assuming office. On the voluntary sector side, the Coalition of National Voluntary Organizations and the Canadian Centre for Philanthropy are currently without presidents and have announced their intention to co-found a new organization by June 2004. A third voluntary sector giant, Volunteer Canada, is engaged in a search for a new leader upon the sudden resignation of Paddy Bowen in May 2003. Given the role these agencies have played in the genesis and life of the VSI and VSF, the changes could impact upon the state-sector relationship in a tangible way. The promise is there but the potential for obtaining meaningful change for the benefit of Canadians is less clear at this stage.

THE STATE OF RESEARCH

The field of research on the nonprofit and voluntary sector has changed in significant ways since this series began. Three developments in particular stand out. Each deserves to be highlighted here.

First, there has been a growth in the study of the nonprofit and voluntary sector. As researchers have become more aware of the nonprofit and voluntary organizations as constituting a sector as well as a vital component of civil society, more researchers have identified their work as falling within this purview. As a result, research networks and awareness of overlapping or relevant studies are growing within the sector studies, just as the place of the third sector within traditional disciplines is being realized. So, for example, the study of international relations has shifted to respond to this new area. Using a more traditional approach, the Capling and Nossal chapter examines the rise of the third sector as a third force in Canadian foreign policy along with the challenges that the aftermath of 11 September 2001 poses in order for these organizations to maintain policy influence and relevance. From a different perspective, the Smith and Smythe chapter examines the impact of new technologies on the ability of third sector organizations to develop global networks for the purpose of influencing transnational decisions. Heidi MacDonald's chapter uses an historical approach to understanding the impact of government policy on two charitable organizations, challenging conventional wisdom about the expansion of the welfare state. Wiktorowicz, Lapp, Brodie and Abelson begin the exercise of measuring third sector influence on health policy by the vital first step of mapping the sector. They offer a new lens for appreciating the development of health policy with some surprising findings. Georges LeBel uses a third sector lens to re-examine judicial decisions interpreting freedom of association as an individual right and to argue for a reconsideration of this freedom as a collective good. Rasmussen, Malloy and Agarwal extend a methodology normally associated with the public and private sectors to understand the ethical climate within the nonprofit sector in a comparative perspective. Pross and Webb and Phillips test and expand current theories of public administration. The chapters all embody the evolving state of research within traditional disciplines and within the specific field of third sector studies as they interact, and, in some cases, collide.

Second, a significant undertaking arising out of the VSI has been the national surveys and identification of the nonprofit and voluntary sector as an entity. The National Survey on Giving, Volunteering and Participating has become the Canadian Survey on Giving, Volunteering and Participating (CSGVP) and, owing to the work of the Joint Tables and subgroups, the survey will be funded on a triennial basis. This will provide the longitudinal data so desperately required to map the sector and its trends and to inform policy decisions. The identification of the third sector in the satellite accounts of Statistics Canada will provide more exact information on the contribution of the sector to the nation's social and economic life. Both of these developments allow for a more profound understanding of the nature and development of the sector both within Canada and in comparative international studies. They coincide with the inclusion of Canada in the Johns Hopkins comparative country studies of the third sector — a significant omission over the past 20 years. Further, the National Survey of Nonprofit and Voluntary Organizations (NSNVO) being undertaken by a consortium of voluntary sector, government, and academic organizations under the purview of the Capacity Table, will provide in-depth material on the state of financial, human, and administrative capacity within the sector for the first time.[3] The qualitative portion of the study was released in spring 2003 and the quantitative study is due to be released in spring 2004.[4] Finally, a smaller study of globalization and the voluntary sector, published in spring 2003 and funded by Human Resources Development Canada, has generated a new wave of thinking about the role of third sector organizations in the global economy.[5] In sum, these national surveys are significantly expanding our factual base for thinking about the sector while stimulating new ideas and directions for action.

The third development in research involves the active promotion of ideas across sectors. Certainly, the Social Sciences and Humanities Research Council is promoting the fertile exchange of ideas through collaborative projects under the Community-University Research Alliances (CURA) program and through wide dissemination of research projects under the new social movements component of the Federalism and Federations program. The Public Policy and Third Sector Initiative at Queen's University brings together government, third sector, and academic researchers and practitioners at its annual national forum to debate different, topical aspects of the state-sector relationship. Over the past three years, the Ottawa-Carleton Centre for Voluntary Sector Research and Development, the Coalition of National Voluntary Organizations, and the Canadian Centre for Philanthropy have engaged in an ambitious undertaking to bring voluntary sector and academic researchers together to explore the prospects for a collaborative research agenda that would embrace the diversity and energy of the sector. Funded by Human Resources Development Canada, this newly named Nonprofit and Voluntary Sector Network Community of Inquiry is directed by a steering group with five working groups engaged in developing a vision, mission and principles, Web site and newsletter, regional activities, conference planning to serve over 200 members throughout Canada. The creation of a Voluntary Sector Knowledge at the University of Victoria and of the Alliance de Recherche Universités-Communautés en Économie Sociale at UQAM, as well as emerging coalitions of voluntary sector organizations at both the provincial and national levels will only foster this dynamic research discourse between sectors. In turn, this research energy is likely to drive further developments in practice that affect the state-sector relationship.

THE CONTRIBUTION OF THIS BOOK

These chapters contribute significantly to our understanding of the voluntary sector and state relationship in Canada. Individually they provide rich commentaries on specific aspects of the relationship. Collectively, they provide guidance and cautions to decisionmakers in both sectors as they move ahead together.

The Phillips chapter offers a thoughtful examination of the Accord signed by the federal government and voluntary sector from its conception, through its birth and to its first steps forward. The odyssey includes the difficulties encountered in the process of negotiations, the similarities and departures from the sister documents in England and Wales and Scotland, the mechanisms to operationalize the principles, and an independent assessment of the viability of the Accord. Apart from the detailed and informative description and analysis of the process and content, Phillips' chapter contributes more broadly to our theoretical understanding of why particular policy ideas emerge and move forward on the policy agenda. She offers wise words of advice to policy leaders as they continue the duet put in motion by the Accord.

Paul Pross and Kernaghan Webb continue this journey with their insightful analysis of the state of federal regulations affecting the voluntary sector. They ask whether the corpus of federal regulations affecting advocacy activities of groups may be characterized as a regime and, if so, how this regime affects voluntary sector organizations. After a thorough examination of state policy and law and extensive interviews with state and sector officials, they concede that the linkages are weak between the seven various components of federal government regulations but conclude that a regime does indeed exist with unintended cumulative effects for the voluntary and nonprofit sector. While their analysis of federal regulations is illuminating and useful in itself, they manage to extract the even more poignant meaning for public debate and open critique of government that is so vital to a liberal democracy. They advise decisionmakers in the government and sector alike who are contemplating changes to think in terms of the whole corpus of law rather than just in increments if they are to enhance the contribution of these organizations to the vibrant interaction between state and society.

The focus shifts from the relationship between the sector and government to the actors themselves in the chapter by Ken Rasmussen, David Malloy and James Agarwal. In a twist on studies of accountability in the public and nonprofit sectors, these authors ponder whether the ethical climates are sufficiently different to warrant special consideration in determining the appropriate balance between public accountability and the autonomy of nonprofit organizations. Utilizing both quantitative and qualitative surveys with government and nonprofit officials to probe the organizational cultures in the two sectors, the authors conclude that while points of convergence do exist, the ethical mindsets of the two types of officials are significantly different. These findings have important implications for how accountability and autonomy are to be managed in contractual arrangements between the state and sector. Like Pross and Webb, these authors conclude that the creative potential of nonprofit organizations can improve the quality of democratic public administration and discourse if harnessed appropriately. If the two sectors dance to the tune of different drummers, then latitude for discretion, advocacy, and different understandings of client needs and satisfaction are essential when governments contract out service delivery to nonprofit organizations.

Heidi MacDonald steps into the past to analyze the impact of legislation and increased state funding on the evolution of the role in health care of the Sisters of Charity who operated the Halifax Infirmary and the Sisters of St. Martha in who administered the Charlottetown Hospital from 1944 to 1982. In a meticulous comparative study of the actions and reactions of the state and the congregations, MacDonald challenges the received wisdom that the welfare state expanded in the 1960s as traditional institutions failed, and specifically that the sisters retreated from hospital work during the expansion of the welfare state due mainly to a shortage of sisters available to work in the hospitals. She ably demonstrates that the sisters were driven out of the hospitals by the escalating health-care costs, especially after the introduction of national health-care insurance in 1959. As Keith

Banting noted in the workshop, this significant finding "turns our theories of the welfare state on their heads." MacDonald's chapter has two further important admonitions for state policymakers when dealing with the nonprofit sector: when nonprofit organizations are providing superior and needed expertise in a social service or health-care area, the state should make greater efforts to alleviate the financial burden imposed on those organizations, especially if that burden is a result of state action; and, if the sector has a professional, experienced workforce in an essential service, then the state policymakers should pause before making any reforms to listen to them and benefit from their experience. Both sides are less likely to trip if this advice is followed.

Following along the theme of health care and the duet of the state and the voluntary sector, Wiktorowicz, Lapp, Brodie and Abelson use a quantitative approach to chart the current composition and involvement of interest groups in health policy in Ontario, and the tactics these groups use to influence policy. In a comprehensive mapping exercise, these authors outline the health policy network, portraying all its rich diversity. They note the correlation between the differences in mandates, priorities, and resources and the differences in strategies to influence policy. While some groups may choose to operate within the policy circle at close contact with government, others will keep their distance choosing other partners, like the media, to apply pressure for policy change. By documenting the complexity of the policy network(s) within health care, the authors prepare a solid foundation for further studies to measure both perceptions of interest group influence on policymakers and the relevance of organizations to the process. The chapter is a quiet caution to researchers against drawing generalizations about a complex field of interaction or assuming influence without careful empirical work.

Georges leBel steps carefully in his analysis of the cumulative impact of administrative and fiscal regulations on associations. Like MacDonald and Pross and Webb, he argues that the cumulative impact of state actions on the sector must be weighed carefully. In this case, court-sanctioned legislation has put in peril the guarantee of freedom of association contained in the *Canadian Charter of Rights and Freedoms*. Through judicial interpretation by courts unduly influenced by a North American corporate and neo-liberal ideology, freedom of association has been denigrated from a collective freedom to the instrumental role of operationalizing individual rights, and even worse, limited to its caricature, the right not to associate. To achieve this interpretation, the courts have all but ignored accepted principles of judicial interpretation, the Quebec Civil Code, Canada's signature on international treaties and covenants, and the commitment to principles of democracy contained in the first section of the Charter. Like Pross and Webb and Rasmussen *et al.*, he regrets the impact that such a short-sighted interpretation may have on group actions that are so critical to social life and democracy. He takes no solace in the moral admonition that a state that should not attack such a fundamental freedom since the Canadian state does just this in its new legislation dealing with terrorism and associations. He asks, "que faire alors?" Rather than posing prescriptions, leBel appeals to the good sense of his reader in his conclusion that we must ask if we should restore this freedom in its robust sense, and if so, how?

The final two chapters take us into the twinned halls of foreign policy and international relations. Ann Capling and Kim Richard Nossal challenge the positive view of the rise of the third sector as a force in the development of Canadian foreign policy, especially trade policy. They link domestic developments with global ones, arguing that the rise of civil society groups and transnational social movement organizations in international politics and global governance was the result of shifts in contemporary politics. Carrying this logic forward into current circumstances, they observe the response of governments to the anti-globalization movement of moving sensitive talks to more secure locations. In a parallel line of logic, they suggest that the re-emergence of the foreign policy focus on security in the wake of the decision of Canada, the United States and its allies to thwart the transnational movement of radical Islamism as a consequence of the terrorist acts of 11 September 2001 will have a profound effect on another transnational social movement, the anti-globalization forces. Already, the concern of policymakers and the public for the input of this engaged sector of civil society has diminished. Further, they venture that gains in public trust of governments will come at the expense of civil society organizations, especially transnational ones. As these organizations come under closer and more critical scrutiny, public demands for increased transparency and accountability could result. Unlike some of the previous authors, Capling and Nossal suggest that the state may re-emerge as a positive force in community life without the third sector as a mediating force.

Elizabeth Smythe and Peter J. Smith are more positive, albeit cautious, in their assessment of the role of transnational networks of non-governmental organizations in challenging new institutions and instruments of global governance. They sketch the impact of new technologies on the rise of transnational social movements and their influence on globalization and international trade negotiations. While they begin to chart how new information and communication technologies have facilitated links between various local and global movements, they concede that it is much harder to gauge the impact of these social movements on policy content. Like Wiktorowicz *et al.*, they suggest that a new framework of analysis would be necessary for measuring the policy influence of interest groups. However, they do not suggest that these groups are marginal to the foreign policy process. On the contrary, the anti-globalization movement has forced trade negotiators to consult more broadly with representatives of civil society to maintain the legitimacy of the international trade policy process using the new technologies to do so. In addition, the domestic rhetoric around trade negotiations has shifted to reflect the concerns of civil society organizations for equality and social justice. Like Capling and Nossal, they question the longevity of this influence but for different reasons; and unlike Capling and Nossal, they suggest that the continued vigilance of civil society organizations will be instrumental in maintaining their place in the international forum.

In sum, the chapters depict both the new moves and old steps as the state and civil society organizations continue their intricate, often frustrating and sometimes harmonic relationship. As this phase of the series of books draws to a close, the third sector is struggling to ensure that the federal government has not decided to sit this one out on both the domestic and global fronts. Keeping their partnership on the floor, if not in the spotlight, will be the challenge of the next phase of the relationship between the two sectors.

Notes

[1]See Joint Coordinating Committee, *Progress to Plan Report*, Ottawa, 5 September 2002. At each meeting, in the latter stages of the JCC, the committee would review the *Progress to Plan* by outcome, deliverable, Joint Table responsibility, progress, and issue/assessment.

[2]From east to west, the selection committee included John Perlin (Newfoundland), Jean Panet-Raymond (Quebec), Kathy Brock (Ontario), Wayne Helgason (Manitoba), and Colleen Kelly (BC). The size of the VSF has been increased subsequently to 22 people in order to enhance its representativeness.

[3]Consortium members include Canadian Centre for Philanthropy, Alliance de Recherche Universités-Communautés en Economie Sociale at UQAM, the Canada West Foundation (CWF), the Canadian Council on Social Development (CCSD), the Capacity Development Network at the University of Victoria, the Community Services Council of Newfoundland and Labrador (CSC), Queen's University School of Policy Studies, the Secretariat on Voluntary Sector Sustainability of the Manitoba Voluntary Sector Initiative, and Statistics Canada.

[4]Both the results of the CSGVP and the NSNVO are available at <www.ccp.ca>.

[5]Kathy Brock, David Brook and Jan Elliott, *Globalization and the Voluntary Sector*. Ottawa and Kingston; Public Policy Forum and Queen's School of Policy Studies Third Sector Program, April 2003.

2

In Accordance: Canada's Voluntary Sector Accord from Idea to Implementation

Susan D. Phillips

The Government of Canada and the voluntary sector have long worked side-by-side. Now, the *Accord Between the Government of Canada and the Voluntary Sector* marks the launch of a new era of cooperation and respect.

Jean Chrétien
5 December 2001

With these words, the prime minister announced the signing of the framework agreement between the federal government and Canada's voluntary sector. This Accord, which is the product of a year-long collaborative process involving federal officials and voluntary sector representatives, sets out shared values and principles and expresses general commitments by both parties as to how they will build a stronger relationship. Under the auspices of the Accord, very specific codes of good practice related to policy dialogue and funding have been developed that, if fully implemented, hold considerable promise to promote better working relationships in these areas. Within the federal government, new institutional arrangements, including the first ever federal minister responsible for the voluntary sector, have been created to carry the Accord and the codes forward and to monitor the state of the relationship over time. Within the sector, a new national coalition, the Voluntary Sector Forum, has been established to provide political leadership and to help ensure that effective implementation ensues.

In spite of the interdependence between the two sectors noted by the prime minister, their relationship over the past two decades has been a rocky one at times, particularly given tensions arising from welfare state restructuring (Brock and Banting 2001; Hall and Reed 1998). Over this period, services were downloaded to voluntary organizations, often without any consultation regarding their ability to carry the additional load; funding to a wide variety of organizations, particularly those engaged in advocacy was cut dramatically; members of Parliament (MPs) questioned the credibility of voluntary organizations as to whom they really represent, and one MP led a campaign to bring in much stricter regulation of the sector (see Jenson and Phillips 1996). In every respect, then, the signing of the Accord is a landmark event which appears to represent a dramatic turn in the federal government-voluntary sector relationship. Given the recent history of the relationship, how did the idea of an accord ever get on the public policy agenda?

Although a novel policy instrument in the Canadian context, the idea of a framework agreement is a transplanted one. It is copied directly from the United Kingdom where the Blair government negotiated "Compacts" with the voluntary sectors in each of England, Scotland, Wales, and in Northern Ireland in 1998. Although the idea of an accord was borrowed, the process for shaping it into an actual document was uniquely Canadian, taking the form of a Joint Table involving an equal number of public servants and voluntary sector representatives. How did the distinctively home-grown process of developing the Canadian Accord affect its form and content?

By the declaration of its own developers, the Accord will be judged a success "when it results in a more effective working relationship based on the shared values and principles outlined in [it]" (Government of Canada/ Voluntary Sector 2001, iii). The collaborative Joint Table process and the politics surrounding it produced an agreement that is much less concrete in its commitments than the original British Compacts. This is not necessarily problematic, but it puts much more weight on the unfolding second phase, that of implementing the Accord and the more specific codes of good practice and of using the newly established mechanisms to monitor adherence to them. What will it take to successfully implement the Accord and enable it, in fact, to shape a new era of cooperation and respect?

This case study of a critical moment in the history of relationship-building between the federal government and the voluntary sector in Canada addresses these questions. The analysis is based on direct observation of the process, interviews with both voluntary sector and federal government participants, and review of primary documents.[1] We begin by exploring how the idea of an accord got on the political agenda in Canada in the first place. Why does an idea's time come when it does? In responding to this question, Kingdon (1995) argues that ideas do not become policy simply because they are good ones or because they have been successful elsewhere. Rather, they are taken up as a result of a convergence, often unplanned, of a problem, a policy instrument, and political imperatives that push the idea through an open policy window and onto the decision agenda. The coming together of these independent streams necessarily involves a variety of different actors, often with competing interests and agendas. The development of Canada's Accord is, indeed, a story of differing agendas and Kingdon's framework provides a useful approach for understanding how various perspectives and interests converged on action that led to its signing.

HOW AN IDEA'S TIME COMES

The traditional way of understanding policy development is as a rational, linear process in which a problem becomes apparent, a variety of options for how to fix it are identified, their merits assessed and compared, the best selected and then implemented. Although this rational model is logically compelling, the reality of policy-making is usually much messier and normally enveloped by political interests that make the process more circuitous than linear. Just because a problem exists, does not mean it gets addressed by governments. Nor does the policy development process necessarily start with a problem. Often political actors may be enamoured with particular policy instruments and wait for the right problems to come along in order to apply their favoured solutions (Cohen, March and Olsen 1972).

The framework developed by John Kingdon is useful in analyzing the politics of the policy process and, in particular, the agenda-setting stage.[2] He suggests that at any time, three largely independent streams flow through policy-making. The *problem* stream denotes the existence of problems which are defined as conditions with the potential to do something about them. Problems may be quite ill-defined or framed in different ways by different sets of political actors, however, making the naming and framing process an important act in itself. In the *policy* stream constantly float a variety of policy ideas and instruments for dealing with problems, but they do so without necessarily being attached to a particular problem. These ideas are carried by a variety of agents both within government and outside it, with a special role played by political entrepreneurs (e.g., think-tanks, independent experts, and voluntary sector leaders) who learn and trade in ideas as a result of their embeddedness in policy networks and epistemic communities (Haas 1992). Although quite a range of ideas, all possible in principle, may be carried in this stream, not all are capable of surviving. As Kingdon notes, "they bump into one another, they combine with one another; some survive, some die out, and some survive in a form quite different from their origins. Even if the beginnings are somewhat haphazard, the survival is not" (1995, 131). Survival of an idea depends on a number of factors including its technical feasibility, its cost and fit with budget considerations, and its likelihood of winning political champions and meeting with public acceptance. Finally, the *political* stream refers to electoral politics, public opinion, intergovernmental and intragovernmental tensions and other factors that shape the motivations, goals, and attention spans of policymakers.

Action occurs when these three streams converge. This happens when a policy window is opened, usually by a change in either the problem stream (such as a crisis or release of new indicators about the magnitude of the problem) or the political stream (such as an impending election, a change in personnel, or the actions of a political entrepreneur in pushing a pet proposal or shaping public opinion). The opening of a window provides an opportunity for proposals, which are constantly in the policy stream, to become suddenly elevated on the governmental agenda because "they can be seen as solutions to a pressing problem or because politicians find their sponsorship expedient" (Kingdon 1995, 172). If the opportunity of an open policy window is seized, the three streams may be joined, with the result that the idea rises on the decision agenda: its time has come. Just as policy windows may open quite quickly and without advance warning, they may also close as readily. The value of Kingdon's approach is that it highlights the fact that the policy process is not a linear progression from problem identification to problem solution and that the result is seldom fully predictable in advance.

GETTING AN ACCORD ON THE POLICY AGENDA

An accord is both a framework document *and* a process. As a document, an accord is not simply another form of a legally binding contract. The compacts that have been established to date are not based on an articulation of rights, but on the creation of a shared vision and principles, joint responsibilities of equal partners, and a process for ongoing monitoring and review. As frameworks, they are not long or complicated documents — running a mere seven or eight pages for the British Compacts and four pages for the Canadian Accord. Nevertheless, as frameworks, they are intended to *frame* key issues and provide mutual guidance about how to deal with some of the potentially contentious aspects of a relationship between two sectors. While the framework document is important, an accord is much more than this. Experience clearly demonstrates that the process of getting to an agreement and the ongoing means for monitoring and reporting are as important, if not more so, than the content of the agreement itself.

In the development process, a challenging issue is how to make a commitment on such a grand scale: the whole of government to an entire sector, particularly one as diverse and lacking in hierarchy as the Canadian voluntary sector. For government, the questions of who signs, which agencies are covered, and where lies responsibility for implementation are relatively straightforward because a government is ultimately a single entity with delineated authorities and reporting relationships. For the voluntary sector, the legitimacy of an accord springs from its endorsement by representatives who have credibility, not necessarily authority, to act on behalf of the sector, and who are well positioned to help change cultures and practices.

In short, an accord is about relationship-building: between the voluntary sector and government, *and* between the leadership of the voluntary sector involved in the development of the accord and the rest of the sector. It has been seen as both a starting point and as a consolidation of a variety of related efforts at relationship renewal. As a starting point, an accord requires a means of moving from general, relatively uncontestable principles and commitments to more specific and potentially problematic ones (Morison 2000, 118-19). In addition, there is a clear expectation that it is not just government that is making commitments, but the voluntary sector as well. The ultimate success of an accord is judged mainly on whether greater trust has been instilled on both sides and whether practices change to the satisfaction and mutual benefit of both partners. As Morison notes, framework agreements do not stand alone or occur in isolation. However, there is a "sense that something bigger than the present exercise in simple recognition is going on here" (ibid.). Compacts or accords are, he notes, "perhaps a first stage in a much wider process involving bigger changes in the state and a new configuration of the relationship of government and civil society" (ibid.). So, what were the bigger things going on in the Canadian case that got the Accord on the political agenda and configured it in particular ways?

Depends on How You Look at it: The Problem Stream

Getting the idea of an accord on the federal government policy agenda was a two-stage process. First, the voluntary sector had to bring itself to the government's attention, then it had to get the idea of using a framework agreement as a means of relationship-building on the agenda. Beginning in the late 1980s, serious problems were evident in the relationship between the federal government and the voluntary sector. Part of this was a direct result of neo-liberalism and the financial crisis, and the welfare state restructuring spawned by them (see White 2001). The downloading of services and cuts to the core funding of a wide range of voluntary organizations that began in the late 1980s has been well documented (Hall and Reed 1998; Juillet *et al.* 2001; Phillips 1991; Pross and Webb 2003). But the problem was not just about funding. It was also about the nature of representation. It became commonplace in the 1990s to question whom voluntary organizations really represented and cuts to core funding were specifically targeted at groups engaged in advocacy. Indeed, the Mulroney government made this point in a budget in the late 1980s by redirecting the money saved from cutting funding to voluntary organizations, not to deficit reduction, but to industrial milk subsidies (Phillips 1991). The charge against the credibility of voluntary organizations was led by the populist Reform Party and by a Liberal backbench MP, John Bryden, who saw the organizations as usurping the role of MPs and "lunching at the public trough" while criticizing government. In a series of reports issued in the mid-1990s, Bryden asserted that charities lacked accountability and he argued in favour of heavy-handed regulation of the sector by the federal government. At the same time, the government's reliance on the sector was increasing. Program review and the massive public service restructuring of the mid-1990s not only downloaded services, but reduced in-house policy capacity so that the federal government increasingly needed both the expert advice and experiential knowledge of voluntary organizations as their source for information in making policy (see Laforest 2002).

Initially, the voluntary sector was slow to react to the combined crises of funding, legitimacy, and impending regulation. In order to recast itself and begin to construct a better relationship with the federal government, the voluntary sector first had to come to terms with the limits of its own structure. From early days, the structure of the voluntary sector, outside Quebec, has mirrored federalism: local chapters are generally organized into regional or provincial umbrellas that are part of national federations (see Coleman 1987; Pross 1992). The result has been the development of relatively isolated silos of activity based on subsector. These divisions have been reinforced by the absence of a truly "peak" national association that could be said to represent or speak for the sector as a whole. Another significant divide has been between the more service-oriented organizations, often registered as charities, and the more political, advocacy focused organizations and social movements. In addition, although a broad range of organizations representing minority and cultural communities emerged in the 1970s and 1980s, they tend to exist in relative isolation from either the mainstream service organizations or issue-focused advocacy groups (Kobayashi 2000).[3] In the mid-1990s when a handful of sector leaders started discussions around the need for voluntary organizations to mobilize collectively in order to be more proactive in contesting the negative consequences of public sector restructuring, one of the first steps was to establish a national coalition that could exercise more effective, broadly-based leadership than existed at the time (see Johnston 2000).

This resulted in the creation of the Voluntary Sector Roundtable (VSR), an unincorporated association comprised of 12 representatives of the main subfields of voluntary activity, including among others arts and culture, social services, sports and recreation, health, faith communities, and environment. The strength of the VSR structure lay in its lack of institutionalization which has allowed it to act quickly, remain nimble and avoid direct head-to-head competition with the existing national umbrellas, many of which were members. As a loose coalition, the primary weaknesses of the VSR were its inability to reach the grassroots (and thus make national level initiatives relevant to organizational life on the ground), its limited inclusivity, and its lack of accountability to a membership. Its critical challenge at the time lay not in creating a vertically integrated governance structure, however, but in reorienting the federal government's perspective on the sector.

One of the first major initiatives of the VSR was to establish an independent panel to make recommendations on improving accountability in the sector. The [Broadbent] Panel on Accountability and Governance in the Voluntary Sector not only addressed issues of self-regulation in its more than 40 recommendations, but saw a window of opportunity to lay out for the federal government a blueprint for reform of its relationship with the sector (PAGVS 1999). In this respect, the Broadbent Panel was a political entrepreneur, trading in ideas, and hoping to pry open a policy window. Relationship-building from the Panel's perspective involved a variety of institutionalized means for sustaining a dialogue that would lead to increased understanding. As the Panel was conducting its work in 1998, it studied the recommendations of the 1996 Deakin Commission, an independent commission established by England's largest umbrella organization, and specifically the idea of a compact that had been suggested by Deakin and was then being discussed by a few voluntary sector leaders in Canada. The Panel was clear, however, that a compact was only one of several vehicles for reshaping government-sector relations and that other institutional changes, such as assigning responsibility for the sector to a minister(s) and creating an administrative unit within the central machinery of government to provide greater horizontal coordination across departments, were also essential.

At this same time, an important shift in thinking was already beginning to occur within the federal government. In preparation for the 1997 election, the Liberal Party produced its second *Red Book* which made a commitment to increasing the capacity of the voluntary sector to contribute to Canadian life (Liberal Party of Canada 1997). The renewed interest in the voluntary sector was the result of several convergent forces. In one respect, it was related to enabling the federal government to better respond to the challenges of a smaller state by relying on the voluntary sector for service delivery and partnerships. There was also a push by key individuals, especially in the Prime Minister's Office, who understood the value of the sector from a democratic perspective and who saw this as a way of moving the party from its recent neo-liberal actions to its liberal roots of being a force of good in society. At this time, the federal government was keenly interested in advancing an initiative known as "Engaging Canadians" that would better connect individual citizens to government departments in a variety of ways or, at least, make citizens *feel* a closer connection to the federal government, thereby restoring some of the visibility and credibility it had lost with Canadians.[4] The peculiarly Canadian interest in forging such connections is that they could be used to support national unity; when relationships with the provinces are tense, the federal government could fall back on its direct links with citizens. At this crucial point, representatives from the voluntary sector convinced key government officials that the best way to engage Canadians was to reach out to those who were already engaged through the voluntary sector. Thus, the link was forged between building stronger ties with individuals and with organizations and the voluntary sector as a whole. It cannot be said that the federal government shared the sector's analysis or deep concern about the problematic nature of the relationship, nor the solutions as to how to improve it, although it was now publicly committed to the vague notion of helping the sector to realize its potential as the "third pillar" of Canadian society. At last, the voluntary sector was on the federal radar screen.

Following its re-election in 1997, the Liberal government created a Voluntary Sector Task Force housed in the Privy Council Office (PCO) to begin to give substance to its rather vague *Red Book II* promises.[5] The sector's demands to be full partners in the process of relationship-rebuilding led to a novel experiment in government-voluntary sector collaboration. In March 1999, three Joint Tables were created, which consisted of 14 members each with equal representation from the voluntary sector and the federal government and were jointly co-chaired. They were charged, respectively, with making proposals for building the relationship, strengthening capacity, and improving the regulatory framework. The Joint Tables had only a few months to complete their work, which in part accounted for their success as people could throw themselves into voluntary participation knowing it would not last long. Given the short period, the Joint Tables had to focus on policy solutions, particularly ones acceptable to both government and the sector, rather than on underlying policy problems (Good 2003, 124). During this period, there was also a series of important dinner meetings involving voluntary sector leaders and ministers (with a remarkable turnout of 14 ministers at one meeting). This reinforced expectations on both sides that concrete action would be forthcoming in a timely manner. The collaborative process was judged by both sides to be an enormous success and the Joint Tables' combined report entitled, *Working Together*, produced a set of consensual recommendations that quite closely reflect those of the Broadbent Panel (Government of Canada/Voluntary Sector 1999). The *Working Together* report reinforced the idea of developing a framework agreement — named an "Accord" — and went even further than Broadbent in laying out a number of options for enhancing ministerial and parliamentary leadership for the sector. Now, the federal government not only had available the idea of an accord, but a process modelled after the *Working Together* Joint Tables for developing it.

Something Borrowed, Something Blue: The Policy Stream

The idea of a government-voluntary sector framework agreement was borrowed directly from the UK. Canada looked most closely at the English Compact, the first to be developed and the best known, and secondly to that of Scotland whose collaborative process was seen to be instructive. Although Canada could try to emulate both the form of the British Compacts (a document outlining shared values, principles, and mutual undertakings) and the process of engagement with the sector that surrounded their development, it could not easily embrace the bigger package of ideological and institutional arrangements that support the Compacts in vital ways. Understanding what could be copied and what was distinctive to the UK experience is helpful in assessing where Canada ended up.

The context and history of the development of the compacts in the UK, particularly the prototype of England, is similar in many ways to that of Canada. During the 1980s and 1990s, downsizing of government in the UK had produced an expansive contracting regime for services with uncertainty about its rules and about funding of voluntary organizations more generally. There was an overriding sense that the sector mattered little to the Thatcher government, which was focused on reshaping the relationship between the state and the market (Kendall 2000). As happened in Canada, an independent commission established by the sector played a key part as policy entrepreneur and it popularized the idea of a "concordant" for the first time.[6] Although the Conservative government responded coolly to the Deakin Commission's suggestion of a concordant, an election was pending so the sector simply bided its time while cultivating closer ties with the opposition Labour Party, which under Blair's leadership was recasting itself and its ideology. New Labour had shed its former statistic orientation to take up the "Third Way" communitarianism which emphasizes the creation of a strong civil society and promotes active citizenship and social inclusion. Not surprisingly, New Labour was very receptive to the idea of a concordant and, indeed, while still in opposition, had publicized its own proposal to reshape government's relationship with the voluntary sector that promised a shift from a contract culture to partnership and advanced the idea of a "compact" and other major institutional reforms (UK. Labour Party 1997). Herein lies an important feature of the UK situation that differed significantly from the Canadian context. The project of government-voluntary sector relationship-building was closely tied to the governing party's political ideology; it enjoyed strong support from senior ministers and, indeed, from the prime minister himself; and supporting governmental structures, notably the Active Communities Unit, were established early on to assist in the process.[7] The enthusiastic political support from the top down not only facilitated the development of Compacts in an expeditious manner, but allowed the voluntary sector in England to lead the process, and secured the creation of separate Compacts for Scotland, Wales, and Northern Ireland as their processes of political devolution proceeded.[8]

The development of the Compact in England took seriously the notion of a framework agreement as both document and process. England's largest cross-cutting umbrella and self-declared "voice" of the voluntary sector, the National Council of Voluntary Organisations (NCVO), formed a

Compact Working Group that included other national organizations. The lead taken by the sector allowed it, as a whole, to formulate quite clearly what it wanted in an agreement, which came to include the recognition of independence, a real two-way partnership, stability of funding regimes, inclusivity, and capacity for monitoring in an implementation phase (Gaines 2001). The broad engagement process that followed built up confidence in the potential of the Compact, and affirmed the notion that a compact should not be "merely a set of high minded principles, but that it needed to be essentially a practical document that recognised the contributions and obligations of both government and voluntary organisations" (Etherington n.d.). Since at one point the black and minority ethnic groups felt they should withhold support because a national compact has little relevance to their work, the consultations also showed the need to take into account their particular concerns.[9]

"Negotiations" took the form of meetings between the sector's Working Group and a Ministerial Working Group (representing 13 departments and chaired by the Home Office) with the two parties jointly drafting the final product. Once the breakthrough was made that there was, indeed, a shared vision between government and the sector, it became relatively easy to define principles and mutual undertakings, resulting in a document that was presented to Parliament in November 1998.[10] The English Compact, like those of the other UK jurisdictions, does address the key issues laid out by the sector and does so not only by laying out general principles, but by making concrete commitments on the part of both the government and the voluntary sector.[11] Subsequent to the Compact, five codes of good practice have been developed by the Compact Working Group that address in very specific ways practices related to: funding, consultation, volunteering, black and minority ethnic groups, and community action.[12] Together with the Compact itself, the codes establish more than 200 specific action points and undertakings.[13]

The annual process of reviewing and reporting on the state of the relationship has become the lifeblood of the Compacts. The English approach is built around an annual report to Parliament which is preceded by an annual meeting involving members of the Compact Working Group and relevant ministers. It reviews progress made in implementing the Compact and codes over the past year (based in part on surveys of both voluntary organizations and government departments) and produces an action plan with concrete steps to be taken by each side.[14] As results of the meetings so far reveal, this report can be quite blunt, naming particular departments or consultations for being in violation of the codes, on the one hand, and bestowing praise on specific units, on the other hand.[15] One positive aspect is that the *Black and Minority Ethnic Organisations Code*, whose development has been the result of extensive consultation and support from the Active Communities Unit, appears to be "popular and a rallying point of unity" for minority communities (UK. Compact Working Group and Home Office 2001, 7).

When the national compact was launched in England, there was also a strong commitment by the Blair government to encourage the rapid development of similar compacts between the sector and local governments. These are vitally important to community-based and minority groups because it is at the local level where they have the most direct dealings with government. By 2002, 60 percent of England's local authorities had either published, were in the process or had signalled an intent to develop their own compacts with the sector (UK. Compact Working Group and Home Office 2001, 9).[16]

Finally, the process of relationship-building in the UK has not stopped with the compacts. Rather, the Compacts are embedded in broader processes of incremental change in both England and Scotland.[17] Since the late 1990s, there has been implementation of more extensive tax relief for charitable giving, an expansion of the responsibilities and funding for the Active Communities Unit, and a review of financing practices and charity law in both jurisdictions.[18] This means that most of the big underlying policy irritants — almost invariably related to funding policies, the definition of charity, or governmental institutions for regulation and support of the sector — have not had to be funnelled through the dispute-resolution processes of the Compact and its codes.

In its process of developing an accord, Canada could look to the UK for the basic elements of a novel policy instrument that was already showing evidence of facilitating more constructive relationships between governments and voluntary sectors. What it could not emulate were the underlying political and institutional supports. Although the Liberal Party supported the notion of building a stronger relationship with the voluntary sector and of an accord as a means to do this, it was not fundamental to its ideology nor a personal commitment of the prime minister and a large number of senior ministers, as it was to Labour and Tony Blair. Although Canada has a number of strong national voluntary organizations, there is no encompassing, "peak" association equivalent to England's NCVO or Scotland's Council of Voluntary Organisations. No permanent administrative machinery had been set up within government to advance the cause of relationship-building, nor is Canada's central agency machinery particularly well-suited to hosting a coordinating unit that would do so. As a federal system, the Government of Canada could not promise that local compacts would follow the national agreement, thereby appeasing minority and community-based groups. And, as we will see, the government's commitment to addressing some of the sector's big issues, namely financing, advocacy, and fundamental institutional and regulatory change as part of a broader reform package was not so clear.

Differing Priorities: The Political Stream

By the fall of 1999, the federal government was working on determining how it would move forward on the recommendations of the *Working Together* Joint Tables and beginning to move these through the Cabinet approval process. And, it was doing so under heightened expectations on the part of ministers and voluntary sector leaders that a plan for implementing the consensual recommendations of the Joint Tables would be announced in the near future. Thus, what the federal government needed were, in Ottawa-speak, "early deliverables" that would provide some successes in the short term, demonstrating that progress was being made.

The regular and ritual occasion of the Speech from the Throne, scheduled for October 1999, opened a window of opportunity for the federal government to signal its intentions on the voluntary sector file. If nothing were put through this window, it would suggest that the voluntary sector had fallen off the political agenda, which was not the case.[19] So, the political stream looked to the policy stream for ideas and came up with the Accord as an ideal candidate to meet the criteria: capable of being implemented in a short period of time without the need for passage by Parliament, relatively inexpensive, highly symbolic, and virtually guaranteed to meet with public acceptance. As a result, the federal government indicated in the Speech from the Throne its intention to "enter into a national accord with the voluntary sector, laying the foundation for active partnership with voluntary organizations in the service of Canadians."

For the voluntary sector leaders who had participated in the *Working Together* process, an accord was an attractive option, but it was not a stand-alone one. Indeed, many would not have made it their top priority as regulatory and institutional reform, stability of financing, liberalizing restrictions on advocacy, and addressing which types of organizations could be registered under the tax system were all vitally, if not more important. Nevertheless, an accord had been part of the consensual set of recommendations and was an important signal from the federal government and a promising beginning for moving toward realization of their fuller agenda.

Thus, it was the political stream, and to a lesser extent the policy stream that drove the Accord through the policy window. It was decidedly not the problem stream. In short, the voluntary sector had a policy problem (its relationship with the federal government), and a vision of how to fix it, which entailed a set of fundamental reforms to the process of representation and to regulatory and funding regimes. The federal government had first, a policy instrument and, only secondarily, an understanding of the problems facing the voluntary sector and a policy agenda for addressing them.[20]

The government followed through, not only on its intention to develop an accord, but to implement most of the package of recommendations of the *Working Together* report. In June 2000, it announced the creation of the Voluntary Sector Initiative (VSI), supported by almost $95 million over five years, the details of which would be determined by a second round of Joint Tables that would work over the first two years of the initiative. With this, the voluntary sector and the federal government took on the challenge of comprehensive reform all at once. Not only was an accord on the agenda, but so too were a national volunteerism initiative, some regulatory reform, promotion of awareness of the sector, capacity-building (including the improvement of technology), and enhanced involvement of voluntary organizations in departmental policy development.

STRIKING AN ACCORD: THE VSI AND THE JOINT ACCORD TABLE PROCESS

The Accord as Process

Although the VSI dealt with a broad range of issues, the Accord was to be one of its centrepieces — the other being a national volunteerism initiative. Making a commitment of $5 million over two years to the development of the Accord, the government was keen to move forward with it in an expeditious manner. Because the Accord was part of a broader, collaborative initiative and because the first set of Joint Tables had been so successful, the process for developing the Accord seemed self-evident — a complete "no-brainer" that did not need to be debated. The process simply copied the Joint Table model that had been used in *Working Together*, consisting of seven representatives from the voluntary sector and seven from the federal government, jointly co-chaired. The Joint Accord Table (JAT) was one of six substantive joint tables assigned to deal with different components of the VSI and its work was supported through two separate secretariats, the government's Voluntary Sector Task Force housed in the PCO and a secretariat responsible to the sector (albeit wholly supported by the VSI).[21]

It is important to note that the nature of representation embodied by the JAT is fundamentally different from that of England or the other UK jurisdictions. While in the UK, whether the process was sector-led as in England or a joint process as in Scotland, it was dominated by the leaders of the national umbrella organizations representing their agencies. Participation in the Canadian context was focused on *individuals,* mainly staff of national or regional organizations (and public servants), who were expected to represent broad sectoral interests, not their own organizations or departments.[22] The voluntary sector membership of the VSI tables was selected through a self-nomination process with an independent selection committee sifting through roughly 1,500 nominations to ensure that the 65 available positions were filled by individuals representing all parts of the country, all parts of the sector and local/provincial as well as national organizations. The selection process never managed to be fully inclusive of minority and Aboriginal communities, however. To enhance its outreach, the VSI established two reference groups representing these communities, but their interaction was often more sporadic than regular and more contested than collegial.

All members of the Joint Tables participated as volunteers, initially being asked to give two days a month to the exercise, although in reality participation took much more time than this. The Joint Tables worked with a no-substitution rule in order to maintain continuity. While there was some turnover (for instance, losing two of the seven government members and one voluntary sector member of the JAT), the rule achieved reasonable continuity in Joint Table membership. Where there was a significant discontinuity, however, was with the earlier process that had gotten the voluntary sector to this point. The members of the VSR who, as part of *Working Together*, had proposed the Accord in the first place were not the ones who, collectively, would take the idea forward to implementation. Nor did the structure of the VSI as a whole allow the sector to assume effective leadership and accountability for the development of the Accord.

As joint ventures, the Joint Tables themselves could not be accountable directly to either government or the sector. The government members reported through an executive committee of assistant deputy ministers to a reference group of eight ministers who were responsible for providing political leadership at the Cabinet table (see Brock 2001; Phillips 2001). At several points in the process of developing the Accord, the government members had to go back to the executive committee and the reference group of ministers to obtain guidance or approvals for certain positions. Leadership on the voluntary sector side was even more challenging as there was no national umbrella organization in charge. In order to provide some measure of leadership, the VSR and the voluntary sector co-chairs of the Joint Tables came together to form a Voluntary Sector Steering Group (VSSG) that met regularly to address issues arising from the VSI. Since it was not an organization itself, however, the VSSG tended to lead from behind, away from public attention. Although the JAT and other Tables were intended to work quite autonomously, a Joint Coordinating Committee (JCC) was established to provide guidance on matters of common interest, notably related to communication and community consultation. The JCC had no overlapping membership with the other Tables, however, and, at least initially, laboured under an unclear mandate, uncertain whether it was to provide light coordination or more directive leadership.[23] This meant that it struggled for some time to define an appropriate leadership role for itself, although eventually it was able to assume a more strategic and problem-solving stance. In short, there was no organizational touchstone or strong leadership for the individual sector members of the JAT to help them assess what the voluntary sector as a whole wanted by way of an accord and minimal guidance as to how to respond to particular suggestions that emanated from government.

The federal government's interest in a fast deliverable for the Accord is evident in the time line it first set for the process (see Good 2001). Initially, it was anticipated that an accord could be developed in a year, which would have had it in place by the spring of 2001, with a second year spent on implementation, including the development of codes of good practice. When the Joint Tables were not fully established until August 2000 and the JAT did not meet for the first time until October, it quickly became evident that the original time line was unrealistic. Nevertheless, the government's timing remained driven largely by the symbolism of 2001 as the International Year of Volunteers (IYV) as well as by its eagerness to start rolling out deliverables from the VSI. Thus, the Accord process was very much time bound, attuned to a goal of allowing the Accord to be unveiled in early December 2001, when IYV came to an end and a new volunteerism initiative could also be announced. Although it created significant challenges of workload for the Joint Table members, one distinct advantage of this time frame is that it kept the process moving along.

The voluntary sector members of the JAT came together from across the country and from different parts of the sector with few preconceptions of exactly what an accord would articulate and with no direction from their own organizations or from the VSR as to what they were expected to achieve from the process, other than a signed document. Neither did government have a clear vision of what it wanted out of an accord. Since it was looking at the product as largely symbolic and high level, however, it mattered less what positive commitments it managed to secure for itself. What mattered more was that it did not end up being unduly bound by commitments it could not live with from a political or financial perspective.[24] The exception to this was the staff of the Voluntary Sector Task Force who had had time in the months before the JAT actually met to develop a fairly clear idea of what an accord should look like and become very knowledgeable about the UK experience (and that of Quebec and Newfoundland which had developed "accord-like" policies), as well as to hire consultants, develop communications plans and even develop a draft of an accord so that ministers would have a concrete sense of what they might be in for.[25]

The JAT did not start from the ground up in drafting an accord as it was felt this would be an extraordinarily time-consuming process, nor did it lay out a clear specification of the desired content of the Accord. Instead, it agreed on the general format (shared values, principles, and commitments), and directed staff to bring a draft to the table that could set the stage for discussion. This draft, based on one prepared by a consultant, borrowed heavily from the English and Scottish Compacts, but in contrast to them was long on principles and quite short on specific commitments. From this point on, most of the work of the JAT focused on reviewing, discussing, and rewording drafts prepared by staff or consultants.[26]

Important cultural differences between the two sectors — notably a government culture focused on deadlines and deliverables and a flatter, diverse voluntary sector — were at times evident at both the Joint Table and relationships among staff (Government of Canada/Voluntary Sector Joint Initiative 2003, 32). But, in general, the atmosphere at the JAT meetings was very collegial with little sense of "us" and "them" between the voluntary sector and the government members. Indeed, at one point when a draft came back that had obviously been worked over by Department of Finance officials so as to gut the integrity of the subtle compromises that had been worked out by the JAT, the government members were as quick as the voluntary sector representatives to speak out against the proposed changes (and these were not incorporated). The very nature of the process, however, kept the JAT focused for the most part on detail, not the bigger landscape. But, without entrenched or particularly strong positions on what the content should be in the first place, there seemed little need to keep going back to basics. The key issue for the voluntary sector members was advocacy and, in particular, ensuring the right to engage in advocacy and that this should not imperil funding relationships. This point was negotiated extensively for a six-week period before agreement was reached and acceptable wording developed (ibid., 16). For many on both sides, what the Accord actually says matters less than what follows in the implementation phase of establishing codes of good practice and creating ongoing, collaborative processes for relationship-building.

On the government side, the question of who had authority to accept or approve any particular commitment became an issue and the process illustrated that "government" is by no means unitary in its interests. Due to the concentration of power that has taken place within the federal government in recent years (Savoie 1999), there are really three different sets of players: the prime minister and his office, the Department of Finance, and what Patrick Johnston (2000) calls "TROG," the rest of government. At first, the Department of Finance had little interest in the VSI. Partway through, however, the breadth and potential implications of the initiative sunk in and Finance began to exercise much more direct scrutiny over not only the JAT, but some other Tables as well.[27] Through the ADM executive committee, Finance began to vet proposed content of the Accord more closely to ensure that provisions that would have significant or long-term fiscal implications did not go forward. This behind-the-scenes oversight created some confusion and misunderstanding at the Joint Table about the real lines of accountability and where the buck actually stopped (ibid., 33).

Engaging the Sector

The JAT realized from the beginning, in part based on the UK experience, that the main source of the credibility of the process would stem from its engagement of voluntary organizations across the country in a dialogue about the Accord. By May 2001, a draft was ready for community consultation which took place in two rounds of meetings with local groups across the country, the first in ten major centres in June, and the second round in smaller centres in September. An important part of this process was to have local voluntary organizations host the event, which proved to be empowering for these organizations and began to build a support network for the initiative as a whole.[28] Usually both a government and a voluntary sector member of the JAT as well as staff attended each full-day session and attendance rotated among the members depending on their availability. In many cases, the incurred expenses of groups from outside the urban area were paid. The result is that the consultations were fairly expensive, costing a total of roughly $800,000 to visit 23 communities, but they were able to reach 2,000 Canadians and to facilitate participation by small and rural organizations (Government of Canada/Voluntary Sector 2001, iv). By this time, concerns over the lack of inclusiveness of visible minority and Aboriginal communities had become a serious issue for the VSI. Even though the JAT held meetings with the visible minority and Aboriginal reference groups, these communities never came to feel any real ownership or identity with the process or the product. [29]

By far the greatest challenge in the engagement process was time pressure. In the first round, which was rushed in order to be held before the summer, participants were given only a few days to review the draft accord. It is ironic to note that had these consultations been held under the terms of England's code for consultation, which stipulates a minimum of 12 weeks for comments, the JAT would have been in violation of good practice. Although participants in the second round had the draft well in advance, those who wanted to make follow-up comments had a short window of time to do so. If the Accord was to be signed off in early December, a final version had to go forward for approval no later than October, just as the consultations were concluding.

In spite of the time pressure, the JAT heard quite plainly some strong messages from the voluntary sector. To its credit, the JAT was very transparent in communicating what was learned in the engagement process and in showing how the Accord changed as a result. The main concerns related to a general level of frustration with governmental relations — with provincial and municipal as well as federal government — and to matters of substance and style of the Accord.[30] Just as in England, it is apparent that a national government is seen as much more remote and, indeed, irrelevant, to the daily operations of most community organizations. Unlike the experience in England, however, the federal government could not respond with a plea to be patient that local agreements with municipal governments would follow. In terms of the substance of the Accord, the consultations reinforced the importance of several issues to the sector at large: the need to ensure that voluntary organizations can engage in advocacy, the importance of funding relationships and their stability, and concerns about how the Accord would actually be implemented (One World 2001). There were also a considerable number of participants who said that although they still had reservations, the Accord was "good enough, move on to the next stage" (ibid.). A range of review and discussion sessions were also held with government officials led by the ADM committee. But, by the admission of the JAT's own government members, there is a sense of missed opportunities for building awareness and support for the Accord and the

VSI across federal departments and regions (Government of Canada/Voluntary Sector Joint Initiative 2003, 36).

Based on what was learned from the first round of consultations, the JAT revised the Accord, simplifying the language where possible and adding an introduction which describes the context and underlying rationale. The final version does not deviate dramatically, however, from the draft that formed the basis of the consultations.

Throughout the process of developing and consulting on the Accord, the JAT struggled with the issue of who constitutes the audience. How is "voluntary sector" to be defined? To whom would the Accord apply: to organizations and government departments who have entered into a relationship? Only to national voluntary organizations, or to all of the sector? Does it apply to all government departments, or only those that choose to have a relationship with the voluntary sector? What if a department refuses a relationship even though its constituency in the voluntary sector is seeking one? The JAT chose to resolve this by being inclusive, that the sector is broadly defined as nonprofit and charitable organizations, and that it applies to any organization, local as well as national, with a relationship with the federal government. It was also careful to recognize, however, that many voluntary organizations will never seek out nor develop such a relationship, and this is to be respected.

This raised a related question of who would sign the Accord. This is relatively straightforward for the Government of Canada, but much more complex for the voluntary sector. The realistic solution was to have the final document signed by the prime minister with the JAT co-chairs signing the letter of transmittal and the chair of the Ministerial Reference Group, the Honourable Lucienne Robillard, and the chair of the Voluntary Sector Steering Group, Marlene Deboisbriand, providing a forward. The signing of the Accord met its target date and was commemorated at a major media event on 5 December 2001, the close of the International Year of Volunteers. The media's approach to the signing event was essentially to ignore it. The event received no mention in the national newspapers or broadcast media and limited coverage in the regional papers.[31]

In sum, the process did succeed in producing an accord in a relatively short period of time and in consulting on it quite broadly across the sector. The structure of the JAT and its relationship to the rest of the VSI led to three shortcomings, however. First, neither party started the Accord development process with a clear vision of what they wanted and what specific elements should be incorporated into a framework agreement. Second, while the staff was seen as enormously supportive of the work of the Table, the process was led by government staff, at least at critical stages early on. This occurred not by intent, but by the fact that the PCO task force was the only aspect of the process that had a measure of longevity and continuity.[32] Third, the consultations did little to produce a broadly based sense of ownership of the Accord given the time pressures under which they took place. The latter is a more serious issue for the sector than it is for government because its longer term stakes in the engagement process were higher. It is still not clear whether such a broad sense of ownership of the Accord will yet be built, but one thing it has done is to raise serious questions about how the voluntary sector represents itself to itself and to governments.

The Accord Document

Although the JAT explicitly modelled its agreement on the English and Scottish Compacts, it also reworked and shaped them to fit the Canadian context. Without strong backing from the top political level and with the oversight role played by Finance, the Canadian Accord achieved what was politically viable. On several issues, it appeared that the government was not prepared to go as far as the sector representatives wanted, but since the starting draft did not raise highly contentious issues, the voluntary sector representatives rarely had to test these limits head to head.

The Accord is, as intended, a high-level document that sets out general principles and parameters of the relationship, with the intention that more specific best-practices are dealt with in two subsequent codes of good practice. In a conceptual sense, there are five dimensions that are key to framing a relationship between the voluntary sector and a government. These are the provisions for: autonomy, advocacy and consultation, funding, inclusion, and accountability (that is, mechanisms for ongoing monitoring and reporting). In the Canadian Accord, these elements are addressed as follows.

Autonomy. As an underlying principle, there is an explicit recognition of the independence and autonomy of the voluntary sector (and, for symmetry, of the Government of Canada), including recognition of their unique strengths and separate accountabilities.

Advocacy and Consultation. Using wording copied almost verbatim from the English Compact, the Accord's statement of principles recognizes the independence of voluntary organizations, including their right within the law to challenge public policy policies and to advocate for change, and that advocacy should not affect funding relationships.[33] The value of open, respectful, and informed dialogue also appears as a guiding principle and the government commits to "*recognize the need* to engage the voluntary sector in open, informed and sustained dialogue" [emphasis added]. Note that this is a commitment to recognize the need for dialogue, not necessarily to consult the sector on issues that affect it (as in the UK counterparts).

Funding. The Accord is relatively silent on funding relationships. The only mention is that the government commits to *recognize and consider* the implications of its legislation, regulations and policies, including the importance of funding policies and practices for the further development of the relationship and for strengthening the capacity of the sector. As with the need for dialogue, the federal government could recognize and consider the impact of its funding policies, but not do anything about them. It is for this reason that the subsequent funding code, which does make commitments regarding good practice, is so important.

Inclusion. Respect for diversity, inclusion, and social justice are recognized as three of six Canadian values that are most relevant to the Accord. The only positive commitment to promoting greater inclusion, however, is made by the voluntary sector in that it agrees to "serve as a means for the voices and views of all parts of the voluntary sector to be represented."

Accountability. The Accord is more open-ended than the UK Compacts regarding the mechanisms for monitoring and review, with greater faith that these will evolve rather than needing to be specified in the document. The most concrete requirement is a regular (not necessarily an annual) meeting between ministers and sector representatives. In addition, the parties agree to develop in a timely manner appropriate organizational structures; processes for monitoring, reporting to Canadians and resolving disputes; and codes of good practice for policy dialogue and funding (and other issues as identified). They will also take ongoing actions to increase awareness of the Accord.

When we compare the Canadian Accord to the prototypes of England and Scotland on which it was modelled, along these five dimensions, it is evident that the Canadian document makes fewer and less specific commitments and deliberately avoids the more contentious points of a relationship (Table 1).

Table 1: Key Dimensions Compared: The Agreements of England, Scotland and Canada

Elements	Autonomy	Advocacy and Consultation		Funding	Inclusion	Accountability
England	√√	Advocacy √√ Consultation √√		√√√	√√√	√√
Scotland	√√	Advocacy √ Consultation √√		√√	√√	√√√
Canada	√√	Advocacy √ Consultation √		√	√	√

Notes: √   weak in number and/or specificity of principles and commitments.
     √√   moderate.
    √√√   strong.

Indeed, the Accord holds the Canadian government and the voluntary sector to only four rather minimalist shared commitments and three particular ones each (Table 2). None of these are particularly powerful undertakings that would provide a vision for or could direct a major change in the government-sector relationship.

So what, if anything, is achieved in the Accord? In contrast to its British counterparts, most of the potential impact of the Canadian agreement lies in its principles rather than in specific commitments. These principles are not unimportant, however, because the parties agree to act in a manner consistent with them. Among these, four may have enough teeth to change how government and the voluntary sector interact. The first is the right to engage in advocacy (within the law) without having an effect on funding relationships. The second is the provision that dialogue be open and respectful and that sustained dialogue have appropriately designed governance structures, suggesting an onus on government to be more innovative in

Table 2: Summary of the Accord's Commitments

Shared Commitments

- Act in a manner consistent with the Accord's values and principles;
- work together as appropriate to achieve shared goals;
- promote awareness and understanding of the contribution that each makes; and
- develop the mechanisms to put the Accord into action.

Government Commitments	• recognize and consider the implications of its legislation and policies; • recognize the need to engage the voluntary sector in dialogue; and • address the issue of ministerial responsibility for the continued development of the relationship.
Voluntary Sector Commitments	• continue to identify important or emerging issues; • serve as a means for the voices and views of all parts of the sector to be represented; and • address the issue of responsibility for continued development of the relationship.

creating new vehicles for engagement. Third, the two sectors agree that there is benefit in working together on issues of mutual concern and that such working relationships are to be respectful and flexible. The final one may be the real sleeper of the Accord: that both government and the voluntary sector ensure transparency, high standards of conduct, and that they monitor and report on the results of working together. This is significant because it reinforces the need for effective mechanisms through which such transparency and reporting can occur. Beyond these principles, the general tone of the Accord is promissory in nature, and herein may lie its sustaining value — that the signatories will continue to work on the relationship and mechanisms for improving it.

ROUND TWO: THE MEANS FOR IMPLEMENTATION

The implementation stage is at least as critical to the effectiveness of the Accord as the process leading up to its development or the actual content.

This is particularly so in the Canadian case because, in producing a less specific and less directive accord in the first place, the onus of giving it life rests with a second stage. To this end, the JAT did not stop its work when the Accord was finalized, but continued to meet as three subgroups until July 2002 in order to develop a code for policy dialogue and for funding, and to make recommendations about the structures for monitoring and reviewing the Accord, as per commitments under the agreement.

The Codes of Good Practice

The process of approving the codes was an example of how the VSI could work collaboratively, but only up to a point, because ultimately the central agencies would intervene if what the VSI "decided" upon was not acceptable to them. The two JAT subcommittees charged with developing the policy dialogue and funding codes respectively reached agreement on wording reasonably swiftly as time was short. Feedback was obtained during a necessarily brief round of consultation and at a national forum on the Accord held in March 2002, and drafts were approved by the JAT and the JCC. At this point, concern arose at higher levels within the federal government that the wording gave away too much democratic control and potentially guaranteed a role for the sector in all policy development.[34] The approval of the codes was held up for some time while revisions were made by senior officials in the central agencies. Nevertheless, the final versions signed off by the federal government and released in October 2002 still make substantial commitments to improved dialogue and funding practices.

In contrast to the high level and general nature of the Accord, the draft codes of good practice are concrete, specific, and comprehensive. Building on an earlier draft (but never implemented) set of guidelines for citizen engagement developed under the auspices of PCO, the policy dialogue code commits the Government of Canada and the voluntary sector, in essence, to engage in regular, open and ongoing dialogue about public policy; to be inclusive in how it does so; and to develop the policy capacity to strengthen the quality of such engagement (see Voluntary Sector Initiative 2002a,b).

The funding code is equally positive in its potential for improving direct funding practices, although (appropriately) was never intended to deal with funding amounts. On the government side, a long list of very useful good practices and commitments is delineated that, if followed, would help to promote sustainable capacity and enhance the consistency, stability, and transparency of the federal funding process. A long-standing concern of the federal government has been that the burden of responsibility in such codes of good funding practices is borne disproportionately by government because it is the funder. Ironically, the code goes far in the other direction, placing at least as much responsibility on the voluntary sector as on the federal government.[35] The voluntary sector not only commits to appropriate financial reporting and sound financial management, but to promoting ethical fundraising practices, diversifying funding sources, ensuring that sufficient monitoring and control systems are in place, providing effective board governance, developing evaluation tools for measurement of long-term outcomes of funding, and investing in organizational and human resource development.[36] All of these are, indeed, good practices with which virtually all of the sector would probably concur. To ensure that such practices are in place on a sector-wide basis, however, will require the development of significant new capacity and of mechanisms that can facilitate the sector's self-regulation. Unless the sector can monitor itself, the federal government will do so on a case-by-case basis when organizations apply for funding. And this would represent a considerable loss of sectoral autonomy and authority for self-regulation. It could also present the federal government with some tricky intergovernmental issues since forcing compliance with the commitments related to fundraising, governance, and management potentially take it into provincial territory.[37]

New Political and Administrative Machinery

Perhaps the most important factor in giving life to the Accord will rest on the establishment of institutionalized mechanisms for communication, coordination, review, and reporting. As is evident from the UK experience, machinery in three distinct locales is vital. The first is a joint space that enables senior representatives of government and the voluntary sector to come together on a regular basis to review, report on, and make action plans for improving the relationship. Second, mechanisms are needed to enable political leadership and administrative support and coordination within the federal government. Third, the voluntary sector needs its own means of leadership for monitoring, communicating, and promoting compliance.

The joint and governmental machinery was announced by the federal government, based largely on recommendations of the JAT subcommittee, at the final wrap-up meeting of the Joint Tables in October 2002. A primary consideration for the design of these mechanisms is that the infrastructure be light, yet provide adequate incentives so that the implementation process is taken seriously. They include:

- assignment of ministerial responsibility for the sector (to the minister of Canadian heritage);
- a consultative committee of ministers to continue the work of the Reference Group of Ministers;
- a joint steering committee comprised of assistant deputy ministers and representatives of the voluntary sector;
- an ADM interdepartmental committee to provide horizontal coordination across federal departments;
- accountability for the Accord and the codes vested in deputy ministers as part of their mandate letters; and
- an administrative unit, housed in the Department of Canadian Heritage.[38]

The contentious aspect of this machinery from the sector's perspective was the location of the administrative unit that will replace the PCO secretariat as there is a strong case that such a unit needs to be located in a central agency in order to have the requisite political clout and means of coordination among other departments. The current nature of the central agency machinery in the Government of Canada is not well disposed to house such a unit, however, nor was there support among senior public servants in trying to make a central agency a hospitable home. The limitations of locating the administrative unit in a line department have been compensated to some extent by providing interdepartmental committees at both the ministerial and senior management levels to address the horizontal issues and by vesting responsibility with deputy ministers for drilling attention vertically down into departments.

During the course of the VSI, the voluntary sector was also working to ensure its leadership structures were up to the task of implementation. Realizing that it was not a sufficiently inclusive or democratic organization to carry the policy work of the sector forward post-VSI, the VSR put itself in mothballs in 2001 and the VSSG began the work of creating a successor. The Voluntary Sector Forum, which was launched in October 2002, is a loose, hybrid coalition, with a slightly broader membership than its predecessor. It includes representatives of national umbrella organizations and of the visible minority and Aboriginal communities, with half of its 18 members drawn from the former VSSG and half newcomers. Even if the forum is eventually capable of strong policy capacity, the emergence of such a role will take some time. In addition, leadership in the sector has further been cast in at least temporary turmoil by discussions of the possibility of a merger of two of the largest umbrella organizations, the Canadian Centre for Philanthropy and the Coalition of National Voluntary Organizations, both of which are without permanent executive directors while lengthy merger discussions take place. So, at the very time that national leadership in the voluntary sector is most needed, it has been most in flux.

The Challenges of Implementation

Implementation of the Accord and the codes of good practice are not without significant challenges. Peter Hall (1989, 370-86) argues that how successfully a new policy idea is adopted and implemented depends on its viability in three contexts. First, its congruence with contemporary theories and perspectives that have a claim on defining the problems of the day is of critical importance. It is against this tableau of prevailing ideas, theories, and claims that the utility of the proposal in helping to solve public policy problems is judged and attracts supporters or mobilizes opponents. Second, the policy proposal must be viable politically. People need to be persuaded, supporting coalitions of interests constructed, and detractors brought on side. This remains as important at the implementation stage as at the time of agenda-setting. The third consideration is administrative feasibility, whether the institutions involved have the requisite interest in and capacity for implementation.

In this section, we consider the viability of the Accord and the associated codes in these three contexts: the fit with other ideas and values; the ability

to garner political support, and the capacity of the administrative structures and mechanisms to promote compliance and make them living
instruments.

The Fit with Ideas

Although the joint phase of the VSI has now been completed, the value of
a stronger voluntary sector-government relationship is still entirely con-
gruent as an idea with other prevailing public policy values and is likely to
remain so for at least the intermediate term. The problem is not with fit,
but with competition for attention. In many respects, it appears that the
voluntary sector's policy window is closing, if it is not shut already. Given
the intensity and scale of the VSI, many federal policymakers may assume
that the voluntary sector file has been completed, or at least that the sector
has had its turn. And not by choice, the political agenda has become much
more crowded since 11 September 2001, notably with matters of security
and the economy, but on the domestic policy front with health-care reform
as well. In addition, the implementation stage begins at a time of leadership transition within the federal government, creating uncertainty about
priorities and tentativeness about making any medium or long-term resource commitments.

Even if the idea of relationship-building with the voluntary sector maintains a space on the policy agenda, implementation of the Accord will need
to be squared against another idea that has a central claim on all federal
departments that deal with the sector — accountability, or at least the restrictive interpretation of accountability and the stringent accountability
regimes that have come into play since the alleged boondoggle of mishan-
dled grants and contributions at Human Resources Development Canada
(HRDC) in 2000. By all accounts, life on the ground for voluntary organizations that receive direct funding from federal departments has become
considerably worse since the imposition of very strict reporting, monitoring, and auditing requirements in the aftermath of the HRDC scandal (see
Phillips and Levasseur 2002). An important challenge will be to find ways
of reconciling the idea and practices of accountability with those of the
codes, which would undoubtedly enhance both real accountability and the
ongoing process of relationship-building.

The Political Test

The political test is in finding champions for the Accord, both within government and the voluntary sector. Although the ministers who were part of the reference group have been supporters of the Accord, they have not been highly visible champions of it. While there is now a minister with named responsibility, the sector's relationships and activities touch on the mandate of most departments to some extent. Thus, the new minister will need to coordinate implementation of the Accord and mobilize broad political support across many departments, a task that is at the best of times difficult for a minister in a line department. While the Joint Table process clearly promoted mutual understanding and policy learning between the government and voluntary sector participants, it is less evident that this learning has been institutionalized within departments and central agencies. One reason for this is the incredible mobility among public servants who often do not stay long enough in one position to build trust relationships, either with relevant constituencies in the sector or horizontally among relevant colleagues in other departments or regions.

For the voluntary sector, an important new political dimension emerged during the VSI process that will require considerable sensitivity and leadership. This is the importance of inclusion and responsiveness to ethnocultural and Aboriginal communities. Inclusion is by no means a new issue for the voluntary sector and, indeed, many voluntary organizations have worked seriously to address it in recent years. Due to the lack of representation and connection with minority communities in the early days of the VSI, however, issues of inclusion were put squarely on the sector's agenda. And, they appeared not as a potential strength of the sector, but as a faultline. Over the course of the VSI, there was considerable movement toward being more inclusive of minority communities as is evident in the explicit and extensive attention paid to inclusion and equity of access in the codes of good practice, compared to the bare mention of inclusion in the Accord's principles and commitments. Nevertheless, minority communities are more mobilized and more attuned to how they are treated by the rest of the sector and by government as a result of the VSI, and will need to be taken seriously in relationship-building over the longer term. The new Voluntary Sector Forum will need to figure out not only how to be inclusive in its work, but how to bring along the leaders of the national umbrella organizations, some of whom are initially sceptical of its relevance and concerned about competition for funding.

Administrative Support

Perhaps the most important factor in giving life to the Accord will rest on how effectively the new joint governmental and voluntary sector mechanisms work. Although it is still very early days in the life of this machinery, three challenges are apparent. The first is that the weight of implementation and coordination in both the joint space and within the federal government rests on relatively "soft" mechanisms, that is, not on new institutions with dedicated resources and political clout, but on working committees. Although understandably there is no appetite in government to create heavy machinery, nor is it necessary, it has to be recognized that attracting the right individuals and establishing the right incentives for continued participation in these committees is critical in the present scenario. Most horizontal initiatives have a tough time maintaining momentum over the long term and the high degree of mobility within the public service makes this even more challenging. Although there is a permanent administrative unit charged with supporting implementation, its location in a line department means that it will be dependent on political leadership, at both the ministerial and senior management levels within the public service, to give it the requisite credibility to promote adherence to the codes within other departments.

A second challenge is that the transition from the VSI mechanisms to the new administrative unit in Canadian Heritage has been slow because the creation of the new machinery was not announced until the Joint Tables wrapped up in October 2002. Consequently, there has been an apparent loss of momentum of at least six months while the new unit is staffed and resourced. The ensuing implementation would do well to consider one of the imperatives of the creation of the Accord in the first place, that quick hits help in building credibility and political support.

Finally, at the end of this intense period of collaborative work with the VSI, there remains a sense among many voluntary sector leaders that the initiative has not adequately dealt with the sector's key concerns. In particular, financing, the treatment of advocacy, reform of regulatory institutions, and regulation of access to the tax system to issue tax receipts for donations remain outstanding issues which will continue to be pressed by the sector. If these more contentious elements of the government-voluntary sector relationship are channelled through the joint processes for review of the Accord and the codes, the high stakes involved and entrenchment of positions may quickly gum up this joint machinery. One element learned from the UK experience is that such highly political issues need to be dealt with, and are perhaps better done so through separate processes in which politics can and will play out to the fullest extent without jeopardizing a new joint process that is still in its infancy.

CONCLUSION: AN ACCORD DANCE

Compared to the past two decades, the voluntary sector and the federal government have come a long way toward improving their relationship with each other. The Accord is an important benchmark in the relationship and it is a remarkable achievement to get agreement on a set of principles and general commitments, including institutionalizing a regular meeting for review of the relationship. In comparison to the Compacts of England and Scotland, however, the Canadian Accord is much less specific in the commitments that it extracts from either the federal government or the voluntary sector. Is this a failure of the Canadian process? Not necessarily. The JAT chose to get a general agreement in place and, in a second round, deal with the detail. This may not have been a conscious tactic so much as it was a natural outcome of how the process was designed: the JAT comprised individuals working without the organizational support of a membership national umbrella, as was the case in the UK. In the absence of an organization to connect the representatives working on the Accord to the broader sector, there was no clear collective agenda that could serve as a touchstone.

There is much to be said for a more incremental approach, however. Given that the Department of Finance was very cautious about the Accord and the VSI in general, it is realistic to assume that not much more could have been achieved in the first round anyway. But a strategy based on incremental change is also risky. Since the VSI was initiated, the political agenda has become more crowded with other issues. In addition, there is unexpectedly less money available to support the Accord, although once developed it is not a particularly expensive proposition to support. While the VSI process drew considerable support from within the senior bureaucracy of the public service, this support was rather narrow in its breadth, and has become increasingly so due to the incredible mobility within the public service which reduces its corporate memory. The implementation of codes of good practice that touch on the very areas that the federal government has astutely avoided dealing with in a joint manner under the VSI, notably funding and advocacy, will prove to be a tricky political process.

The ultimate success of the VSI also depends on how it plays within a diverse voluntary sector. At the grassroots level, there is already considerable questioning of what all this relationship-building has done for community-based organizations, particularly given the pressures they are facing from the very demanding federal accountability regime that has been imposed in recent years. Although even in the best-case scenario, an accord could not quickly transform life at the grassroots, there are nevertheless real concerns about the longer term benefits, and the sector's leadership will need to communicate widely about how implementation is proceeding and build confidence that it is a worthwhile endeavour. At the same time, a major impact of the VSI has been to put a spotlight on how well the leadership and governance structures serve the sector as a whole. The VSR brought the sector an incredible distance in its relationship with the federal government on the basis of the voluntary effort of a handful of individuals, but the next two to five years will have to concentrate on making a new leadership mechanism work. Indeed, commitments under the Accord hold the sector to dealing with this matter.

So, the future of the Accord is unlikely to be a neat linear march toward full implementation whose success is predetermined at this stage. Rather, the process is more likely to be played out as an accord "dance" among its supporters, its detractors and those who question its relevancy. Cha-cha-cha.

Notes

My thanks to David Good, Kathy Brock and the participants at the authors' workshop for their thoughtful comments on an earlier draft of this paper. I am also grateful to the members and staff of the Joint Accord Table for allowing me to be an observer to the process.

[1]I was granted the only observer status at the Joint Accord Table that developed the Accord. This allowed me to attend all of the meetings that led to its development and to have access to all of the minutes and background documents prepared for the Table as well as interview members of the Table and secretariat staff.

[2]I am grateful to David Good for suggesting that Kingdon's framework be developed more fully than it had been in an earlier draft of this paper. Kendall (2000) has undertaken a similar analysis of the development of the English Compact which served as a useful comparison in making these revisions.

[3]A number of traditional "charities," perhaps most significantly the YM and YWCA, had reinvented themselves over the course of the 1980s to become much more inclusive organizations with strong outreach to minority communities.

[4]I am thankful to Gordon Floyd of the Canadian Centre for Philanthropy for drawing this to my attention.

[5]Before the Voluntary Sector Task Force was created, the responsibility for developing a strategy to meet the *Red Book* commitments was given to the Canada Customs and Revenue Agency (CCRA) which worked for a short time with an interdepartmental committee and minimal resources contributed by other departments. Little progress was made under this arrangement, however, as the narrow mandate and focus of CCRA on registered charities did not give it enough political clout, nor were there adequate resources to make the work sufficiently horizontal.

[6]The idea was fashioned after the experience of Northern Ireland where in 1993 civil servants (who dominate government power) had developed a framework for conduct of relations with voluntary and community organizations (see NICVA n.d.; McCall and Williamson 2001). Even more directly, the idea of a framework agreement was modelled (and named) after the "concordants" that were being developed within the national government as a means of facilitating accountability between the centre and the host of departments and agencies whose operations had been so significantly decentralized as part of NPM (Kendall 2000).

[7]Once Labour formed the government in 1997, the voluntary sector enjoyed unprecedented access and its new status was reflected in the creation of a centrally placed administrative unit which is known as the Active Citizenship Unit and is housed in the Home Office. The Conservative government had also had a commitment to active citizenship, but it was focused to a much greater extent on promoting volunteerism than on civic participation or social inclusion than its Labour successor.

[8]Wales has gone further than any of the other UK jurisdictions in institutionalizing the Compact in formal ways. As part of devolution, a Voluntary Scheme was embedded in the *Government of Wales Act* that establishes legally binding requirements on the government to have regular dialogue with voluntary organizations. In addition, a Voluntary Sector Partnership Council, comprised of representatives of the sector and elected members of the Welsh Assembly, has been created as a means of facilitating this dialogue on an ongoing basis.

[9]To this end, a reference group of 67 members representing diverse parts of the sector was established to provide ongoing advice to the Working Group and enabled minority and community-based groups to at least go along with the national process until their turn came. Consultation was not limited to engaging the voluntary and community sector, however. The government also consulted internally with a range of departments and agencies on the draft in order to understand existing differences in practice, coordinate responses, and build commitment for a compact.

[10]The Compact Working Group took an additional step in getting agreement from the Opposition Conservative Party so that the Compact is truly a bipartisan policy, not merely an agreement with the Labour Government (Straw 1999)

[11]These include undertakings on the part of governments to: recognize and support the independence of the sector, including its right to comment on and challenge any government policy; respect the right of the sector to advocate within the law in order to advance its aims; and consult the sector on issues affecting it in a manner that takes into account the interests and needs of women, minority groups and the socially excluded. The voluntary sector commits to ensuring that it informs and represents the view of its constituents and supporters; promotes equality of opportunity in the sector's activities, employment and involvement of volunteers; (in Scotland) demonstrates how organizations consult and how they are accountable to their constituencies; and promotes the development of infrastructure to allow particular interests and groups to communicate their views to government. In no compact is it expected that assurances of certain levels of funding will be given. What is relevant, however, is the fairness and stability of funding regimes. In both England and Scotland, issues of funding relationships are addressed in concrete terms, including provisions for the development of detailed codes of good practice for funding. Beyond dealing with funding regimes, however, both of these Compacts could be read as creating positive funding obligations on the part of government. This comes in the form of undertakings in the Scottish document to "support umbrella bodies and the infrastructure of the sector" and in the English, "where appropriate" to support the sector's development. In return, the voluntary sector makes commitments to maintain high standards of good management and practice.

[12]These codes lay out quite detailed guidelines for practice. See, for instance, *Funding: A Code of Good Practice* (London: Home Office and Working Group on Government Relations, NCVO, 2000).

[13]A comparable, comprehensive code had been developed in Scotland, but it is the product of the executive rather than a more collaborative process.

[14]All of this takes administrative support: NCVO serves as secretariat to the Compact Working Group, and the Active Communities Unit in the Home Office supports the government's participation. A key aspect of the implementation phase has focused on making the sector aware of the Compact, and training voluntary organizations to use and comply with it effectively. To this end, NCVO has disseminated the codes widely, provided training seminars, and hired a full-time compact development officer to work with community organizations in ensuring that they know what to expect.

[15]See, for example, the report of the second annual meeting in October 2001 (UK. Compact Working Group and Home Office 2001, 7).

[16]The impact on local government-community sector relations was described in the recent review of the English Compact as nothing short of "spectacular," significantly improving understanding and providing the foundation for a beneficial future partnership between local authorities and community-based organizations (UK. Compact Working Group and Home Office 2001, 9). In Scotland, all of the 32 local authorities have established voluntary sector policy statements. Independent of the compact process, the Blair government had embarked on a major reform and modernization of local government that has given local authorities more power, but also submitted them to greater scrutiny. As part of this process, there is an expectation that local strategic partnerships involving private and voluntary sector organizations will be created and that they will tackle issues of social exclusion. In Scotland, the idea of framework agreements between local governments and the voluntary and community sector actually predated the national compact, although they had been destabilized to some extent by a centralized approach to local government reform. In Wales, the development of local compacts has been made mandatory. For a discussion of the local compacts see Craig and Taylor (2002); Craig et al. (2001); and Ross and Osborne (1999).

[17]Northern Ireland and Wales have gone beyond incremental change in involving the voluntary sector and have created new institutions, the Civic Forum and Voluntary Sector Partnership Council respectively. On the developments in Northern Ireland, see McCall and Williamson (2001).

[18]A major review of financing released by the Treasury in 2002 has also been important in addressing both policy and practice. In Scotland, as comprehensive review of charity law (and regulatory institutions governing the sector) was led by the McFadden Commission and in England separate reviews have been led by a task force (chaired by NCVO) and by the Charity Commission. In addition, a broader review by the Cabinet Office addressed the law and the regulatory structures (see UK. Cabinet Office, Strategy Unit 2002).

[19]I am grateful to David Good, who was at this time a senior public servant, for his thoughtful analysis and commentary on this period.

[20]In his application of the Kingdon framework to the development of the Compact in England, Kendall (2000) argues that there was a higher degree of connectedness between the political and the policy stream than is suggested in Kingdon's formulation.

[21]There were also several sector-only or government-only working groups dealing with issues such as advocacy and funding that the federal government was not prepared to address in a fully joint manner at the time.

[22]The terms of reference for the Joint Accord Table were explicit in stating that the role of the voluntary sector members is "not to represent the interests of their organizations, but rather to advance the interests of the sector as a whole in establishing a closer working relationship with the government." See Voluntary Sector Initiative, "Terms of Reference," available at <http://www.vsi-isbc.ca>. The voluntary sector participants were staff of national organizations, such as the YWCA and John Howard Society, but with one exception they are not national *umbrella* organizations that have broad cross-sectoral memberships.

[23]See Brock (2003). The design was intentionally decentralized because the VSI was based on voluntary participation by Joint Table members. To ask individuals to sit on more than one Joint Table was seen to be unreasonable.

[24]The first two meetings were spent getting to know each other and addressing the basic question of the purpose and nature of an accord as a policy instrument. This became a rather circular discussion with little direction so that for the third meeting a facilitator was called in to help the JAT acquire more focus on what they wanted to accomplish. At this time, the voluntary sector representatives and the government members were asked to caucus briefly, which is the first and only time separate caucuses were held at the JAT meetings.

[25]This work was done by the PCO staff rather than the VSI secretariat because the latter was still being staffed. The delay in getting the sector's secretariat fully operational was in part due to the fact that the contribution agreement from the federal government which supported the secretariat took an inordinate amount of time to be signed. See Phillips (2001, 164-65). Although the processes in Quebec and Newfoundland were examined by the JAT, these were always described as only "accord-like" because they are government policies rather than the product of joint development with the sector. Thus, these were never taken as seriously as those of the UK. For a discussion of the policies in Quebec, see White (2001); and Laforest and Phillips (2001).

[26]The JAT held 24 meetings either in person (in Ottawa) or by teleconference, from October 2000 to July 2002. My observation of the process is confirmed by the final report of the Joint Accord Table which recommends that future processes would be better to focus volunteer participation on broad, substantive issues, rather than using their skills for "wordsmithing" tasks (Government of Canada/ Voluntary Sector Joint Initiative 2003, 5).

[27]Approval of the final draft of the Accord was delayed so that Finance could review it. As Brock (2003) notes, had Finance thought the Accord would apply to tax policy, it would never have been approved.

[28]The consultation process is described in detail in the Joint Table's final report (Government of Canada/Voluntary Sector Joint Initiative 2003, 16-20).

[29]The meetings with the Aboriginal community were particularly disturbing for the JAT as it was evident that there seemed little common ground that would enable it to feel any ownership of the Accord. One basic difference is that the whole concept of "voluntary sector" is quite foreign to Aboriginal communities. While it is widely understood that Aboriginal communities would define themselves as nations rather than as part of the voluntary sector, there is little conception of a voluntary sector within Aboriginal communities. Of course, voluntary action occurs in Aboriginal communities, but it is seen as a natural part of helping each other and occurs in a more informal manner or through family networks, rather than being structured into formal organizations and labelled.

[30]The style of the draft accord received an overwhelming thumbs down. It lacked poetry and passion, and the language was often obscure, described as "fuzzy wuzzy."

[31]The announcement of $50 million for the Canada Volunteerism Initiative made at the same time received more coverage, eclipsing that of the Accord, which had always been a fear of the Joint Accord Table members. The only Canadian newspaper to devote any significant attention to the signing was the *Victoria Times Columnist* which ran the story in its second section. ("Ottawa Pledges $50 million to Volunteerism Initiative," *Time Colonist*, 6 December 2001, p. B6). The two major weekly news magazines, *MacLean's* and *L'Actualité* later carried stories.(Media summary provided by the VSI Secretariat).

[32]In its self-assessment, the JAT members commented on the unnecessarily large number of staff present at meetings and the tendency for staff to steer the overall direction of the Table (Government of Canada/Voluntary Sector Joint Initiative 2003, 35).

[33]The phrase, "within the law" is important and intentionally somewhat ambiguous: it could mean within the criminal law (which is not contested), or within the 10 percent regulation of the *Income Tax Act* (which restricts advocacy activities by registered charities to expenditures of no more than 10 percent of all of their resources and is being contested by the sector). By not being specific, the wording was able to pass muster from Finance officials because it puts no pressure on government to change the 10 percent rule. For a discussion of this rule, see Webb (2000) and Harvie (2002).

[34]Even the name of the code, whether it was to be policy "development," as the voluntary sector preferred, or policy "dialogue," as government insisted, was contested.

[35]Note that the funding code applies only to direct funding by the federal government, that is, to grants, contributions and contracts, not to indirect funding through the tax system.

[36]The diversification of funding sources is by conventional wisdom assumed to be beneficial and a desired goal for a voluntary organization. Recent work by Keating and Frumkin (2003) questions the efficiency and benefit of such diversification. Nevertheless, diversification is now a commitment by voluntary organizations.

[37]It would be difficult for the federal government to set up monitoring and compliance mechanisms for these practices in general, outside of reviewing individual organizations when they apply for federal funding, because regulation of voluntary organizations (outside of those that are tied to the *Income Tax* Act) is a provincial jurisdiction.

[38]There was also the announcement that the PCO would continue to work to develop a "voluntary sector lens" that would be applied to all new policies and initiatives going to Cabinet for approval.

References

Brock, K.L. 2001. "State, Society and the Third Sector: Changing to Meet New Challenges," *Journal of Canadian Studies* 35 (4):203-20.

_____ 2003. "A Final Review of the Joint Coordinating Committee of the VSI 2000-2002." Unpublished paper.

Brock, K.L. and K.G. Banting. 2001. *The Nonprofit Sector and Government in a New Century*. Montreal and Kingston: School of Policy Studies, Queen's University and McGill-Queen's University Press.

_____ 2001. "The Nonprofit Sector and Government in a New Century: An Introduction," in *The Nonprofit Sector and Government in a New* Century, ed. Brock and Banting, pp.1-20.

Cohen, M., J. March and J. Olsen. 1972. "A Garbage Can Model of Organizational Choice," *Administrative Science Quarterly* 17 (March):1-25.

Coleman, W.D. 1987. "Federalism and Interest Group Organization," in *Federalism and the Role of the State*, ed. H. Bakvis and W.M. Chandler. Toronto: University of Toronto Press.

Craig, G. and M. Taylor. 2002. "Dangerous Liaisons: Local Government and the Voluntary and Community Sectors," in *Partnership, New Labour and the Governance of Welfare*, ed. C. Glendinning, M. Powell and K. Rummery. Bristol: The Policy Press.

Craig, G., M. Taylor, C. Szanto and M. Wilkinson. 1999. *Developing Local Compacts: Relationships between Local Public Sector Bodies and the Voluntary and Community Sectors*. London: York Publishing Services.

Etherington, S. n.d. "Developing Collaborative Relationships between Civil Society and Government: The Compact between the British Government and the Voluntary and Community Sector in England." Paper presented to the World Conference on Governance.

Frumkin, P. and E.K. Keating. 2002. "The Risks and Rewards of Nonprofit Revenue Concentration." Paper presented to the annual conference of the Association for Research on Nonprofit Organizations and Voluntary Action (ARNOVA), Montreal, November.

Gaines, A. 2001. "Voluntary and Community Sector Involvement in the Development of the Compact in England." Presentation to the Joint Accord Table, Ottawa.

Good, David. A. 2001. "A Government-Voluntary Sector Accord," *ISUMA* 2 (2): 46-52.

_____ 2003. "Promises and Pitfalls: Experience in Collaboration between the Canadian Federal Government and the Voluntary Sector," *Journal of Policy Analysis and Management* 22 (1):122-27.

Government of Canada. 2000. *Partnering for the Benefit of Canadians: Government of Canada-Voluntary Sector Initiative*. Ottawa: Privy Council Office.

Government of Canada/Voluntary Sector. 2001. *An Accord between the Government of Canada and the Voluntary Sector*. Ottawa: Voluntary Sector Initiative Secretariat.

Government of Canada/Voluntary Sector Joint Initiative. 1999. *Working Together: Report of the Joint Tables*. Ottawa: Privy Council Office and Voluntary Sector Roundtable.

_____ 2003. *Final Report of Joint Accord Table*. Ottawa: Voluntary Sector Initiative.

Haas, P. 1992. "Introduction: Epistemic Communities and International Policy Co-ordination," *International Organization* 46 (2):1-35.

Hall, M. and P. Reed. 1998. "Shifting the Burden: How Much Can Government Dowload to the Non-Profit Sector?" *Canadian Public Administration* 41 (1):1-20.

Hall, P. 1989. *The Political Power of Economic Ideas*. Princeton, NJ: Princeton University Press.

Harvie, B. 2002. "Liberalizing the Limits on Advocacy by Registered Charities," Unpublished Master's Project Thesis. Kingston: School of Policy Studies, Queen's University.

Jenson, J. and S.D. Phillips. 1996. "Regime Shift: New Citizenship Practices in Canada," *International Journal of Canadian Studies* 14 (Fall):111-36

Johnston, P. 2000."Strengthening Voluntary Sector/Government Relations in Canada." Paper presented to the Independent Sector 2000 annual conference pre-session, Washington DC, October.

Juillet, L., C. Andrew, T. Aubry and J. Mrenica. 2001. "The Impact of Changes in Funding Environment on Nonprofit Organizations," in *The Nonprofit Sector and Government in a New Century*, ed. Brock and Banting, pp. 21-62.

Kendall, J. 2000. "The Mainstreaming of the Third Sector into Public Policy in England in the Late 1990s: Why and Wherefores," *Policy and Politics* 28 (4):541-62.

Kendall, J. and M.R.J. Knapp. 1996. *The Voluntary Sector in the UK*. Manchester: Manchester University Press.

Kingdon, J.W. 1995. *Agendas, Alternatives, and Public Policies*, 2d ed. New York: HarperCollins.

Kobayashi, A. 2000. "Advocacy from the Margins: The Role of Minority Ethnocultural Associations in Affecting Public Policy in Canada," in *The Nonprofit Sector in Canada: Roles and Relationships*, ed. K.G. Banting. Kingston and Montreal: School of Policy Studies, Queen's University and McGill-Queen's University Press, pp. 229-61.

Laforest, R. 2002. "Rethinking the Contours of Advocacy." Paper presented to the annual conference of the Canadian Political Science Association. Toronto, May.

Laforest, R. and S.D. Phillips. 2001. "Repenser les relations entre gouvernement et secteur bénévole: à la croisée des chemins au Québec et au Canada," *Politque et Sociétés* 20 (3):37-68.

Lewis, J. 1999. "Reviewing the Relationship between the 'Voluntary Sector' and the State in Britain in the 1990s," *Voluntas* 10 (3):255-70.

Liberal Party of Canada. 1997. *Securing our Future Together: Preparing Canada for the 21st Century*. Ottawa: Liberal Party of Canada.

McCall, C. and A. Williamson. 2001. "Governance and Democracy in Northern Ireland: The Role of the Voluntary and Community Sector after the Agreement," *Governance* 14 (3):363-83.

Morison, J. 2000. "The Government-Voluntary Sector Compacts: Governance, Governmentality, and Civil Society," *Journal of Law and Society* 27 (1):98-132.

Northern Ireland Council of Voluntary Associations (NICVA). n.d. "Review of the Strategy for the Support of the Voluntary Sector and for Community Development in Northern Ireland." Available at <http://www.nicva.org/millennium/review_of_the_strategy.htm>.

One World. 2001. "Expanding the Dialogue: Overview Report of the June, 2001 Consultations on *An Accord between the Government of Canada and the Voluntary Sector*. Ottawa: One World.

Panel on Accountability and Governance in the Voluntary Sector (PAGVS). 1999. *Building on Strength: Improving Governance and Accountability in Canada's Voluntary Sector*. Ottawa: Voluntary Sector Roundtable.

Phillips, S.D. 1991. "How Ottawa Blends: Shifting Government Relationships with Interest Groups," in *How Ottawa Spends: The Politics of Fragmentation*, ed. F. Abele. Ottawa: Carleton University Press, pp. 183-228.

_____ 2001. "From Charity to Clarity: Reinventing Federal Government-Voluntary Sector Relationships," in *How Ottawa Spends 2001-2002*, ed. L.A. Pal. Toronto: Oxford University Press, pp. 145-76.

Phillips, S.D. and K. Lavasseur. 2002. "The Snakes and Ladders of Accountability: Sliding between Accountability and Collaboration in Canada." Paper presented to the annual conference of the Association for Research on Nonprofit Organizations and Voluntary Action (ARNOVA), Montreal, November.

Pross, A.P. 1992. *Group Politics and the Policy Process*, 3d ed. Toronto: Oxford University Press.

Pross, A.P. and K.R. Webb. 2003. "Embedded Regulation ....," in this volume.

Ross, K. and S.P. Osborne. 1999. "The Voluntary Sector Compact in the UK: Enabling or Constraining Government-Nonprofit Relationships?" Paper Presented to the ARNOVA Conference, Arlington VA, November.

Savoie, D.J. 1999. *Governing from the Centre: The Concentration of Power in Canadian Politics*. Toronto: University of Toronto Press.

Stowe, Sir K. 1999. "England's New Model — a Compact." Presentation to the Canadian Centre for Philanthropy's Fifth Annual Symposium, Toronto.

United Kingdom. Cabinet Office, Strategy Unit. 2002*a*. *Private Action, Public Benefit: A Review of Charities and the Wider Not-for-Profit Sector*. London: Cabinet Office, September.

United Kingdom. Compact Working Group and Home Office. 2001. *Report of the Second Annual Meeting to Review the Compact between Ministers and Representatives from the Voluntary and Community Sector*. October.

United Kingdom. Home Office. 1998. *Compact: Getting it Right Together*. London: HMSO.

United Kingdom. Labour Party. 1997. *Building the Future Together: Labour's Policies for Partnership between Government and the Voluntary Sector*. London: Labour Party.

Voluntary Sector Initiative. 2002*a*. *A Code of Good Practice on Funding*. Ottawa: VSI.

_____ 2002*b*. *A Code of Good Practice on Policy Dialogue*. Ottawa: October.

Webb, K.R. 2000. *Cinderella's Slippers?: The Role of Charitable Tax Status in Financing Canadian Interest Groups*. Vancouver: SFU-UBC Centre for the Study of Government and Business.

White, D. 2001. "Citizenship and the Welfare State: Formalizing Relations between States and Voluntary Sectors." Paper Presented to the ISA-RC19 Conference, Oviedo Spain, September.

3

Embedded Regulation: Advocacy and the Federal Regulation of Public Interest Groups

A. Paul Pross and Kernaghan R. Webb

Optimistic forecasts for the role of the state in Canada emphasize a paradigm shift from government to governance.[1] Voluntarism is at the centre of the new paradigm. "By necessity," as Susan D. Phillips points out,

> the process of governance is much more embedded in civil society institutions than was traditional government. Effective governance requires both a strong private and strong voluntary sector [which] ... includes not only those organizations providing direct services, but intermediary umbrella groups and those, either as independent interest groups or as part of social movements, that are dedicated primarily to advocacy activity.... In governance, the sector is necessary not only to deliver programmes that the state wishes to contract out or vacate, but to provide input into policy-making processes and to promote strong communities capable of helping themselves. Active citizenship, in which citizens engage in civic life through voluntary associations, supports governance by providing better input and monitoring of policy and, as a by-product of participation, by producing greater trust in other citizens and in government (2000/2001, 183-84).

This chapter, which is part of a larger study of the advocacy role of the voluntary sector, focuses on the difficult terrain currently occupied by groups that aspire to the roles attributed to them by civil society ideology and the proponents of the governance paradigm. Its central preoccupation is with the freedom to advocate and with how government regulation affects the exercise of that freedom. In a world where, according to Naomi Klein (2000), the logo may be more important than the product, and where reality shimmers only briefly on the screen, it is instructive to look at the contrast between what is being said about relationships between the voluntary sector and the state and the day-to-day reality of groups — even very significant, highly respected groups — that are attempting to "make a difference." Despite the enormous effort that leaders of the voluntary sector, politicians, and public servants are putting into building the new paradigm, we will show that there is a long way to go to before it will be brought to life.

The discussion is built around two questions: first, it asks whether the advocacy activities of groups are governed by a body of regulation that can be described as a regime. Second, if such a regime exists, how is it experienced by these groups?[2] The chapter is based on a longitudinal study of more than 20 public interest groups. The first part of the study was conducted in 1991–94 and involved interviews with leading officials of 33 groups. The interviews, most of which lasted two hours, touched upon the groups' policy activities and roles; their organizational characteristics and the backgrounds and attitudes of the officials themselves. In the winter of 2000–2001 further interviews were carried out with comparable officials of 20 of the groups. These interviews elicited some information updating the earlier study but focused on the groups' relations with government and their participation in public policy processes.

The groups all meet certain criteria: first, they are all Canadian groups. Most have international connections, but their primary orientation is toward domestic policies and programs. Second, they are all public interest groups.[3] Third, their concerns are national in scope. Fourth, for practical reasons, they had to be located in Ottawa or Toronto. Fifth, they operate in one of the study's selected policy fields: health, "good government," and social justice.[4] Finally, they had to be sufficiently large, in 1992, to be listed in the *Directory of Associations*.

Before addressing the two questions upon which our discussion builds, we must first remind ourselves that the advocacy activity of no group is responsive exclusively to government regulation. In fact, it is likely that official regulation usually has less of an impact on advocacy activity than a host of broader environmental factors, not the least of which are a set of accountability requirements that pertain to the groups themselves and the communities they serve and that support them. In the next section we discuss these accountability requirements as setting the context in which government regulation plays its part. We will then look at the federal government's regulatory framework and examine the impact it has on groups. Before concluding our discussion we will return to the regime question and briefly consider recent developments in regulation.

ACCOUNTABILITY: THE CONTEXT OF REGULATION

The 1990s were a testing time for Canada's charities. Difficulties had emerged initially in the public sector during the 1980s. Inflation and burgeoning government debt gave credibility to conservative attacks on "the nanny state" and fuelled demands for cuts in expenditures and the abandonment of programs. By the beginning of the 1990s a political swing to the right was maturing rapidly. All of this might have encouraged an expansion of voluntary activity, had it not been for two conditions that undermined the ability of the "third sector" to fill the vacuum created by the retreat of the welfare state.

The first condition was inherent in the relationship between governments, charities, and nonprofit organizations (NPOs). Theoretically independent of the public sector, in reality these organizations were highly dependent on it. In 1994 it was estimated that the federal government paid interest groups $3.3 billion, or 2 percent of budgetary spending (Canada.Treasury Board Secretariat 1994, 7).[5] Inevitably, cut-backs in government spending were to have a major impact on the budgets of these organizations, notwithstanding the fact that governments were simultaneously looking to the voluntary sector to provide many of the services that could no longer be provided by public agencies.[6]

The second condition was that Canadians were suddenly given dramatic evidence that highly respected charitable institutions had violated the public's trust. A series of high-profile investigations into abuse at residential schools operated by religious organizations and into the failure of the Canadian Red Cross to protect the blood supply led many to lose confidence in charitable organizations in general (see Picard 1995; Stewart 1996).

Also contributing to public suspicion of the charities was a growing tendency for politicians and the media to attack advocacy groups as special interests. The most strident critic was John Bryden, Liberal MP for Hamilton-Wentworth who conducted a vigorous campaign against government funding for special interest groups. In March 1994 he introduced in the House a private member's bill which sought to secure disclosure of income received by senior officials of charities and nonprofit organizations.[7] Later the same year he published a report which claimed to bring to light "an almost complete lack of government oversight — and the likelihood of widespread abuse — within Canada's $100-billion not-for-profit industry (Bryden 1994, 1). Although Bryden's proposed legislation suffered the usual fate of private members' bills, and did not survive second reading, it did provoke a debate which made it clear that other members had similar criticisms of the third sector.[8]

More authoritative criticism came from the Auditor-General whose review of the Citizenship Branch at Secretary of State and of the Department of National Revenue's management of charities and nonprofit organization under the *Income Tax Act*, found "cause for concern" at both agencies (Canada. Auditor General 1989–90, 674-77). The audit found that 31 percent of charities did not file returns on time; that the rules did not provide a sufficient check on the right of official charities to continue to qualify, or on the validity of deductions and credits allowed to taxpayers or the reliability of information in the Public Information Return (ibid., 258). The report charged that departmental leniency weakened incentives for compliance. The Public Accounts Committee of the House of Commons also looked at the funding mechanisms, grants and contributions, used to provide government financial support to charities and nonprofit organizations. Although the committee did not attack group funding, it "strongly endorsed" the Auditor-General's view that "because there is less accountability for grants than for contributions, grants should only be used rarely and should be reserved for situations where the payment of public funds is truly unconditional and where the use of grants is cost-effective" (Canada. House of Commons 1990).

In his 1994 budget speech Finance Minister Paul Martin made it clear that the government was sympathetic to these views, promising to "review its policy on funding interest groups." With this, Treasury Board began a major assessment of interest group funding, so that by 1995 Martin was able to promise that

> our approach to interest group funding will change as well. Some groups will continue to be funded as is. For others in a position to secure financial support from outside government, we will move toward a system based on the provision of matching funds. For still other groups, continued funding will not be possible due to our financial situation (Martin 1994, 1713; 1995, 1709).

But the chilling effect of public concern and governmental dissatisfaction had been felt in the third sector long before Martin gave official sanction to the campaign to discipline charities and nonprofit organizations. As early as 1991, Susan Phillips had noted "increasing selectivity in how Ottawa spends money on interest groups, resulting in cuts to some groups, and ... greater requirements for financial accountability" (1991, 184-85). Core funding, in particular, was becoming less readily available and was being replaced by "project funding that is more easily controlled and more visibly accountable" (ibid., 185). She also detected a trend toward penalizing advocacy groups speaking out against government policies, but rewarding those whose voice was "integral to the campaign for national unity and the quest for a Canadian identity" (ibid.).

This trend seems to have been clear to the groups themselves. Of the 20 organizations we interviewed in 2000 and 2001, eight could be considered to be engaged in high-profile advocacy. That is, they relied heavily on media exposure to promote their cause in Ottawa.[9] Six derived more than 51 percent of their funding from government, five depending on government for more than 75 percent of their revenues.[10] Four experienced declining revenues in the 1990s, three of them reporting that their revenue situation became turbulent during the period.

Despite growing concern amongst charities and nonprofit organizations, it was not until 1995 that the sector began to organize a clear response.[11] In an article in *Front and Centre*, a publication of the Canadian Centre for Philanthropy, Gordon Floyd reported on government and media criticisms of the sector and warned that higher standards of accountability were not only essential, but should be introduced by the sector itself. The centre was part of a group of national organizations that had begun to address these issues. Calling itself the Voluntary Sector Roundtable, the group, in October 1997, established a panel of six prominent individuals, headed by former NDP Leader Ed Broadbent, to look into the issue of the account-ability of Canada's charities. They were charged with reviewing governance and accountability practices within the sector; proposing guidelines for more effective governance and accountability and were expected to "lead a broad consultation on these proposals" (PAGVS 1998).

The Broadbent Panel is pertinent to this discussion for two reasons. First, it placed the issue of accountability squarely on the agenda of Canada's major charities and nonprofit organizations. Second, it went some way toward defining accountability as it applies to these organizations in this country.[12]

During the 1980s the concept of accountability had been much discussed in Canada, particularly apropos the public sector. However, concern was slow to spread to the third sector. For example, the term does not appear in the index to Samuel A. Martin's 1985 ground-breaking study, *An Essential Grace: Funding Canada's Health Care, Education, Welfare, Religion and Culture*. He focuses his attention on declining government support and the need for charities to develop new income sources. This is not to say that organizations in the sector paid no attention to accountability issues. Rather, there seems to have been a general assumption that trustees, directors, and other officials of charities in particular, but also of many nonprofit organi-zations, had an appropriate sense of their responsibilities and exercised due diligence in meeting them. The residential school scandals, the tainted blood crisis, and government insistence on higher levels of accountability, forced the third sector to recognize that its standards of accountability needed review and reform.[13]

The second factor making the Broadbent review relevant to this discus-sion was its attempt to state precisely what constitutes accountability in the third sector. The panel suggested that "accountability is an obligation to explain how a responsibility for an assigned mandate has been discharged.

It is particularly important in situations that involve public trust" (PAGVS 1999, 12/86). The panel emphasized that this is a complex, multi-layered task, involving "accountability to different audiences, for a variety of activities and outcomes, through many different means." In its largest aspect, accountability holds organizations and their leading officials answerable to a very broad public; not only their immediate members, but also those who have given financial or voluntary support; governments and private sector organizations that have engaged their services; those who have received their services, and sometimes individuals who have been affected indirectly by their activities. This broad public has numerous ways of reviewing the performance of third sector organizations and holding them to account. These include the internal processes of review established by organizations' constitutions and bylaws; examination through media and academic commentary; review by peer associations, and, in extreme cases, the rigours of litigation. Furthermore, different audiences are inclined to scrutinize various aspects of charities' work: some will look directly at outcomes, but others are more concerned with how decisions are arrived at, the means used to accomplish goals, how the organizations comport themselves, the representativeness of the governing body, and so on.

We were interested in using our interviews to discover whether, after a decade of debate, even turmoil, within the third sector, concepts of accountability were widely appreciated and considered significant. Early in the interview we read to our respondents a provocative statement drawn from a British study, which suggested that the accountability standards required of non-governmental organizations (NGOs) are very low, comparing unfavourably with those that corporations must meet.[14] The effect was nearly always instantaneous. The respondent would bristle, obviously wondering whether the rest of the interview would proceed along the same lines. Sometimes the interviewer had to hastily disown any personal agreement with the statement. Only one of the 20 officials interviewed "strongly agreed" with the statement, explaining that he is "very sceptical of NGO accounting practices" and believes that there are "no standard accounting principles used by charities." Officials of two nonprofit organizations agreed with the statement,[15] and one other charity official sat on the fence, while the remaining 16 of our respondents disagreed with it, ten of them strongly. Eight followed this firm rejection of the view that accountability regimes rest lightly on NGOs by agreeing — three strongly — that "the regulatory regime governing Canadian NGOs is comparable to that governing corporations."[16] Six had no comment on this issue, most of them explaining that they did not know enough about accountability regimes in the business community, but another six did disagree. Paradoxically, 15 respondents agreed — seven strongly — that "in order to retain charitable status Canadian NGOs are forced to police themselves more rigorously than are business interests."[17]

We concluded from these responses that concepts of accountability have certainly arrived at centre-stage since S.A. Martin's day. We also inferred, from the responses to a further question about accountability, that some, at least, of this awareness could be attributed to the consultations fostered by the Broadbent Panel. When asked whether "adoption of a voluntary code of accountability developed by and for NGOs, but not a law, would provide useful information to government, the public, the private sector and other stakeholders and increase NGO accountability," an option proposed by the Panel, 16 respondents agreed, four of them strongly. Three, one an NPO, had no opinion and the charity official sceptical of accounting practices disagreed.

While the aggregate responses to these statements are interesting, the supplementary comments made by most respondents are illuminating. The executive director of one charity, for example, disagreed with the suggestion that the regulatory regime governing NGOs can be compared to that governing corporations, "because corporations are less affected by regulations than are charities and NPOs. Furthermore, the voluntary sector has far more accountability mechanisms built in. Volunteers expect to be accountable — their overriding push is collective." Another commented that "as far as accountability goes, an NGO is no different than a corporation with shareholders, especially at the local level. The degree of accountability will vary with the organization. There is always a tug of war between the national body and the provincial organizations and there is a great tension between volunteers and professionals." From another we heard that the issue of accountability "makes people pretty sensitive to their responsibilities. Organizations that are run by volunteers tend to be sensitive to accountability issues. The whole purpose of a volunteer board is to bring members' personal reputations to the service of the organization. Board members don't want to put their reputations at risk."

A senior official of a nonprofit organization commented wryly on the range of accountability mechanisms that her group must work with. Where government funds are involved there are audits and reporting mechanisms that have to be complied with. Her organization has to report four times a year on its federal grant. Both narrative and financial reports are required. When the organization is a registered charity it is required to file the T3010 form annually and may be subjected to a Canada Customs and Revenue Agency (CCRA) audit. It is also accountable to its own annual general meeting board.

These responses reinforce the contention of the Broadbent Panel that accountability is complex and multi-faceted, deriving from many points in the organization's environment, not simply, or even primarily, from government.[18]

FEDERAL GOVERNMENT REGULATION: AN ASPECT OF ACCOUNTABILITY

Thus far we have spoken of accountability in its broadest configuration. Doing so has reminded us that organizations advocate their policy positions in a multi-faceted context of accountability. The vigour and persistence with which a given policy will be promoted, as well as the words used to formulate it, will reflect the expectations of supporters, the sensitivities of volunteers and benefactors, coalition partners, clients, and business associates, as well as the constraints of government regulation. Each, to a greater or lesser degree, is capable of holding the advocacy group to account for its position and the way in which it has delivered its message. But our research is concerned with how government participates in these processes. It recognizes that the concept of third sector accountability is much larger than the level of accountability imposed, in various ways, by the state. At the same time, it does assume that government intervention in the third sector is multi-faceted, influential, and warrants examination in its own right.

The state is variously umpire, guardian of the public interest, and interested party. As umpire it requires third sector organizations to adopt structures and procedures through which their officials can be held to account by members at large. At the federal level the *Canada Corporations Act* is the chief vehicle through which the state plays this role. In this capacity, too, as we shall see, political actors may foster or participate in public discussion of third sector ethics, with a view to creating a climate of opinion that raises the public's expectations of organizations' behaviour. As guardians of the public interest, the state imposes certain rules on third sector organizations, notably the rules that specify what charities and nonprofit organizations may, or may not, do. Finally, in sharing responsibilities with third sector organizations, or commissioning them to perform "paragovernmental" services, including, sometimes, advocacy, governments have a direct interest in holding charities and nonprofit organizations to account for the way in which they carry out their commitments.

Previous research had suggested to the authors that these diverse governmental interventions in third sector accountability could be treated as a "regulatory regime." That is, rather than being discrete regulations which have no discernible systematic or cumulative effect, these various regulations interact as "a mode of rule or management" to encourage certain kinds of behaviour and to suppress others.[19] Interviews with association officials in 1992–93 and documentary research, led us to conclude that associations experience federal government regulation as a regime, and that it would be advantageous to examine the interactive and cumulative effect of charitable status regulation, the requirements of corporate status, the rules surrounding direct funding and other government-imposed standards of accountability.

The literature generally focuses on one element or another of what we believe is the current regulatory regime. The law respecting the tax treatment of charities has received considerable attention (Webb 2000). In recent years the regulation of advocacy groups during elections has been studied by a royal commission and has been the subject of several academic papers (Royal Commission on Electoral Reform 1992, ch. 5; Cross 1994; Bakvis and Smith 1997; Hiebert 1998). Issues in accountability have received much attention from those interested in the delivery of services by charities and nonprofit organizations, though the greater part of that literature examines these organizations in quite different environments, the United States in particular. Very few of these studies look at the regulatory regime in the round.[20] This has consequences for the development of policies intended to encourage these institutions to play an optimal role in service delivery and policy debate, but it is referred to here because it means that there is no consensus in the literature as to what constitutes the regulatory regime. In a later section we will discuss our findings on the regime question and consider their implications for public policy. Our immediate task, however, is to show which federal regulations affect charities and nonprofit organizations and how they are experienced.

We identified seven elements which we believed constituted the federal regulatory regime operating in this field.[21]

1. Accountability

2. Regulation of access to policy formation

3. Corporate status

4. Direct funding

5. Tax expenditure funding

6. Regulation of lobbying

7. Regulation of participation in elections

We asked our respondents whether their organizations were affected by each, and then asked them to indicate the extent to which each kind of regulation affects them. Does it have a major effect? Or is it minor? We followed this question by asking whether the respondent felt that this list "adequately encompasses the field of regulation that affects your organization."

As Table 1 demonstrates, the majority of respondents reported that six of the seven regulatory elements do affect their organizations. The one exception — the regulation of participation in elections — is discussed below; for the moment, we can note that almost all the organizations we contacted make it a policy not to engage in partisan politics. Consequently their officials tend to consider election regulation irrelevant to their activities. Similar factors explain most of the responses in the "no" column. For example, the four groups unaffected by regulations associated with direct funding were nonprofit organizations and major charities receiving no significant government support, whilst three of the four groups reporting that they were not affected by regulations governing charities were nonprofit organizations. By definition, those regulations would not apply to them.[22]

Table 1: Assessing the Impact of the Regulatory Regime

Regulatory Element	Affects your Organization ...					
	1 Yes	2 No	3 N/A (1&2)	4 Major Impact	5 Minor Impact	6 N/A (4&5)
Regulation of access to policy formation	13	6	1	9	6	5
Regulation of participation in elections	4	14	2	3	4	13
Regulation of lobbying	11	8	1	3	8	9
Accountability	11	6	3	7	6	7
Tax expenditure funding	14	4	2	7	3	10
Direct funding	15	4	1	9	5	6
Corporate status	16	4	0	2	10	8

Notes: Regime adequately defined: Yes – 11; N/A – 3; additional elements suggested – 6.

We were also struck, however, by the fact that group officials seemed at times to be quite unaware of the less prominent regulations, even while observing them. This was most noticeable in the case of the response to the question "is corporate status a regulatory element that affects your organization?" Four executive directors replied that it did not, yet all 20 reported later in the interview that they were registered under the *Canada Corporations Act*, or, in a few cases, under the Ontario *Societies Act*. This observation suggested the possibility that the regulatory regime is so embedded that it is almost invisible, even to those who work with it on a daily basis. Hence the title we have given this chapter.

Of the 17 respondents who addressed the question of whether or not we had adequately defined the regulatory regime, 11 felt that we had. Six said that there are additional regulatory elements, but on closer examination we concluded that most of these could be treated as part of one or other of the regulatory elements we had identified.[23] The question of whether a regulatory regime actually exists will be explored later.

ACCOUNTABILITY TO GOVERNMENT AND THE
CONSEQUENCES OF POLICY PARTICIPATION

When we asked respondents whether their organizations were affected by government regulations defining their accountability, we were answered in terms that reflected both the many dimensions of the term and their sector's current preoccupation with it. No fewer than 12 respondents made supplementary comments, some of which help interpret the opaque figures presented in Table 1. Several asked how the term was defined for the purposes of our question. Prior to the interview, we had provided the respondents with definitions of each of the regulatory terms we were using, and explained that in this case we were looking at those aspects of accountability actually described in law.[24] This, however, was ambiguous, since it could include those fiduciary responsibilities the law imposes on charities and nonprofit organizations, as well as the obligations associations might have toward government itself.

Several respondents had in mind the former version of accountability, but pointed out that a sense of obligation to supporters and clients was a far more powerful force than government regulation. One spoke of the "internal forces" that influence her performance and went on to comment that "the members feel that it's their responsibility to oversee the work I do. They can and do challenge me and hold me accountable." Another found the federal government's interest in the accountability of charities and foundations irritating and of much less concern than the internal accountability mechanisms of his own organization: "I have ten organizations looking at every dime I spend." These internal forces may be especially noticeable in coalition organizations, particularly in imposing informal controls. An executive director of a group participating in a social justice coalition noted, for example, that "we wouldn't talk of 'workfare.'" These respondents were often interested in the voluntary code proposed by the Broadbent Panel, referring to it and noting in some cases that it had been discussed with their boards.

The obligations that associations might have toward government itself were clearly on the minds of a second group of respondents. These spoke of the audits and evaluations associated with government grants or of the "product" which their organization delivers.

Six organizations reported that they were not affected by accountability regulations. Their responses reflect the ambiguity we have noted. Some considered their internal controls more significant than government controls; others thought in terms of obligations stemming from contractual relations with government, and since those were, for them, relatively few, they answered our question negatively.

For all of our respondents, though, the issue of accountability is significant. Their views could be summed up in these words:

> There should be accountability. It is not intrusive. Some fundamental elements of accountability intelligently defined and overseen by government can be helpful for organizations. It allows them to say "We met these criteria." On the other hand, there is a danger that it might become bureaucratic. Currently the accountability imposed from outside is light. Level of accounting to the general public is on a par with the tax form T30-10 that is filed annually.

When we asked group leaders whether they felt that their organizations were affected by regulations stemming from access to policy formation we had in mind the possibility that admission to policy discussion might be accompanied by an obligation to accept conditions laid down by sponsoring agencies.[25] This after all, is the crux of the frequently heard complaint that co-optation too often results from accepting agency invitations to contribute to the formation of public policy. Although a significant majority of our respondents, 13 out of 20, reported that their organizations were affected by regulations associated with access, and nine of these felt that the regulations had a major impact, very few commented further. Of those that did, two were clearly not part of an inner circle cultivated by the agencies they wished to influence. One commented that her organization "would like access, but hasn't had and doesn't expect to get it." The other described a constant battle to obtain information from the agency.

Other groups were generally satisfied with their levels of access to agencies, although most appeared to have only infrequent influence in policy areas where their views might have been sought. As one director put it, "access would bring major constraints if [we] were to be involved continuously in policy formation. However, [our organization] does not have access on an on-going basis." Another confessed to having been "pleasantly surprised by the openness of officials. Key is to develop trust. Must not misuse trust. There's a responsibility and ethical challenge to know when being you're co-opted and when respect for confidentiality is a way of getting something done."

In short, while being admitted to bureaucratic policy conclaves might constrain some participating organizations, and was recognized as a possible problem by the majority of those we spoke to, we were not able to delve deeply enough into this issue to determine what form informal regulations might take and how significantly they affect advocacy.

THE REGULATORY IMPACT OF CORPORATE STATUS ON PUBLIC INTEREST ORGANIZATIONS

There are many reasons why individuals wishing to join together to engage in public interest advocacy might choose to adopt the nonprofit corporate form:[26]

- the corporate structure can be used to limit the liability of a corporation's directors and members;[27]

- legal transactions such as entering into contracts or leases, owning property, or participating in legal proceedings are facilitated when an organization is incorporated;

- as noted earlier, to be eligible for government contributions funding, organizations typically are required to be incorporated as nonprofit corporations (or to be in the process of incorporation);

- to obtain charitable status under the *Income Tax Act*, an organization must first be registered either as a nonprofit corporation or be governed by a legal document called a trust or a constitution; and

- some public interest organizations find that corporate status has a prestige and credibility value.

Thus, there are strong incentives for groups to incorporate as nonprofit corporations.

At the federal level, the key legislation pertaining to nonprofits is the *Canada Corporations Act*, and in particular, Part Two of that Act (at the provincial level, see legislation such as the BC *Society Act*). As is discussed below in greater detail, this Act is widely regarded as being in need of significant revision, and is currently the subject of review by federal authorities. For purposes of the *Canada Corporations Act*, a nonprofit corporation is defined as "a body corporate and politic, without share capital, for the purpose of carrying on, without pecuniary gain to its members, objects, to which the legislative authority of the Parliament of Canada extends, of a national, patriotic, religious, philanthropic, charitable, scientific, artistic, social, professional or sporting character, or the like objects" (section 154). Nonprofit corporations must have bylaws in place with provisions pertaining to: the conditions of membership, the mode of holding meetings, what constitutes a quorum, the rights of voting, enacting and amending bylaws, appointment and removal of directors, trustees and officers, and their respective powers and remuneration, audit of accounts and appointment of auditors (section 155).

Of the 20 public interest organizations surveyed, 16 indicated that corporate status had an impact on their activities, but only 2 of the 16 suggested that the impact was major, and nine suggested it had a minor impact.[28] One respondent noted that corporate status "gives some protection and respectability. It encourages donors and increases our responsibility to donors." Another indicated that they "keep an eye" on the *Canada Corporations Act*.

Researchers have suggested that the requirements associated with federal or provincial incorporation may be unduly formal, expensive, and time-consuming for some interest groups: electing a board of directors and establishing bylaws, maintaining publicly accessible records and submitting reports, as is required by federal and provincial law, are significant undertakings for many volunteer organizations. An official in one Canadian nonprofit organization is reported by a researcher as suggesting that rifts can develop between the board (formerly volunteers, but elevated to director status as part of incorporation) and paid staff, with the incorporation process introducing "a hierarchy into the agency" (Ng 1988, 71-78).

Since at least the 1970s (see Cumming 1974; Canada. Consumer and Corporate Affairs Canada 1977), it has been widely acknowledged that the provisions of Part Two of the *Canada Corporations Act* are incomplete, confusing, and out-of-date, leaving the Act silent on major issues of corporate governance (Canada. Industry Canada 2000; Hirshhorn and Stevens

1997). Ministerial discretion and administrative policies currently cover off some of these inadequacies (similar to the situation with respect to charitable tax status), which leaves nonprofit officials at the mercy of administrative whim, and does not provide the sort of up-front clarity that engenders certainty and confidence. The Act lacks critical accountability features that would help sustain public confidence in the sector in its expanded role. Accountability features which are needed pertain to such issues as standard of care provisions for directors, voicing mechanisms for members and other stakeholders, the provision of timely information to directors, members, donors, beneficiaries and the public.

Clarification of the rules with respect to directors' and officers' liability could reduce a considerable amount of current uncertainty — uncertainty that can have a chilling effect on attracting good volunteers.[29] This uncertainty may be particularly relevant to advocacy activities of nonprofits, with directors, officers, and other nonprofit corporate officials particularly vulnerable to legal suits for the statements they make. Under a modernized nonprofit corporate law, as long as directors, officers and other officials acted in good faith, honestly, and exercised the care, diligence, and skill that a reasonably prudent person would exercise in the circumstances, they would likely escape legal liability.

Requirements that the board include a minimum number of directors from outside the organization, or a minimum number of member-directors for membership organizations, but not for other types of organizations, might also have some impact on the advocacy activities of the organization. Currently, the *Canada Corporations Act* has no stakeholder-interest provisions which would allow directors and officers to consider interests beyond those of the organization's members. Such provisions may or may not be appropriate for nonprofits.

Our survey and research to date suggests that the requirements associated with nonprofit corporate status can have an important if subtle effect on the advocacy activities of public interest organizations, and that public interest group representatives recognize this. Current federal efforts to review the antiquated provisions of Part Two of the *Canada Corporations Act* suggest awareness that a streamlined and modernized federal nonprofit corporations law could improve the effectiveness, efficiency, and accountability of public interest groups in Canada.

REGULATION THROUGH DIRECT FUNDING

A recent Treasury Board study identifies five "mechanisms" through which federal government support flows to third sector organizations (Canada. Treasury Board Secretariat 2000, 7).

- in-kind support
- fee-for-service
- contributions
- grants
- tax measures.

The last of these is discussed below. Support in-kind does not appear to figure prominently in group-government relations; it was not mentioned by any of our respondents. Fee-for-service arrangements are identical to those the government enters into with commercial organizations. The constraints attached to a fee-for-service contract are negotiated between the parties. Such commercial contracts between non-governmental organizations and the federal government have to be awarded in a way that is open to competition from other possible suppliers. Most nonprofit organizations and charities have a non-commercial relationship with the federal government. Consequently, the greater part of federal government funding reaches them through instruments that are designed to govern such non-commercial relationships. These are grants and contributions. Grants are more open-ended and less subject to restrictions than contributions, or, to quote the Auditor General: "Contribution programs contain clear obligations to account for funds expended. Grant programs, however, place major emphasis on the decision to allocate funds, but not on their use" (Canada. Auditor General 1988, ch. 9 para. 9.78). Earlier we described how, in the early 1990s, criticisms of the provision and management of group funding had led the federal government to cut back financial support to groups. Grants, the vehicle for core funding were severely restricted.

Initiated in the early 1970s to help Aboriginal groups to find a voice, core funding was extended to a number of groups seeking social justice (Faulkner 1982). It was particularly effective in fostering women's groups, until, in the early 1990s prominent critics of organizations like the National

Action Committee on the Status of Women succeeded in linking core funding to growing concerns over the public debt (Pal 1993). Critical reports from the Auditor General (1990, 1991) contributed to a public impression that funding for these groups was growing out of control and that public money was being wasted. Irritated by the confrontational character of some demonstrations, the government of Brian Mulroney threatened to cut back on core funding, and then the government of Jean Chrétien carried out the threat. Today, although core funding has not entirely disappeared — five groups told us that they still receive it — it is far less significant than it was.

A contribution agreement is a financial agreement between an organization and a government agency. By accepting the contribution, the organization agrees to carry out the work and be accountable for the amounts received. A number of conditions are set out in the contribution agreement (such as quarterly progress reports and financial reports, and at the end, a final third-party assessment report). Although many contributions programs are aimed at the provision of services, some are aimed at "representation" activities. For example, the Office of Consumer Affairs (OCA) Contributions Program for nonprofit consumer and voluntary organizations is intended "to strengthen the consumer's role in the marketplace by assisting consumer and voluntary organizations to represent the consumer interest efficiently and effectively." More specifically, the program provides such groups with "the means to produce high quality and timely research on consumer issues affecting the marketplace, and to develop policy advice on these issues that are credible and useful to decision-makers" (Office of Consumer Affairs 2003). Eligible applicants are voluntary organizations that are:

- incorporated as nonprofit corporations under appropriate provincial legislation, under Part Two of the *Canada Corporations Act*, or under a special Act of Parliament;

- have demonstrated competence, credibility, and accountability in carrying out projects;

- are capable of reaching consumers who are not members of the organization itself; and

- are guided by objectives that are consistent with the program objective of "strengthening the consumer's role in the marketplace by representing the consumer interest efficiently and effectively."

In the application form, applicants are to provide a statement of incorporation, an audited statement of the organization's previous year's income and expenses, along with the auditor's name and address, and the organization's forecast budget for the current year, and background information on the aims, objectives, and structure of the organization. The application should also provide information concerning membership (categories, fees, and number of paying members), donors (number and amount), magazines/newsletter information (number of subscribers, paying subscribers, readers). Applicants must provide a detailed description of the project, objectives, workplan, expenses, marketing strategy. The applicants must fill out declarations concerning conflict-of-interest and post-employment codes for public office-holders and the registration of any person lobbying on its behalf pursuant to the *Lobbyist Registration Act*, other sources of government funding (contributions and contracts).

Assessment of the organization focuses on the competence, credibility, and accountability of the group, its financial situation, the group's ability to manage the project, and its past experience, results of assessment of the most recently completed project undertaken by the group, and the group's ability to deliver the project results on time. Organizations that receive funding must report expenses every financial quarter and are subject to audit. At the end of the project, and before making the results public, organizations receiving project contributions will be required to submit an independent review of the project methodology, conclusions, and recommendations. The reviewer must have appropriate qualifications and experience to assess the validity of the research methods employed in relation to the subject matter of the study. The reviewer is to provide a one to two page opinion on the validity of the conclusions and policy recommendations, given the methodology employed in the study.

Fifteen of the 20 groups in our study reported that their activities are affected by government direct funding.[30] Eleven of these are significantly affected by the way in which direct funding is administered.[31] From what they told us, we concluded that government funding moderates public interest group advocacy (Table 2).

Table 2: Funding Dependence of Groups Related to Service/Advocacy Character and Budget Experience in 1990s

Identification	Status		% Government Contribution to Budget				Sector*	Character			1990s Budget History			
	Charity	NPO	<20	21–50	51–75	>75		Service	High-key Advocacy	Low-key Advocacy	<	0	>	~
1	X		X				1	X		X	X			
2		X	X				4		X		X			
3	X					X	2	X	X				X	
4	X		X				1	X		X		X		
5		X				X	2	X	X	X			X	X
6	X				X		2	X			X			
7	X					X	1	X	X	X			X	X
8	X		X				1	X		X		X		
9	X					X	4	X	X	X			X	X
10		X	X				2	X		X			X	X
11	X		X				1	X		X	X			
12	X		X				4	X		X				
13	X		X				2	X	X	X			X≠	
14	X				X		2	X		X		X		
15	X			X			2	X		X			X	
16	X			X			1	X		X	X+			
17		X				X	2		X	X	X			
18		X			X		3		X	X	X^		X	X
19	X				X		3	X		X	X		X	X
20		X	X				3			X			X	X

Notes: * Sectors: 1 = health; 2 = social justice; 3 = good government; 4 = other.
≠ Lower government funding related to termination of program.
+ Group reported a substantial increase in donations.
^ Budget increased, but proportion represented by government contributions declined.
Budget history symbols: < budget increased in 1990s.
　0 budget stayed essentially the same.
　> budget decreased.
　~ budget turbulence during the period, related to fluctuations in government contribution.

We reached this conclusion from the following evidence: (i) executive directors told us that this was the case; (ii) some described instances where funding was used to limit advocacy; (iii) some reported the effects on their groups' activities of long-term reduction of government funding; and (iv) nonprofit organizations with limited government funding and lacking charitable status appear to be more vigorous in advocacy than groups with charitable status and a significant degree of government funding.

In our interviews we asked our respondents whether they agreed that "core funding by governments significantly constrains the advocacy activities of NGOs." Twelve did; six of them strongly. No one strongly disagreed, though four did disagree and four others stated that they did not know.[32]

To verify this finding, and also to secure opinion on the extent to which informed observers feel it is safe for organizations to depend on government funding, we also asked whether members of the group agreed with the statement that "NGOs deriving more than 25 percent of their revenues from government are circumspect in advocating policies." This produced a slightly different result. Eleven agreed with the statement, though none of them strongly; two did not know, but six disagreed and one disagreed strongly. We take this to mean that while being dependent on government funding is believed to constrain group advocacy, it does not entirely compromise a group's willingness to pursue its goals. As the director of a women's group put it, "If there is a need to advocate a position in order to secure equal rights for women, then it has to be done."

This attitude became apparent in the conversations leading from this question. Several directors asked why we had fixed on 25 percent to divide the circumspect from the bold. We explained that Jeffrey Berry, in his survey of American public interest groups, had categorically excluded from his sample any group that received more than 20 percent of its revenue from government, on the grounds that such groups could not pretend to be independent and would in fact have to be considered an arm of government.[33] Previous research had led us to believe that on this dimension, at least, Canadian public interest groups are quite different from their American counterparts, and we were anxious to test both Berry's assumption and our own earlier conclusions. The usual reaction to this explanation was summed up by the director who commented that "Canadians have a stronger tradition of government funding. It's hard to transpose Berry's views to Canada." Another invoked this sense of tradition when she commented that "When direct funding began in the early seventies there were supposed to be no strings attached. It was supposed to ensure that a community-based voice was heard."

We concluded, then, that though government support may constrain public interest group activity, it does not necessarily lead to co-optation. This conclusion was reinforced by the comments several directors made about their relations with the agencies that fund their groups. One of those who disagreed with the view that core funding restrains advocacy pointed out that core funding often is given to encourage advocacy and active participation in policy-making. Clearly it has some limiting aspects and puts some restraint on groups, but "I can't think of any important issue that we've backed away from because we've had core funding." Another, who felt that non-governmental organizations dependent on government funding are circumspect, pointed out that though 90 percent of her group's budget comes from one agency, it still challenges that agency. Perhaps the effect of the budget dependence is that "it forces us to think seriously about criticizing them." A third put it more dramatically: "You can see the fear. There is always that worry about next year's grant. It may colour what you say about the government. I do keep that in mind when I'm writing to Jane Stewart or the PM. These people are keeping us alive." Despite qualms, this director still writes critically to the minister and the prime minister.

If government funding is believed to moderate activity, it is quite possible that some officials will attempt to use the power of the purse to discourage attacks on specific policies or events. Several examples were given. When it voiced concerns about the way in which its funding agency had handled a major incident, one group became aware of memos circulating in the agency "asking questions about our grants and suggesting that we were 'biting the hand that feeds us.'" The group's leadership was told to "think about our resources," and as it worried about the future funding of its programs, tensions developed in the organization. These did not dissipate until the government, facing persistent media and opposition attacks, set up an inquiry which ultimately concurred in the group's view of the incident.

Standing up to this type of coercion not only takes courage on the part of groups and their officers, it also depends on a certain security of tenure. The group just referred to has considerable standing in its field and provides services that its funding agency depends on and cannot duplicate. Not all groups have this leverage. An organization taking part in the coalition to promote tobacco control experienced severe cuts in funding, ultimately reaching a point at which it prepared to close down a widely used service. Faced with this possibility, its funding agency agreed to enhance its grant, but only on condition that the organization stop participating in lobbying activities.

Of the 20 groups we studied, only two reported that they had experienced coercive behaviour of this magnitude.[34] It was clear, however, that there has been a steady attrition of the assumption that there is a tradition of tolerance for diverse views and a commitment to ensure that such views are heard. This attrition has been expressed through funding mechanisms, and has implications for the tendency of group leaders to voluntarily regulate their advocacy activities.

What are the implications of this for public interest groups?

The majority of groups in our sample are working in the fields of health or social justice, and in these sectors eliminating or reducing core funding has severely constrained the ability of groups to do what they set out to do. Childcare, for example, has been a central concern for several of these groups. Two reported to us that their ability to advocate for better childcare has been compromised by changes in funding programs and procedures.

> There is no more core funding; no long-term funding. We are strongly impacted by this. It has had a huge impact. We used to have a staff of ten, now we have two-and-a-half. We used to get money to carry on advocacy; now we only get project money. We have to advocate in our spare time. It's very difficult.

The other organization had to severely curtail its activities:

> Project funding has become less accessible. There is a process of attrition. The delay in ... funding [from a key supporting agency] has meant that [we have had] to be closed in the summer. We lost our administrator and this meant that we lost opportunities to participate in policy consultations. Borderline organizations don't have the resources to weather these storms.

While these two organizations were the most severely affected by the government's retreat from core funding, others, including some of the country's leading and highly respected organizations in this field, indicated that they, too, had found their advocacy work curtailed. All in all, one organization reported, its budget had increased, but the capacity to act on many fronts had decreased since project funding has meant that action is linked to specific activities. Because the greater part of its funding is derived from research projects, research has become the main activity. It can no longer do advocacy or consultation. Furthermore, although the group's budget as a whole is secure, funding for specific activities is more vulnerable.

The ramifications of these changes are complex, and in some respects profound, for the groups affected as well as for the development of public policy. The examples we have given illustrate some of these effects, but not all.[35]

From a group perspective the most immediate and striking effects have been reductions in staff and staff capacity. Uncertain cash flow has meant that more staff is hired on a part-time basis. Fringe benefits are reduced or eliminated. Inevitably this means that these groups have difficulty retaining staff, particularly professionals, and as one director pointed out, "we have to have experienced professionals in order to deal with the social service agencies." This group worries that it may not be able to maintain services at the calibre that is necessary. In addition to the problem of maintaining quality, groups must worry about continuity. Smaller groups, as we have seen, lose the ability to operate on a year-round basis, which makes it difficult for them to participate in the policy process, a short-coming that affects other groups. Organizations that are overly dependent on variable funding from government tend to be unable to sustain partnerships in coalitions, and as the director of a leading health group pointed out, this "does constrain the ability of groups to work together on advocacy."

Core funding, as the term implies, was initiated by governments to assist groups to build an administrative core and to sustain their activities over a period of time. Core funding consequently not only ensured that groups could afford to hire staff for the longer term, which in the case of most advocacy groups might mean two or perhaps three years, it also meant that group leaders, freed of the immediate need to raise funds, were able to devote a good deal of energy to their groups' central missions, including advocacy. Conversely, the reduction of core funding has meant that group leaders must now spend more time on fundraising. Hand in hand with this trend has come increased demands for detail in applications and account- ability in the administration of projects. Demands that put further pressure on the limited staff resources of groups.

Given this level of detail, it is hardly surprising that group officials find the application process onerous. One executive director spoke of the grant her organization received annually from a federal agency. Nowadays the grant applications not only require a great deal more detailed information up-front, "increasingly there are regulations that affect what we do and how we do it. Applying for the last grant probably took two times the amount of time as earlier ones." This director estimated that she devoted four weeks to the most recent application, each week comprising about 35 hours. The application form itself was complex and there were unexpected add-ons. Another director, whose organization is able to raise the bulk of its revenue from non-governmental sources, confessed that he avoids ap- plying for government assistance. "The amount of work needed ... almost makes applications ... not worth it."

Groups varying considerably in size and policy orientation commonly complained about the complexity and the extent of regulations. The direc- tor of a major health organization commented on the nature of the reporting regulations, considering them "stringent in terms of their timing and the kind of information that is required." The evaluations conducted at the end of projects were referred to on several occasions as "onerous," particularly for small organizations. "Evaluation can be helpful for future projects, but the extent of evaluation creates difficulties for organizations of different sizes."

Most of the directors we spoke with accepted the need for a high degree of accountability for contribution funding. As one put it, "an organization funded by government has to meet tight accountability requirements. Get- ting more so. I don't say this negatively. When you write a proposal you have to accept the conditions that go with a government grant."

What does rankle is the impression that charities and nonprofits are more closely scrutinized than private sector organizations offering similar serv- ices. Once again, the childcare field offers a striking example: "Commercial childcare programs have to account publicly for places that are funded by government, but otherwise (other than meeting income tax requirements) don't have to open their books. But nonprofits have to submit budgets and have their statements audited." Furthermore, "the regulations that come with government contracts," in the words of one director, "often force us to do things differently. Not always the way we would choose to do them, or that would be best for us." At times these regulations can threaten the existence of a group. For example, some groups with long-standing relations with supporting agencies have been able to renew project funding annually, and while this does not give the groups the same degree of flexibility and independence that core funding once provided, they have given a degree of financial stability. Recently, however, this stability has been threatened by the more stringent observance of Treasury Board regulations which require that agencies not renew projects until a final report from the previous year has been received and reviewed. Since it may take up to 12 weeks to review the report and approve a renewal, smaller groups can experience a cash crisis during the period. For one group, the delay has meant closing in the summer; loss of the group's administrator and lost opportunities to participate in policy consultations. Borderline organizations do not have the resources to weather these storms. "You reach a point at which you can no longer meet the organization's needs." "Government officials [who design regulations] have no idea how they affect us," was the resigned conclusion of one director.

Advocacy is generally not envisaged in project funding. At times, we were told by a number of our informants, it is specifically prohibited. Even when not excluded, project funding is, in the view of one director, "far more important than core funding in constraining advocacy. Especially locally. You may be taking a chance when you criticize the local [field] service, for example. You may have an apprehension that it might lead to vindictive treatment in the management of a local contract."

Although contribution funding is less rigid in its definition of deliverables, it is essentially project funding and "will only cover the actual costs of the project itself." Here, too, the opportunity for advocacy is limited. Agencies will define priority areas for contribution funding and may specifically exclude educational activities, conferences, workshops, exhibitions, training programs, and the development of promotional materials.[36] Of course, they may specifically encourage these and other activities that are closely related to advocacy. Status of Women, for example, has for many years supported advocacy work on the part of women's groups. One group that we studied is very closely allied with an agency mandated to promote a particular government policy. Not surprisingly, this group is encouraged in its advocacy work.

Overall, it is apparent that the process of applying for contribution funding, the subsequent obligations associated with fulfilling the terms of the contribution, as well as the suggested guidance concerning priority areas, when taken together, could have significant influence over the advocacy activities of interest groups. Indeed, if the group was small and heavily dependent on government funding, it would be possible for the selection and priorities of projects by groups which apply for funding to overwhelm the group's own priorities.

Some groups have moved to more fee-for-service contract funding, instead of contribution funding. Contracts that involve less paperwork, was the reason given. Contributions are really tough. It is not necessary for contractors to provide information about members, incorporation, and so on. Contract funding, however, has its own set of disadvantages. It is not restricted to voluntary groups; they must compete with professional consultancy firms. With this more competitive environment comes greater uncertainty. Furthermore, contracts offer less scope for the soft-edged, holistic services that many groups wish to provide and which are consistent with their founding mandates. This is because, as we have noted, contracts are more precise than contributions in their definition of deliverables. Often these deliverables have been determined before tenders are called and there is little scope for modification.

Looking back over our interviews with both executive directors and government officials we see evidence that the cumulative effect of changes to regulations has encumbered the advocacy work of the groups we studied. Two directors described their relations with funding agencies as tense and conflict-ridden. They gave specific examples, which we have quoted, of instances in which officials have stifled, or attempted to stifle, their advocacy activities. On the other hand, the majority of directors spoke of their relations with officials as cordial, even warm. One group administrator, who described the budget process as "a scramble all the time" reported that she frequently begs for support from sympathetic public servants who are able to find money in their budgets. That may be unusual, but it is clear that officials frequently assist groups to find projects that will keep them going. Our own conversations with officials gave ample evidence that there has been a significant debate within policy circles over the restrictive impact of the policies Ottawa embraced in the 1990s. This debate has been conducted as well through the Joint Tables and working groups associated with the Voluntary Sector Initiative. The official endorsement of the Government-Voluntary Sector Accord, in December 2001, as well as recent discussion papers, suggest that a more nuanced understanding of the impact of direct funding may be taking hold.

THE REGULATORY IMPACT OF TAX EXPENDITURE FUNDING ON PUBLIC INTEREST ORGANIZATIONS

The award of nonprofit organization or registered charitable status under the *Income Tax Act* has distinctive benefits for public interest organizations.[37] In particular, both nonprofit organizations and registered charities are exempt from paying income tax under Part I of the *Income Tax Act*. In addition, charities can provide receipts to donors who, if they are individuals, are entitled to claim a tax credit for their donations, and if a corporation, may claim a deduction from their taxable income for their donations. The ability of charities to provide tax credit or deduction receipts creates a distinct inducement for individuals and corporations to give to charities which non-charities do not possess.

Government is engaging in *tax expenditure funding* with these groups in the sense that, were it not for their status as nonprofit organizations or registered charitable organizations, these types of organizations would otherwise be providing income tax revenue to government. In the case of charities, forfeited revenue otherwise forthcoming into government coffers is estimated as costing the federal treasury in the order of $850 million per year (Eade 1995). With income tax-exempt and tax-credit/deductible receipt privileges associated with tax-expenditure funding come certain requirements for public interest organizations — what we refer to as a *regulatory* component. Fourteen of 20 respondents to our survey are registered charities and said that the tax-expenditure funding regulatory element affected their organization.[38] Eight of these felt that tax-expenditure funding had a major regulatory impact.

Following a brief discussion of the *Income Tax Act* obligations associated with nonprofit status, the focus of attention here will be on the charitable tax regime.

Nonprofit Organizations and the *Income Tax Act*

Compared with the requirements pertaining to registered charities, the rules under the *Income Tax Act* associated with nonprofit organizations are minimal. Unlike a charity, a nonprofit organization does not have to first register either federally or provincially to maintain its nonprofit tax status. Instead, nonprofit organizations generally file returns only if they earn more than a certain amount of income per annum ($10,000) or have more than a designated amount of assets ($200,000), or if an organization takes the form of a corporation. The Revenue Canada return form for nonprofit organizations contains modest obligations, requiring only that basic information be provided to correctly identify the organization, its type (see below), the amounts received, the assets, liabilities, and remuneration paid to all employees and officers, a brief description of the organization's activities and location of those activities, as well as the location of the organization's books and records.

To be an organization exempt from paying taxable income, a "club, society or association" must:[39]

- not be a charity;[40]

- "be organized exclusively for social welfare, civic improvement, pleasure, recreation or any other purposes except profit."[41]

- in fact operate exclusively for the same purpose for which it was organized; and

- not distribute or otherwise make available for the personal benefit of a member any of its income unless the member is a registered Canadian amateur athletic organization.[42]

It should be apparent that the scope of what constitutes a nonprofit organization as defined here is much broader than simply public interest groups, potentially encompassing clubs and industry associations with no public interest component.

There are no explicit rules pertaining to nonprofit organizations' political or policy advocacy activity contained in the *Income Tax Act* or Revenue Canada interpretation bulletins and other guidelines and documents. The major constraints which affect a nonprofit organization's ability to engage in advocacy activity are those associated with registration as a corporation. While it is difficult to make generalizations about the numbers of public interest organizations which are registered as corporations, we note that all twenty of the respondents in our survey have federal or provincial corporate status. The regulatory impact of corporate status on public interest organizations was discussed earlier.

Charities Registered Under the *Income Tax Act*

To obtain and maintain registered charitable status, an organization must observe requirements pertaining to political activity, advocacy of policy, and the application of funds to non-charitable purposes. Our survey provided evidence that for several of the respondents, the rules associated with political activity and policy advocacy for registered charities had a significant constraining impact on their activities. One respondent said: "We are always aware of the limits to advocating positions. We constantly ask whether a proposed action is educational, or research or advocacy." This same respondent noted that their participation in elections was affected by their charitable status: "[Charitable status] makes the organization very cautious. We have to avoid breaching our charitable status." Another organization stated:

> It [charitable status] affects how we think about what we do. We discuss whether participating in advocacy would affect our charitable status. But we have an advocacy image. I keep track of my time so that if there is an audit I can show that most of my time is not spent on advocacy.

Another respondent spoke of its efforts to be "careful not to be partisan."

These comments bespeak organizations that are consciously measuring and noting their own policy-oriented activities — in a sense, imposing limits on themselves. One organization directly spoke of this phenomenon, confirming that "self-limitation is a significant factor. NGOs respond negatively to lobbying.... But when I look across the table ... I realize that [industry] does not play by the same rules.... industry plays by the rules of the rich and powerful." One could argue that a subtle form of internalization of the regulator may be taking place. It is our position that the *Income Tax Act* charity regime, and in particular the rules restricting political and policy advocacy, seem to play a major role in instilling a risk-averse, cautious approach to lobbying by many public interest organizations, whereas commercial lobbying bodies are not so constrained — by the *Income Tax Act* or any other legislation. Arguably, this puts charities engaged in lobbying at a considerable financial, regulatory, and psychological disadvantage when compared with their private sector counterparts. It is perhaps not surprising, then, that 15 of 20 respondents felt that in order to retain charitable status Canadian non-governmental organizations are forced to police themselves more rigorously than are business interests.

With these general points in mind, we examine the *Income Tax Act* regime associated with charitable registration and administration, as well as the reactions of survey respondents to this regime.

The *Income Tax Act* Charitable Regime

Revenue Canada has indicated that, to qualify for registration, an organization must be established and operated for charitable purposes, and it must devote its resources to charitable activities (Canada. Revenue Canada 2000; Webb 2000; Drache 1998).[43] A charity must also meet a "public benefit test," pursuant to which it must show that: (i) its activities and purposes provide a tangible benefit to the public; (ii) those people who are eligible for benefits are either the public as a whole, or a significant section of it, in that they are not a restricted group or one where members share a private connection, such as social clubs or professional associations with specific membership; and (iii) the charity's activities must be legal and must not be contrary to public policy.

Following guidance from court cases extending back to the nineteenth century, Revenue Canada requires that the purposes of charity must fall within one of four categories: relief of poverty, the advancement of education (in the sense of formal training of the mind or balanced research, not simply provision of one-sided information), the advancement of religion, or certain other purposes that benefit the community in a way the courts have said are charitable. A charity's purposes must be set out in its corporate charter or trust or constitution document, and must be accompanied by a statement of activities indicating how the organization will accomplish the purpose.

Revenue Canada has stated explicitly that "[u]nder common law, political purposes are not charitable and an organization will not qualify for charitable registration if at least one of its purposes is political." Revenue Canada has interpreted this to mean not only that a charity cannot explicitly be created to further the aims of a political party or promote a political doctrine, but also "to persuade the public to adopt a particular view on a broad social question" or attempt "to bring about or oppose changes in the law or government policy." Thus, while it would be acceptable to devise a charity devoted to relief of poverty through means of a food bank, a charity devoted to relief of poverty through changes in the social welfare legal system would not be acceptable. In effect, there is an explicit orientation in favour of public interest organizations with a *direct service orientation*, as opposed to a public policy orientation

This is buttressed by other requirements which state that a registered charity can engage to a limited extent (i.e., devote no more than 10 percent of its resources) in "non-partisan political activities" which directly help accomplish the charity's purposes. This includes, for example, distributing publications or holding conferences, workshops or other forms of communication intended primarily to sway pubic opinion to the charity's point of view. However, the Act specifically prohibits a registered charity from engaging in any "partisan political activity," which has been defined by Revenue Canada as "supporting or opposing, monetarily or otherwise, a political party or candidate for public office" (Canada. Revenue Canada 2001).

Several survey respondents noted the difficulties they had experienced with the practicality of the current regime. One said "the rules governing charitable status are mystifying. The current definition is problematic." Another said that the "definitions of charitable and advocacy [are] problematic." Ten of 20 respondents wanted revision of the 10 percent ancillary and incidental political activities rule. "The 10 percent rule is not functional or realistic," one respondent said. A non-charity respondent said, "The laws governing charitable status should be less restrictive. We work with educational organizations [registered charities] but find their status restricts [them]. For example, when we organize conferences we have to be very careful because other organizations' status might be jeopardized." The respondent indicated that their movement was "fragmented by Revenue Canada regulations. They force us to duplicate our work and they restrict coalition-building. The movement includes [other organizations], but we can't work with them for fear that they would lose their charitable status."

Six of the respondents wanted a new tax status for groups engaging primarily in political activities (another two wanted more information concerning this option).[44] One respondent suggested that the separate status "could be supported as a different class of organization. It would recognize that there is a certain public interest in ensuring that these groups exist." Another agreed, but said there should still be some restrictions. Five respondents said they agreed with the current restrictions but indicated that the rules needed clarifying.

Administration of the Regime

The Broadbent Panel on Accountability and Governance in the Voluntary Sector examined four models for regulating charities: an expanded Revenue Canada (providing information to the general public and helping to promote the sector), an independent federal Voluntary Sector Commission, a federal-provincial independent Voluntary Sector Commission, or an independent non-governmental agency drawn from the voluntary sector. When offered these choices, the most popular model (favoured by eight respondents) was the non-governmental agency. Seven preferred an independent federal commission. Although two selected an expanded Revenue Canada model, others vehemently rejected it. No respondents preferred the federal-provincial commission model.

Eighteen of 20 respondents thought that charities should play an important role in setting standards of behaviour for groups with charitable tax status, and 16 of 20 thought that charities should also play an important role in monitoring such standards (another two thought that charities should play a minor role in monitoring). One respondent noted that, with respect to monitoring, the danger was that "charities must avoid putting a particular *imprimateur* on the role of charities that suits only a few of them."

In conclusion, our research concerning tax-expenditure funding suggests that this form of regulation has a considerable impact on the public interest community, particularly with respect to the rules constraining political activities and advocacy of policy by registered charities. Survey responses indicated confusion and frustration with the current restrictions, a desire by many for reform or clarification, including considerable support for the creation of a new status for advocacy-oriented organizations. There was also commentary from a number of respondents on their efforts to consciously measure and constrain their activities in order to stay "in bounds. It was suggested that this sort of self-imposed or internalized regulation of public policy activities puts public interest organizations at a considerable disadvantage when compared with business organizations which are not so constrained. The perception by 15 of 20 respondents that they had to police themselves as charities in their activities more rigorously than did the private sector is general support for this observation. In terms of administration, there was little support for Revenue Canada assuming an expanded role, with a preference being voiced for independent commissions, be they federal or non-governmental in nature. An overwhelming majority of respondents wished to play a greater role in charity rule development and monitoring.

THE REGULATION OF LOBBYING

The *Lobbyists Registration Act* (LRA) creates a registry which public office holders and the public can consult in order to learn "who is attempting to influence [the] government [of Canada]."[45] The coverage of the Act is not as extensive as this phrase suggests. From the inception of the registry federal authorities have disclaimed any desire to "impede free and open access to government" and so have required registration only of those who practise a trade of lobbying, either by working as consultant lobbyists or through their employment in a corporation or other organization, including charities and nonprofit organizations (Canada 1989).

> For the most part there will be no impact on private citizens who deal with the government. Communication with public office holders on the day-to-day functions of government does not require registration. Neither does lobbying on a volunteer basis or on one's own behalf (ibid., 2799).

These limitations are described more fully in the Act itself and in the various explanatory documents issued by the Lobbyists Registration Branch, but this excerpt from the regulations suffices to demonstrate the ambiguity that led half of the organizations we interviewed to decide that they were not required to register, and the other half to decide that they should.[46]

Of the 14 charities in our sample, six registered and one intends to register. Of the six nonprofit organizations, three registered. Several reasons were given for the decision to register. One organization registered because "the LRA forces groups to register," but others have more pragmatic reasons. Several of our groups are engaged in a bitter struggle with industry over the regulation of tobacco products; all registered. The spokesman for one of them explained that all members of his staff are registered because his organization "wants to be sure that industry cannot accuse [it] of failing to report any person engaged in lobbying."[47]

The fact that half of the groups we interviewed have decided not to register is probably indicative of a wider uncertainty in the lobbying community about the intent and requirements of the Act. This uncertainty became apparent when we asked the executive directors of three groups why they had decided to discontinue registration. The first told us that

> she used to register. She had been told by officials that she should. However, she found that executive officers of similar groups were not registering and that the organization's lobbying was actually being done by volunteer board members, who would not be required to register. Consequently, she ceased registering.

This person works in the criminal justice field; a colleague in the same field reported a similar experience. He concluded that his organization "does very little 'pure lobbying'; most of its contacts with government come in the form of responses to government requests for consultation or in the form of appearances before inquiries, parliamentary committees, and so on." These are forms of communication with government that are explicitly outside the Act's coverage. He accordingly wrote to the Registrar stating that in view of the limited amount of time he devotes to pure lobbying (which he defines as seeking to obtain a benefit for the organization itself) and in view of the fact that much of the rest of his organization's advocacy vis-à-vis the federal government occurs as a result of invitations to present briefs, appear before committees, and so on, the organization did not appear to be required to register. This view was apparently not challenged by the Registrar.

Other organizations have noted that the Act requires the registration of only those paid employees who spend a significant part of their time in lobbying. The Registrar considers "a significant part of the duties of one employee to be 20 percent of that employee's time."[48] The fact that paid employees are not significantly engaged in lobbying was generally given as the reason for not registering. Or, as one director put it, "I read through the LRA and decided [we] were not exclusively doing it." Several directors also pointed out that the greater part of their organizations' lobbying was actually done by volunteers, who are specifically excluded from an obligation to register.[49]

In general, lobbyist registration is not considered onerous. Eight of our 20 organizations thought that lobby regulation had only a minor effect on their operations and nine went so far as to report that it had no effect at all. Not surprisingly, all but one of these last did not register and seven had no opinion on the efficiency of the registration process. Of the 13 that did register an opinion on the efficiency of the process, three considered it undemanding and seven thought that it was "reasonably efficient." However, one executive director did consider the process "cumbersome and time-consuming," though no reason was given for this assessment.

Although the ambiguities in the *Lobbyists Registration Act*, and its administration, clearly give officials of organizations valid reasons for not registering, we came away from several interviews with the impression that they only partially explain why some directors, and their organizations, avoid registration. To some extent avoidance may reflect a distaste for being treated as lobbyists. As one director put it, "why lump [my organization] with the Canadian Medical Association. [We are] focusing on the public interest; CMA primarily on the self-interest of doctors." Another drew a distinction between advocacy and lobbying, seeing lobbying as "obtaining benefits for your organization; advocacy as promoting a public benefit — not an advantage for your organization." A colleague managing a major health organization took a similarly moral view of this distinction, considering himself to be "an advocate on behalf of members and individuals suffering from..... ." He rejects the suggestion of a former federal minister of health that his organization is a special interest group, arguing that it is "simply putting forward the situation of ... sufferers and their caregivers. [It] is motivated by altruistic considerations, not from selfish special interests," and, by implication should not have to register. These respondents would like to see the *Lobbyists Registration Act* distinguish between NGOs so that there is "some kind of threshold for identifying a lobbying organization." In effect, recognizing that "charities are not lobby groups when they promote policy that does not reflect a self-interested position."

Another explanation, and one that supports our regime hypothesis, emerged from our attempt to explain the claim by the representatives of three major charities that the Act had a major effect on their organizations. Their reasons for holding this view were not clear, though it appeared to be rooted in a fear that registration could expose their organizations to a review of their charitable status. One of these executive directors did express concern that charities engaged in advocacy may find that compliance with the registration requirements of the *Lobbyist Registration Act* will lead to stricter control and perhaps loss of charitable status.[50]

While few of our respondents considered lobbyist registration a significant influence on their organizations, even fewer were aware of any benefits to be derived from the registration service. Given an opportunity to indicate whether they considered the registry useful or ineffective, only three thought that it is useful, six believe that it is ineffective and 11 had no opinion. One director pointed out that "you never hear about it" while another confessed that she had "no idea what the result is." Although registration was introduced to assist Canadians to identify who is attempting to influence government, it was apparent that the majority of those we interviewed did not use the registry for that purpose. Of the few that did, the most generous assessment was that "it tells us which people are doing things, but not *what* they are doing. It's a good start. That's it." This last commentator was one of the few who had a suggestion for improving the registry. He believes "it would be useful to know how much time and money they are spending on different contracts, and also to know whom they visit." Another, the representative of a group active in the coalition for tobacco regulation, would like the registry to provide more complete information about groups the coalition believes to be acting as fronts for the tobacco industry.

REGULATING ELECTION ADVERTISING

After reading a draft of this chapter one participant remarked that we had overlooked the fact that "most organizations interested in public policy agree that charities should not be engaged in partisan politics." In fact, this was the overall impression left by the interviews. Very few of the groups we met had involved themselves in elections.[51] Only three groups reported running advertisements during elections. Only four of our 20 respondents felt that their groups were affected by election advertising regulations and a mere two of these believed that the regulations have a significant impact on their advocacy activities.

The reasons for abstaining from election activity seem to have little to do with the rigours of the *Canada Elections Act.*[52] Eight of our respondents maintained that their groups' decisions not to advertise were not influenced by the Act, and nine did not know whether the Act had had any effect. The groups abstained for other reasons. Sometimes strategic, as in the case of the organization that stays away from direct participation in elections because "it's not a wise policy [to be partisan]. We must be non-partisan. Also our provincial organizations must cover a broad panoply of government parties; we don't want to embarrass them."

More frequently, financial constraints were given as the principal reasons for holding back. As one executive director said, "it's never discussed. We don't have the resources." Another questioned whether expensive advertising was worth the investment, whilst a third also combined a hard-nosed financial approach with a sense of strategy when he commented that it is not wise for charities to be seen to be paying large sums for advertising: "Supporters ask where the money is coming from."

There is a difference, however, between partisan involvement in elections and using an election to advocate a change in policy. Hence, advocacy groups do not ignore elections. Most track party positions on their issues and often, as well, the positions of individual candidates. This information is circulated to members and supporters, posted on Web sites and printed up as press releases and hand-outs that are given to interested voters. The description given by one executive director is typical: "We simply present the parties' positions. [We] ask questions. Parties are given an opportunity to respond to [our] position. Their responses are circulated, usually through a letter to supporters." Even one of the few groups that believes in election advertising prefers this approach.

> We usually put out [the parties'] stated positions. Criticizing a party or candidate wouldn't go over well. We interview candidates and publicize their position on our issues — abortion and euthanasia — and then send out a flyer quoting them. Perhaps we will run an ad if we decide to target a riding. First, we obtain the candidate's position. Second, we publicize it. The rest is up to the public. The strategy varies according to means.

Another stratagem is to mount a public awareness campaign. As one group leader put, "we try to become a news item." Of course, this technique is not employed only during elections. A coalition of groups concerned with children's welfare worked for a number of years to draw attention to the growing problem of child poverty, but in the November 2000 election *Campaign 2000's* message that governments have been neglecting the youngest and weakest members of Canadian society took on special significance (see Table 3).

Although nearly all the groups we interviewed have little interest in conducting the kind of advertising campaign that prompted legislators to introduce restrictions on third-party advertising, two group representatives did state that election regulation does have a major effect on their advocacy activities. One of these, a major charity, has not taken out election advertisements and did not explain how the regulations affect it. The other, a pro-life nonprofit organization, has advertised during elections. The organization states that it has met the requirements of the Act, being careful to avoid criticizing specific parties or candidates, and that its advertisements have not been investigated by the chief electoral officer. Nevertheless its executive director commented that the group endorses the constitutional challenge to the Act which has been mounted by the National Citizens' Coalition, and went on to say that the *Canada Elections Act* worries group members greatly:

> We could put more into a picked riding. The average person [in the organization] sees it as an attempt to stifle debate. These are small people with limited funds, not big bucks. We cannot see the great need [for the law]. We feel the pressure of the law. It is unfair. Others will get by it. We don't have professional lobbyists or a lot of money. Advertising is one of our few means of influencing people at election time. We see it as a way to shut us up.

Table 3: The Impact of Election Regulations

Group Code	Charitable Status		Affected by Regulation			Have Run Election Ads?			Influenced by Act		
	Charity	NPO	Y/N	Major	Minor	Y	N	DK	Y	N	DK
1	X		N		X		X				X
2		X	Y	X		X			X		
3	X		N		X		X			X	
4	X		N		X		X			X	
5		X	N		X	X					X
6	X		N		X		X			X	
7	X		N/A	N/A	N/A		X		X		
8	X		Y	X		X					X
9	X		N		X		X			X	
10		X	Y	N/A	N/A		X				X
11	X		N		X		X				X
12	X		N		X		X				X
13	X		N		X		X				X
14	X		N		X		X				X
15	X		N		X		X		X		
16	X		Y		X		X			X	
17		X	N		X		X				X
18	X	X	N		X		X			X	
19	X		N		X		X			X	
20		X	N		X		X			X	
Totals	14	6	N 15 Y 4 N/A 1	2	16	3	17		3	8	9

Notes: Y – Yes.
N – No.
N/A – Not Applicable.

Some members of Parliament (MPs) might agree. Targeting strategies is amongst those that the *Canada Elections Act* is intended to constrain. As used by pro-life groups in the United States the strategy has resulted in the election of single-issue candidates in a number of Congressional districts and has strengthened the anti-abortion voice in Congress.[53] It is possible that targeting strategies could secure the election of a few MPs single-mindedly committed to a specific issue, particularly if such a strategy could be reinforced by unrestricted advertising,[54] but even with this freedom the possibility seems remote, given the discipline exerted by Canadian parties both inside Parliament and through central party organizations.

This executive director was one of only two who believed that "groups like mine should be allowed to advertise without restriction."[55] At the other extreme two argued that "organizations like mine should *not* be allowed to advertise during an election.' Four did not respond to the question, none of them having advertised during elections or considered themselves affected by the legislation. The remaining 12, however, opted for an advocacy position, ten of them stating that their organizations should be allowed to advertise on policy issues, but on such issues only, and the remaining two taking essentially the same position but specifying strict expenditure limits.

In short, the regulation of election advertising is not a burning issue for the majority of those we interviewed. Most feel that they are not affected by the law because, quite simply, they do not advertise. Their reasons for not advertising varied. Most felt constrained by financial limitations; a couple believe that it is inappropriate for charities to advertise during elections and one executive director confessed that the prospect of election advertising "makes us very cautious. We have to avoid breaching our charitable status." What is significant about their approach, however, is that 12 of the 16 who answered this question believe that policy-related advertising should be permitted. Taken together with the two responses that opted for no advertising restrictions at all, this suggests that further clarification of the *Elections Act* may be called for.[56]

IS THERE A REGULATORY REGIME?

We began our research by asking two questions. First, can the cluster of federal regulations which govern the operations of charities and nonprofit organizations be described as a regime? That is, do these separately developed regulatory structures have, in fact, a cumulative, interactive effect, working together as "a mode of rule or management" to encourage certain kinds of behaviour and to suppress others? Second, how do these regulations affect the advocacy activities of the organizations we studied? In the following paragraphs we will return to our initial question and consider, in light of recent experience, what are its implications for the formation of public policy. In our concluding comments we will make some general observations on the effect that regulation has on public interest advocacy in this country.

The interviews confirmed our hypothesis that there are seven different sets of federal government regulations governing the advocacy activities of charities and nonprofit organizations. They include informal regulations, like those that flow from participation in policy-making, but most derive from statutes such as the *Income Tax Act*, the *Canada Corporations Act*, the *Financial Administration Act*, the *Lobbyists Registration Act*, and the *Canada Elections Act*. We were also reminded that important though government regulation may be, there is a broader framework of accountability that draws great vigour and effect from the expectations of supporters, clients, organizational associates, and professional employees of these organizations. Their relations with charities and nonprofit organizations create a larger realm of accountability into which government inserts a formal, structured set of regulations that articulate those norms and sanctions that must be defined precisely and are enforced by the state.

We found grounds for arguing that a regulatory regime exists. There is evidence in the responses that apparently discrete regulations do conjoin to promote or discourage certain kinds of behaviour. In particular, though a majority of respondents felt that they were not affected by the *Elections Act* and eight believed that they were not affected by the *Lobbyists Registration Act,* group officials were aware of them, particularly the *Lobbyists Registration Act,* and evinced some uneasiness about the effect both pieces of legislation might have on their standing as charities or as recipients of direct funding from government. How groups accommodate some regulations affects the application of others. Issues associated with accountability resonate with regulations applying to charitable status and to contractual relations with the federal government. Certain steps are contingent. It is difficult for an organization to receive a grant or contribution from the

Government of Canada unless it is incorporated under the *Canada Corporations Act* or a comparable provincial statute. Similarly, corporate status facilitates receipt of registered charity status. The *Lobbyists Registration Act* offers a means of monitoring the lobbying activities of charities or of the observance of regulations governing direct funding.

On the whole, however, while we found that a definable regulatory regime does exist, we concluded that the linkages between the various elements of the regime are still relatively weak. The core of the regime is the *Income Tax Act*, which authorizes the Canada Customs and Revenue Agency to determine and monitor the status of charities and nonprofit organizations, and the *Financial Administration Act*, which authorizes Treasury Board to regulate financial relations between third sector organizations and the Government of Canada. The impact of these two pieces of legislation is considerable. In comparison, the *Lobbyists Registration Act* and the *Canada Elections Act* have only a supplementary, limited effect, and the *Canada Corporations Act*, while necessary, does not, as we have seen, loom large in the lives of association officials.

An aspect of the research which did mildly surprise us was the extent to which some of these regulations seemed to have an effect through the "organizational subconscious." Some aspects of the regulatory regime appeared to be so embedded that they are practically invisible. Another way to put this is to suggest that certain kinds of activities produced a conditioned response on the part of officials, who felt that their organizations might be vulnerable to a strict reading of the regulations. This was most obvious in the case of advocacy activity on the part of charities. We were struck by the number of times respondents indicated that their organizations avoided certain kinds of advocacy for fear of jeopardizing their charitable status. Officials of the Canada Customs and Revenue Agency apparently feel the same way, arguing that the constraints of charitable status are not nearly as restrictive as many charitable organizations believe.

Do these observations have public policy implications? Is it relevant to talk about a federal regulatory regime affecting charities and nonprofit organizations?

For two reasons we suggest that it is. First, it simply makes sense that legislative draftsmen should bear in mind that organizations — the objects of regulation — are affected not only by a regulation or law currently under review, but by others, and that there may be unintended cumulative effects. We have shown, for example, how during the 1990s discrete changes in Ottawa's handling of grants and contributions had a considerable and deleterious impact on the advocacy capacity of many organizations.

The second reason why it is useful to think in terms of a regulatory regime is closely related to our last observation. By thinking holistically of a body of regulations, we also open discussions that do not arise when we tinker with specific regulations or statutes; when, as the current saying has it, we work in silos. An example is evident in the current debate over charitable status. An elaborate national consultation has been carried out by IMPACS, the main thrust of which has been to secure third sector agreement on an incremental shift in the definition of charitable status. The thinking behind this strategy is that small steps are all that is possible in the present climate of opinion, but the approach begs an important question: How well is the public interest served by current rules affecting advocacy? At some point this question must be addressed.

Finally, it is worth noting that recent developments present evidence that it is useful to think about in terms of a regulatory regime.

We think first, for example, of the extensive discussions that have taken place between the federal government and leading agencies in the voluntary sector, under the aegis of the Voluntary Sector Initiative. The formal structure of the consultation, as managed by the Privy Council Office, gives scant recognition of the need to discuss such issues as the advocacy role of third sector organizations or the impact that funding regulations have on them. Yet these issues have intruded repeatedly, and have, perforce, been addressed "unofficially" by the Voluntary Sector Working Group on Advocacy, a Working Group on Funding, and by an internal Treasury Board Project group. The history of the Accord project testifies to the persistence with which the advocacy issue, for example, has recurred, despite a reluctance on the part of the government to deal with it at this point in time (Voluntary Sector Initiative 2000). A document that promises to deal "specifically with the relationship between the voluntary sector and the Government of Canada in its full breadth and depth and at every level across the country," invites that inclusion. Unwelcome though this kind of regime thinking may be to certain agencies in the Government of Canada, it seems to the writers that the voluntary sector itself is pulling the debate toward a more inclusive, regime-oriented, appreciation of the regulatory "mode of rule or management."

The recently passed *Charities Registration (Security Information) Act* offers another example. It provides that the minister of the Canada customs and revenue agency and the solicitor general, by issuing a certificate, can effect the nearly immediate removal of an organization's charitable status. This step, which must be reviewed by a judge of the federal Court of Canada, could be taken where the ministers have reasonable grounds, based on security or intelligence reports, to believe that the charity "has made, makes or will make available any resources, directly or indirectly, to an entity that is a listed terrorist organization" (Canada. House of Commons 2001). Critics of the Act have argued that existing regulations governing charities are adequate for this purpose, and that, because it is extremely difficult for international aid organizations to be fully aware of, or able to control, how food and other aid is used, there is a distinct possibility that these organizations will inadvertently breach the new regulations. The Canadian Centre for Philanthropy, in its brief to the House of Commons Standing Committee on Justice and Human Rights also pointed out that it is quite common for some governments to routinely denounce aid organizations (Canadian Centre for Philanthropy 2001; Duff 2001). Without success, they called for a warning period for such organizations, and for a stronger evidentiary basis for issuing the certificate.

Clearly the Act was drawn up without a sufficient understanding of the conditions under which certain charities must operate. The silo, in this case, is national security. Even a limited consideration of the larger aspects of charities administration should have signaled the need for a more nuanced approach. The case illustrates how valuable a regime approach can be, introducing, as it does, a broader perspective on regulatory issues.

GENERAL CONCLUSIONS

This chapter analyzes the information gathered in recent interviews. It draws together responses to key questions relating to the impact of the regulation of public interest groups. We conclude from those responses that direct and indirect government regulation constrains advocacy activity on the part of public interest groups. Constraint is exercised principally through regulations applied to charities and to organizations receiving government funds, but these invoke or reinforce the operation of other elements of the regulatory regime.

Accordingly, the *Lobbyists Registration Act* and the *Canada Elections Act* do not in themselves impose a regulatory burden on the advocacy activities of groups. They do, however, have implications for the treatment of groups as registered charities and as recipients of government funds.

The chief means through which government funding has operated to constrain public interest group advocacy activity are:

- contractual prohibition,

- funding cut-backs,

- shifting the category of support from core funding to project funding, and

- tightening procedures.

The history of government-group relations during the 1990s reveals a pattern of development. As we have noted, a combination of austerity and reaction to some advocacy groups led governments to curtail their support for core funding. A number of the groups in our study reported that they had experienced severe budget cuts in the mid-1990s. Most, however, also reported considerable improvement in recent years, in part because they found other sources of income, but also because government funding increased. Several reasons can be given for this increase. Government agencies often need an articulate attentive public: a forum for developing policy, but also a vehicle for promoting a supportive public opinion. Some of the groups we studied serve this need. A number also can deliver services that government no longer provides and that the private sector is unwilling to take on. During the late 1990s, as the policy capacity and extent of government activity declined, the need for these group functions became increasingly evident and, as the federal government's financial position improved so did the availability of funding for groups.

The new government money, however, came in the form of project funding, either as contributions or as contracts for very specific deliverables. The capacity to advocate policy has, as a result, been significantly constrained. Not only does project funding often implicitly or explicitly exclude advocacy activity, group financing through project funding exacts a heavy toll on the time and energy of group leaders and the key professionals who have the necessary background for advocacy work.

A number of the directors we met described the effect these category shifts and procedural changes have had on their advocacy work; and we have tried to capture their discouragement in this chapter. There is a sense that governments are abandoning a tradition of tolerance for diverse views and a commitment to ensure that such views are heard. "We are moving to a place of having to be more constrained. It hasn't always been that way. In the past there has been a view that government has a responsibility to ensure that multiple values are heard." Or, in the words of another group leader, there has been an increasing emphasis on the provision of services and a decline of "a community-based voice."

Although recent developments lay outside the scope of our study, it is pertinent to note that they suggest conflicting tendencies. On the one hand, the Voluntary Sector Initiative and related exercises offer hope that the trend toward restricting advocacy that emerged in the 1990s may be coming to an end. On the other, the *Charities Registration (Security Information) Act* could portend a period of intense constraint for groups that seek to promote full public debate of important issues. Which of these tendencies will prevail will depend very much on the capacity of the voluntary sector itself to see the regulatory regime in the round and to make an effective case to both the public and the government for full and open discussion of the challenges that confront us.

Notes

The authors acknowledge the support of the Queen's University and Kahanoff Foundation Nonprofit Sector Research Initiative. Pross also acknowledges the support of the Social Science and Humanities Research Council of Canada Grant No. 410.91.1748 (The Public Interest Group in Canada). We are grateful for the patience and kindness of the officials of charities, nonprofit organizations and government agencies whom we interviewed; to David Melvin for his assistance in carrying out the research; and to Gordon Floyd, Susan Phillips, Kathy Brock and our colleagues at the November 2001 Research Initiative workshop who participated with enthusiasm in discussing an earlier draft of the paper.

[1] As in a recent article by Susan D. Phillips,

Whereas governing through a paradigm of government is centred on control, governance involves collaboration and co-ordination, both across sectors and across policy areas. While government works on the strength of hierarchy, governance necessitates horizontality. The advantage of traditional government is the ability to deliver uniform programmes unilaterally to a broad segment of an eligible population; in contrast, governance recognizes difference and the value of flexibility. Whereas the legitimacy of government flows from its authority, that of governance derives from its credibility with citizens and partners. While the success of government hinges largely on programming, governance depends on relationship building (Phillips 2000/2001, 183).

[2]In later articles we will address further questions having to do with how groups adapt to the regulatory regime as they pursue their advocacy goals.

[3]We define public interest groups as formal organizations whose members have come together in order to altruistically promote a common perception of the public interest.

[4]Three policy fields were selected for the initial study when it became clear that it would be extremely difficult to derive useful results from a randomly selected sample of groups listed in the *Directory of Associations*. It was hoped that by choosing groups of different sizes, status, and financial resources in two or three sectors, we would be able to identify commonalties within and across sectors. We hope to explore these methodological issues elsewhere.

[5]These figures were, and remain, controversial. Treasury Board officials arrived at them by subtracting from the general category "grants and contributions" ($17.2 billion in the 1994–95 Estimates) those payments that were clearly not made to interest groups. That is, payments (other than those under the Canada Assistance Plan) to provinces and municipalities, to international organizations, to private sector contractors and to individuals. The residual $3.3 billion, furthermore, did not go in its entirety to charities and nonprofit organizations associated with the charitable sector. Many Aboriginal, business, and professional interest associations were also paid grants and contributions. Nor were payments to charities and related nonprofit organizations exclusively in support of the organizations themselves. The greater part were for services rendered (Interview. Treasury Board. A.P. Pross. March 1996).

Of the 26 associations interviewed in the summer of 1992 during the first phase of this study, 20 responded to a question that asked for an estimate of the extent of annual revenue derived from government. Eleven reported that they received 50 percent or more of their revenues from various governments. Five of these received 75 percent or more of their revenues from government.

[6]Of the 20 associations interviewed in the 2000–2001 phase of this study, eight stated that they had experienced serious cut-backs in the mid-1990s.

[7]Bill C-224 *Charitable and Non-profit Organization Director Remuneration Disclosure Act*. Read for the first time on 15 March 1994 and debated on

second reading on 10 February 1995. See House of Commons *Debates* for that date.

[8]Fellow Liberal, Ian Murray, noting that government funding had allowed groups to "usurp the role of members of Parliament, who are elected to speak for their constituents" complained that the funding of charities and nonprofit organizations had become a field of patronage dominated by bureaucrats. According to Reform MP Daphne Jennings,

> with the advent of the Charter of Rights and Freedoms, Canada gradually has become a society dominated by special interest groups, each group advocating what it deems to be a worthwhile cause.... More often than not these groups receive seed money from some level of government ... The problem with this procedure is that the dependence on government grants begins and carries on. It becomes difficult for the organization to function without federal money. For political reasons it becomes difficult for government, any government, to eliminate that funding *(Debates,* 10 February 1995, 9492).

[9]In contrast, low-profile advocates would rely more on behind-the-scenes lobbying, particularly the presentation of briefs to senior officials and politicians.

[10]Of the four groups whose revenues increased during the 1990s, two derived less than 20 percent of their revenues from government. Another, highly dependent on government funding, reported an increase in revenues, but also experienced budgetary turbulence. Involved as this group is with national unity policy, its experience tends to confirm Susan Phillips' observation that the government was rewarding those whose voice was "integral to the campaign for national unity and the quest for a Canadian identity." The only high-key advocacy group whose budget increased during the period and apparently did not experience financial turbulence was a nonprofit organization in the health sector.

[11]During our 1992–93 interviews several group officials voiced their concerns over the trends in government funding, but did not suggest that any of the sector's leading groups were making concerted action. At least one study published at this time drew attention to the problem of dependence on government funding and asked whether groups were becoming more accountable to government. See Reckart (1994). The diffused character of the charities' community makes it difficult to develop and arrive at a consensus, as Revenue Canada discovered when it consulted the major charities on revision of the *Income Tax Act* provisions relating to charities. See "Reform Delays Puzzling," *Not-for-Profit News,* September 1995, p. 66.

[12]Of course, the primary function of the Panel was to foster consensus within the charities community concerning the meaning and significance of accountability and to set the stage for the consultations with Ottawa that have been held under the aegis of the Voluntary Sector Initiative.

[13]The insistence on higher levels of accountability occasioned in part by the fact that governments themselves were being pressed to improve their own per-

formance. We should not discount the influence of events in other countries. The United Kingdom and Australia, for example, had conducted major inquiries into the governance of the charities and had instituted reforms. In the United States, accountability had become a significant focus of group, government, and academic discussion.

[14]Question 2 reads as follows: "Recently the Institute of Economic Affairs, which is based in the United Kingdom, published a study entitled *A Code of Conduct for NGOs — A Necessary Reform* in which it argued that

> there is no ... public scrutiny of NGOs [comparable to the public scrutiny of corporations], nor is there much evidence of accountability. There is a "double standard" operating here under which companies have to meet extremely high public expectations about their economic, environmental and social performance while their chief critics, NGOs, are able to conduct themselves without formal restraint apart from the criminal law and without any requirement for them to show social responsibility.

Members of advocacy groups on the other hand, might argue that their organizations are subject to various forms of regulation which can be compared to those that govern corporate behaviour. We are interested in knowing which of the following statements most accurately reflect the reality encountered by the groups with which you have worked."

Then followed a series of statements that the respondents were asked to "agree strongly" with, "agree," etc. These statements were: "The Institute statement is correct," "The regulatory regime governing Canadian NGOs is comparable to that governing corporations"; "In order to retain charitable status Canadian NGOs are forced to police themselves more rigorously than are business interests"; "NGOs deriving more than 25 percent of their revenue from government are circumspect in advocating policies"; "Adoption of a voluntary code of accountability developed by and for NGOs, but not a law, would provide useful information to government, the public, the private sector and other stakeholders and increase NGO accountability." Two of these statements directly addressed the comparison between third sector and corporate accountability regimes; one tested an important recommendation of the Broadbent Panel that related to accountability, while two others attempted to assess the extent to which organizations feel that government-managed accountability mechanisms influence the behaviour of groups.

[15]One of them explaining: "As applied to others? Yes. As applied to ourselves? No!"

[16]Several went further, suggesting that charities especially are more closely regulated. One executive director maintained that "corporations have more leeway. Charities must be screened for social responsibility. We are subject to every possible regulation there is." Another maintained that "Our standards of accountability are far greater than government."

[17]Three did not answer while two, the same two officials agreeing with the Institute of Economic Affairs statement, "disagreed" with the statement. No one "disagreed strongly."

[18]In a perverse way, further confirmation of this point came from responses to a question that asked whether "accountability" as a "regulatory element" affected the organization. The questions respondents asked and their further comments indicated that most differentiated various levels and directions of accountability.

[19]*Webster's New Collegiate Dictionary (1953)*. Impressionistic support for our thesis is evident in the pages of major newsletters circulating in the charities community. In Canada the *Not-for-Profit News*, and in the United States the *Non-Profit Times* and *The Chronicle of Philanthropy*, regularly run articles on charities rules, election controls, and lobbying "cheek by jowl" with articles about financial relations with government. In this chapter we show that these separately developed regulatory structures do in fact have a cumulative, interactive effect.

[20]The study by the Panel on Accountability and Governance in the Voluntary Sector, *Building on Strength*, is a partial exception.

[21]Prior to the interviews we provided each respondent with our own definitions of these terms. Here the definitions will be footnoted where we discuss the responses we received.

[22]The response of the fourth is surprising, as it is a major charity. The response might be explained by the fact that its expenditures on "political activities" are so small, in comparison to its total budget, that they would be considered truly "ancillary and incidental."

[23]"Self-discipline," for example, is an elusive concept, but could be considered as part of the complex of formal and informal rules that are bound together under the label of "accountability." Similarly, "stringent reporting requirements" clearly are associated with several of the regulations we listed and do not belong in a category by themselves. Changes in federal-provincial arrangements create organizational difficulties for some groups, that fact alone does not constitute advocacy regulation. Three observations did warrant separate consideration. Groups working with certain types of project grants would agree with the respondent who complained that MPs or MLAs are sometimes invited to review awards to groups in their constituencies, a practice that certainly has the potential to nudge groups into adapting their advocacy to suit the prejudices of local power brokers. This practice, of course, can be treated as part of the grab-bag of rules that are associated with direct funding. One suggestion was made that potentially represented a net addition to the roster of regulatory elements that we have defined as the regulatory regime in this field. We agreed with the respondent who felt that regulations dealing with access to information affect advocacy groups' ability to influence public opinion, but we decided not to include them in the regulatory regime because they relate to the information that is made available rather than to the groups themselves.

[24]Previously, we had referred to accountability in these terms: "The law imposes certain obligations on members of boards of directors toward the members of the associations they lead; toward the public at large and, in some circumstances, toward government. These fiduciary responsibilities and the accountability practices of charities and nonprofit associations affect the operations and activities of public interest groups."

[25]Specifically, we had previously referred to regulation of access to policy formation as follows: in some cases governments provide statutory guarantees of participation in certain decisions. More usually agencies recognize, through practice or policy directive, the claim of certain groups to take part in policy discussions. Agencies and royal commissions inviting this type of participation will often provide financial support for group interventions. Group participation in these exercises implies an obligation to accept conditions laid down by sponsoring agencies. These conditions constitute informal regulation. A special set of rules governs participation in litigation. Groups will often apply to courts for recognition of standing or to be given intervenor status. Here again, in certain circumstances, some financial support may be available to pay some of the costs of intervention.

[26]For an overview description of advantages and disadvantages of incorporation for nonprofit groups, see MacLeod (1986, ch. 6).

[27]Directors of incorporated nonprofit corporations may not fully benefit from limited liability because they may be held personally liable for activities performed in their capacity as directors: see, e.g., discussion in Kreiger (1989).

[28]We had explained our interest in corporate status by pointing out that "associations must meet the registration requirements of either the *Canada Corporations Act* and/or its provincial equivalents."

[29]As, for example, in the dispute between the Friends of the Lubicon and the Daishowa corporation, in which the company sued the group for organizing a boycott of its products. The case was settled out of court following a 1998 decision allowing the activists to boycott the company's customers as part of the Friends efforts to force a resolution to the long-standing land claims of the Lubicon Lake Indian band in northern Alberta. See <http://www.life.ca/nl/74/lubicon.html>.

[30]We had described our interest in direct funding in these terms: "Receipt of funds from government is generally accompanied by the imposition of government policies or standards in relation to, *inter alia*, equity in hiring and pay; tendering; accounting practices; audit and security. This study is particularly interested in the impact of these regulations on the participation of advocacy groups in policy discussion."

[31]Of the four that were not affected, two are major charities whose budgets dwarf the contract grants they receive from government; one is a nonprofit organization that exists almost exclusively as an advocacy organization opposed to government policy. Only one of these four has characteristics shared by the majority of those reporting that they are significantly affected by direct funding.

[32]Some of the latter added that they could not respond to the question because they and their groups did not have any experience with core funding.

[33]No organization that receives 20 percent or more of its funds from the government shall be considered as a public interest group. Any figure is admittedly arbitrary, but the less than 20 percent division assures a high degree of independence on the part of the public interest group in choosing their advocacy actions (Berry 1977, 9).

[34]In addition, we heard from two groups that the Ontario Trillium Foundation has advised them that it will not fund organizations that are engaged in advocacy.

[35]A more detailed examination of the impact of reductions in funding will be found in Juliet *et al.* (2001). Our research confirms their findings that some groups have been more resilient in the face of government cuts than many had predicted, but it also challenges their conclusion that the central mission of these groups was not seriously affected. Where advocacy was integral to their central mission some effects were felt.

[36]Note, however, that these are activities considered to be part of the educational functions of charities and may be funded through charitable donations.

[37]We had previously noted that our chief interest in tax-expenditure funding lay in the fact that "the award of charitable or not-for-profit status obliges groups to observe regulations concerning partisan political activity, advocacy of policy, and the application of funds to non-charitable purposes."

[38]Four said that it had no impact, one said that they did not know and felt that the question was not applicable to them.

[39]This phrase is from section 149(1) (l) of the *Income Tax Act*. An "association" is considered general enough to include a corporation. See Revenue Canada, IT-496, (2 August 2001) *Non-Profit Organizations, Discussion and Interpretation, General.*

[40]Note that under the *Income Tax Act*, registered charities are also exempt from income tax, but under different provisions.

[41]While the terms "social welfare," "civic improvement," "pleasure," etc. are not defined in the Act, they are elaborated on in a non-binding Revenue Canada *Income Tax Interpretation Bulletin* (IT-496, 2 August 2001). Pursuant to paragraph 5 of the bulletin, "In general terms, **social welfare** means that which provides assistance for disadvantaged groups or for the common good and general welfare of the people of the community. **Civic improvement** includes the enhancement in value or quality of community or civic life. An example would be an association that works for the advancement of a community by encouraging the establishment of new industries, parks, museums, etc. Under the categories of social welfare and civic improvement, care must be taken to ensure that the purposes of the association are not those of a charity.... The phrase **any other purpose** except profit is interpreted as a catch-all for other associations that are organized and operated for other than commercial or financial reasons."

[42]As set out in IT-496.

[43]The following discussion of the charitable tax regime draws directly on T4063 (E)(00) 2000-01021.

[44]For more detailed elaborations on what this separate status might be and how it might operate, see Webb (2000). The suggestion that a separate status might be an option was contained in the following question:

Do you agree with current *Income Tax Act* rules whereby charities can only engage in "ancillary and incidental political activities of a non-partisan nature," devoting no more than 10 percent of the resources of the charity to such activities? [Check more than one response if necessary.]

❑   yes
❑   yes, but the rules regarding what constitutes acceptable activities need to be clarified in lay-person's language.
❑   yes, but the rules regarding what constitutes acceptable activities need to be better enforced.
❑   no, there should be no ancillary and incidental political activities allowed
❑   no, ancillary and incidental political activities should be permitted without restriction.
❑   no, there should be separate tax status, with tax deductions, available for donors, for groups engaging primarily in political activities.
❑   other:

[45]Preamble, the *Lobbyists Registration Act* RS 1985 c. 44 (4th Supplement). See also *An Act to the Amend the Lobbyists Registration Act* SC 1995 c.12.

[46]We had previously referred to regulation of lobbying in these terms: "A cluster of regulations relating to corrupt practices associated with lobbying are set out in the *Criminal Code* and, of course, apply to interest groups, their supporters and employees as well as to other citizens. In recent years lobbying activity has had to be registered under the *Lobbyists Registration Act* and consequently has come under increasingly close scrutiny, if not regulation."

[47]At the same time, he noted, "Industry has an unknown number of people engaged in research and back-up work."

[48]If lobbying activities are performed by several employees, registration is required "when the accumulated lobbying duties by all paid employees would constitute 20 percent or more of the duties of one employee" (Canada. Industry Canada 1996, 8).

[49]There is a fascinating variety in the structure and legal status of public interest groups. One of the rare groups to be designated a trustee of the Crown considered that its status rendered registration unnecessary:

At one point most of the ... team were registered, but we looked at the LRA very carefully and eventually concluded that because of the organization's special relationship with government, the Act does not apply. In some respects it seemed appropriate that [the organization] should be considered a Tier II organization, but as a trustee of the Crown [it] has special access.

[50]It is worth noting that all three organizations are major charities whose lobbying expenditures would be unlikely to violate the current *Income Tax Act* rule whereby charities can only engage in "ancillary and incidental political activities of a non-partisan nature," devoting no more than 10 percent of the resources of the charity to such activities.

[51]We had introduced the subject of regulation of participation in elections by noting that: "There is a ban on partisan activity by charities, but in addition several jurisdictions have legislated limits on policy advocacy by charities and, during elections, on expenditures by third parties to promote or oppose candidates or to advocate or oppose policy positions."

[52]*RSC* 1983 C-E2, s. 259; 42 Eliz 2 c. 19, s. 259. *SC* 1993.Vol. 1.; 48 Eliz. 2 c. 9, Part 17 *SC* 1999.

[53]This view was stated most explicitly at an early stage in Parliament's attempts to regulate third-party advertising by the NDP's Rod Murphy who commented that "some of the most partisan vicious and one-sided advertising takes place during election campaigns on behalf of so-called third parties. I believe it is incumbent upon the House not to follow the American example where all sorts of groups spend enormous amounts of money during an election campaign to emphasize a single issue while not always being bound by the truth, fairness or honesty. They are simply pushing a very emotional issue to the extent that it clouds the real political issues of a campaign." House of Commons *Debates*, 25 October 1985, p. 28299.

[54]Which this group favours.

[55]The second was a group working in general public policy fields. It does not advertise during elections, or at any other time, and its executive director offered no reason for selecting this position from the six available.

[56]Respondents were also asked whether the chief electoral officer had ever investigated their advertisements, issued warnings to them or prosecuted. None had had any contact of this sort. When asked how they would prefer election advertising regulation to be monitored, the executive directors registered no strong preference. The majority of those responding, nine, opted for surveillance either by the chief electoral officer, or by a group in which the officer would be represented. Seven did not respond to the question.

References

Bakvis, H. and J. Smith. 1997. "Third-Party Advertising and Electoral Democracy: The Political Theory of the Alberta Court of Appeal in *Somerville v. Canada (Attorney General)* [1996]" *Canadian Public Policy/Analyse de Politiques* 23 (2):164-77.

Berry, J.M. 1977. *Lobbying for the People: The Political Behavior of Public Interest Groups*. Princeton, NJ: Princeton University Press.

Bryden, J. 1994. *Special Interest Group Funding: M.P.'s Report*. Mimeo.

Canada. 1989. "Lobbyist Registration Regulations," *Canada Gazette: Part 1*, 125, 10 June, p. 2797.

Canada. Auditor General of Canada. 1988. *Report 1987–88*. Ottawa: Supply and Services Canada.

_____ 1989–90. "The Departments of National Revenue, Taxation and Finance: Charities, Non-profit Organizations and the *Income Tax Act*," *Annual Report*. Ottawa: Supply and Services Canada, ch. 10.

_____ 1990. *Report: 1989–90*. Ottawa: Supply and Services Canada.

_____ 1991. *Report: 1990–91*. Ottawa: Supply and Services Canada.

Canada. Consumer and Corporate Affairs Canada. 1977. *Detailed Background Paper for the Canada Non-Profit Corporations Bill*. Ottawa: Supply and Services.

Canada. House of Commons. 2001. 49-50 Eliz. II. Bill C-36 *An Act to Amend the Criminal Code...* Part 6 "Registration of Charities – Security Information," section 4. Ottawa: House of Commons.

Canada. House of Commons. Standing Committee on Public Accounts.1990. *Sixth Report*. Ottawa: Supply and Services Canada.

Canada. Industry Canada. 1996. *Lobbyists Registration Act: A Guide to Registration*. Ottawa: Supply and Services Canada.

Canada. Industry Canada. Corporate Law Policy Directorate. 2000. *Reform of the Canada Corporations Act – The Federal Nonprofit Framework Law*. At Industry Canada Strategis Web site <Strategis.ic.gc.ca>.

Canada. Revenue Canada. 2000. *Registering a Charity for Income Tax Purposes*, No. T4063(E)(00), "What Standards Does the Canada Customs and Revenue Agency Use to Register Charities?" Ottawa: Supply and Services Canada.

_____ 2001. *Registered Charities: Education, Advocacy, and Political Activities*. Ottawa: Supply and Services Canada.

Canada. Treasury Board Secretariat. 2000. *The Voluntary Sector: Third Pillar of Canadian Society – Partnering with the Voluntary Sector for the Benefit of Canadians – Framework for the TBS Study of Funding Issues*. Ottawa: Voluntary Sector Project Office.

Canada. Treasury Board Secretariat. Program Branch. 1994. "The Review of Interest Group Funding: A Consultation Paper" (Marked "Draft"). Ottawa: Supply and Services Canada. Mimeo.

Canadian Centre for Philanthropy. 2001. "Submission to the House of Commons Standing Committee on Justice and Human Rights of The Canadian Centre for Philanthropy Re: Bill C-36 Anti-terrorism Act. Toronto: The Centre. Mimeo.

Cross, W. 1994. "Regulating Independent Expenditures in Federal Elections," *Canadian Public Policy/Analyse de Politiques* 20 (3):253-64.

Cumming, P. 1974. *Proposals for a New Not-for-Profit Corporations Law for Canada,* Volume I. Ottawa: Information Canada.

Drache, A. (with F. Boyle). 1998. *Charities, Public Benefit and the Canadian Income Tax System: A Proposal for Reform.* Ottawa: Non-Profit Sector Research Initiative.

Duff, D.G. 2001. "Charitable Status and Terrorist Financing: Rethinking the Proposed *Charities Registration (Security Information) Act,*" in *The Security of Freedom: Essays on Canada's Anti-Terrorism Bill,* ed. R.J. Daniels, P. Macklem and K. Roach. Toronto: University of Toronto Press, pp. 321-40.

Eade, R. 1995. "Too Many Charities Begin at Home," *Ottawa Citizen*, 22 April, pp. A1, A2.

Faulkner, J.H. 1982. "Pressuring the Executive," *Canadian Public Administration* 25 (2):240-54.

Floyd, G. 1995. "Charities Pressed to be more Accountable," *Front and Centre*, July, p. 7.

Hiebert, J. 1998. "Money and Elections: Can Citizens Participate on Fair Terms Amidst Unrestricted Election Spending?" *Canadian Journal of Political Science* 31 (1):91-112.

Hirshhorn, R. and D. Stevens. 1997. "Organizational and Supervisory Law in the Nonprofit Sector," CPRN Working Paper No. CPRN/01. Ottawa: Canadian Policy Research Network.

Juillet, L., C. Andrew, T. Aubry and J. Mrenica with C. Holke. 2001. "The Impact of Changes in the Funding Environment of Nonprofit Organizations," in *The Nonprofit Sector and Government in a New Century,* ed. K.L. Brock and K.G. Banting. Montreal and Kingston: School of Policy Studies, Queen's University and McGill-Queen's University Press, pp. 21-62.

Klein, N. 2000. *No Logo: Taking Aim at the Brand Bullies.* London: St. Martin's Press.

Krieger, S. 1989. *Duties and Responsibilities of Directors of Non-Profit Corporations.* Toronto: Canadian Society of Association Executives.

MacLeod, F. 1986. *Forming and Managing a Non-Profit Organization in Canada.* Vancouver: International Self-Counsel Press Ltd.

Martin, Hon. P. 1994. House of Commons *Debates*, 21 February.

_____ 1995. House of Commons *Debates*, 27 February.

Martin, S.A. 1985. *An Essential Grace: Funding Canada's Health Care, Education, Welfare, Religion and Culture.* Toronto: McClelland & Stewart.

Ng, R. 1988. *The Politics of Community Services: Immigrant Women, Class and the State.* Toronto: Garamond Press.

Office of Consumer Affairs. 2003. *Applicant's Guide* for the OCA Contributions Program. The information provided below is derived from the *Guide*, which is available at <http://strategis.ic.gc.ca/pics/ca/app guide e.pdf>.

Pal, L.A. 1993. *Interests of State: The Politics of Language, Multiculturalism, and Feminism in Canada.* Montreal and Kingston: McGill-Queen's University Press.

Panel on Accountability and Governance in the Voluntary Sector (PAGVS). 1998. *Helping Canadians Help Themselves: Improving Governance and Accountability in the Voluntary Sector,* Discussion Paper. "Introduction: The Panel – A Mirror and a Compass." Ottawa: PAGVS. At <www.pagvs.com>.

_____ 1999. *Building on Strength: Improving Governance and Accountability Canada's Voluntary Sector,* Final Report. Ottawa: PAGVS. At <http://www.ccp.ca/information/documents>.

Phillips, S.D. 1991. "How Ottawa Blends: Shifting Government Relationships with Interest Groups," in *How Ottawa Spends, 1991–91: The Politics of Fragmentation,* ed. F. Abele. Ottawa: Carleton University Press, pp. 183–228.

_____ 2000/2001. "More than Stakeholders: Reforming State-Voluntary Relations," *Journal of Canadian Studies* 35 (4):182–201.

Picard, A. 1995. *The Gift of Death: Confronting Canada's Tainted Blood Tragedy.* Toronto: HarperCollins.

Reckart, J. 1994. *Public Funding, Private Provision: The Role of the Voluntary Sector.* Vancouver: UBC Press, 1994.

Royal Commission on Electoral Reform (Lortie Commission). 1992. *Reforming Electoral Democracy: Report.* Ottawa: Supply and Services Canada.

Stewart, W. 1996. *The Charity Game: Greed Waste and Fraud in Canada's $86-Billion-a-Year Compassion Industry.* Vancouver/Toronto: Douglas and McIntyre.

Voluntary Sector Initiative. 2000. *Report of the First Round of Cross-Canada Consultations on the Draft Accord.* At <http://www.vsi-isbc.ca/eng/joint_tables/accord/fall_consultations.cfm>.

Webb, K.R. 2000. *Cinderella's Slippers? The Role of Charitable Tax Status in Financing Canadian Interest Groups.* Vancouver: SFU-UBC Centre for the Study of Government and Business.

4

Ethical Climate, Accountability and Autonomy: A Comparative Analysis of Nonprofit and Government Managers

Ken Rasmussen, David Malloy and James Agarwal

INTRODUCTION

Among the issues emerging from the increase in contracting activity between nonprofit organizations and governments is the question of accountability and organizational autonomy (Phillips and Graham 2000). The often expressed concern is that when governments use contracts with nonprofit organizations for the delivery of social services, these same governments can lose public accountability for tax dollars. Equally troubling for nonprofit organizations is that they can see their cherished autonomy erode due to the influence of government funding (Ferris 1993). As increasing numbers of government services come to be delivered by nonprofit organizations, questions are rightfully being asked about effective methods of ensuring public accountability while maintaining nonprofit autonomy (Dicke and Ott 1999; Milward, Provan and Else 1993).

While cost-conscious governments often turn to nonprofit models of service delivery from a desire to trim budgets, governments are also legitimately concerned about bringing the delivery of services more in line with the needs of clients. This dual concern clearly implies that the broad policy directives and discretion given to nonprofits by governments will be fine-tuned through adaptation at the local level, resulting in services that are more efficiently delivered and tailored to community needs. Indeed, there is a well-entrenched tradition that suggests that parcelling out of discretion to nonprofit delivery agents can be very positive and contribute effectively to the policy process, especially when this discretion allows the implementing agency to play an active role in defining the policies that they are implementing (Burke 1990).

While the goals of meeting budget targets, getting closer to the needs of citizens and achieving administrative innovation are all important, a key question that is rarely asked is whether individual managers in nonprofit organizations are committed to the democratic and ethical values of transparency, fairness, equal treatment, accountability, and due process (Brehm and Gates 1997; Leazes 1997). There is, in fact, a critical view within the literature which suggests that nonprofit organizations are by definition inefficient, unaccountable, and inequitable creatures of government (Bennett and DiLorenzo 1989). Still others have argued that nonprofit organizations are particularized in dealing with problems, create client dependence, and tend to be run by well-meaning amateurs (Salamon 1987). Governments also have voiced legitimate concerns about losing accountability in the face of their insuperable difficulties in coordinating decision-making authority among institutions that have their own independent sources of authority and support (Barrados, Mayne and Wileman 2000).

It is possible that the nature of these conflicting assessments of the role of nonprofit organizations stems from differences in value preferences or orientations in the two sectors. Government, of course, has a commitment to protect and promote the "public interest" which would include commitments to fairness, equality, and transparency. The nonprofit sector's obligation is to clients or individual members of some subgroup based on strong commitments to individually sensitive service and social compassion. If different values lead to questions about accountability, not to mention problems with implementation, it would be useful to understand what these differences in values are and how they might cause distortions in the delivery of services that would be inconsistent with the norms of democratic public administration. Equally, these value differences, if properly understood by both parties might well result in services that are more closely allied to the needs and desires of the clients receiving the service.

At the core of this tension are apparent differences in the ethical orientations of the two environments. Evidence from previous research points to the fact that nonprofit managers will often push the boundaries of overhead control and contract compliance. Bernstein even suggests managers in the nonprofit sector "do not consider it 'wrong' and indeed may consider it 'right,' to effect the illusion of compliance, which baldly, is to lie, in order to benefit clients" (1991, 124). This orientation contrasts with the ethical orientations of public sector managers which require a commitment to protecting and promoting the "public interest" with its commitments to fairness, equality, and transparency (Gortner 1991). Such differences in ethical orientation, if they are widespread and deeply held, can potentially have a major impact on how contracts are established and how accountability is defined in those contracts. Furthermore, if different ethical climates do exist It would be useful for governments to understand what these differences are and how they might cause distortions in the delivery of services that would be inconsistent with the norms of democratic public administration.

The utility of exploring the concept of "ethical climate" is that potentially it adds a useful dimension to our understanding of the complex relations between policy designers in government and policy implementers in the nonprofit sector. The reason for an optimistic assessment is that the concept of an ethical organizational climate has received increasing amounts of attention in the literature on organizational theory as both theorists and practitioners search for a means of explaining and enhancing work-related behaviour and satisfaction (Bartels *et al.* 1998; Jones and Hiltebeital 1995; Schwepker, Ferrell and Ingram 1997). That a positive or strong climate within an organization is a necessary antecedent for high performance and satisfaction is accepted theoretically and, to a limited extent, empirically by the scholars studying organizations. Generally, ethical climate has been considered to be the informal interpreter and judge of an individual's organizational behaviour. Such an understanding may provide insights into the ethical reasoning of both partners in the delivery of government services and ways in which the differences can be more effectively combined.

If these differing ethical climates are present and do manifest themselves in different behaviours, then governments which are devolving more service delivery activity to nonprofit organizations, will need to consider the concept of ethical climate in determining public accountability. Thus, the belief that the nonprofit delivery agency should be unambiguously linked to the government department that it is contracting with in an essentially hierarchical relationship will clearly give a false sense that accountability is present and is easily attainable. Such an approach, which reflects the preoccupations of public service managers, might well be at odds with the view of nonprofit managers. Nonprofit managers may well feel that because they are closer to the source of the problem they should have maximum discretion on matters where the problem is most immediate.

What we can predict from our understanding of the existing literature is that public sector managers, with their much greater interest in rules, legal definitions, and responsibility to an abstract public interest, will try and develop relationships based on "organizational management" (Cline 2000; Lester and Googin 1998). That is, they will try and create accountability through goal specification and control of subordinate organizations. This gives rise to the issues of funding formulas, authority relationships, regulations, and administrative controls (budget, planning and evaluation items), and rule setting. All of these will be used by governments to try and prevent what they would view as the illegitimate policy preferences of nonprofit delivery agents from dominating the delivery process. This framework tends to pose the problem of accountability as something that is related to the administrative process and not a conflict over values. Should public servants favour such an approach, they would be ultimately reducing the reliance on knowledge and skill at the delivery level and increasing reliance on abstract, standardized solutions that are more comfortable for government officials.

Another approach addresses the problem of accountability as a conflict of interest between the various participants in the process. As such, the existence of differing ethical climates will naturally produce conflicts that cannot be overcome by simply relying on managerially based approaches. Instead, the government will be required to find new methods of extracting cooperation. Power is seen to be shared in the process of implementation, and conflict of interest and problems with accountability are really a legitimate struggle over basic values (Cline 2000, 552). In this view, power in the implementation process is distributed among the partners so that participants must bargain in order to gain a capacity to act. If it is true that the conflict over values more often than not hinders the implementation of policy and thus accountability, the best solutions become ones requiring governments to enter relationships that create a cooperative context for those who participate in the implementation process. In particular, governments would require public sector managers to ensure that they recognize and accept the client orientation of nonprofit organizations and the advocacy role that the client orientation will encourage.

The purposes of this chapter are to explore these questions through both a qualitative and quantitative survey of key informants in government departments and nonprofit organizations, and to begin a process of providing some more precise meaning to the differing ethical climates in the two sectors and examining the possible impact this might have on accountability. This chapter will try to determine the extent to which differences in ethical climate exist and how these differences might help us understand and, eventually resolve, some of the dilemmas associated with securing public accountability while maintaining nonprofit autonomy.

ETHICAL CLIMATE

Ethical climate is a concept that describes the shared perception of organizational norms, values, and behaviour (Schneider 1975). It informally assists the members of an organization to define acceptable behaviour within the confines of that organization. Specifically, many in the field have suggested that the ethical climate in organizations influences the moral conduct of the membership (Cohen 1995; Schneider 1975; Victor and Cullen 1987, 1988). Ethical climate is therefore an organizational variable worthy of considerable attention, particularly in light of governments' increased interest in using nonprofit organizations to deliver government programs.

The ethical nature of organizational conduct has received increased attention in all administrative sectors (e.g., Tait 2000; Ford and Richardson 1994). Public administration scholars have been particularly interested in how ethical values such as integrity, fairness, and accountability have been affected by contracting (Boase 2000; Kettner and Martin 1993). More specifically, there are questions raised about "the extent to which it is possible to infuse programme delivery agencies with core public service values" (Kernaghan 2000, 99). However, despite this interest, relatively little research has been carried out with regard to intersectoral differences in ethical climate. While there is some limited evidence that suggests that variations do exist (e.g., Agarwal and Malloy 1999; Brower and Shrader 2000), no comparative research is available which has explored the nature of differences in the ethical climates in government and the nonprofit sector.

Victor and Cullen (1987, 1988) developed a framework for measuring the perception of ethical orientation. It consists of nine theoretically derived climate types that result from the juxtaposition of three ethical theories and three decision-making reference points or loci of analyses. The ethical perspectives include egoism, benevolence, and principled ethical grounding. Egoism refers to behaviour that is fundamentally self-interested. The focus of benevolence is toward the greatest good for the collective or for the greater number (e.g., the immediate work group, the firm, the community, and the society-at-large). The principled perspective places greatest emphasis on duty to adhere to laws, rules, policies, and procedures (e.g., the organization's code of ethics, the policies of government, or the laws of society).

The second aspect of this framework consists of three decision-making reference points (i.e., the construct termed "locus of analysis"). The individual locus of analysis reflects a self-driven referent for decision behaviour. The local referent is the immediate work group or the organization generally as well as the individual's community of significant others. Norms, values, and behaviours derived from this immediate work or social community are internalized or at least generally operationalized by the individual actor. The cosmopolitan locus of analysis extends beyond the group and the organization. At this level, behaviour is shaped by normative systems that have the potential to operate within the organization, but are generated and maintained externally (e.g., professional codes of ethics as opposed to organization-specific behavioural norms). The juxtaposition of ethical theory and locus of analysis results in a 3x3 matrix consisting of nine theoretically based ethical climates (see Figure 1).

Though Victor and Cullen's theoretical framework represents generic organizational climates, much of the empirical work has been done in the

Figure 1: Ethical Climate Matrix

		Locus of Analysis		
		Individual	**Local**	**Cosmopolitan**
	Egoism	self-interest	company profit	efficiency
Ethical Theory	**Benevolence**	friendship	team interests	social responsibility
	Principle	personal morality	organizational rules and procedures	law and codes

Source: Victor and Cullen (1987, 1988).

for-profit sector. While there has been limited research conducted in nonprofit contexts, there has as yet been no published research based on the public sector. Further, other than a study by Brower and Shrader (2000), there has been no intersectoral comparison of ethical climate. Based on the implicit organizational goals of these three realms (i.e., for-profit, nonprofit, and government), one would expect to find some variation in the perception of what is and what is not acceptable behaviour. For example, responsibility and commitment of the nonprofit employee/volunteer and organization may lean more toward welfare of the client as opposed to the explicit commitment of the for-profit organization to the shareholder (e.g., Brower and Shrader 2000; Hansmann 1987). Similarly, in a governmental organization the focus is upon the commonweal as opposed to individual clients or shareholders. In his report of the Task Force on Public Service Values and Ethics, Tait suggests that "a professional public service implies three things: a body of knowledge, skills and expertise that those outside the profession are unlikely to possess; a set of values and attitudes that determine the culture of the profession; and a set of standards for both of these" (2000, 23). It is likely therefore that public service professionals will have a different ethical orientation than managers in the nonprofit sector.

Our aim in this research is to explore ethical climate in the realm of nonprofit and government organizations in order to assist policymakers in understanding the nature of ethical conduct in their organizational setting and how the differences might affect the implementation of public policy and the nature of the partnership arrangements between the two sectors (see Burns 1970; Tait 2000).

METHOD

The method for this study involved both a qualitative and a quantitative survey. The major basis for this chapter was a series of one-on-one, face-to-face, and in-depth unstructured interviews conducted through a process of ethnographic interviewing (Fontana and Frey 1994). This involved a selected sample of 24 mid-level managers from both the government and the nonprofit sector in the health and social services sectors in a single Canadian province, each of whom was interviewed one hour and asked to provide answers to a number of open-ended questions. The nine primary questions were designed to elicit responses that would correspond to one of the dimensions of ethical climate (Table 1). However, interview subjects were encouraged to engage in a conversation and provide more detail when they wanted. All interview subjects were required to sign a consent form that guaranteed their anonymity and privacy. The sample was divided equally between men and women, but it was dominated by individuals with an undergraduate university education or higher. The average age in our sample varied between 47 in the government sector to 42 in the nonprofit sector. Those who were employed in the nonprofit sector worked in organizations with over 15 employees and those in government worked in large social service, or justice departments with over one hundred employees. In order to make consistent judgements about the strength of perception, we considered climates to be relevant in the organizations when more than 50 percent of respondents were in agreement (see Table 1). We did not use two judges and a inter-judge reliability test; thus single rater bias may be evident.

The second part of this research involves a survey questionnaire sent to 500 managers in each sector. There was a response rate of 147 (29 percent) in the government sector and 89 (17 percent) in the nonprofit sector, and these results are used to further support our propositions. In this sample,

Table 1: Frequency Response from Survey Questionnaire

EGOISM

(1) In this organization, decisionmakers are mostly out for themselves? (EGO INDIVIDUAL)

Government (N-147)

Completely false	Mostly false	Somewhat false	Somewhat true	Mostly true	Completely true
14.29	44.90	14.29	19.05	7.48	0.00

Nonprofit (N=89)

Completely false	Mostly false	Somewhat false	Somewhat true	Mostly true	Completely true
47.19	35.96	4.49	7.87	1.12	3.37

(2) Decisionmakers are concerned with the organization's interest — to the exclusion of all else? (EGO LOCAL)

Government (N=146)

Completely false	Mostly false	Somewhat false	Somewhat true	Mostly true	Completely true
10.96	24.66	27.40	32.19	4.79	0.00

Nonprofit (N=89)

Completely false	Mostly false	Somewhat false	Somewhat true	Mostly true	Completely true
15.73	33.71	22.47	16.85	8.99	2.25

(3) The most efficient way is always the right way in your organization? (EGO COSMOPOLITAN)

Government (N-147)

Completely false	Mostly false	Somewhat false	Somewhat true	Mostly true	Completely true
4.08	25.85	40.14	26.53	3.40	0.00

Nonprofit (N=89)

Completely false	Mostly false	Somewhat false	Somewhat true	Mostly true	Completely true
5.62	23.60	40.45	19.10	7.86	3.37

BENEVOLENT

(4) In this organization, our major concern is what is best for the other person. (BENEVOLENT INDIVIDUAL)

Government (N=147)

Completely false	Mostly false	Somewhat false	Somewhat true	Mostly true	Completely true
2.04	12.25	33.33	36.74	14.29	1.35

Nonprofit

Completely false	Mostly false	Somewhat false	Somewhat true	Mostly true	Completely true
2.25	4.49	15.73	30.33	35.96	11.24

(5) Our major concern is what is best for everyone in the organization? (BENEVOLENT LOCAL)

Government (N=147)

Completely false	Mostly false	Somewhat false	Somewhat true	Mostly true	Completely true
2.72	9.52	29.25	38.10	19.73	0.68

Nonprofit (N=89)

Completely false	Mostly false	Somewhat false	Somewhat true	Mostly true	Completely true
0.00	4.49	10.11	24.72	40.45	20.23

... *continued*

Table 1 (Continued)

(6) In this organization, it is always expected that people in the organization will do what is right for the client and the public. (BENEVOLENT COSMOPOLITAN)

Government (N=147)

Completely false	Mostly false	Somewhat false	Somewhat true	Mostly true	Completely true
1.35	2.03	9.46	22.30	51.34	13.51

Nonprofit (N=89)

Completely false	Mostly false	Somewhat false	Somewhat true	Mostly true	Completely true
0.00	0.00	3.37	6.74	55.06	34.83

PRINCIPLE

(7) In this organization people are expected to follow their own personal and moral beliefs? (PRINCIPLE INDIVIDUAL)

Government (N=144)

Completely false	Mostly false	Somewhat false	Somewhat true	Mostly true	Completely true
2.08	13.20	18.75	39.58	24.31	2.08

Nonprofit (N=89)

Completely false	Mostly false	Somewhat false	Somewhat true	Mostly true	Completely true
2.25	7.87	11.24	38.20	34.83	5.61

(8) Successful people in this organization go by the book? (PRINCIPLE LOCAL)

Government (N=147)

Completely false	Mostly false	Somewhat false	Somewhat true	Mostly true	Completely true
3.38	6.75	30.41	43.24	15.54	0.68

Nonprofit (N=89)

Completely false	Mostly false	Somewhat false	Somewhat true	Mostly true	Completely true
2.25	12.36	19.10	35.96	25.84	4.49

(9) In this organization people are expected to strictly follow legal or professional standards? (PRINCIPLE COSMOPOLITAN)

Government (N=147)

Completely false	Mostly false	Somewhat false	Somewhat true	Mostly true	Completely true
1.35	1.35	5.41	25.68	45.27	20.94

Nonprofit (N=89)

Completely false	Mostly false	Somewhat false	Somewhat true	Mostly true	Completely true
0.00	2.25	6.74	23.60	37.08	32.58

the average age of the government managers was 47.7 and their gender distribution was 40 percent female and 60 percent male. A total of 85 percent of government managers had either a bachelor's degree or a master's degree. Nonprofit managers had a somewhat different profile in that they were marginally younger, with an average age of 45, but the gender balance substantially favoured women with 71 percent of respondents female and only 29 percent male. This group differed in its educational profile as well in that only 70 percent had either a bachelor's or a master's degree.

RESULTS AND DISCUSSION

What became clear was that different perceptions of ethical climate exist and these differences point us in a very interesting direction. There are some predictable tensions between the two sectors. In the nonprofit sector there were frustrations and cynicism about the way governments are off-loading services, knowing that the nonprofit sector will be there to fill the gaps and exploit the caring values of these organizations. Nonprofit managers also wanted more training for staff coupled with the need to have wages and benefits reach the levels found in government. Equally strong was the support for stable funding, so that programs are no longer ad hoc and based on short-term program funding which is reviewed by government on an annual basis and subject to easy termination. There is a strong sense in the nonprofit sector that government has lost touch with the grass-roots needs of the citizens they service. Thus, in general, nonprofit managers wanted to see the sector mirror the government delivery of services, but retain the caring values.

Government managers were aware of the frustrations faced by the nonprofit organizations, but felt that as public sector managers, they add a much more important commitment to be accountable for taxpayer dollars. This duty was paramount to them as public servants. In this regard they had some resentment that government is seen as the "big bad brother" — uncaring and uncooperative. Yet by-and-large there appears to be an aware-ness that the government-nonprofit relationship is still emerging and that there is room for creativity and innovation in the partnerships with com-munity and nonprofit organizations. There is clearly an awareness on the part of government managers that better ways should be found to make partnership agreements less cumbersome so that clients are indeed better served.

There were a number of generalized responses to various questions which brought to the surface differences on the issues of the role of rules, organizations, orientations, and the nature of different ethical climates. From the responses to the nine statements, it is possible to group the responses into our three ethical categories: egoism, benevolence, and principle. We then observe how these ethical orientations conform to three different loci of analysis: the individual, the organizational, and extra-organizational. The following is a brief discussion of some of the differences we noted, followed by an ethical climate matrix that offers a systematic presentation of these findings.

Egoism

Respondents to the survey questionnaire in both sectors displayed a lack of identification with ego or strong Machiavellian drives at either the individual level or the local (organizational) level. The responses were similar in both sectors, as were the levels of intensity. The response to all three questions (see Table 1) was typically "completely false" or "mostly false." Curiously, only those in the volunteer sector were seen as individuals who were out for themselves. As one nonprofit manager noted in his response: "If a person is going to volunteer they need to get something out of it. Whether it's satisfaction that they've helped somebody, whether it's something on a resumé or something for a university or college class or high school class."

Some differences did, however, show up in our interviews, differences that we did not see in the survey, particularly at the cosmopolitan locus of analysis when managers were asked about the role of efficiency and cost-effectiveness in decision-making in their organizations. Officials in both government and nonprofit organizations disagreed strongly with the statement that "the efficient way is always the right way in your organization," and neither group was placed in this section of the final matrix. However, their reasons for the disagreements with this statement were very telling and deserve to be noted. There is a strong sense from government managers that they try to be cost-effective and efficient in the way they deliver their programs, but there are other factors that are important and take precedence over efficiency and cost-effectiveness. Government managers are looking at issues such as the long-term effectiveness of programs, how to maintain relationships, and overall value for money over more than one budget cycle. Consistently they look at the survival of the system in the long term and rarely admit that cost-effectiveness was a leading criterion in decision-making. In contrast, respondents from the nonprofit sector disagreed in almost the same numbers that the cost-effective way is not always the right way, but they put cost-effectiveness at the very top of their agenda because they had no alternative. The nonprofit sector clearly feels that it faces a much greater squeeze on its resources than does the government sector — an impression shared by both parties. While nonprofit managers would like to follow their public sector counterparts and not be obsessed with cost-effectiveness, they find that their yearly budgetary renewals depend on their ability to demonstrate this to government decisionmakers. Nonprofit managers would ultimately like to mirror the behaviour of their government counterparts, but their perceptions of their current climates are clearly different.

Benevolent

The three climates based upon benevolent theory were fully represented in the findings of this study (i.e., greater than 50 percent agreement). Interestingly, the nonprofit respondents identified each of the three climates (i.e., benevolent-individual, benevolent-local, and benevolent-cosmopolitan) as existing in their realm, though their responses were more pronounced in the individual and local foci (78 percent and 85 percent agreement, respectively in the nonprofit sector, and only 52 percent and 58 percent agreement in the government sector). Respondents in the government sector, predictably, identified nearly as strongly with the cosmopolitan-benevolent ethical climate as existing in their organizations (87 percent for government respondents and 96 percent for nonprofit respondents). Thus, the divergence between the two sectors was found outside the cosmopolitan realm, that is, within the individual and local foci.

In interviews, government managers consistently suggested that in their environment there were always multiple stakeholders who had to be taken into consideration. In contrast, those in the nonprofit sector tended to see the "other person" exclusively as the client. There were also substantial differences in the area of "caring" that really began to point out potential value conflicts between the two sectors. While both sectors identified the cosmopolitan-benevolent climate as existing in their sector, the government respondents appear to be intensely focused on this climate. Those working directly for government universally acknowledged that doing right for the public is their primary concern. They often suggested that in their organization they "take the role of public service really seriously. We're spending or we're influencing two billion of taxpayers' dollars so that's the primary focus. People in this branch take that seriously." Those in the nonprofit sector tended to be much more client-focused, characteristically arguing, "I think we tend to do what's best for our clients and the people we serve, rather than looking at the public as a whole." These somewhat contrasting views were present in most interviews, and this is indeed predictable. Previous research suggests that the client-based concerns are to be expected in the nonprofit sector because of the underlying communitarian assumptions of this sector (Agarwal and Malloy 1999; Jeavons 1994). This sector is by definition and design more focused on the interests and needs of clients and immediate colleagues (i.e., the identification of benevolent-local climate). In contrast, public servants appear oriented exclusively toward the larger values associated with the maintenance of social systems through serving the public interest.

This dichotomy is further emphasized by public servants who generally see their responsibility to the public in terms of following policies and procedures that in turn assure good service to clients and protect and defend the public interest. In this regard, one government manager noted, "It's important to have clear policies and procedures. We would expect that these policies and procedures would ensure good service or would contribute to it. Not ensure, but would contribute to good service and what's good for the client." Thus, even when a client focus was seen as being important and positive, this focus came from a duty to ensure fairness to all clients and to treat all clients in a similar manner. On the other hand, within the nonprofit sector it was often felt that "the culture, for example, is one where I might not ask for support in professional development activities because my colleagues and superiors might, maybe, think that I shouldn't be taking money from the mouths of the poor. The whole focus is really client-oriented." This intense focus on the needs of the client is both a strength and a weakness of the nonprofit sector, but is clearly something that must be part of the ongoing dialogue between the two sectors as they shape their relationship.

Principle

When the questions turn to ethical criteria based on principles or duty, we begin to witness some rather notable differences. First, public servants strongly assert that the organization has priority over individual moral beliefs. For example, one public service manager noted that "often times there's a larger overriding perspective and if your moral beliefs don't correspond with that overall direction, I think the expectation is that you put those aside in your work life." Similarly, another public service manager noted that "in my program with problem gambling you know I can have my own personal beliefs on whether gambling is good or bad but at the end of the day I don't ever get into debates about whether we should or shouldn't have gambling. That's not my job." Even more forceful is the conviction that if the manager's values conflict with those of the government then the manager should leave the job. "I think people could have personal prejudices or beliefs that may not be consistent with what policies or directions we want to take — they would have to follow those things or seek alternative employment in those cases." The overall conclusion for those in government was made quite well by one official who noted that organizational values include:

> things like inclusivity, transparency, consensus building — those are some of the important principles that we work with here in this department and probably, generally, you could say, in government. So it's within that framework that people have to assess the measure of their personal and moral beliefs against, and if people don't want to work in that kind of environment then, maybe they should work somewhere else.

This contrasts somewhat with nonprofit managers, one noted that he agreed, because "I think personal and moral beliefs walk hand in hand with what the objectives are here — that people in conflict with the law can be rehabilitated." While there is a sense that employees in the nonprofit sector have some latitude with their own personal values, they should not conflict with those of their clients.

Curiously, during the interviews both sets of respondents were disinclined to see themselves as individuals who strictly "follow the book," but in the survey they did agree with this. What became clear through the interviews was that public servants, while respectful of legal and professional responsibility, were not inclined to take this a step further and see themselves as being bureaucratic. Their answers tended to suggest most often that "successful people in this branch are risk-takers and innovators" or that "successful people are creative and flexible and aggressively seeking change." This is sometimes seen as an individual virtue, as when one public servant noted that "what we promote is innovation and encouraging new approaches, which means it might not be in 'the book.' But as long as you're not breaking the law or breaking legislation ... then we encourage looking for innovative approaches and solutions." Yet even this desire to be creative and innovative is circumscribed by the observation that "we try and make sure we're treating people fairly and equitably. That's probably the closest we have to 'the book.'" Interestingly, this notion of fair and equitable treatment which is key to public sector managers, was never once mentioned by the managers working in the nonprofit sector.

Those in the nonprofit sector also did not believe in the "book," but they used their flexibility in a much more client-focused manner. They are not abstractly "seeking change" or trying to be "risk-takers" but rather they are trying to ensure that each client is treated separately. Thus, a typical observation would be: "We don't have a book. We add a chapter every day every time a new situation arises." It was noted that "there is a sense that the rules are really not something that can help the client and that you must constantly be open to 'gray areas.'" There is a sense in which managers in both sectors do not want to be seen as doing something by the book, but when they go beyond the book they are using the discretion implied by this for much different purposes. Public servants are pursuing an organizational mission and generally want to promote the goals of the organization or the public, whereas managers in the nonprofit sector once again have a client focus.

Public servants generally expressed the belief that they expect people to follow strict legal and professional standards. There is a strong recognition of the environment of public service they operate in, given the response that "we have legislation that we need to abide by and we're answerable to courts. So we do need to follow and live within those guidelines.... It also fits in professionally with how we would view looking at people. It fits in with the social work profession as well." However, once again, we noticed a contrast in the nonprofit sector where they are clearly going to follow legal rules, but regard this as an imposition, as opposed to being a positive means of achieving accountability or transparency. It is in some sense the classic front-line worker response to gather discretion and use it in a variety of ways to both differentiate among clients and make their scarce resources of time and money go as far as possible. Yet clearly for nonprofit managers, serving the client sometimes means approaching a situation without the same concern for the implications for superiors within a hierarchy. Government managers, however, are always aware of political superiors who want both accountability for performance and accountability for process. Thus, a regime of rules exists within government that is as much about ensuring that decisionmakers are not surprised as it is about ensuring that citizens get all the services they need. Those in the nonprofit sector are clearly more interested in using discretion in a way that is more client-focused than would public servants with client responsibilities who are more inclined to use discretion in a way that might benefit themselves or avoid embarrassing mistakes. It is not surprising to find managers of nonprofits who say, "We abide by all the constraints of our contract, but meeting them, at times, we may be more creative and walk away from set policies and procedures to find ways to do it." The attitude that "rules are meant to be bent" is not the attitude expressed by public servants in our sample. Rather, they tend to see much more virtue in legal rules, which they tend to equate with the public interest.

CONCLUSIONS: IMPLICATIONS FOR ACCOUNTABILITY

Preliminary indications from both our qualitative and quantitative surveys are that there are some noticeable similarities and differences between the two sectors. Respondents from both nonprofit and government organizations perceived the existence of the cosmopolitan locus of analysis. Cosmopolitan sources of ethical reasoning tend to be abstract concepts generated outside organizations but used inside organizations as part of the institutionalized normative system. This finding would lead one to assume that global issues and standards of ethical conduct are perceived and valued by both nonprofit and government employees. When we examine the second matrix (Figure 2) we can see that the government and nonprofit sectors share the organizational referent or locus of analysis described as

Figure 2: Ethical Climate Matrix (nonprofit and government)

		Locus of Analysis		
		Individual	Local	Cosmopolitan
Ethical Criteria	Egoism			
	Benevolence	nonprofit **individual caring**	nonprofit **team caring**	government and nonprofit **social caring**
	Principle	nonprofit **independence**		government and nonprofit **law and code**

cosmopolitan within two of the ethical theories (principle and benevolent). At the cosmopolitan level the source of principles is extraorganizational (the legal system or professional norms) and was strongly supported by both government and nonprofit sector managers. Ethical thinking appears to be greatly influenced by referents who are external to the individual and organization. Within this category, role definition is found in the social system external to the system in which the actor is embedded.

However, the two sectors differ once other loci are considered. While there is congruence at the cosmopolitan locus, the nonprofit sector respondents identified three additional climate types as existing (benevolent-local, benevolent-individual, and principle-individual) whereas no other climates were perceived by the government sector. The identification of two climates within the individual locus is similar to Agarwal and Malloy's (1999) quantitative finding in which respondents scored friendship and personal morality as being shared perceptions of organizational climates. Unlike the findings of the current study, the benevolent-local climate was not found in this earlier research. It appears that while nonprofit respondents do not perceive the presence of a thrust toward organizational survival (ego-local) or organizational duty per se (principle-local), they do recognize that the group dynamic or team caring as a shared perception among employees.

The nonprofit managers expressed a concern at the individual level for the consideration of other people without reference to organizational membership, and at the local level, nonprofit managers experienced a greater consideration for the organizational collective (team-play, *esprit de corps*) than found in the government context. Within the principle criterion nonprofit managers tended to have stronger beliefs that principles are to be self-chosen and the climate is to be guided by personal ethics, whereas government managers did not regard such a view as legitimate.

Such findings may have significant implications for how accountability and autonomy are to be managed, particularly when seen in the light of previous research into the use of administrative discretion in the implementation of public policy. Much of the previous research suggests that public servants who actually deliver social services, the so-called "street-level bureaucrats," display a variety of behaviours toward their clients. These behaviours range on a continuum from reluctant, to routine, to extraordinary treatment representing fundamentally different levels of service. The more traditional street-level bureaucrat, the social worker or police officer, tends to determine who gets what kind of service on the basis of judgements about the worthiness that organizes the nature of the services that the individual client will receive. There are "values switches" which turn off and on various levels of services (Scott 1997).

Equally important in this is our existing understanding of public servants at street level who tend to be very resistant to attempts at change based on traditional organizational change tactics. That is, "street-level actions are guided less by rules, training or procedures and more by beliefs and norms, especially beliefs and norms about what is fair. Beliefs and norms are more elusive and resistant to change than rules and procedures; they are shadowy, never fully articulated, and often inconsistent" (Maynard-Moody and Musheno 2000). Even more troublesome is the fact that as governments attempt to control discretion through more direct overhead control there is a real possibility that they will push this discretion underground, thereby weakening their own control and accountability. If this is the case, then the strong support of the values of caring found in this survey among nonprofit managers may easily come to be seen as a source of strength that furthers the goals of government.

What needs to change within government is the idea that the adaptive behaviours of nonprofit managers are illegitimate. Instead, these behaviours should become a welcome part of the process and part of contracts. If you look at the difference in the ethical climate and the discretion that flows from this fact, partnerships should capture and allow for adaptive responsibility to highly specialized problems. Stated somewhat differently, any attempt to reject the positive use of discretion through increased overhead control is probably doomed to fail. Indeed, partnerships with nonprofit organizations can probably be made more effective when governments consider the tremendous creative potential they represent in solving problems and making policy (Rubin 1993). However, in order to take advantage of this, nonprofit organizations must be seen as having a legitimate role as representatives of clients before they can be told to adopt the broader citizen-based concept. This may also require definitions of accountability that give consideration to nonprofit policy systems in which there may be few explicit standards of performance, matrix organizational structures, and unpredictable channels of compliance reporting (Kearns 1994).

For this to occur, a number of changes will have to take place, beginning with an end to both the obsessive top-down approach and the unrealistic expectations that governments often have regarding nonprofit organizations. To achieve this partnership, agreements should include the clear right of a nonprofit organization to continue with its advocacy roles without any fear that it will be in jeopardy of losing funding. Nonprofits can be very effective eyes and ears for the government and can add a new dimension to the idea of democratic administration. They can also be effective in the creation of a "learning organization," but only if they are allowed to point out errors and provide some audit role. This will mean that nonprofits must be seen as partners not only in implementation but also in policy-making. If they are seen simply as implementers they will continue to engage in illicit policy-making which will be hidden from government and may result in the imposition of new restrictions on the behaviour of nonprofit organizations.

If governments are concerned about losing authority they may want to include strategies for capacity-building within partnership agreements. In other words, they might want to pursue a strategy of mild convergence, in which nonprofit managers move slightly toward the norms associated with public management. Governments can do this by increasing training and development budgets and providing a much more stable funding environment. But governments also have to accept the advocacy role of nonprofits. This is a contribution to the democratic dialogue, and governments need to get used to formulating policy in partnership with their critics. What appears to be required is a move from the narrow hierarchical relationship of funder/provider to a new model based on partnership agreements that take into consideration the reality of differing values held by those represented in the partnership agreement.

Much of the evidence in this research points in this general direction. That is to say, many managers of nonprofit organizations feel that basic fairness and equity have little in common with the traditional bureaucratic definitions of these terms which demand that all citizens be treated the same and that laws and policies be fairly implemented. Instead, in the nonprofit sector, the fairness, justice, and equality appear to mean providing the client services based on their intrinsic worth. Yet it is important to note that the image of street-level bureaucrats who replace the rule of law with their own moral judgements and stereotypes is more complex than it first appears. Street-level definitions of "worthiness" involve a complex balancing of client needs, the ability to respond to services, and the concern for husbanding of scarce resources (Maynard-Moody and Leland 2000). Based on both our interviews with managers and the responses to our survey questionnaire, those respondents from the nonprofit sector lead us to believe that we can and should expect the same kinds of behaviour from these actors. That is, their client focus is likely to see them ignore more traditional, bureaucratically imposed prescriptions of how to define client needs and choose definitions independently of those that public servants might be inclined to use.

If these differing ethical climates are present and do manifest themselves in different behaviours, then governments wishing to establish contractual relations with nonprofit organizations should consider these differences when establishing agreements. The idea that the implementing agency, in this case the nonprofit organizations, will be unambiguously linked to the contracting agency in a hierarchical relationship is a bad premise upon which to base public accountability. Such an approach reflects the preoccupations and value orientations of public sector managers, and is at odds with many of the views of nonprofit managers. Nonprofit managers see themselves as being closer to the source of the problem and as a consequence feel there should be a maximization of discretion at the point where the problem is most immediate. Finding a way to manage these differing ethical climates may not by itself overcome the dilemmas associated with contracting-out the delivery of government services. However, it may provide an avenue to ensure better contractual agreements that recognize and acknowledge the importance of ethical differences and use the recognition of ethical differences to improve the quality of democratic public administration and just not hinder it.

Note

Research for this chapter was supported by a generous grant from the Kahanoff Foundation Nonprofit Sector Research Initiative.

References

Agarwal, J. and D.C. Malloy. 1999. "Ethical Work Climate Dimensions in a Not-for-Profit Organization: An Empirical Study," *Journal of Business Ethics* 20:1-14.

_____ 2000. "The Role of Existentialism in Ethical Business Decision-Making," *Business Ethics: A European Review* 9 (3):143-54.

Barrados, M., J. Mayne and T. Wileman. 2000. "Accountability for Collaborative Programme Delivery Arrangements in Canada's Federal Government: Some Consequences for Sharing the Business of Government," *International Review of Administrative Sciences* 66:495-511.

Bartels, L.K., E. Harrick, K. Martell and D. Strickland. 1998. "The Relationship Between Climate and Ethical Problems within Human Resource Management," *Journal of Business Ethics* 17:799-804.

Bennett, J.T. and T.J. DiLorenzo. 1989. *Unfair Competition: The Profits of Nonprofits*. New York: Hamilton Press.

Bernstein, S. 1991. *Managing Contracted Services in the Nonprofit Agency*. Philadelphia: Temple University Press.

Boase, J.P. 2000. "Beyond Government? The Appeal of Public-Private Partnerships," *Canadian Public Administration* 43:75-91.

Brehm, J. and S. Gates. 1997. *Working Shirking and Sabotage: Bureaucratic Response to a Democratic Republic*. Ann Arbor: University of Michigan Press.

Brower, H.H. and C.B. Shrader. 2000. "Moral Reasoning and Ethical Climate: Not-for-Profit vs. For-Profit Boards of Directors," *Journal of Business Ethics* 26:147-67.

Burke, J.P. 1990. "Policy Implementation and the Responsible Exercise of Discretion," in *Implementation and the Policy Process: Opening up the Black Box,"* ed. D.J. Palumbo and D.J. Calista. New York: Greenwood Press.

Burns, J.M. 1970. *Leadership.* New York: Harper & Row.

Cline, K.D. 2000. "Defining the Implementation Problem: Organizational Management versus Cooperation," *Journal of Public Administration Research and Theory* 10 (3):551-71.

Cohen, D.V. 1995. "Creating Ethical Work Climates: A Socio-economic Perspective," *The Journal of Socio-Economics* 24:317-43.

Dicke, L.A. and S.J. Ott. 1999. "Public Agency Accountability in Human Services Contracting," *Public Productivity & Management Review* 22:502-16.

Ferris, J.M. 1993. "The Double-Edged Sword of Social Service Contracting: Public Accountability vs Nonprofit Autonomy," *Non-profit Management and Leadership* 3 (4):363-79.

Fontana A. and J.H. Frey. 1994 "Interviewing: The Art of Science," in *Handbook of Qualitative Research*, ed. N.K. Denzin and Y.S. Lincoln. Thousand Oaks, CA: Sage Publications.

Ford, R and D. Zussman. 1997. *Alternative Service Delivery: Sharing Governance in Canada.* Toronto: Institute of Public Administration of Canada.

Ford, R.C. and W.D. Richardson. 1994. "Ethical Decision-Making: A Review of the Empirical Literature," *Journal of Business Ethics,* 13:205-21.

Gortner, H.F. 1991. *Ethics for Public Managers.* New York: Praeger.

Hansmann, H. 1987. "Economic Theories of Nonprofit Organization," in *The Nonprofit Sector: A Research Handbook*, ed. W.W. Powell. New Haven: Yale University Press, pp. 27-42.

Jeavons, T.H. 1994. "Ethics in Nonprofit Management: Creating a Culture of Integrity," in *The Jossey-Bass Handbook of Nonprofit Leadership and Management*, ed. R.D. Herman. San Francisco: Jossey-Bass Publishers, pp. 184-207.

Jones, S.K. and K.M. Hiltebeitel. 1995. "Organizational Influence in a Model of the Moral Decision Process of Accountants," *Journal of Business Ethics* 14: 417-31.

Kernaghan, K. 2000. "The Post-Bureaucratic Organization and Public Service Values," *International Review of Administrative Science* 66:91-104.

Kearns, K.P. 1994. "The Strategic Management of Accountability in Nonprofit Organizations: An Analytical Framework," *Public Administration Review* 54 (2):185-92.

Kettner, P.M and L. Martin. 1993. "Performance, Accountability and Purchase of Service Contracting," *Administration in Social Work* 17 (Winter):61-79.

Leazes, F.J., Jr. 1997. "Public Accountability: Is it a Private Responsibility?" *Administration and Society* 29:395-413.

Maynard-Moody, S. and M. Musheno. 2000. "State Agent or Citizen Agent: Two Narratives of Discretion," *Journal of Public Administration Research and Theory* 10 (3):329-58.

Maynard-Moody, S. and S. Leland. 2000. "Stories from the Front-Lines of Public Management: Street Level Workers as Responsible Actors," in *Advancing Public Management*, ed. J.L. Bruney *et al.* Washington, DC: George Washington University Press, pp. 109-26.

Milward, H., K. Brinton, G. Provan and B.A. Else. 1993. "What Does the 'Hollow State' Look Like?" in *Public Management: The State of the Art*, ed. B. Bozeman. San Francisco: Jossey-Bass, pp. 309-22.

Phillips, S.D. and K.A. Graham. 2000. "Hand-in-Hand: When Accountability Meets Collaboration in the Voluntary Sector," in *The Nonprofit Sector in Canada*, ed. K.G. Banting. Montreal and Kingston: School of Policy Studies, Queen's University and McGill-Queen's University Press, pp. 149-90.

Rubin, H.J. 1993. "Understanding the Ethos of Community-Based Development: Ethnographic Descriptions for Public Administrators," *Public Administration Review* 53:429-37.

Salamon, L.M. 1981. "Rethinking Public Management: Third-Party Government and the Changing Forms of Government Action," *Public Policy* 29 (3):255-57.

_____ 1987. "Partners in Public Service: The Scope and Theory of Government-Nonprofit Relations," in *The Nonprofit Sector: A Research Handbook*, ed. W.A. Powell. New Haven, CT: Yale University Press, pp. 99-117.

_____ 1995. *Partners in Public Service: Government-Nonprofit Relations in the Modern Welfare State*. Baltimore, MD: Johns Hopkins University Press.

Schneider, B. 1975. "Organizational Climate: An Essay," *Personnel Psychology* 28:447-79.

Schwepker, C.H., Jr., O.C. Ferrell and T.N. Ingram. 1997. "The Influence of Ethical Climate and Ethical Conflict on Role Stress in the Sales Force," *Academy of Marketing Journal* 25:99-108.

Scott, P.G. 1997. "Assessing Determinants of Bureaucratic Discretion: An Experiment in Street-Level Decision Making," *Journal of Public Administration Research and Theory* 7:35-57.

Tait, J.C. 2000. *A Strong Foundation: Report of the Task Force on Public Service Values and Ethics*. Ottawa: Canadian Centre for Management Development.

Victor, B. and J.B. Cullen. 1987. "A Theory and Measure of Ethical Climate in Organization," *Research in Corporate Social Performance and Policy* 9:51-71.

_____ 1988. "The Organizational Bases of Ethical Work Climates," *Administrative Science Quarterly* 33:101-25.

5

The Impact of Increased Health-Care Funding on the Evolution of Two Congregations of Religious Women in Nova Scotia and Prince Edward Island, 1944–1982

Heidi MacDonald

B efore World War II, provincial governments supported health care in a scattered, minimal way, according to what they could afford. In the Maritime provinces, most hospitals were nonprofit and were affiliated strongly with either the Roman Catholic or Protestant Churches. As in the rest of North America, Catholic sisters operated most Catholic hospitals. Their virtually unpaid labour and their coordination of donations provided affordable health care and social services for thousands of clients.[1] Agitation for improved health care took on new urgency following World War II, however, as the federal government promised to compensate Canadians for the war by improving their quality of life. In particular, the Marsh Report, formally entitled, *Report on Social Security for Canada* (1943), made six social security proposals, including a comprehensive system of health care. As many recommendations for improved funding were implemented gradually over the next quarter-century, Catholic sisters were unable to adapt to the new conditions for a variety of reasons.

This chapter will consider how new health-care funding and legislation affected two congregations of Catholic sisters that administered hospitals: the Sisters of Charity of Halifax who administered the Halifax Infirmary, and the Sisters of St. Martha who operated the Charlottetown Hospital. The period examined in this article, 1944 to 1982, reflects the significant infusion of government funding to hospitals that began with the Veterans Charter of 1944, through the closure or transfer of ownership of both of the Catholic hospitals under study, the second of which occurred in 1982.[2] It is widely assumed that sisters retreated from hospital work in the late 1960s solely because of the decreasing number of sisters available to do the work. This essay will argue that this explanation is inadequate.

The impact of increased government funding had both positive and negative effects on congregations of sisters. In some cases, government funding allowed the sisters to improve their educations, and consequently improve the quality of care in their institutions. Some sisters were also pleased that the government took more responsibility for institutional care because it allowed them to work at other endeavours more closely connected to serving the poor. In other cases, however, new government funding regulations frustrated sister health workers by interfering with how they operated and governed institutions. While increased government funding was not the only, or even perhaps the greatest, influence on sisters in the postwar era, it was certainly a significant contributor to their decreasing involvement in Canadian health care by the mid-1960s. For example, between 1970 and 1975, the number of Catholic hospital beds in Canada fell by 50 percent, from 60,954 to 26,356, and the number of sisters involved in hospital work dropped by more than 30 percent between 1970 and 1980 (Cellard and Pelletier 1990, 170 and 199). Several scholars have drawn a correlation between the decline of sisters working in health care and the decline in their membership. The greatest authority on demographic change in American congregations of sisters, Helen Fuchs Ebaugh, notes that by the 1960s, the result of "death, defections, and reductions in new recruits" was "higher median ages, an increase in the number of elderly and retired nuns no longer able to work" (Ebaugh 1993, 41 and 85). Between 1967 and 1976, the number of sisters in Canada fell by 33.5 percent, from 61,942 to 41,145

(Murphy 1996, 362; Catholic Council of Bishops 2003). I will argue that the complicated financial situations created by hospital insurance and rising health-care costs have forced congregations of sisters to withdraw from hospitals prematurely.

BACKGROUND ISSUES

While several congregations of sisters served in Nova Scotia and Prince Edward Island in the twentieth century, each province had a single congregation that acted as the foremost provider of diverse Roman Catholic institutional care. In the 1960s, the Sisters of Charity of Halifax, who numbered about 1,500, served the 30 percent of the Nova Scotia population that was Roman Catholic and administered social institutions all over Canada and the United States, including the prominent 500-bed Halifax Infirmary. In PEI, approximately 160 Sisters of St. Martha served the 45 percent of the provincial population that was Catholic, operating many institutions, including the 180-bed Charlottetown Hospital. Two decades later, each congregation had withdrawn from the major city hospital it administered.

The period under study was a very complicated one. The baby boom, consumerism, suburbanization, second-wave feminism, improved access to education, Cold War concerns, and increased focus on youth made the postwar era a cauldron of change and reform. The Roman Catholic Church established the Second Vatican Council in 1962 in order to respond to these societal changes. Although major changes were implemented in liturgy and church government, Vatican II failed to bring Catholics back to church: the number of Catholics regularly attending church in Canada dropped from 83 percent in 1965 to 61 percent in 1975, and to 43 percent in 1986 (Bibby 1987, 17). The upheaval in both the church and the secular world trickled down to congregations of sisters who were urged to reassess their mission and purpose. Some congregations responded by strengthening their commitment to working more directly with the poor, and therefore closed large institutions, including hospitals (McKenna 1998, 201; SCHA 1958). Many individual sisters were dissatisfied with Vatican II directives and left congregations in the late 1960s, while few young women were drawn to enter. Increasing education and career opportunities in the secular world may have also convinced potential aspirants that ministries that formerly could be accomplished only inside the convent were just as tenable outside the convent.

The lack of new entrants created a rapidly increasing average age of sisters in North America, which greatly reduced the number of sisters available to work in various institutions by the early 1970s. In 1966, for example, 17 percent of American sisters were more than 65, a figure that jumped to 38 percent by 1982 (Ebaugh 1993, 81).[3] In 1967, of the 1,625 members of the Sisters of Charity of Halifax, 28.6 percent were more than 60 years of age; a decade later, 52.5 percent of the 1,287 members were more than 60 (SCHA 1958). Among the 160 Sisters of St. Martha in 1967, 24 percent were more than 60, while in 1975, 32.6 percent of the 132 members were more than 60 (SSMA 2003, 10-11). While such figures suggest that many congregations in English Canada surrendered their institutions at this time because they could no longer staff them, this chapter will consider another cause for surrendering: the impact of increased government funding on Catholic hospitals.

CANADIAN HOSPITAL FUNDING IN THE EARLY 1940s

While hospital insurance was not fully implemented in all provinces until 1961, it was preceded by increased government support for health care, most notably in hospital construction grants for veterans in 1944, and soon after with provincial government subsidization of per diem rates. Thus, to understand the changes brought by increased government spending toward health care, it is useful to consider the year 1944, which was the eve of change.

There was no standard for funding general hospitals in the first half of the twentieth century.[4] Health care was a provincial responsibility, but most provinces could not afford much and/or did not consider it their duty (Lindenfield 1980, 166-67).[5] There is no simple answer to how hospitals were funded before federal construction grants and national health insurance were implemented in the postwar era. It should be noted that with the exception of a handful of provincial hospitals — not all provinces had them — Canadian general hospitals remained open through a complex and very tenuous system of receipts and expenditures. In addition to getting what they could from provincial and municipal governments, general hospitals charged patient fees, with varying degrees of success in obtaining payment. Hospitals also encouraged endowments, some of which were large enough to fully fund the construction of a wing of a hospital, while smaller endowments furnished patients' rooms. Ladies' auxiliaries raised funds on behalf of hospitals by operating canteens or holding annual bazaars or picnics. Needless to say, there was diversity in the types of funding that a hospital could generate in any given year.

David Gagan, writing about Ontario public general hospitals, argues that the dependence on private funding, and especially patients' fees, rather than government funding, grew out of hospitals' Victorian tradition of caring for the impoverished. In Gagan's words, "government social policies continued from the 1870s until the 1950s to define the hospitalization of indigents as a community responsibility primarily dependent on the deployment of hospital resources for medical philanthropy well below the rapidly escalating costs of providing 'scientific' medical care to all patients, and sharply differentiated care to some" (1989, 154). The result, Gagan continued, was that by 1949, private donations "had become an insignificant proportion of total revenue, while government grants represented only 15 percent of hospital income" (ibid., 155). Hospital boards of directors struggled to keep hospitals open and were forced to depend on middle-class patients to subsidize hospital care for all. Unfortunately, no studies of other provinces exist. Given that Ontario was the country's wealthiest province in the mid-twentieth century, it is doubtful that poorer provinces, including Nova Scotia and Prince Edward Island, could have depended on subsidization by the middle-class as Ontario hospitals did. Regarding PEI's commitment to health-care funding, it is worth remembering closely related evidence: as Douglas Baldwin notes, in the mid-1920s, PEI had the lowest provincial revenue per capita and "one of the highest tuberculosis rates, [but] was the only province lacking sanatoria, diagnostic clinics, and government preventive health work" (Baldwin 1990, 122). The more impoverished provinces really struggled to fund health care, and in the case of tuberculosis in PEI, the government was so cash-strapped it took no responsibility in the early twentieth century.

Understanding how Canadian hospitals were funded before federal government initiatives in the postwar era is further complicated by examples of great disparity in the provincial assistance that hospitals received. Some provinces even administered funding disproportionately to hospitals in the same city, as was the case with Halifax's two major hospitals, the Halifax Infirmary and the Victoria General.

According to Colin Howell, the Victoria General, which served about 7,000 patients in 1943, had "evolved from a charity institution serving the sick poor to a highly competent ... component of the modern public welfare system" (1988, 76-77). The Victoria General was provincially owned, a situation solidified in the hospital's position as the teaching hospital for Dalhousie University, the region's only university that offered medical degrees (ibid., 88-89). Paying patients were cared for in separate areas of the hospitals, while non-paying patients stayed in wards. In 1944, only one in five patients paid hospital fees (ibid., 91). The province regularly paid any deficit the hospital accumulated.

By the end of World War II, the Halifax Infirmary had also become a large hospital. It was administrated by the Sisters of Charity and operated under Catholic Hospital guidelines, but served as a public general hospital under a civic advisory board.[6] Although the hospital had evolved significantly since its denominational beginnings, it still received only a small amount of provincial funding compared to its parallel institution in the city, the Victoria General. The Infirmary depended heavily on user fees as well as the virtually unpaid administrative and nursing labour of the Sisters of Charity, while the Victoria General depended on government funding in every aspect of its operation. In fact, Colin Howell's history of the Victoria General, published in 1988, barely mentions the hospital's sources of revenue beyond saying it was supported by the provincial Department of Health. The histories of most Canadian general hospitals, published or not, are more likely dominated by the financial struggle necessary to keep such expensive institutions afloat (Howell 1988, 91, 105 and 109). In both the wealthy provinces, such as Ontario, and the impoverished provinces, such as PEI, hospitals struggled for decades to provide the most up-to-date medical care despite many patients' inability to pay.[7] Hospitals were thus eager to benefit from the federal government's postwar funding promises.

ISSUES RELATING TO CATHOLIC HOSPITALS

At the end of World War II, many Canadian general hospitals were operated by or affiliated with churches. Catholic and Protestant hospitals were
common in most provinces. Catholic provinces were run very much like
other general hospitals in the mid-twentieth century. Funding came from
the same variety of sources, including small amounts from government
and larger amounts from patient fees. Some dioceses made additional donations through special collections. Catholic hospitals were owned by the
diocese in which they resided, by the congregations of sisters who administered them, or by a local board of directors.

The Roman Catholic Church hierarchy was very concerned about providing *separate* health care for Catholics. The roots of separate Catholic
social institutions and services are found in nineteenth-century
Ultramontanism, a conservative Roman Catholic clerical movement that
sought to strengthen the institutional church's relationship with its flock
by meeting its members' social needs completely. It was important that
Catholics have access to hospitals run according to Catholic health-care
moral guidelines, which did not permit those procedures that violated natural
law, including therapeutic abortion, sterilization, euthanasia, and instruction in birth control. Furthermore, special regard for the patient was
imperative in certain areas, such as informing the patient of imminent death
so that he or she could prepare spiritually and make a last confession (Cellard
and Pelletier 1990, 71-72).

Most Canadian Catholic hospitals have belonged to the Catholic Hospital Association of the United States and Canada since 1916, but formed
their own association, the Catholic Hospital Council of Canada (CHCC)
in 1939 (ibid., 19 and 55). According to the CHCC's 1952 mission statement: "The object of the Association shall be to promote and realize ideals
in the religious, moral, medical, nursing education, social and other phases
of hospital activity pertaining to Catholic hospitals and schools of nursing
in Canada" (ibid., 69). Sister-nurses were the mainstay of this organization, although they were sometimes represented by priests because sisters
had restrictions on travelling and going to meetings at night. The sisters
were more active in the association as they, and not priests, had practical
experience in dealing with hospitals' day-to-day affairs (ibid., 24). The

effect of proposed national health insurance was a great concern to the council. In fact, one of the main reasons the association separated from its American parent group was the need to focus on the implementation of national health insurance that was expected to be a significant part of post-war reconstruction (ibid., 79-80). The CHCC was determined to protect Catholic health care in the postwar era. The association expected its members to benefit from additional government funding while maintaining the Catholic medical and moral code in existing Catholic hospitals.

CASE STUDY: FINANCING THE HALIFAX INFIRMARY AND THE CHARLOTTETOWN HOSPITAL AT MID-CENTURY

The remainder of this chapter will focus on the impact of increased federal funding on two Catholic hospitals, the Halifax Infirmary, operated by the Sisters of Charity since 1887, and the Charlottetown Hospital, operated by the Sisters of St. Martha of Charlottetown since 1925. Just as Gagan has argued for Ontario hospitals, before the introduction of health insurance, both hospitals were dependent on user fees, while provincial and municipal government funding accounted for a minor part of these two general hospitals' budgets.[8]

Since the early twentieth century, the provincial government of PEI had paid a flat-rate grant to the two Charlottetown area general hospitals. In the early 1940s, the amount was $6,000 annually, which accounted for under 5 percent of the Charlottetown Hospital's annual operating budget (SSMA 1925-1960; PAPEI 1950). During the same period, 22 sisters of St. Martha worked full-time, six days a week, at the hospital. The hospital was a very labour-intensive undertaking for the sisters. The 22 sisters who served there in 1940 comprised 32 percent of the congregation's entire membership (SSMA 1940). Each sister received only a meager allowance of about $15 a month to cover her personal expenses, and thus the hospital was able to save a great deal of money in wages.[9]

Beginning in 1944, the PEI provincial government paid $0.75 a day for the "medically indigent." This acknowledgment that a significant number of patients were unable to pay their hospital bills was a big help to the sister administrators, but the government cash infusion was still $36,000 short of the costs incurred for these patients (SSMA 1951).[10] In fact, in the mid-1940s, approximately 40 percent of the clientele at the Charlottetown Hospital were unable to pay their entire bills.[11] In 1947, the provincial government increased their contribution to the Charlottetown Hospital. Instead of the flat-rate grant, the government began to pay $0.50 per "day's treatment" for every patient, and the amount was then increased to $0.75 per patient-day in 1948. Even then, the hospital did not balance its budget as hospital expenditures were $229,990, an amount that exceeded revenue by $13,161 (PAPEI 1950, Table 10). Government contributions still averaged only 15.1 percent of the Island's five general hospitals' budgets in 1949. Patient fees comprised a larger contribution to hospital budgets at 52.3 percent of the year's revenue. Another 19.3 percent came from pre-paid insurance plans. Most significant to the budget was the sisters' labour. Between 1946 and 1950, an average of 25 sisters served at the hospital annually and continued to be paid their small $15 monthly allowance. For some idea of how much the hospital saved by employing sisters rather than secular health workers, consider that wages at the Toronto General Hospital in 1947 were $140 to $150 monthly for regular nurses, and $160 to $200 monthly for head nurses and nurse administrators (McPherson 1996, 225). Using their sister-health workers instead of secular health workers probably saved the Charlottetown Hospital $40,000 annually.

It is more difficult to paint a financial picture of the Halifax Infirmary in the 1940s because the sisters' archives burned in a major fire in 1949.[12] The records that remain, however, indicate that the hospital received little, if any, provincial government funding before the late 1940s.[13] In the early 1940s, the City of Halifax contributed a paltry $500 annually. Before the introduction of national health insurance, the Sisters of Charity did not receive any wages or allowances for their work at the infirmary, although they lived at the hospital and their food and board came out of the hospital's general budget. Patient fees were by far the greatest source of hospital income and financed both the operating and capital costs of the hospital. Although the sisters expressed a desperate need to eliminate overcrowding in the 1930s by building a new wing, they did not begin construction until the government accepted more financial responsibility in the late 1940s.

By the late 1940s, the Halifax Infirmary received $0.45 for the first 5,000 patient-days and $0.30 thereafter, which was still a very small proportion of actual costs.[14] Of course, their greatest financial asset, as for any Catholic hospital, was actually invisible in their budgets: the sisters' virtually unpaid labour.

The Halifax Infirmary started to measure the value of the Sisters of Charity's labour after 1948. From 1948 until the introduction of national health insurance in 1959, the labour was valued at over half a million dollars. As a general rule in secular hospitals, salaries were expected to account for 60 to 65 percent of total operating costs, excluding doctors' wages which were separate from hospital expenses (SCHA 1965). Thus, in the era before provincial governments provided funding for health care, sisters were absolutely essential to the operation of Catholic hospitals in Canada. After that time, new government funding had a significant impact on sisters, their work, and the evolution of their congregations. While the funding was welcomed, it was far from complete. As a result, it created new financial expectations and increased debt-load significantly.

THE IMPACT OF POSTWAR FUNDING AT THE CHARLOTTETOWN HOSPITAL AND THE HALIFAX INFIRMARY, 1944–1982

During the postwar era of significant hospital expansion, sisters were still largely responsible for balancing Catholic hospital budgets, which had increased greatly due to technological innovations and the vastly increased utilization of hospitals. The first major postwar federal government funding initiative for hospitals was assistance for the construction of veterans' wings. Like many postwar funding initiatives, these construction grants did not fully pay the required costs and thus left the sisters financially responsible for the difference. Both the Charlottetown Hospital and the Halifax Infirmary suffered from poor government planning.

The Department of Veterans' Affairs determined that PEI required one hundred new hospital beds for veterans, and requested that they be evenly split between the Catholic and Protestant hospitals in Charlottetown. This aid, however, fell far short of funding the necessary renovations. When the Charlottetown Hospital Corporation took advantage of federal funding to renovate and expand their 1925 building, the hospital received only

$198,000 to offset the $850,000 expansion cost, or 23 percent of the total cost (RCDCA 1947, 8). Similarly, between 1933 and 1968, the cost of land, buildings, and equipment for the Halifax Infirmary totaled $15,379,349, of which only $5,296,892, or 34 percent was borne by federal, provincial, or municipal governments (McKenna 1998, 287).

The Sisters of Charity and the Sisters of St. Martha bore the financial burdens of their hospitals to different degrees. The Sisters of St. Martha were responsible for the daily operating costs of the hospital but not the construction costs, which were the responsibility of the Diocese of Charlottetown, and, ultimately, of PEI Roman Catholics. The sisters nevertheless shared the financial burden in many ways, including their reliance on out-of-date equipment and occasionally, at the request of the bishop, relinquishing their salary to the building fund. The Sisters of Charity, on the other hand, owned the Halifax Infirmary. In order to keep the hospital open, they were forced to take out large loans from Mutual of New York to finance much of the $10 million in capital costs for necessary renovations by the mid-twentieth century. Traditionally, congregations preferred to own the social institutions they administered because it allowed them greater autonomy from the bishops in whose dioceses they served (Oates 1995, 91). The Sisters of Charity did not seem to benefit, however, from owning the Halifax Infirmary.

The financial responsibility of operating each hospital, though clearly greater for the Sisters of Charity, was a tremendous burden on both congregations of sisters. Though both congregations realized that government assistance came at a cost, the Sisters of Charity and the Sisters of St. Martha were eager to obtain the relief promised by the government in discussions of postwar reconstruction (McNamara 1996, 629). As noted, the first significant funding program, which subsidized construction of hospital beds for war veterans, was disappointing for the Charlottetown Hospital. Congregations involved in hospital care were hopeful for more widespread relief in the form of national health insurance. Again, while this program brought money to the sisters' hospitals, it also increased hospital costs a great deal, with the demands of both an increased number of patients and changes in technology.

National health insurance was the most significant funding to hospitals in the postwar era. Although the Marsh Report (1943) recommended government health insurance and the federal government offered to pay 60 percent of such a program in 1946, federal-provincial agreement was not reached until 1958, when the federal and provincial governments each agreed to pay 50 percent of hospital patient fees, excluding medical bills (Lindenfield 1980, 167). By 1961, all provinces had implemented the funding through the *Hospital and Diagnostic Services Act* (Naylor 1986, 127).

As mentioned at the beginning of this chapter, additional funding to hospitals had both positive and negative effects on Catholic hospitals and the sisters who administered them. To qualify for national insurance, hospitals were required to submit annual budget estimates. Catholic hospitals were asked to assign their sister-hospital workers a salary equivalent to that of a layperson with the same qualifications. This was meant to reflect hospitals' true operating costs and to distinguish the finances of sisters' congregations from the hospitals they administered. Both governments and hospitals wanted it made clear that congregations were not skimming money from the hospitals, but rather that sisters were finally being remunerated fairly. The sisters' salaries were added to their congregations' general coffers just as sister-teachers' salaries had been for decades. While the negative repercussions of health insurance on congregations will be discussed later in the chapter, I will first note the positive impact. In particular, hospital insurance greatly increased the congregation's financial stability.

The introduction of health insurance allowed hospitals to pay sisters at the same rate as lay employees. The cash infusion was significant. In 1960, for example, salaries of the 17 sister-employees of the Charlottetown Hospital totaled $80,491 while in 1970 the 42 sisters working at the Halifax Infirmary each received between $10,620 and $12,540 in salary. The new salaries were very timely and allowed for the development of both the sisters and the congregations. Salaries also permitted the hiring of more secular staff because additional money made the sisters' unpaid labour less crucial;[15] and, more sisters could be redirected from hospitals to other missions, particularly social work, which received less government subsidization.[16] The salaries of those sisters who continued in hospital work were extremely valuable in providing educational opportunities, building retirement savings, and, most noticeably, constructing sisters' housing.

It is no coincidence that the Sisters of St. Martha and the Sisters of Charity both built new mother-houses around the same time that national health insurance was implemented. For the Sisters of St. Martha, their new mother-house, which opened in 1964, was their first. Successive bishops had not allowed the congregation to build because of a lack of financial resources or stability. For the Sisters of Charity, a new mother-house was needed after theirs was destroyed by a major fire in 1949. Both congregations went into debt constructing these necessarily large buildings. The Halifax congregation, with ten times the membership of the Charlottetown congregation, hired a Montreal architect to design the building, estimated at $7 million (McKenna 19998, 79). When it opened in 1958, it was said to be the largest single building east of Montreal, and could house over 600 sisters in addition to a great deal of administrative space (ibid., 69). In order to pay the high cost, the mother-general requested that, "every sister ... renew her effort to contribute in every way possible" (ibid., 79). Certainly the increased income to hospital sisters helped to pay off the mother-house debts of both congregations.

On a less financially positive note, the implementation of insurance also meant that hospitals required expanded space and services because more patients sought care. This had a great impact on congregations of sisters, including the Sisters of St. Martha (Charlottetown) and the Sisters of Charity (Halifax), each of whom expanded their hospitals in the 1950s to meet the demands required by the increasing numbers of patients. The Sisters of Charity expanded the number of beds at the infirmary from 223 to 498, and the infirmary also became a teaching hospital for Dalhousie University medical and health professional programs in 1961. The sisters argued that a teaching hospital required the most current equipment, which put additional financial burdens on the hospital (ibid., 286).[17] The Sisters of St. Martha also expanded the Charlottetown Hospital's capacity during this time from 122 to 180 beds.

Although government funding increased a great deal in the late 1950s, hospital costs increased at the same time and many of the expenses were not covered by the new funding. The problems of incomplete funding were compounded by governments' explanations that Canadians' higher post-war taxes were converted into essential services such as health care. In fact, national health insurance covered only the cost of daily patient care and not hospital construction or equipment costs. It proved difficult to convince Catholics to contribute to hospital buildings and equipment funds when they believed they were already doing so through their taxes (Oates 1995, 114). Once again, the financial burden fell to the sisters. Furthermore, the sisters were more limited in how they could pay for hospital capital construction and equipment costs. Before national health insurance paid patient costs, sisters had some flexibility in setting fees that could include some funding for capital costs. In contrast, national health insurance funds were meant to go entirely toward patients' per diem rates, and consequently, separate fundraising had to be developed to finance capital costs.

Funding capital costs was complicated by the rapid depreciation of hospital buildings. New technology and standards in patient care regularly required new buildings or major renovations, but because there was no market in which the old buildings could be sold, the initial costs could not be recovered. Often hospitals were still paying off existing debt when new financial loans were required to update their buildings. Depreciation was a major concern of Catholic hospitals nationally. Many public hospitals were regularly bailed out of debt by their provinces, while smaller, voluntary hospitals, such as Catholic hospitals, were forced to accumulate debt, particularly for construction costs. The board of directors of the Halifax Infirmary perceived real injustice in the way that Halifax's other general hospital had avoided a debt. The president of the Nova Scotia Hospital Association confirmed this lack of debt a year before hospital insurance was implemented. He explained that although patient-days at the Victoria General Hospital accounted for 157,000, or 19 percent, of the province's total of 847,000 hospital days, the Victoria General accumulated 50 percent of the total provincial hospital deficit in 1955. That debt was paid in full by the province. The amount of actual funding worked out to $4.81 per patient-day at the Victoria General, whereas other hospitals were paid the equivalent of only $0.50 a patient-day (SCHA 1957). Though it was not considered a regional referral hospital, the Halifax Infirmary was, like the Victoria General, a large general hospital and a teaching hospital. The sisters and the board of directors of the infirmary were often frustrated by the fact that the provincial government contributed much more capital funding to the Victoria General than to the infirmary.

The Sisters of Charity never regained financial stability at the infirmary once they began their postwar expansion to a 500-bed teaching hospital.

While they received major government grants and continued to fundraise for capital expenses, the money was never enough and the hospital's debt began to accumulate. The infirmary's expansion, completed in 1962, cost the congregation $6.3 million. In 1960, the infirmary received almost $2.5 million of combined federal and provincial grants and $700,000 in donations, but a $518,244 mortgage had to be obtained for the immediate costs. The congregation lent the hospital another $131,020 in 1961. The chartered accountant who audited the infirmary's books that year wrote that "the necessity of increased borrowing from the sisters to refinance the repayment of existing and future capital debt we feel cannot be avoided (while not recommended)" (SCHA 1962).

Despite the acknowledgment that the sisters were contributing a great deal financially, a large portion of which they borrowed from Mutual of New York, there seemed to be no alternative if the hospital were to remain open. Needless to say, the sisters' practice of loaning such large sums to the hospital put them at real financial risk; because hospitals depreciate so rapidly, the sisters knew they could never sell the hospital for the amount they had invested. By 1967, the hospital owed the Sisters of Charity $2.7 million. The financial crisis became public in the late 1960s. On 17 February 1969, a headline in the Halifax *Mail Star* read, "3 Million Debt to Sisters."

By 1970, the hospital was unable to meet either operational or capital expenses. Over-expenditures in the operational budget of 1971 totaled $190,766, including nursing ($66,327), medical and surgical supplies ($80,000), and laboratory expenses ($49,411). A report from the hospital's board of directors argued that "all of these expenditures were legitimate and required to meet the demands of patient care" (SCHA 1972, 2). The capital expenses were more concentrated, stemming from repayment of existing debt, equipment, and capital for physical changes. These necessary expenditures had not only accumulated debt, but required further expenses immediately. For example, the repayment of the existing debt, from 1973 to 1982, was expected to average almost $400,000 a year (ibid., Appendix 1). By the early 1970s, the need for equipment in the Halifax Infirmary was so dire that physicians argued that the acute shortages of equipment justified the closure of the hospital (ibid., 3). The necessary equipment was estimated to cost $500,000 in 1972, an amount that would have increased the capital debt, thereby creating a domino effect.

The Halifax Infirmary board of directors, which included several Sisters of Charity, expected the province to step in to save the hospital. They expected this, in part, because "government legislation — federal and provincial has precluded the locally sponsored (?), controlled (?), owned (?) hospital from practicing sound financial dictums in relation to capital commitments" (SCHA 1968, 1; question marks appear in the original). The main issues were debt-financing and depreciation.

Clearly, many medical and social changes had occurred in Nova Scotia and PEI since the introduction of national health insurance. The increased baby-boom population, in addition to increased accessibility and expectations, especially in diagnostic services, meant that more people sought health care. The several million-dollar debt the hospital incurred was far beyond the usual definition of charity that could be expected of the Sisters of Charity. The degree of debt, combined with the sisters' decreasing human resources meant that the Sisters of Charity were at very serious financial risk in the early 1970s, risk they could not tolerate as they had in the past.

Halifax Catholics feared that the moral-medical code would not be respected if control of the hospital shifted out of the hands of the sisters, or more broadly, the Catholic Church. They also worried that secular administration could lead to decreased efficiency; whereas the sisters had devoted their lives to charitable works and had no family commitments which could interfere with their work, such would not be as likely with lay hospital workers. Nevertheless, the sisters themselves were certain that they could not continue administering the Halifax Infirmary given the immense and steadily increasing debt.

Public reaction to, and misunderstanding of, the Halifax Infirmary's financial crisis certainly did not help the sisters. An editorial in the *Scotian Journalist* on 8 February 1973 questioned whether any compensation should be paid given that, according to the editorial, the hospital "had done very well at the expense of the public treasure for some years." The editorial objected strongly to the Roman Catholic Episcopal Corporation gaining anything from the sale of the hospital to the province. The editor did not realize that it was, in fact, the sisters who had shouldered the debt for several decades.

Eventually the sisters were "bought out" of the hospital with $5,000,000 payable in ten annual installments. Although the sisters managed to have the initial offer raised, it was nowhere near the actual cost of the hospital, estimated at $17 million. In return for the sale and the acceptance of a $4.6 million debt to Mutual of New York, the province obtained the building, all assets, and the ability to appoint the board of directors, in 1973 (SCHA 1973, 1). The financial crisis that finally forced the Sisters of Charity to relinquish their flagship Nova Scotian health institution, the 500-bed Halifax Infirmary, is the clearest example of how nonprofit and government organizations failed to work together effectively.

The Charlottetown Hospital also experienced dramatic changes during the postwar era, although for a variety of reasons it avoided the deep financial crisis that the Halifax Infirmary suffered. The Charlottetown Hospital was much smaller, having increased the number of beds from 122 in 1947, to180 in the mid-1960s. Some of the sisters' new salaries, acquired through national health insurance, were redirected into capital costs. In addition, the sisters shared more of the financial burden of the hospital with the Diocese. Although the sisters managed it on a daily basis, the hospital was owned by the Episcopal Corporation and the Bishop was the chair of the board of directors. In fact, whereas most congregations became more autonomous from bishops in the postwar era, the Sisters of St. Martha's primary mission, the Charlottetown Hospital, came increasingly under the Bishop's control.

Given the Bishop's degree of control over both the hospital and the sisters, his scepticism about national health insurance determined how the money generated by it would be spent. In 1944, for example, the Bishop of Charlottetown, Bishop James Boyle, warned that, "if the National Health Insurance Plan becomes effective, let no one imagine that the government will be a Santa Claus. The People will have to pay the bill." He continued, writing that the advocates of national health insurance wrongly argued their scheme was inevitable because the voluntary (user pay) system had failed. He summarized: "In other words the voluntary system has failed and therefore must be supplanted by compulsion" (RCDCA 1947, 1). Boyle was clearly wary of surrendering the health-care system to the state and associated such a system with communist-socialist Europe (ibid., 4). The sisters themselves, however, must have looked forward to the increased funding that hospital insurance would provide.

In the early 1950s, the sisters struggled to pay for their own basic personal expenses. In 1952, Mother Frances Loyola requested, in vain, that Bishop Boyle increase the hospital sisters' monthly allowance, citing cost-of-living increases, educational expenses, and the tripling of sisters' personal expenses for "footwear and clothing, etc."[18] It was thus a great relief to the congregation to receive salaries similar to equally qualified laypeople.

Whereas the Sisters of Charity at the Halifax Infirmary accepted salaries, loaned that money to the hospital corporation to reduce the debt, and hoped to reclaim the loan in the future, the Sisters of St. Martha were expected to donate, not loan, their new salaries to the hospital debt. The 17 sisters working at the hospital started to receive salaries in accordance with their training and experience, at the same rate as lay-staff. In 1959, they returned $46,000, or 57 percent of their salaries to the hospital. In 1961, they gave $62,380, or 88 percent, of their salaries, $62,692 or 89 percent in 1963, and $62,956 or 83 percent in 1965 (SSMA 1959–1965).

After 1965, fewer sisters were assigned to the Charlottetown Hospital because of the hospital's increasing ability to pay laypeople through the national health insurance. A decade after the introduction of health insurance, the Sisters of St. Martha began to slowly withdraw from the Charlottetown Hospital. From the time the hospital opened in 1925, until 1960, the proportion of the congregation who were employees at the Charlottetown Hospital fluctuated between 20 and 32 percent. In 1966, the number had fallen to 16 sisters, or 10 percent of the congregation, and in 1976, the percentage of sisters was just 5 percent: six of the congregation's 127 members. In comparison to the Sisters of Charity, whose control of the Halifax Infirmary was surrendered relatively quickly, the Sisters of St. Martha lost their control of the Charlottetown Hospital over two decades. This can be partly attributed to national health-care initiatives.

Once the provincial and federal governments began to fund health care in the small province, they tried to eliminate the duplication of services in the two referral hospitals: the Charlottetown Hospital and the Prince Edward Island Hospital. Several reports recommended amalgamation, including the Andrew Peckham Report in 1966; the *Premier's Task Force on Alcoholism and Welfare* in 1969; and the Rosenfield Report of 1972 (Andrew Peckham Hospital Consultants 1966). The sisters themselves favoured amalgamation. Sister Stella MacDonald wrote a guest editorial in the local newspaper apologizing for failing to communicate the need for a new hospital sooner.

We never told you how difficult it is to keep patching worn out things and places ... But do you the public, have any idea how difficult it is to make a hospital designed 25 years ago meet present health care needs? We should have been telling you about the equipment that was not even dreamed about 25 years ago but must be part of today's hourly use (MacDonald 1975).

Clearly the Sisters of St. Martha, for the most part, would have been happy to give up the Charlottetown Hospital rather than keep operating it with its rapidly rising costs and out-of-date equipment. But in spite of financial difficulty, the sisters continued to operate it until 1982.

The extra time permitted an agreement to be reached in which the board of directors of the new, amalgamated, provincial Queen Elizabeth Hospital agreed not to offer therapeutic abortions at the new hospital. The Catholic Church had long been involved in the anti-abortion movement. The Chancellor of the Diocese, the Reverend Eric Dunn, stated publicly that he did not intend to contribute to the equipment fund of a new hospital until the abortion issue was resolved. It was noted in the same newspaper article that because Roman Catholics comprised almost half of the province's population, their threat to refuse to fund the equipment could be crucial; a hospital could not operate without equipment (*Guardian* 1980). The issue came to a vote at the annual meeting of the Queen Elizabeth hospital in June 1981. It was resolved that the hospital would not create a therapeutic abortions committee. Effectively, the non-denominational Queen Elizabeth Hospital had implemented the Catholic medical-moral code.

CONCLUSION

Both congregations of sisters worked extremely hard to keep their hospitals running, in spite of real financial adversity. This financial adversity, in conjunction with decreasing human resources, led both congregations to want to surrender their hospitals in the early 1970s. A $10 million debt and inadequate equipment forced the Sisters of Charity out of the infirmary in 1973, while the Sisters of St. Martha held onto the Charlottetown Hospital another decade in order to negotiate medical-moral guidelines for the proposed amalgamated hospital. In each case the sisters were unable to keep up with rapidly increasing health-care costs, especially after the introduction of national health-care insurance in 1959. By the late 1960s, these congregations, like congregations all over North America, needed to consider how to plan for the retirements and geriatric care of hundreds of their members, knowing that very few younger women were joining their congregations.

If provincial governments had more generously subsidized the capital costs of the larger, modern hospitals that resulted from national health insurance, the sisters could have continued longer in hospital administration. Patients would have benefited from their experience and expertise. It can be argued that this expertise was greater on average than that of lay women because the sisters, as single women, were free to receive ongoing education, work irregular hours and benefit from the congregation's experience in operating other hospitals. The experience of the Sisters of St. Martha and the Sisters of Charity in hospital administration offers an important lesson for governments today: more effort should be made to accommodate nonprofit groups willing and capable of working in essential services, but unable to carry huge burdens of debt.

Clearly, government funding had a strong impact on the evolution of sisters' work in health care in the postwar era. On a positive note, the funding allowed congregations to better prepare for sisters' retirements as well as to provide education for their members and thus improve the quality of care, which the sisters provided to thousands of clients.

Unfortunately, the governments of PEI and Nova Scotia did not talk with the sisters or benefit from their experience. In the words of one elderly, but very active, sister who worked as a nurse and administrator in a hospital for 40 years, "Most people in government have no experience in health care. [But] they wouldn't have time to listen to us."[19]

Notes

I would like to sincerely thank the following archivists who generously gave me permission to study various parts of their collections: Sister Carmelita Soloman of the Sisters of St. Martha (Charlottetown); Sister Marie Gillen and Joanna Andow of the Sisters of Charity, Halifax; Father Art O'Shea of the Diocese of Charlottetown Archives, and Karen White of the Archdiocese of Halifax Archives. I would also like to thank James Roche of the Catholic Health Association of

Canada for helping me with research, and Dr. Femida Handy of York University for giving extensive advice on this chapter.

[1]Often used imprecisely, the term *nun* refers to contemplative, professed women religious, while the term *sisters* refers to those women religious active in teaching, nursing, or other related endeavors. Similarly, the nineteenth- and twentieth-century groups to which these women belong are called *congregations,* while the more commonly used term *order* implies one of the founding groups of nuns or sisters, usually of the seventeenth century. For an excellent overview of the role of congregations of sisters in Catholic philanthropy in the United States from the early nineteenth century until the present, see Oates (1995). Unfortunately, there is no similar study on Canada.

[2]The Mackenzie-King government, determined not to repeat the mistakes of World War I, one of which was the alleged "betrayal of those who had served overseas," implemented a comprehensive Veterans Charter in 1944. See Neary (1998, 3). The Charter emphasized rehabilitation, which required significant hospital construction, and for which the federal government provided a great deal of funding.

[3]No similar figures exist for Canada.

[4]By "general hospitals" I mean hospitals that provided a variety of services for a variety of illnesses.

[5]Some tuberculosis sanatoriums, mental hospitals, and public health services such as immunization were federally funded, but standard hospitals continued to be run on patient fees.

[6]The civic advisory board was created in 1940 and replaced in 1961 by a board of directors. See McKenna (1998, 285-87).

[7]The two largest hospitals, the Charlottetown Hospital and the PEI Hospital, were general hospitals which served the province as a referral hospital as well as the Charlottetown area as a more general hospital. Although one was identified as Catholic and the other as Protestant, both had roughly the same number of beds and received equal funding, which amounted to $6,000 annually in the mid-1940s from the provincial government. Studies of other provincial hospitals are not complete so it is uncertain how representative the Halifax example of two general hospitals with such widely varying amounts of provincial funding due to one of the hospitals having provincial status, really was. Certainly the city hospitals of Prince Edward Island were virtually equal in the amount of government aid they received.

[8]Special care institutions such as mental health hospitals and tuberculosis hospitals were exceptions as many were federally funded by the 1930s.

[9]The Charlottetown Hospital was also able to set lower per diem rather than the other Charlottetown area hospital, the Prince Edward Island Hospital, which was known as a Protestant hospital. Figures are not available for wartime, but in 1937 the per diem rate at the Charlottetown Hospital was $1.33, while it was

$2.34 at the PEI Hospital. Roman Catholic Diocese of Charlottetown Archives (RCDA), "O'Sullivan," Bishop O'Sullivan, Circular (1938).

[10]In 1951 the provincial grant for wards of the state was $30,000 and thus covered less than 10 percent of the hospital's operating costs.

[11]RCDCA: "Bishop MacEachern," Pastoral Letter, 12 February 1961.

[12]SCHA. "Finding Aid," Halifax Infirmary. I had hoped to be able to piece together more of the financial history of the Halifax Infirmary through Department of Health records at the Nova Scotia Archives and Records Management, but six months after submitting my request to the department through the *Freedom of Information and Protection of Privacy Act* (Application 5200-30/00-003), I was refused research access.

[13]For example, an annals style Halifax Infirmary "Information Book" notes that in 1948 the hospital's board of directors was reorganized to include a representative from the city and one from the province so the hospital could be eligible for "receiving grants." See SCHA. Halifax Infirmary Information Book 1:3, p. 3.

[14]"Report on the Survey of Health Facilities and Services in Nova Scotia under the Federal Survey Grant 1949-1950," p. 209, National Library of Canada, COP NS 1047.

[15]Oral Interview, Sister Mary Angela O'Keefe, Charlottetown, 20 July 2001.

[16]Oral Interview, Sister Rebecca Sark, Charlottetown, 20 July 2001.

[17]The infirmary's affiliation with Dalhousie Medical School was also valuable in that it proved the quality of the institution.

[18]SSMA (1940). Letter to Bishop Boyle from Mother Loyola, 24 November 1952. The Bishop's refusal, which he based on the previous superior being happy with the small increase in allowance granted 15 years earlier, was quite consistent with the paltry allowances in other North American social institutions. Carol Oates cites an example of a 93 percent cost-of-living increase between 1940 and 1953 that was met with only a 25 percent salary increase in the same period to American parochial school sister-teachers. See Oates (1995, 155).

[19]Oral interview, Sister Pauline Grant, 20 July 2001.

References

Andrew Peckham Hospital Consultants. 1966. *Report on a Single Hospital in Charlottetown.*

Baldwin, D. 1990. "Volunteers in Action: The Establishment of Government Health Care on Prince Edward Island, 1900-1931,"*Acadiensis* 19 (2):121-47.

Bibby, R. 1987. *Fragmented Gods: The Poverty and Potential of Religion in Canada.* Toronto: Irwin.

Boyle, Bishop James to [Hospital Directors], 1951, SSMA: Series 12, Box 1, No. 7, "Financial Statements, Charlottetown Hospital."

Catholic Council of Bishops Web Site: <http://www.cccb.ca/CatholicChurch. htm?CD=96> [28 March 2003].

Cellard, A. and G. Pelletier. 1990. *Faithful to a Mission: Fifty Years with the Catholic Health Association of Canada*. Perth, ON: BAC Communications.

Ebaugh, H.R.F. 1993. *Women in the Vanishing Cloister: Organizational Decline in Catholic Religious Orders in the United States*. New Jersey: Rutgers University Press.

Gagan, D. 1989. "For Patients of 'Moderate Means': The Transformation of Ontario's Public General Hospitals, 1880-1950," *Canadian Historical Review* 70 (2):151-79.

Guardian. 1980. "Abortion Controversy Growing," 23 April, p. 3.

Howell, C. 1988. *A Century of Care: A History of the Victoria General Hospital in Halifax, 1887-1987*. Halifax: The Victoria General Hospital.

Lindenfield, R. 1980. "Hospital Insurance in Canada: An Example of Federal-Provincial Relations," in *Perspectives on Canadian Health and Social Services*, ed. C. Meilicke and J. Storch. Michigan: Health Administration Press.

MacDonald, Sister Stella. 1975. "Editorial," *Guardian* (Charlottetown), 21 December.

Marsh, L. 1975. *Report on Social Security for Canada, 1943*. Toronto: University of Toronto Press.

McKenna, M.O. 1998. *Charity Alive: Sisters of Charity of St Vincent de Paul, Halifax 1950-1980*. Boston: University Press of America.

McNamara, J. 1996. *Sisters in Arms: Catholic Nuns through Two Millennia*. Cambridge, MA: Harvard University Press.

McPherson, K. 1996. *Bedside Matters: The Transformation of Canadian Nursing, 1900-1990*. Toronto: Oxford University Press.

Murphy, T. 1996. "Epilogue," in *A Concise History of Christianity in Canada*, ed. T. Murphy and R. Perin. Toronto: Oxford.

Naylor, C.D. 1986. *Canadian Health Care and the State*. Montreal and Kingston: McGill-Queen's University Press.

Neary, P. 1998. "Introduction," in *The Veterans Charter and Post-World War II Canada*, ed. P. Neary and J.L. Granatstein. Montreal and Kingston: McGill-Queen's University Press.

Oates, M.J. 1995. *The Catholic Philanthropic Tradition in America*. Bloomington and Indianapolis: Indiana University Press.

Public Archives of PEI (PAPEI). 1950. Untitled Report on PEI Health Care. RG 34, Series 11, n.p.

Roman Catholic Diocese of Charlottetown Archives (RCDCA). 1947. "Bishop Boyle," Report by Bishop James Boyle [to Hospital Board of Directors]."

Sisters of Charity Halifax Archives (SCHA). 1957. "Halifax Infirmary Board of Directors: Letter to the Executive, Nova Scotia Section, Maritime Hospital Association from H.F. Mackay, President, NS Section, Maritime Hospital Association," 3 April. Box 4:5.

_____ 1958. "Halifax Infirmary Board of Directors Annual Reports," Box 2:4. Halifax: SCHA.

_____ 1962. "Financial Report of the Halifax Infirmary," Box 1:33.

_____ 1965. Halifax Infirmary Financial Statements [1965], "Re Financial Statements–Hospital," Box 3:8.

_____ 1968. "Walter W.B. Dick (Chartered Accountant) to Frank Covert (Chair, Halifax Infirmary Board of Directors)," 22 November.

_____ 1972. "Report on Financial Crisis [of the Halifax Infirmary], 1972," (Green Binder).

_____ 1973. "Agreement between the Provincial Department of Health and the Sisters of Charity," January, (Blue Binder).

Sisters of St. Martha Archives (SSMA). 1925–1960. "Statistics and Financial Information, Charlottetown Hospital," Series 12, Box 1, No. 7.

_____ 1940. "Sisters' Ministries," Series 3, subseries 4, No. 1.

_____ 1959–1965. "Financial Statements, Charlottetown Hospital," Series 12, Box 1, No. 3,

_____ 2003. "Centre for Applied Research in the Apostolate, Personnel Projections to the Year 2003, Sisters of St. Martha, Canada, (Draft)," Series 1, Box 7, subseries 7, No. 10. Charlottetown: Bethany Archives.

6

Nonprofit Groups and Health Policy in Ontario: Assessing Strategies and Influence in a Changing Environment

Mary Wiktorowicz, Miriam Lapp, Ian Brodie and Donald Abelson

The involvement of nonprofit groups in Ontario health policy is currently undergoing a significant evolution at a time when health policy itself faces tremendous challenges. The current policy environment has become destabilized as a result of the combined effect of shrinking budgets, escalating costs, and health-system restructuring. Considerable pressure has been brought to bear in most provincial jurisdictions for health policy to change, including a shift in emphasis from traditional institutional models of care to more community-based and integrated approaches (Baumann *et al.* 1996; Rondeau and Deber 1992); primary care reform (Canada. Health Canada 1995); and the regionalization of health authority (Church and Barker 1998). At the federal level, initiatives for national homecare and drug-benefit programs have been proposed to ensure service consistency among provinces in areas not protected by the *Canada Health Act*, and to maintain a federal presence in health policy as its funding role through transfer payments has diminished (Maslove 1996). The fiscal restraint sustained by the provinces during the 1990s also led provincial governments

to consider various alternatives in order to achieve efficiencies in the provision of publicly insured health care and to create political incentives for
cost-shifting among program areas. These involve shifts from institutional
to community care as evidenced by hospital downsizing, transferring acute
and convalescent care to the community, and introducing "managed competition" to the delivery of homecare services (Williams *et al.* 2001; Maioni
1998; National Forum on Health 1998). At the same time, both the changes
occurring within the traditional policy community and the emergence of
new groups are transforming the context of the current health-policy arena.

As governments consider a range of policy alternatives to address current issues, opportunities have been created for interest groups in the
nonprofit sector to put forward various options and to assert competing
views (Maslove 1996). At the federal level, the Panel on Accountability
and Governance in the Voluntary Sector has considered various models of
engagement with nonprofit groups, and the Government of Canada-
Voluntary Sector Accord has been advanced as a framework to facilitate
the role of nonprofits in the policy process (Armstrong and Lenihan 1999;
Phillips 2002). In this way, health policy initiatives occurring at the national, provincial, and regional levels have created multiple points of
intervention for such groups and the potential for a diverse range of actors
to assert their policy positions. Such a process affects not only the nature
of the groups that choose to mobilize, but also the strategy and manner
through which they assert their interests (Lowi 1972).

The purpose of this research is to acquire a better sense of the current
make-up and involvement of the health-policy interest group population in
Ontario. Our analysis seeks to answer two main questions. First, which
groups are currently involved in health policy at the provincial level? And
second, how do they seek to influence health policy? Our description of
group involvement includes an examination of resources (both tangible
and intangible), membership, and nature of involvement in government
activities. In responding to the second question, we examine the internal
workings, priorities and agendas of our sampled groups, and compare their
activities based on group type, jurisdictional basis, annual budget and "prestige." Our overall objective is to develop a clearer understanding of the
strategies and mechanisms through which interest groups seek to exert
influence in the health-policy arena in Ontario. It is important to note that
our current study focuses on interest groups and associations only;

policymakers are not included at this stage, but will be the subject of future research. Thus we make no attempt to assess the overall effectiveness of group involvement, other than to describe how groups perceive their own influence. We hope that through a careful mapping of the health-policy interest group population in Ontario, we will gather the necessary insights to lay the foundation for a more sustained examination of group impact.

THEORETICAL PERSPECTIVE AND ANALYTIC FRAMEWORK

The role of interest groups in the policy-making process has been studied extensively in both the United States and Canada. While early works were concerned primarily with the normative implications of interest group activity for democratic government (Dahl 1961; Truman 1964), more recent treatments have sought to take a more analytical approach to group activity (Presthus 1973, 1974; Coleman 1988; Pross 1992). Our study situates itself within the work of those scholars who view interest groups as part of larger policy communities and networks that seek to influence government policy. This approach assesses the policy salience of groups by describing their characteristics and their policy capacity (Pross 1992, 101). Its premise is that by mapping out the network of relationships among relevant interests within a particular sector, the influence of policy communities on policy outcomes may be discerned.[1] A growing inventory of case studies has allowed scholars to identify relationships between such characteristics as the "pluralist" or "corporatist" orientation of a policy network and the types of policies likely to ensue. Coleman and Skogstad (1990) developed a sixfold typology of policy networks based on differences in their organizational cohesiveness and level of state autonomy.[2] Such analyses led to hypotheses regarding the stability of policy networks and the ability of different types of networks to respond to certain policy challenges (Tuohy 1996).

At the same time, we recognize the importance of alternate theoretical orientations that emphasize the influence of the institutional framework (Hall 1986; Maioni 1998; Immergut 1992) and the climate of ideas in which policy is developed (Kingdon 1995; O'Reilly 2001).[3] Nevertheless, given the emphasis of our research on assessing the role of nonprofit groups in the policy process, the most meaningful framework and potential for contribution is within the "policy network" orientation. While our present study does not address the issue of group influence directly, it is our intention to use the current findings as a basis from which to conduct specific case studies which incorporate the institutional and ideational perspectives. A comparative analysis of such cases will allow us to develop a framework for measuring and assessing group effectiveness.

In adopting the "policy network" orientation, our study differs from previous contributions that involve case studies based on two dimensions. First, our methodology involves a large mail survey of nonprofit organizations and associations in the health-policy sector in Ontario.[4] We draw on the survey to describe group characteristics (type, jurisdiction, financial resources, and prestige), and compare group access and contributions to the policy process (consultation, coordination, cooperation in policy formation, and implementation) (Van Waarden 1992).[5] Second, in broadly casting our net across actors and issues, we characterize the richness of nonprofit groups' behaviour, and types of networks being formed across the health sector.

Our goals are therefore to describe the characteristics of nonprofit organizations in the health-policy arena, and compare their approaches to advocacy and involvement in the policy process based on such characteristics as group type, jurisdictional basis, financial resources and "prestige" (using "year established" as a proxy for prestige),[6] and the tendencies for policy coalitions and networks to emerge. As such, we seek to clarify relationships between group characteristics, the manner in which they work together through coalitions and policy networks, and the nature of their access and contributions to the policy process.

RESULTS

Respondent Organizations

Of the 244 eligible organizations and associations to whom the survey was sent, 155 completed questionnaires were returned (following two mailed reminders to non-respondents), for a response rate of 64 percent. Respondent organizations are listed in Appendix 1.

Respondents were categorized according to the following *types* of nonprofit organizations: charitable (24 percent), health-service agencies (23 percent), hospitals (17 percent), health professional associations (13 percent), health professional regulatory colleges (10 percent), health-service agency associations (10 percent), and research institutes (4 percent).[7] Of the organizations surveyed, 41 percent provided regional representation, 35 percent provincial representation, and 22 percent were national organizations.

As prestige was not a straight-forward characteristic to measure, we used the year established as a proxy. In the comparisons, the sample was divided between those established from 1850 to 1974 (52 percent; the Canadian Medical Association in 1857), 1975 to 1990 (22 percent), and 1991 to 2001 (26 percent).

Organizations' Activities

The main activities of the organizations surveyed included: patient/client services (34 percent), professional regulation (9 percent), advocacy (8 percent), serving the needs of their profession (8 percent), research (6 percent), education (5 percent), health promotion (5 percent), protecting the public (4 percent), and fundraising (3 percent). Less frequent were activities in the areas of public awareness, family assistance, and the provision of services for members (each with less than 2 percent). Twenty-three percent indicated multiple main roles, while 15 percent were involved in other activities.

Thirty-seven percent of the organizations reported having branches in Ontario, and 19 percent have branches throughout Canada, with some overlap between the two categories. The average number of branches at the provincial level is 18 (Ontario) and at the national level is 43.

Membership

Membership-based organizations accounted for 67 percent of those surveyed. The following descriptive statistics refer to organizations with a membership, with percentages based on the whole sample of 155 organizations. The membership of the organizations consists of the following categories: professionals/practitioners (27 percent), health-care consumers (8 percent), health-care organizations (6 percent), and other organizations (5 percent). "Other members" (30 percent) consisted of individuals and organizations: 8 percent reported their membership to concurrently include health-care consumers, professionals/practitioners and health-care organizations, retirees (3 percent), the general public (3 percent), researchers, and volunteers (less than 2 percent, respectively). Membership was voluntary for 55 percent, and compulsory for 12 percent of the organizations (the remaining 33 percent were not membership-based). Fifty-seven percent of the organizations collect dues from their members. The number of members varies greatly, whether based in Ontario (average of 6,545 members) or nationally (average of 25,394 members).

Resources

The majority of organizations (66 percent) had annual budgets of over $1 million for the fiscal year 2000–2001, and 44 percent had budgets over $5 million (see Figure 1). Organizations' budgets were derived from a variety

Figure 1: Organizations' Annual Budgets, 2000–2001

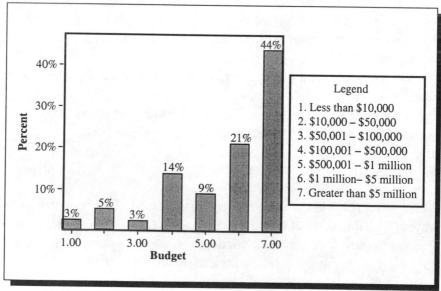

of sources: provincial government (45 percent of organizations), membership fees (44 percent), federal government (14 percent), contracts (11 percent), and local government (8 percent). Nine percent of organizations obtained their funds exclusively from the provincial government and 10 percent exclusively from membership fees. Charitable donations from individuals and corporations comprised a portion of the budgets of 29 and 22 percent of organizations, respectively. Forty-four percent of organizations received funds from other sources including: foundations and charities such as the United Way (6 percent), income investments (7 percent), services (3 percent), special events and fundraising (3 percent), grants and sponsorships (3 percent), and education (3 percent).

Priority Activities

In terms of budget allocation, 48 percent of organizations allocated at least 10 percent of their budget to *patient/client services*, while 9 percent allocated their entire budget to *client services*. Forty-two percent devoted a portion of their budget to *public education*, with 27 percent allocating more than 10 percent of their budget to educational activities. While *professional affairs* was supported by 19 percent of organizations, only 7 percent applied more than 10 percent of their budget, and no organization over 35 percent. Thirty-four percent assigned funds to *research*, and 25 percent to *other activities*. Budgets were assigned to *fundraising* and *membership* by 23 and 26 percent of organizations, respectively. Interestingly, 34 percent assigned part of their budget to *advocacy*.

Patient/client services were considered among the most important activities for 40 percent, and were a first priority for 30 percent (see Table 1). *Advocacy* ranked among the top three priorities for 29 percent, and 10 percent considered it a first priority. *Public education* was mentioned as an important activity by 33 percent, but only 4 percent consider it a first priority. *Research* and *membership* rank among the top three priorities for 24 and 21 percent, respectively.

Health-Policy Areas

The organizations surveyed were active in a variety of health-policy areas. Organizational type and jurisdiction (national, provincial, or regional) was

Table 1: Importance Attributed and Funds Allocated to Specific Activities

Area of Activity	Organizations that Allocate Funds (%)	Three Most Important Activities			Total* (%)
		1st priority (%)	2nd priority (%)	3rd priority (%)	
Patient services	47	30	6	4	40
Public education	41	4	12	17	33
Advocacy	34	10	12	7	29
Research	34	8	8	7	24
Membership	26	8	5	7	21
Fundraising	23	4	3	5	8
Professional affairs	19	1	8	5	14

Note: *The remainder to 100 percent consists of missing cases and N/A.

significantly related to both their areas of involvement, and the nature of their activities and strategies. While 57 percent were active in health-service restructuring, hospitals were particularly active (93 percent) with most (85 percent) indicating involvement in the area of hospital closures/amalgamations. Such regional organizations as hospital and health-service agencies (73 percent) were therefore most involved in health-service restructuring, followed by those with provincial (54 percent) and national representation (27 percent) (see Table 2). Regional organizations were also most active in the area of hospital closures/amalgamations (52 percent), while those at the provincial (13 percent) and national level (7 percent) were significantly less active (p = 0.000).

Community services was another key area of involvement for many (47 percent), most of which were health-service agencies (71 percent).[8] Community services were more likely to receive the attention of provincial and regional organizations (both 54 percent), than national organizations (23 percent). Other areas in which organizations were active included long-term care (43 percent) and homecare (32 percent). Indeed, most regional organizations (57 percent) mentioned long-term care as an area in which they were involved, as did national (40 percent), and provincial organizations (32 percent).

Table 2: Involvement in Policy Areas based on Regional Jurisdiction

Policy Area Involvement	Jurisdictional Representation Percent of Organizations at Each Jurisdictional Level Active in a Policy Area			Pearson Chi-Square		
	National (30) (%)	Provincial (54) (%)	Regional (63) (%)	Value	Df	Signif.
Health-service restructuring	27	54	73	18.02	2	0.000*
Hospital closures	7	13	52	31.00	2	0.000*
Long-term care	40	32	57	8.04	2	0.018*
Community services	23	54	54	8.91	2	0.012*
Pharmacare	40	6	5	27.04	2	0.000*
Homecare	43	28	32	2.16	2	0.339

Notes: *Statistically significant at the level p = 0.05.
( ) number of organizations in each category.

Other policy issues in which organizations were involved included: clinical services (30 percent),[9] primary care reform (29 percent), and women's health (27 percent). Although a smaller percentage of associations/organizations were active in the area of pharmacare policy (12 percent); 40 percent of these were national, compared to provincial (6 percent) and regional (5 percent) organizations. Indeed, none of the hospitals were involved in pharmacare policy.[10] National groups were also most active in the area of homecare policy (43 percent), followed by those at regional (32 percent) and provincial (28 percent) levels. As national pharmacare and homecare programs have been the subject of ongoing debate among federal and provincial governments, it is not surprising that national organizations are most active in these areas.

Other areas in which organizations were active include: professional regulation (5 percent), health care and research funding (5 percent), accessibility to health and social services (4 percent), homelessness and other community issues (3 percent), health and environment (3 percent); 2 percent were active in each of the following: research, mental illness, and education.

Seeking to Meet with Government Representatives

Although most respondents (91 percent) indicated their organization had wanted to meet with government representatives to discuss policy issues, there were significant differences among them based on organizational type and prestige. While *all* health professional associations, professional regulatory colleges, hospitals, and health-service agency associations (except one) sought to meet with government representatives, fewer charitable organizations (76 percent), research institutes (83 percent), and health-service agencies (91 percent) sought such contact ($p = 0.002$).

In terms of organizational prestige, the most prestigious organizations (established before 1975) (98 percent), and those initiated in the last decade (95 percent) were most likely to *seek* to meet with government representatives, compared to those founded in 1975 to 1990 (71 percent) ($p = 0.000$). While it is not surprising that the most prestigious organizations are most actively engaged in advocacy, more recently established organizations involved in such social movements as "upholding medicare" were also among the most active in their efforts to meet with government (Gais and Walker 1991; Kriesi *et al.* 1992).

While there was no association between the organizations' jurisdiction (national, provincial, or regional) and their seeking to meet with government, such representation was related to the nature of groups' strategies to influence policy (Table 3). Indeed, most national organizations sought to meet with the federal government (93 percent), while far fewer provincial and regional organizations (37 percent, respectively) attempted to do so.

Although all regional and provincial organizations made efforts to meet with the provincial government, only 59 percent of national organizations indicated having done so. And while many regional organizations (56 percent) sought to meet with municipal governments, far fewer provincial (25 percent) and national organizations (15 percent) did so. Even though most organizations directed their concerns to the level of government most closely tied to their jurisdiction, a majority of all levels of organizations sought contact within the provincial government, which is not surprising given the management and funding of health care is largely within provincial jurisdiction.

Comparisons based on group type revealed that charitable organizations (74 percent) were more likely to convey their concerns to the federal gov-

Table 3: Meeting with Elected Representatives

	National (26) (%)	Provincial (47) (%)	Regional (56) (%)	Pearson Chi Square		
				Value	Df	Signif.
Sought to meet elected representative	33	46	79	19.86	2	0.000*
Met elected representative	42	51	79	13.06	2	0.001*

Notes: *Statistically significant at the level p = 0.05.
( ) number of organizations in each category.

ernment than were the other types of groups (p = 0.004). The majority of the other organizations (84 percent or over) instead directed their concerns to the provincial government (p = 0.029). In contrast, most charitable organizations addressed their concerns to *both* federal and provincial levels. Another difference was that over half of hospitals and health-service agencies directed their concerns to the municipal government compared to other groups which did so to a far lesser extent (p = 0.000). The majority of organizations (80 percent) therefore directed their concerns to the provincial government; less than half (45 percent) contacted the federal government, while fewer (35 percent) sought contact with their municipal government. Five percent directed their concerns to other organizations such as regional health authorities (3 percent) and international bodies (2 percent).

Organizations sought to meet with representatives from federal and provincial government ministries, including Health Canada (35 percent) and Human Resources Development Canada (4 percent). Most organizations (72 percent) attempted to initiate contact with the Ontario Ministry of Health and Long Term Care (MOHLTC), while 13 percent also sought to meet with one or more of the following Ontario ministries: Community and Social Services, Education, Training, Colleges and Universities, Finance, Labour, and the Environment. Organizations that attempted to contact regional/municipal governments directed their concerns to city councils (14 percent), and institutions providing health and social services (5 percent).

In exploring possible associations between organizations' annual budgets and their initiatives to communicate with government representatives, we found that as organizations' financial resources increased, they were more likely to seek to meet with government representatives (p = 0.003). While *all* organizations with a budget greater than $5 million sought to meet with government, 73 percent with an annual budget of less than $100,000 did so.

When specifying the type of government representative with which their organization wished to discuss health-policy issues, the majority indicated high-level government representatives that included the minister of health (68 percent), the deputy minister (57 percent), and an assistant deputy minister (64 percent). A majority (64 percent) also sought to meet with a senior civil servant; most commonly a director (22 percent).

In comparing activities across group types, health professional associations and regulatory colleges (91 percent) were most likely to seek to meet with the minister of health (p = 0.004). Alternatively, health-service agency associations and research institutes (79 percent) and charitable organizations (76 percent) were most likely to seek meetings with the deputy minister (p = 0.036). In contrast, all hospitals sought to meet with an assistant deputy minister, as did most health-service agency associations and research institutes (84 percent) (p = 0.001).

Other agencies our respondents sought to meet with included the Health Service Restructuring Commission (HSRC) director or board members (30 percent), and representatives of District Health Councils (DHCs) (43 percent). While hospitals (57 percent) and health-service agencies (60 percent) were more likely to want to meet with the HSRC than other organizations (p = 0.015), their efforts are less than might be expected given their involvement in health-services restructuring.[11] In addition, more hospitals (85 percent) and health-service agencies (69 percent) directed their concerns to District Health Councils compared to other groups (p = 0.000). Given DHCs' roles as planning and advisory bodies without decision-making power, community organizations nevertheless view DHCs as an important consultative body. This is likely because DHCs are responsible for reviewing hospitals' operating plans on which they advise the MOHLTC.

Half of the respondents also reported that they had sought meetings with *elected officials*, the most commonly mentioned were members of provincial parliaments (MPPs) (33 percent), members of Parliament (MPs) (14 percent), and municipal representatives (8 percent). In particular, hospitals (88 percent) and health-service agencies (69 percent) were more likely to seek to meet with *elected representatives* than other types of organizations (p = 0.000).

Meeting with Government Representatives

Our survey revealed that not only had most organizations sought to meet with high-level government representatives, but that a majority were given this opportunity. Indeed, respondents reported having had the opportunity to meet with the minister of health (58 percent), deputy minister (51 percent), and assistant deputy minister (58 percent); although the highest proportion (62 percent) met with a director or other senior civil servant. Thirty-five percent had met with the HSRC director or board members, while 43 percent met with a DHC. Interestingly, half (52 percent) had the opportunity to meet with an elected official.

In terms of *seeking* and having the *opportunity* to meet with elected representatives, there were no significant differences among group types. However, differences were evident among organizations based on jurisdictional representation, as shown in Table 3. In particular, most regional organizations (79 percent) sought and had the opportunity to meet with elected representatives. In contrast, while fewer provincial (46 percent) and national organizations (33 percent) sought to meet with elected officials, a greater percentage were given this opportunity than had sought it; 51 percent of provincial and 42 percent of national organizations met with elected representatives. Members of provincial parliaments and MPs would therefore appear to be responsive to organizations by making themselves available to them.

In comparing across organizations, similar proportions of all group types had the opportunity to meet with the minister of health ranging from between 76 percent (health professional associations and regulatory colleges) and 52 percent (health-service agencies). Hospitals (96 percent) and health-service associations (78 percent) were, however, significantly more likely to have met with an assistant deputy minister than the other groups (p = 0.006). This is likely because of the administrative programs and operations within the MOHLTC responsible for institutional and community care. Hospitals were also more likely to meet with the Health Services

Restructuring Commission (p = 0.010) and District Health Councils (p = 0.000) than other groups. Moreover, hospitals (88 percent) and health-service agencies (81 percent) were more likely to meet with *elected officials* than other types of organizations (p = 0.000). Whether this is a transient phenomenon associated with health-system restructuring remains to be seen. Indeed, hospitals may have drawn on their symbolic stature as important health, social, and economic community institutions to appeal to local MPPs in an effort to influence the restructuring process.

Invitations by Government

In pursuing their interests in priority areas, most respondents (81 percent) reported that their organization was invited to be involved in government activities. Although we found no statistically significant association between group type and group involvement in government activities, the proportion of organizations in each group type varied. We did, however, find a relationship between organizations' annual budget and the likelihood of being *invited* to participate in government activities (p = 0.011). Organizations with the largest budgets were more likely to be involved in government activities.[12]

In assessing the effect of prestige, a higher percentage of organizations established prior to 1975 (86 percent), and after 1990 (87 percent) were given the opportunity to meet with government than those founded in 1975 to 1990 (72 percent). However, the association between organizations' year of establishment and their access to government was not statistically significant (p = 0.145).

In exploring the extent to which organizations' budgets were related to their access to specific government representatives, we found no relationship between annual budget and the ability to meet with the minister of health, the deputy minister of health, a senior civil servant, or the HSRC. However, organizations with the largest budgets were more likely to have met with an assistant deputy minister (p = 0.007), District Health Council (p = 0.001), and an elected official (p = 0.003). As hospitals and health-service agencies are among those organizations with the largest budgets, these data confirm (triangulate) our earlier results which show that hospitals and health-service agencies were more likely to meet with assistant deputy ministers, District Health Councils, and elected representatives than other organizations.

Invited Roles and Contributions

The organizations that participated in government activities were asked to describe the roles they were invited to play. The highest proportions served on task forces (56 percent), policy development committees (50 percent), disseminated information (47 percent), or served as consultants/policy experts (45 percent). Involvement as a special advisor (19 percent) or in other roles (14 percent) was less common.

We found that different types of organizations played divergent roles. In serving as a consultant, research institutes (100 percent), health professional associations (82 percent), and health-service agency associations (79 percent) were more likely to serve as consultants or policy content experts than were regulatory colleges (60 percent), health service agencies (39 percent), or charitable organizations (39 percent) (p = 0.004). In terms of task forces, hospitals (86 percent), health professional associations (82 percent) and health-service agencies and associations (79 percent) were more likely to serve as members of a task force than were health professional regulatory colleges (20 percent), research institutes (60 percent) and charitable organizations (54 percent) (p = 0.000). Moreover, health-service agencies (82 percent) and health professional associations (71 percent) were more likely to be members of policy development committees than were regulatory colleges (33 percent), health-service agency associations (50 percent), charitable organizations (50 percent), research institutes (60 percent), and hospitals (64 percent) (p = 0.046).

Organizations' levels of participation differed significantly for only two of these roles based on jurisdictional representation. A majority of provincial (66 percent) and national (63 percent) organizations were invited to act as consultants or policy content experts, compared to regional offices (38 percent). The reverse was the case for serving on task forces; while 82 percent of regional offices were invited to serve on task forces, only 56 percent of national and 57 percent of provincial offices had been involved in task forces. National and provincial organizations were therefore more likely to become involved as consultants or policy experts, while regional offices were most often involved through task forces.

In terms of groups' prestige, the only type of contribution that reflected a difference was to have facilitated information dissemination (p = 0.005). Government was more likely to ask the more well-established organizations (1850–1974) (68 percent) to disseminate information to their members, compared to those founded between 1975–1990 (54 percent), and in the last decade (37 percent).

Respondents were also asked about the nature of their organization's contributions in these invited roles. The highest proportion provided information on policy issues (67 percent), identified potential problems with policy or legislation (59 percent), provided feedback on policy implementation (54 percent), provided guidance on policy goals and objectives (52 percent), provided feedback on a draft policy following consultation with its members (52 percent), facilitated information dissemination (49 percent), provided policy advice without a formal request (46 percent), responded to a general request for policy direction (45 percent) and developed a position paper (45 percent).

The largest proportion of respondents (24 percent) considered providing guidance on policy goals and objectives to be their most important contribution. Providing feedback on a draft policy was the next most frequently chosen contribution in terms of its importance (10 percent). Providing information on policy issues, and identifying potential problems with policy or legislation was considered most important by 9 and 7 percent of organizations, respectively. Since less than 5 percent of respondents considered 1 of 13 other possible contributions as most important, the results suggest a diversity in organizations' roles in the policy process.

We therefore found significant differences in organizations' contributions based on group type. For example, health-service agency associations (93 percent), professional associations (71 percent), and regulatory colleges (73 percent) were more likely to develop a position paper than research institutes (20 percent), hospitals (36 percent), health-service agencies (39 percent) and charitable organizations (54 percent) (p = 0.003). In terms of responding to a general government request for policy directions, health professional associations (82 percent), regulatory colleges (80 percent) and health-service agency associations (79 percent) were far more likely than the other groups to respond (40 percent, respectively) (p = 0.002). There were also differences among groups in the extent to which they were asked to provide feedback on a draft policy following consultation with their members. Health-service agency associations (93 percent), regulatory colleges (80 percent), health professional associations (71 percent), and health-service agencies (64 percent) were more likely to be asked to consult with their members on policy issues and provide feedback to government than were hospitals (41 percent), research institutes (40 percent), and charitable organizations (54 percent) (p = 0.026). Moreover, health-service agency associations (71 percent) and health professional associations (65 percent) were more likely to be asked by government to identify stakeholders with an interest in a health policy issue than the other groups (p = 0.014). In addition, health-service agency associations (86 percent), health-service agencies (82 percent), health professional associations and regulatory colleges (81 percent) were more likely to be asked to identify potential problems with policy or legislation than were other groups (p = 0.043).

There was also a relationship between the nature of organizations' contributions and their jurisdictional representation in three types of roles. Provincial organizations (72 percent) were more likely to have developed a position paper than their national (52 percent) and regional (40 percent) counterparts (p = 0.006). Similarly, provincial organizations (72 percent) were more likely to respond to a general request for policy direction, compared to national (52 percent) and regional (38 percent) organizations (p = 0.003). Finally, provincial (79 percent) offices were more likely than regional (54 percent), and national offices (48 percent) to provide feedback on a draft policy (p = 0.01). Provincial organizations and associations were therefore more likely to be engaged in specific roles than their national and local counterparts. For local organizations, this may at times be a function of the resources available to address policy issues, as opposed to focusing on their primary roles which often include service provision.

Organizations' roles and contributions also varied based on their annual budget. For example, those groups with budgets over $5 million (81 percent) were more likely to have served on a task force, than those with lower budgets (p = 0.021). In contrast, those groups with budgets of between $100,000 to $1 million (79 percent) and less than $100,000 (67 percent) were more likely to respond to a general request for policy directions than were organizations with budgets over $1million (p = 0.019). However, groups with an annual budget of between $100,000 to $1million (71 percent), and $1 million to $5 million (68 percent) were more likely to develop a position paper than those with budgets less than $100,000 or over $5 million (44 percent, respectively) (p = 0.042).

Groups differed in their contributions on the basis of organizational prestige in two respects. Government was more likely to ask groups established between 1850–1974 (68 percent) and 1975–1990 (54 percent) to disseminate information than those founded in the last decade (37 percent) (p = 0.012). Established groups (between 1800–1974 and 1975–1990) (57 to 71 percent) were also more likely to be asked to identify stakeholders with an interest in a health-policy issue than those founded in the last decade (23 percent). Our findings confirm that the more established and prestigious groups are more likely to be key players in health-policy networks and are called upon when the government wishes to send, or gather information from, relevant stakeholder groups.

Forums Used to Meet with Government Officials

Respondents were asked about the types of forums their organization uses to meet with government officials, and the frequency of these meetings (Table 4). Only 5 percent of organizations used one-on-one meetings with government representatives "weekly or more." Most indicated their organization met with government officials "several times a year" in such forums

Table 4: Type and Frequency of Meetings with Government Officials

	Weekly or More (%)	Monthly (%)	Several Times a Year (%)	Once a Year or Less (%)	Never (%)
One-on-one meetings	5	13	52	20	3
Meetings that include other associations	1	8	50	25	5
Public hearings	1	1	35	35	9
Telephone meetings	16	14	39	6	8
Letters	7	26	45	7	2
E-mail	13	12	37	6	7
Other types of forums	0	1	1	3	1

as one-on-one meetings (52 percent), meetings that included other association representatives (49 percent), telephone meetings (38 percent), letters (44 percent), and e-mail (36 percent) correspondence. The exception was public hearings; in which respondents were involved either "once a year or less" (35 percent) or "several times per year" (34 percent).

Publishing Reports

A significant proportion (39 percent) of the respondents published reports to clarify policy debates. Organizations intended these reports to be read by their membership (85 percent), the government (75 percent), other health-related organizations (74 percent), the general public (56 percent), and by the media (56 percent), while 8 percent indicated another type of readership.

The areas in which these organizations published reports included: health-service restructuring (56 percent), long-term care, community services, clinical services, homecare (31 percent respectively), hospital closures/amalgamation, primary care reform (23 percent respectively), women's health, pharmacare (15 percent respectively), as well as such "other" areas (51 percent) as legislation (10 percent), human resources, and funding (8 percent respectively).

Certain groups were more likely to rely on published reports as part of a strategy of advocacy than others. Indeed, health-service agency associations (73 percent), health professional associations (70 percent), and research institutes (60 percent) were more likely to publish reports than were hospitals (11 percent), charitable organizations (27 percent), health-service agencies (37 percent), and regulatory colleges (50 percent) (p = 0.000). And while there was no relationship between organizations' prestige and their tendency to publish reports, there was an association with budgets. As such, organizations with budgets in the mid-range of $100,000 to $1 million (59 percent) and $1 million to $5 million (52 percent) were more likely to publish reports than those with budgets under $100,000 (27 percent) and those over $5 million (32 percent) (p = 0.026). As hospitals represent a large proportion of the organizations with the highest budgets, they publish modestly (11 percent). At the same time, smaller organizations and regional offices may not have the capacity to develop reports.

Communication Channels

Most organizations (93 percent) indicated that they used media or other public venues to communicate issues. A high percentage of organizations mentioned using Internet Web sites (58 percent) and radio and television interviews (48 percent respectively). Thirty-five percent relied on newspaper editorials, and 24 percent on public hearings. A smaller proportion of respondents communicated their issues through advertisements in the newspaper (20 percent), on the radio (14 percent), and on television (7 percent). Twelve percent relied on newsletters as a channel, while 4 percent of organizations adopted forms of public protest. Other channels were used by 37 percent of organizations.

At the same time, there was divergence among groups in the channels on which they relied. For example, health-service agency associations (67 percent) were far more likely to rely on public hearings to communicate their concerns than were other groups (p = 0.012). Radio interviews were used by 50 to 60 percent of most groups, except regulatory colleges (7 percent) and research institutes (33 percent) (p = 0.017). Newspaper editorials were more likely to be used by health-service agency associations (67 percent) and hospitals (58 percent) than other types of organizations (p = 0.002). In addition, hospitals (42 percent) and research institutes (33 percent) were more likely to use newspaper advertisements than the other group types (p = 0.016). Moreover, television interviews were used by more than half of most groups, except for health professional regulatory colleges (7 percent) and research institutes (33 percent) which did not rely as much on this channel (p = 0.025). Most organizations also communicate issues via their Web sites. While almost 80 percent of all organizations post such information on their Web sites, fewer hospitals and health-service agencies did so (p = 0.005).

Twelve organizations (8 percent) indicated that they had challenged health-policy decisions through the courts or other tribunals in the last five years. Three of these cases related to issues of discrimination.[13] Interestingly, there was no association between respondents' decision to challenge health-policy decisions through the courts and their group type, jurisdictional representation, budget, or prestige, respectively.

Indicators Used to Evaluate Effectiveness

Respondents were asked about the types of indicators their organization uses to evaluate its effectiveness in conveying health-policy concerns to government. The largest percentage of respondents (25 percent) indicated they assess their effectiveness by the degree to which the government acts in accordance with their recommendations in its policy or funding decisions. Some organizations indicated using government contact (19 percent) and media exposure (17 percent) as measures of their effectiveness. A low percentage consider the testimony they provide to legislative committees (9 percent) as an indicator. Finally, 3 percent used surveys, polls, or qualitative research to assess their effectiveness.

In assessing differences among groups, health-service agency associations (46 percent) and research institutes (33 percent) were more likely to use testimony to legislative committees to gauge their effectiveness, compared to the other groups (p = 0.020). Otherwise, groups generally relied on similar indicators to gauge their effectiveness. As a quarter of the respondents chose not to answer this question, many organizations may not assess their effectiveness as a matter of course.

Policy Communities

We asked respondents about the nature of their organization's involvement in their priority area in relation to other groups. Eighty percent indicated working with other groups active in their policy area, and 84 percent included the names of those with whom they worked. The largest proportion (45 percent) indicated they were one of several organizations involved in that area. Only 16 percent indicated they were one of a handful of organizations, 9 percent were the dominant organization among several, while 7 percent indicated they were the only organization involved in that area. Another 16 percent indicated that the nature of their involvement varied according to the issue addressed.

While there was no significant variation among different types of groups in the role they played within policy networks, some differences were apparent on the basis of prestige (year established). Organizations established in 1850–1974 (10 percent) and 1975–1990 (17 percent) were more likely to be dominant among several organizations compared to those founded in the last decade (3 percent). Associations established in the last decade (69 percent) were more likely to be one of several organizations active in a particular area, compared to those founded in 1850–1974 (10 percent) and 1975–1990 (27 percent) (p = 0.002). There were also differences in organizations' role in policy networks based on their budget. Interestingly, groups with annual budgets of between $1 million and $5 million (23 percent) were more likely to be the dominant among several organizations compared to those with budgets over $5 million (8 percent) and less than $1 million (4 percent) (p = 0.005).

When compared on the basis of jurisdictional representation, few respondents indicated they were the dominant organization among several (13 percent national, 10 percent provincial, and 7 percent regional). However, national and provincial organizations perceived themselves as the dominant or only organization in a policy area more often than regional organizations (p = 0.006) likely due to their broader jurisdictional base. The variety in the results suggests the diversity of policy networks within the health sector.

In assessing differences among group types, we found that research institutes were the least likely to work with other organizations (50 percent). Similar proportions of respondents within the other group types reported working with other associations (range of 82 to 100 percent). The most frequently mentioned organization to work with others was the Ontario Hospital Association (by 14 percent). Others mentioned less frequently included: the Canadian Nurses' Association (7 percent), the Heart and Stroke Foundation (5 percent), and the Ontario Medical Association (4 percent). Two to 3 percent mentioned the following organizations: the Canadian Cancer Society, the Registered Nurses Association of Ontario, the Canadian Medical Association, the Lung Association, the Federation of Health Regulatory Colleges of Ontario, the Kidney Foundation, and the Easter Seals Foundation.

In working with other organizations, the largest percentage of groups indicated they worked on the policy issue of funding (17 percent). Other issues included human resources (staff recruitment, retention, and shortages) (11 percent), and privacy regarding electronic health records (7 percent). Other (5 percent or less) worked in concert with related associations on the following issues: homecare, health-system restructuring, primary health care, long-term care, the *Regulated Health Professions Act,* and access to services. The most often cited capacity in which respondents worked with associations in their area was in making joint presentations, submissions, or joint proposals (9 percent). The next most frequently mentioned capacity was sharing information (7 percent). However, there was no association between whether groups worked with other organizations involved in their policy area and their jurisdiction, group type, or budget, respectively.

Policy Coalitions

In order to better understand the composition, membership, and nature of the coalitions and networks operating in the health-policy environment, respondents were asked to include the names of the other organizations active in their priority area, those with whom they coordinate their advocacy initiatives, and in what capacity and on what policy issues they worked with these organizations. In drawing on their responses, we identify several coalitions (Appendix 2). While not exhaustive, the range provides an understanding of the networks and coalitions currently operating in Ontario's health-policy community. We refer to these alternatively as coalitions or policy networks. Coalition refers to organizations that work together toward a common vision. However, networks is used to describe the diversity of coalitions that either work together or alone in developing agendas to influence government policy. An assessment of the formal and informal institutional frameworks through which government and interest associations interact comprises the second stage of this research.

The diversity and breadth of these coalitions and networks allow us to develop an initial framework of three types of coalitions within the health-policy community (i) horizontal coalitions: comprised of similar organizations that share a common professional or organizational affiliation; (ii) vertical coalitions: comprised of such different organizations as professional associations and health service agency associations which coalesce on the basis of a common issue (Heclo 1978); and (iii) hybrid coalitions: comprised of similar and different types of organizations (Pross 1992).

Horizontal coalitions are the most enduring given their history of working together on common concerns and established relations with government. Some of the horizontal coalitions active in Ontario include several Ontario Hospital Association Coalitions such as the GTA/905 Hospital Alliance, the Managed Competition Stakeholders Group, the Long Term Care Coalition, and the Chronic Care Coalition. And while *vertical* coalitions are more transient, the diversity of the organizations working toward a shared goal can highlight the salience of the issue addressed to government. Moreover, the implementation and sustainability of policy reforms face fewer obstacles when governments, providers, and consumers resolve issues through consensus (Eager, Garrett and Lin 2001). Vertical coalitions include the HIV/AIDS Network, the Canadian Health Coalition, the Interagency Coalition for the Disabled, and the National Children's Alliance (see Appendix 2).

At the same time, many coalitions are comprised of *hybrids* which include subgroups of organizations with a common professional or organizational affiliation and a history of working together through which formal and informal links have been established. Such established channels of communication can facilitate the integration of additional organizations with different professional/organizational orientations (Glaskiewicz 1979). Examples of hybrid coalitions in the health-policy community include the Health Action Lobby, the Coalition for Primary Health Care, the Health Research Coalition, and the Mental Health Network. The extent to which such coalitions incorporate groups considered part of the subgovernment, participating in policy formation and the attentive public engaged in advocacy varies from one coalition to another (Pross 1992). The incentive for groups in the attentive public to become involved in coalitions is partly due to their ability to leverage the insider status of the cooperating subgovernment groups. Alternatively, the associations routinely in contact with the government may wish to present a unified position to government, rather than have their message diluted by the other groups.

Interviews with members of the Ontario mental health-policy community revealed that provider and community groups form separate (horizontal) coalitions in order to develop a unified position that will carry more weight. At the same time, an overarching vertical alliance, which includes community service, provider, and hospital specialty associations, has formed in an attempt to find positions on which there is common ground and to present policy positions to the government with a unified voice. However, as the Ontario Medical Association is seldom in agreement with the Canadian Mental Health Association (CMHA), which represents community service agencies, associations must inevitably send issues back to their membership for consultation. Such an approach has been adopted in lieu of the previous case in which 15 associations would propose a series of different positions to the government. Instead of hearing from 20 groups, the government instead receives submissions from three or four (Lindquist 1992).

Moreover, as the Ontario Ministry of Health has been disaggregated into seven regional offices and mental health planning has been delegated to nine Mental Health Implementation Task Forces, community groups perceive program development to be occurring through a regionally based, disparate process. As a result, such groups as the CMHA view government bureaucrats involved in policy development as having little influence over policy implementation. Instead, they perceive power to be centralized with elected officials, particularly ministers and those in Cabinet. In response, the Ontario CMHA develops monthly briefing notes summarizing its key issues, which it distributes to its regional branches for their use in meetings with MPPs and to assist them in forming relationships with local opinion leaders (Wiktorowicz forthcoming).

DISCUSSION

Our survey results identify the characteristics of the organizations and associations engaged in the health-policy arena in Ontario and nationally where common issues intersect. The results also shed light on the processes through which groups contribute to the policy process and how they work with others in attempting to exert influence in their priority areas.

Respondents represented different nonprofit groups within the health sector: charities (24 percent), health-service agencies (23 percent), hospitals (17 percent), health professional associations (13 percent), health professional regulatory colleges (10 percent), health-service agency associations (10 percent), and research institutes (4 percent). The membership of most associations surveyed varied from professionals and practitioners, health-care consumers, to health-care and other types of organizations, with more than half receiving dues from their membership. The majority of the organizations had annual budgets over $1 million, while a large plurality had budgets over $5 million. Their budgets were derived from a range of sources, the two largest being the provincial government and membership fees. Organizations' allocation of funds was as diverse as their main areas of activity; a significant percentage allocated at least a third of their budgets to client services, public education, research, and advocacy.

These groups were active in a variety of health-policy areas including funding of health services, health human resources, health-system restructuring, privacy of electronic health records, long-term care, homecare, primary health care, and the *Regulated Health Professions Act*. A smaller percentage of the organizations were involved in pharmacare and francophone services.

Organizational type, financial resources, and jurisdiction (national, provincial, or regional) were significantly related to groups' areas of involvement, and the nature of their activities and strategies. Indeed, such regional organizations as hospitals and health-service agencies were most active in the areas of health-service restructuring and long-term care. Alternatively, both provincial and regional organizations were active in the area of community services, most of which were health-service agencies. On the other hand, national organizations were most engaged in policy issues related to pharmacare and homecare. These results appear to reflect the ongoing debates among the federal and provincial governments over responsibility for pharmacare and homecare policies.

While the vast majority of organizations indicated they sought to meet with the government to discuss policy issues, nonprofit groups differed in the extent of their efforts; the most active were health professional associations and regulatory colleges, hospitals, and health-service agency associations. Moreover, the most prestigious groups, and those initiated in the last decade were most likely to want to meet with government. While the most prestigious organizations are members of established policy networks, recently created associations such as the Medical Reform Group are motivated by such social movements as preserving medicare.

Although most groups directed their concerns to the provincial government, nearly half targeted the federal, while just over a third sought contact with the municipal government. In exploring differences on the basis of group type, charitable organizations addressed their concerns to both federal and provincial levels, while hospitals and health-service agencies were most likely to seek contact with municipal governments, MPPs, MPs, the HSRC, and District Health Councils.

Organizations' jurisdictional representation was also associated with the nature of their strategies to influence policy. As such, national organizations sought primarily to meet with the federal government, and provincial and municipal organizations with their respective levels of government. At the same time, most organizations sought contact with the provincial government. This is not surprising given the provincial government's jurisdiction in the health-care sector.

Our results also revealed that not only had the majority of organizations sought to meet with government representatives, but that a majority were given this opportunity. More that half of the organizations reported having had the opportunity to meet with the minister of health, deputy minister or assistant deputy minister at federal and provincial levels. Many also had the opportunity to meet with a senior civil servant. More than half also reported having had the opportunity to meet with an elected official. This latter result is somewhat surprising, given the relatively minor role assigned to elected officials in much of the interest group literature, which we would like to explore further.

Different groups also targeted their strategies at diverse government representatives. While health professional associations and regulatory colleges were most likely to want to meet with the minister of health, health-service agency associations and charitable organizations were most likely to seek meetings with the deputy minister. In contrast, all hospitals sought to meet with an assistant deputy minister, as did most health-service agency associations and research institutes.

Jurisdictional representation was also related to organizations' meetings with elected representatives. While the vast majority of regional groups had the opportunity to meet with elected representatives, far fewer provincial and national organizations did so. However, the number of provincial and national organizations that met with elected officials was actually greater than the number that sought to meet with them. Elected representatives would therefore appear to be making themselves available to meet with a range of groups even when such meetings were not requested. Elected representatives may have several reasons for doing so, including apprising themselves of organizations' positions in the current environment. Moreover, hospitals and health-service agencies were more likely to meet with elected representatives than other groups. This may be a transient phenomenon associated with health-system restructuring, in which hospitals may have drawn on their symbolic community stature to appeal to local MPPs and MPs in an effort to influence the restructuring process. Nevertheless, MPs' and MPPs' influence over policy issues is highly variable depending on their status as members of Cabinet, ministers, backbenchers, members of the Opposition, or legislative committee members. Further exploration of the types of representatives with which organizations meet would therefore be valuable. Initial interviews suggest that groups perceive power to be polarized between such elected officials as ministers who appear to control broad policy development, and regional MOHLTC offices which oversee program management and implementation. The perception of disparate points of power appears to be leading groups to focus their efforts on elected officials, including the ministers responsible.

In exploring the association between organizations' annual budgets and their initiatives to communicate with government representatives, the analysis revealed that as organizations' budgets increased, so did their tendency to seek to meet with government representatives. In pursuing their interests in priority areas, a large majority of groups reported they had been invited by government to be involved in its activities. However, the larger an organization's budget, the more likely it was to be involved in government activities. The highest proportion of organizations served on task forces or policy development committees, disseminated information, or served as a consultant/policy expert. For the most part, there were no differences in rates of participation in these roles based on jurisdictional representation. However, national and provincial organizations were more likely to become involved as consultants or policy experts, while regional offices were most often involved in task forces.

Organizations' roles in the policy process also varied depending on the nature of their group. As such, research institutes, health professional associations, and health-service agency associations were more likely to serve as consultants or policy content experts than were other groups. Alternatively, hospitals, health professional associations, health-service agencies and their associations were more likely to serve as members of a task force than were other groups. However, health professional associations and health-service agencies were more likely to be members of policy development committees than were other groups (regulatory colleges, health-service agency associations, charitable organizations, research institutes, and hospitals).

When jurisdictional representation was considered, nonprofit groups' levels of participation differed for only two of these roles. A majority of provincial and national organizations had been invited to act as consultants or policy content experts, compared to regional offices. The reverse was the case for serving on task forces; while 82 percent of regional offices were invited to serve on task forces, slightly more than half of national and provincial offices were involved in task forces.

In terms of groups' prestige, the government was more likely to request the more well-established organizations to disseminate information to their members, compared to those more recently founded (1975 or thereafter).

Respondents were also asked about the nature of their organization's contributions in such invited roles. The highest proportion provided information on policy issues (67 percent), identified potential problems with policy or legislation (59 percent), provided feedback on policy implementation (54 percent), provided guidance on policy goals and objectives (52 percent), provided feedback on a draft policy following consultation with its members (52 percent), facilitated information dissemination (49 percent), provided policy advice without a formal request (46 percent), responded to a general request for policy direction (45 percent) and developed a position paper (45 percent).

The largest proportion of respondents (24 percent) considered providing guidance on policy goals and objectives to be their most important contribution. Providing feedback on a draft policy was the second most frequently chosen contribution in terms of its importance (10 percent). Providing information on policy issues, and identifying potential problems with policy or legislation was considered most important by 9 and 7 percent of groups, respectively. Since less than 5 percent of respondents considered 1 of 13 other possible contributions most important, the results reveal a diversity in organizations' roles and contributions to the policy process.

Nonprofit groups' contributions differed according to the nature of their group. As such, health-service agency associations, professional associations, and regulatory colleges were most likely to develop a position paper, respond to a general government request for policy directions, and to consult with their members on policy issues and provide feedback than were other groups. In addition, health-service agencies and associations, health professional associations, and regulatory colleges were more likely to be asked to identify potential problems with policy or legislation than were other groups.

Organizations' contributions were also associated with their jurisdictional representation for three types of contributions. Provincial organizations were more likely to have developed a position paper, responded to a general request for policy direction, and provided feedback on a draft policy than their national and regional counterparts. In terms of organizations' sense of the importance of their contributions, the largest percentage considered providing guidance on policy goals and objectives to be most important, followed by providing feedback on a draft policy.

In terms of meetings with government, most organizations indicated they met with government officials "several times a year" in a variety of forums that included one-on-one meetings, meetings with other associations, telephone meetings, letters, and e-mail. Whether such meetings assist in bringing organizations' concerns to Cabinet and other policy forums is not clear at this stage, and requires further research, including interviews with the government officials involved. We intend to pursue this question in a second stage of our research.

Most groups recorded very high levels of participation and involvement in the policy process. At the same time, further research is required to clarify whether the interest in elected officials was because MPPs and MPs were reaching out or whether groups desire contact on their own. Nevertheless, our findings represent a departure from the traditional Presthus (1974) analysis.

In terms of policy networks in the health sector, almost half of the respondents indicated they were one of several organizations involved in their priority area, thereby reinforcing the importance of the concept of the policy community. Relatively few considered themselves to be the dominant organization, or the only organization involved in that area. Many organizations indicated the nature of their involvement varied based on the issue addressed. National and provincial organizations were more likely to perceive themselves as the dominant or only organization in a particular policy area than regional organizations.

Our results also identify the diversity of policy coalitions and networks through which organizations work with other groups and associations in the health sector (Appendix 2). These can be classified variously as horizontal, vertical or hybrid coalitions or networks depending on the types of groups involved. Such coalitions most often engaged in sharing information among member groups, and make joint presentations, submissions, or joint proposals to government. The variety in the results suggests the diversity of policy networks operational in the health sector.

CONCLUSIONS

Among other things, the findings of our survey demonstrate the enormous diversity in the types of nonprofit organizations that populate Ontario's health-policy community. As we discovered, the 155 respondent organizations have very different mandates, priorities, and resources. Indeed, they seek to exercise policy influence in very different ways. For many of these organizations, contacting elected officials at various levels of government is considered the most effective way to communicate their recommendations on various health-policy areas. For others, it is by relying on the media or by working closely with other groups that they can have the greatest policy impact.

While the literature on interest groups can help to shed light on why interest groups with access to various resources may or may not rely on particular strategies to exercise policy influence (Pross 1992; Presthus 1974), it tells us very little about how to properly evaluate the impact of these organizations on public opinion and public policy. In other words, our findings illustrate the types of organizations engaged in health policy in Ontario and how they seek to influence public policy, but the more important question of policy influence must still be addressed.

Assessing the policy influence of interest groups is notoriously difficult because the leaders of these organizations, not to mention the scholars who study them, have very different perceptions of what constitutes influence and how it can best be measured. What makes this methodological problem even more complicated is that it is often difficult to trace the origin of an idea to a particular person or organization. Every successful policy idea has a hundred mothers and fathers. Every bad policy idea is an orphan. The factors that contribute to an idea's incorporation into the policy agenda can also be difficult to determine. Nevertheless, our analyses suggests that depending on the issue, the medical profession is not necessarily the most dominant group in terms of policy influence. This is particularly evident in light of the MOHLTC's shift in policy focus to care in the community which involves a diversity of groups, reflected in mental health sector restructuring (Wiktorowicz forthcoming) and the Health Professions Legislative Review (Bourgeault and Fynes 1996/97; O'Reilly 2001).

Recognizing the many obstacles that scholars must overcome to assess the impact of interest groups, we suggest building on the work of Kingdon (1995) and Stairs (1977/78), who, among others, recognize that all groups do not share the same commitment or desire to become involved at each stage of the policy-making cycle. Some, as this chapter has shown, are more committed to educating policymakers and the public about the potential risks to our health-care system and as a result, devote considerable resources to enhancing their media exposure. Others, however, are committed to becoming more deeply involved in the policy-making process by serving as consultants to ministers and testifying before appropriate legislative committees.

With this in mind, we must develop an appropriate analytical framework which not only permits a greater understanding of how groups measure their own impact, but how policymakers view their relevance at each stage of the policy-making cycle. This can be accomplished by analyzing the subgroups of health-policy organizations that share the same priorities, and by polling policymakers about organizations to which they turn for policy advice. However, it is difficult to assess the impact of interest groups before we know *which* organizations are relevant actors in the policy-making process. Now that we have a fairly good idea of who the players are, and the coalitions through which they work, we can build on this research in the next stage of this inquiry by undertaking a more systematic examination of how much of a difference the groups have made through their work. The purpose of this study has been to lay the initial groundwork for further analysis of interest group behaviour in health policy. Now that this groundwork has been laid, it is critical to develop a framework to measure their impact.

Notes

[1] See, for example, Bourgeault and Fynes' (1996/97) analysis of the policy networks inherent in the integration of midwifery into the Ontario health-care system.

[2]See also Atkinson and Coleman's (1989*a,b*) framework of network typologies, and subsequent elaborations by Linquist (1992, 1996) and Van Waarden (1992).

[3]As O'Reilly's analysis of health-care practitioner groups in the Ontario Health Professions' Legislative Review suggests, traditional groups' historical connections to the state were not sufficient to lead to success in the policy process; rather, linkages in policy communities in combination with changing ideational contexts contributed to policy outcomes.

[4]The survey was sent to the executive directors of 274 associations and nonprofit organizations in Ontario and their national offices. Thirty organizations were ineligible either because they no longer existed, or were local organizations with limited staff and resources who forwarded their questionnaires to their provincial office. Our final survey population consisted of 244 groups. The unit of analysis is the organization or association, which we identified from a variety of sources: the Directory of Associations in Canada, Internet sites, and annual reports. As the survey will form the basis of case studies related to health-system restructuring in five regions in Ontario (Toronto, the Greater Toronto Area, Hamilton, Ottawa, London), hospitals, community care access centres, public health units, and regional branches in these regions were included.

[5]The survey instrument identified the size, funding sources, membership of each organization, the various governmental and non-governmental channels that groups rely on to convey their concerns to policymakers, and the nature of their involvement in the policy process. Frequency analyses describe group characteristics, approaches, and activities. Cross-tabs analyses with chi-square tests of significance assessed relationships between organizational type, jurisdictional representation (national, provincial or regional), budget, year established (as a proxy for prestige) and groups' strategies and activities.

[6]As the Ontario *Health Disciplines Act* was implemented in 1974, we chose the division date of 1974. Associations and organizations established by 1974 are considered to have greater "prestige" associated with their historical role than the less-established organizations initiated after 1974.

[7]In several chi-square analyses, the groups were collapsed to ensure statistical validity (fewer than 20 percent of cells with expected counts of five or less). The collapsed categories include: health-service agencies (26 percent), charitable organizations (24 percent), health professional associations and regulatory colleges (23 percent), hospitals (17 percent), and health-service agency associations and research institutes (10 percent).

[8]The *community services* in which organizations are involved are summarized as follows: specific diseases/disorders (asthma, autism, speech and language, etc.) (7 percent); public health (5 percent); fostering community or regional health centres (3 percent); home and long-term health care (2 percent).

[9]The organizations involved in *clinical services* were mostly engaged in cancer care and prevention (5 percent), as well as cardiac/stroke and arthritis care (5 percent).

[10]While pharmacare generally refers to a program of out-patient public drug insurance, some of the most expensive drugs and biologics are used in hospitals, and consume an increasingly larger portion of their budget. It is therefore interesting that hospitals indicated not being active in this policy area.

[11]However, hospitals and health-service agencies were given the opportunity to submit their recommendations to the HSRC in writing, and most likely chose to do so.

[12]The association between organizations' budget and being involved in government activities was found in cross-tabs with Pearson chi square test of significance ($p = 0.011$), and confirmed in an analysis of variance ($p = 0.008$).

[13]Including the case involving the planned reconfiguration of the Montfort Hospital to an ambulatory facility and its claim of language discrimination, on the basis of which it successfully challenged the government's policy through judicial appeal.

References

Armstrong, J. and D. Lenihan. 1999. *From Controlling to Collaborating: When Governments Want to Be Partners — a Report of the Collaborative Partnerships Project.* New Directions No. 3. Ottawa: Institute of Public Administration of Canada.

Atkinson, M.M. and W.D. Coleman. 1985. "Corporatism and Industrial Policy," in *Organized Interests and the State*, ed. by A. Cawson. London: Sage Publications.

_____ 1989a. "Strong States and Weak States: Sectoral Policy Networks in Advanced Capitalist Economies," *British Journal of Political Science* 19:48-67.

_____ 1989b. "State Tradition, Bureaucratic Culture, and Industrial Policy," in *The State, Business and Industrial Change in Canada.* Toronto: University of Toronto Press, pp. 53-76.

Baumann A.O., L.L. O'Brien-Pallas, R.B. Deber, G. Donner, D. Semogas and B. Silverman. 1996. "Downsizing in the Hospital System: A Restructuring Process," *Healthcare Management FORUM* 9 (4):5-13.

Bourgeault, I.L. and M.T. Fynes. 1996/97. "Delivering Midwifery in Ontario: How and Why Midwifery was Integrated into the Provincial Health Care System," *Health and Canadian Society* 4 (2):227-62.

Canada. Health Canada. 1995. *Primary Care Organizations.* Federal-Provincial Discussion Paper. Ottawa: Supply and Services Canada.

Church, J. and P. Barker. 1998. "Regionalization of Health Services in Canada: A Critical Perspective," *International Journal of Health Services* 28 (3):467-86.

Coleman, W.D. 1988. *Business and Politics: A Study of Collective Action*. Montreal and Kingston: McGill-Queen's University Press.

Coleman, W.D. and G. Skogstad, eds. 1990. *Policy Communities and Public Policy in Canada*. Toronto: Copp Clark Pitman.

Dahl, R.A. 1961. *Who Governs?* New Haven: Yale University Press.

Eagar, K.P. Garrett and V. Lin. 2001. *Health Planning: An Australian Perspective*. Sydney: Allen & Unwin.

Gais, T.L. and J.L. Walker, Jr. 1991. "Pathways to Influence in American Politics," in *Mobilizing Interest Groups in America: Patrons, Professions and Social Movements*, ed. J.L. Walker, Jr. Ann Arbor: University of Michigan Press.

Glaskiewicz, J. 1979. *Exchange Networks and Community Politics*. Beverly Hills, CA: Sage.

Hall, P. 1986. *Governing the Economy: The Politics of State Intervention in Britain and France*. New York: Oxford University Press.

Heclo, H. 1978. "Issue Networks and the Executive Establishment," in *The New American Political System*, ed. A. King. Washington, DC: American Enterprise Institute for Public Policy Research, pp. 87-124.

Immergut, E. 1992. *Health Politics: Interests and Institutions in Western Europe*. Cambridge: Cambridge University Press.

Kingdon, J.W. 1995. *Agendas, Alternatives, and Public Policies*, 2d ed. New York: HarperCollins College Publishers.

Kriesi, H., R. Koopmans, J.W. Duyvendak and M.G. Giugni. 1992. "New Social Movements and Political Opportunities in Western Europe," *European Journal of Political Research* 22:219-44.

Lindquist, E.A. 1992. "Public Managers and Policy Communities: Learning to Meet New Challenges," *Canadian Public Administration* 35 (Summer):127-59.

_____ 1996. "New Agendas for Research on Policy Communities: Policy Analysis, Administration, and Governance," in *Policy Studies in Canada: The State of the Art*, ed. L. Dobuzinskis, M. Howlett and D. Laycock. Toronto: University of Toronto Press, pp. 219-41.

Lowi, T. 1972. "Four Systems of Policy, Politics and Choice," *Public Administration Review* 32:298-310.

Maioni, A. 1998. *Parting at the Crossroads: The Emergence of Health Insurance in the United States and Canada*. Princeton, NJ: Princeton University Press.

Maslove, A.M. 1996. "The Canada Health and Social Transfer: Forcing Issues," in *How Ottawa Spends 1996-97*, ed. G. Swimmer. Ottawa: Carleton University Press.

National Forum on Health. 1998. *Striking a Balance: Health Care Systems in Canada and Elsewhere.* Sainte-Foy, PQ: Éditions MultiMondes.

O'Reilly, P.L. 2001. *Health Care Practitioners: An Ontario Case Study in Policy Making.* Toronto: University of Toronto Press.

Phillips, S. 2002. "In Accordance: Canada's Federal Government-Voluntary Sector Accord from Idea to Implementation." Paper prepared for the Kahanoff Nonprofit Sector Research Initiative.

Presthus, R. 1973. *Elite Accommodations in Canadian Politics.* Toronto: Macmillan.

_____ 1974. *Elites in the Policy Process.* Toronto: Macmillan.

Pross, A.P. 1992. *Group Politics and Public Policy*, 2d ed. Toronto: Oxford University Press.

Rondeau, K.V. and R.B. Deber. 1992. "Models for Integrating and Coordinating Community-Based Human Service Delivery: An Analysis of Organizational and Economic Factors," in *Restructuring Canada's Health Services System: How Do We Get There from Here?* ed. R.B. Deber and G. Thompson. Proceedings of the Fourth Canadian Conference on Health Economics. Toronto: University of Toronto Press, pp. 387-92.

Stairs, D. 1977/78. "Public Opinion and External Affairs Reflections on the Domestication of Canadian Foreign Policy," *International Journal* 33 (1):128-49.

Truman, D. 1964. *The Governmental Process: Political Interests and Public Opinion.* New York: Knopf.

Tuohy, C.H. 1996. "National Policy Studies in Comparative Perspective: An Organizing Framework Applied to the Canadian Case," in *Policy Studies in Canada: The State of the Art*, ed. L. Dobuzinskis, M. Howlett and D. Laycock. Toronto: University of Toronto Press, pp. 317-45.

Van Waarden, F. 1992. "Dimensions and Types of Policy Networks," *European Journal of Political Research* 21:29-52.

Wiktorowicz, M. Forthcoming. "Mental Health Policy Reform in Ontario: Restructuring Processes and the Policy Community." Paper submitted to *Canadian Public Administration*.

Williams, A.P., R. Deber, P. Baranek and A. Gildiner. 2001. "From Medicare to Home Care: Globalization, State Retrenchment, and the Profitization of Canada's Health-Care System," in *Unhealthy Times*, ed. P. Armstrong, H. Armstrong and D. Coburn. Toronto: Oxford University Press.

Appendix 1

Organizations Included in the Survey

NAME OF ORGANIZATION

1. Canadian Nurses Association
2. College of Audiologists and Speech-Language Pathologists of Ontario
3. College of Chiropodists of Ontario
4. College of Dental Hygienists of Ontario
5. Royal College of Dental Surgeons of Ontario
6. College of Dental Technologists of Ontario
7. College of Denturists of Ontario
8. College of Massage Therapists of Ontario
9. College of Nurses of Ontario
10. College of Occupational Therapists of Ontario
11. College of Optometrists
12. Ontario College of Pharmacists
13. College of Physicians and Surgeons of Ontario
14. College of Physiotherapists of Ontario
15. College of Psychologists of Ontario
16. College of Respiratory Therapists of Ontario
17. Nurse Practioners Association of Ontario
18. Ontario Association of Medical Laboratories
19. Ontario Association of Medical Radiation Technologists
20. The Ontario Association of Speech Language Pathologists and Audiologists (OSLA)
21. Ontario Medical Association
22. Ontario Nurses' Association
23. Ontario Physiotherapy Association
24. Ontario Psychological Association
25. Ontario Society of Medical Technologists
26. Registered Nurses Association of Ontario
27. Registered Practical Nurses Association of Ontario

28. Association of Ontario Health Centres
29. Ontario Association of Community Care Access Centres
30. Canadian Association on Gerontology
31. Canadian Healthcare Association
32. Ontario Community Support Association
33. Ontario Home Health Care Providers' Association
34. Ontario Public Health Association
35. Society of Rural Physicians of Canada
36. Cancer Care Ontario
37. Cardiac Care Network of Ontario
38. Canadian Medical Association
39. Canadian AIDS Society
40. Canadian Cancer Society (Ontario Division)
41. Canadian Diabetes Association—Ontario Division
42. Asthma Society of Canada
43. The Migraine Association of Canada
44. Multiple Sclerosis Society of Canada
45. Parkinson Society Canada
46. Toronto People With AIDS Foundation
47. Ontario Lung Association
48. Autism Treatment Services of Canada (Ontario)
49. Ontario Association of Rehabilitation Services
50. Ontario Association for Families of Children with Communication Disorders
51. Canadian Institute of Child Health
52. Bereaved Families of Ontario
53. Psychiatric Patient Advocate Office
54. Canadian Society for Medical Laboratory Science
55. Canadian Transplant Association
56. Canadian Women's Health Network
57. Ontario Health Care Education Association
58. Association of Local Public Health Agencies
59. Canadian Association for Adolescent Health
60. Canadian Coordinating Office for Health Technology Assessment
61. Canadian Health Economics Research Association

62. Canadian Red Cross Society, Ontario Zone, Community Health Services
63. Canadians for Health Research
64. Health Law Institute
65. INFACT (Infant Feeding Action Coalition)
66. Ontario Healthy Communities Coalition
67. Catholic Health Association of Canada
68. Catholic Health Association of Ontario
69. Canadian College of Health Service Executives
70. Ontario Healthcare Housekeepers Association
71. Institute for Clinical Evaluative Services
72. Hong Fook Mental Health Association
73. Ontario Federation of Community Mental Health and Addiction Programs
74. Ontario Mental Health Foundation
75. Hamilton Program for Schizophrenia
76. Toronto Women's Health Network
77. Victorian Order of Nurses, Middlesex-Elgin Branch
78. VON Hamilton-Wentworth
79. Victorian Order of Nurses, Ottawa-Carleton Branch
80. Brain Injury Association of London and Region
81. Canadian Liver Foundation (4 branches)
82. Heart and Stroke Foundation (2 branches)
83. Kidney Foundation of Canada, Eastern Ontario Branch
84. Thyroid Foundation of Canada (2 branches)
85. Lawson Health Research Institute
86. London InterCommunity Health Centre
87. Middlesex London Health Unit
88. Heart and Stroke Foundation of Ontario
89. Ontario Association of Non-Profit Homes and Services for Seniors, Region 5
90. Niagara Ina Grafton Gage Village
91. United Generations Ontario
92. Federal Superannuates National Association (4 branches)
93. Ontario Case Managers Association
94. Ontario Long Term Care Association

95. The Council on Aging of Ottawa
96. Alzheimer Society for Halton-Wentworth
97. Alzheimer Society of Ottawa-Carleton
98. Alzheimer Society of Toronto
99. Canadian Mental Health Association, Ottawa Branch
100. CMHA Metro Toronto Branch
101. St. Joseph's Health Care, London
102. Hamilton Health Sciences Centre
103. Bloorview MacMillan Children's Centre
104. The Hospital for Sick Children, Toronto
105. Mount Sinai Hospital
106. Toronto Grace Health Centre
107. St. John's Rehabilitation Hospital
108. St. Michael's Hospital
109. The Riverdale Hospital
110. Toronto East General Hospital
111. Children's Hospital of Eastern Ontario
112. Hopital Montfort
113. SCO Health Service
114. The Ottawa Hospital Riverside Campus
115. The Ottawa Hospital
116. Halton Region Health Dept.
117. Toronto Public Health Division
118. York Region Health Services Dept.
119. CCAC of York Region
120. Hamilton Community Care Access Centre
121. CCAC of Halton
122. Community Care Access Centre of Peel
123. Ottawa-Carleton Community Care Access Centre (OC-CCAC)
124. North York Community Care Access Centre
125. Scarborough Community Care Centre
126. Toronto Community Care Access Centre
127. York CCAC
128. Rouge Valley Health System (Ajax site)
129. Humber River Regional Hospital
130. Trillium Health Centre (2 branches)

131. Southlake Regional Health Centre
132. Sunnybrook & Women's College Health Sciences Center
133. Lakeridge Health Corporation (2 branches)
134. York Central Hospital
135. The Scarborough Hospital (2 branches)
136. Rouge Valley Health System
137. Providence Centre
138. Humber River Regional Hospital (2 branches)
139. The Arthritis Society
140. Heart and Stroke Foundation of Canada
141. Canadian Lung Association
142. VON Canada
143. Institute for Work & Health

Appendix 2

Health Policy Coalitions in Ontario

COALITION FOR PRIMARY HEALTH CARE

Ten community associations and provider groups in Ontario coordinate their advocacy initiatives around the issue of primary health care. They include the Association of Ontario Health Centres, the Association of Ontario Midwives, the Canadian Pensioners Concerned, Dietitians of Canada, the Medical Reform Group of Ontario, the Older Women's Network, the Ontario Association of Medical Radiation Technologists, the Ontario Coalition of Senior Citizens' Organizations, the Ontario Association of Social Workers, the Ontario Nurses' Association, the Registered Practical Nurses Association of Ontario, and the Registered Nurses' Association of Ontario (RNAO), which have formed a coalition for primary health care. The coalition has developed 12 principles as the foundation for reform, on which its joint advocacy initiatives are based.[1] Its activities include holding public forums, news releases, and meeting with the leader of the opposition, Dalton McGuinty, and MPP Shelley Martel to discuss issues related to primary care reform, and responding to opportunities to communicate their message.

Although neither the Ontario Medical Association (OMA) nor the Canadian Medical Association (CMA) are associated with this coalition, both

---

[1]The principles include: ensure access to a wide range of comprehensive services; provide primary health care 24 hours a day, seven days a week; establish interdisciplinary group practices; service based on community need; primary health care must not be for profit; community boards; enrolment; funding; information management; coordination of care; rights, responsibilities, and accountability; education.

have been very active in this area as primary care reform will affect a significant proportion of their members. The OMA has formed a Primary Care Reform Physician Advisory Group, and developed a report. It has also consulted with such other groups as the Professional Association of Interns and Residents of Ontario, Ontario College of Family Practitioners, College of Family Physicians of Canada, the CMA, and the five chairs of the departments of family medicine in Ontario. The Joint Policy and Planning Committee comprised of members of the Ontario government and the OMA has been a key forum for consultation and joint policy formation on issues that affect the medical profession. Alternatively, the CMA developed an evaluative framework for primary care reform through consultation with CMA divisions, academics, federal and provincial governments, regional health authorities, nurses' associations, and provincial and territorial reform pilot sites, and held an invitational workshop supported in part by Health Canada.

INTERAGENCY COALITION FOR THE DISABLED

A coalition for the disabled combines the efforts of community service and charitable organizations in developing positions and advocating on issues concerning those who are disabled. These groups include the Ontario Brain Injury Association and its regional offices, the Ontarians with Disability Act (ODA) Committee, the Multiple Sclerosis Society of Canada, and the London Academy of Medicine. Subgroups have also formed related to the issue of disability and Canadian Pension Plan Disability benefits that include the Multiple Sclerosis Society of Canada, the Cystic Fibrosis Foundation and the Canadian Mental Health Association. Another subgroup focuses its efforts on issues related to homecare for those disabled, including the Multiple Sclerosis Society of Canada, the Alzheimer Society, and the ALS Society. Representatives of these associations form joint committees to ensure that their concerns are taken seriously by the government, the public, and the news media. They work together by providing information, collaborating in order to develop positions, supplying volunteer speakers, and writing letters.

HIV/AIDS NETWORK

Several organizations coordinate their initiatives to advance the cause of individuals with AIDS, including the Central Secretariat for the Network on Stakeholders for an Appropriate Response to AIDS, the Canadian HIV/AIDS Legal Network (Montreal), and the Canadian AIDS Society. A local subgroup has formed involving the Toronto People with AIDS Foundation, AIDS Action Now!, the Canadian AIDS Society, the Ontario AIDS Network, the BC Compassion Club Society, and the HIV/AIDS Legal Network. The groups involved in this coalition partner with each other on common issues,[2] exchange information, keep each other appraised of their advocacy efforts, and participate in letter/advocacy campaigns.

HEALTH ACTION LOBBY

The Health Action Lobby (HEAL) is a coalition of national health and consumer associations and organizations whose goal is to protect and strengthen Canada's health-care system. HEAL was formed in 1991 by seven founding organizations out of concern over the erosion of the federal government's role in supporting a national health-care system. It works with other organizations and governments to ensure an effective health-care system that meets the needs of Canadians. The coalition is currently comprised of 30 national associations, including health professionals (CMA, Canadian Nurses' Association (CNA), Canadian Pharmacy Association), health-service agency associations (Canadian Healthcare Association, Canadian Home Care Association, Canadian Public Health Association), and the Catholic Association of Canada. Depending on the issue, different associations work together to coordinate their advocacy. The activities of HEAL span several areas, including the protection of medicare, federal

---

[2]Several common issues include: reform of the Trillium Drug Program, national pharmacare, medicare, medication access for developing countries, and medical marijuana.

funding of health care, the impact of international trade agreements on the health-care system, and the need for national homecare and pharmacare programs.

Some of HEAL's initiatives included a pre-budget presentation (2000/ 2001) to the Commons Standing Committee on Finance which outlined recommendations for the federal government to work with health stakeholders, non-governmental organizations, and the public to develop a strategic vision for a seamless continuum of health-care services, address the challenges of funding for insured services, support the transition to community-based services and provide long-term and sustainable funding for Canada's publicly funded health-care system. Other activities include participating in a National Roundtable on Home and Community Care (1999) sponsored by Home Care Development (HCD), Health Canada, and sponsoring research related to the health-care system.

NATIONAL CHILDREN'S ALLIANCE

The National Children's Alliance (NCA) is a group of more than two dozen national organizations who advocate for children, youth, and their families in Canada. It was founded in 1996 to promote the development of a national children's agenda by the federal and provincial governments. Since 1999, NCA representatives have lobbied the federal Cabinet, MPs from all parties and federal officials on children's issues, in order to promote the National Children's Agenda. The Agenda is a federal, provincial, and territorial public commitment to Canada's children, youth, and their families (addressed in the 1999 Throne Speech). The NCA coordinated a community response to the Agenda through consultations, and lobbied local, provincial/territorial, and national governments.

CANADIAN HEALTH COALITION

The Canadian Health Coalition (CHC) is a national nonprofit organization. Founded in 1979, the coalition is dedicated to preserving medicare and improving health care in Canada. Its membership consists of national and provincial organizations representing senior citizens, students, women, health, anti-poverty, education, labour and church groups. The CHC vision for health-care reform is outlined in their document: *Ten Goals for Improving Health Care for Canadians.*

CHILDREN WITH SPECIAL NEEDS "KIDS" COALITION

Several organizations have formed a coalition to address issues related to the support of children with special needs, including the Ontario Association for Families of Children with Communication Disorders, the Ontario Association of Rehabilitation Services, Ontario Association for Community Living, Spina Bifida Association, Ontario Federation for Cerebral Palsy, and the Easter Seals Society. Its goals are an integrated coordinated service system for children with special needs. The coalition has focused its recent efforts on an interministerial agreement on health services for schools. Coalition members work together to draft and review documents, and participate in joint meetings with government ministry representatives.

GTA/905 HOSPITAL ALLIANCE

A hospital-based alliance has developed related to the changes taking place in the Greater Toronto Area-905 region from Oshawa to Oakville in Halton, Peel, York, Durham Regions, North Toronto and Scarborough. It includes the Ontario Hospital Association, Ontario Teaching Hospitals, and individual hospitals (Rouge Valley Health System, Southlake Regional Health Centre). Their concerns span a diverse range of issues, including the funding of operating budgets, funding capital projects, hospital report cards, establishing regionalization of clinical services (cardiac surgery, pediatric services, emergency services). The participating organizations work together in committees to set strategies, and make written and oral presentations to the MOHLTC.

ONTARIO HOSPITAL ASSOCIATION COALITIONS

Hospitals in Toronto (St. Michael's, Sunnybrook, and Women's College Health Sciences Centre, Mount Sinai, the University Health Network, and the Hospital for Sick Children) also actively work together through such organizations as the Toronto Academy of Health Sciences Council, the Ontario Hospital Association, the Cardiac Care Network, the Canadian Association of Academic Healthcare, and the Toronto East Emergency Network. These groups and subgroups of hospitals sponsor think-tanks to conduct projects, and form working groups, steering committees, task forces through which common agendas are established, and through which joint meetings with government officials are organized. Depending on the issue addressed, hospital members will alternatively provide leadership or serve as participants. Recent concerns have included hospital funding and health-services restructuring. A coalition of hospitals has also formed in Ottawa; in other cities hospitals have merged to form large corporations with multiple sites (Hamilton, London, Windsor).

CHRONIC CARE COALITION

A coalition has been established among chronic care hospitals in Ontario (Toronto Grace Health Centre, Riverdale Hospital, Runnymede Hospital, St. Peter's Hospital). Given the recent downsizing in the chronic hospital sector, organizations meet to develop common positions and strategies for advocacy that include holding joint meetings with government. Their primary concerns are related to chronic care reform and coordinated residential care in the community.

HEALTH RESEARCH COALITION

A number of associations work jointly in developing an agenda and strategy to influence policy concerning health research in Canada. These include Canadians for Health Research, the Coalition for Biomedical and Health

Research whose membership includes 16 medical and eight veterinary medicine schools, and the Council for Health Research in Canada (CHRC) comprised of 21 health agencies and research institutions, such as the Heart and Stroke Foundation, that raise funds for health research. Established in different years over the last three decades, these organizations work together to influence Canadian public and private sectors through various strategies.

MANAGED COMPETITION STAKEHOLDERS GROUP

A coalition has formed around the issue of managed competition in the homecare sector, including the Canadian Red Cross Society (Ontario Zone), Ontario Home Healthcare Providers Association, the Ontario Community Support Association (OCSA), the Canadian Home Care Association, the Ontario Association of Community Care Access Centres, the Ontario Case Managers Association and the Victorian Order of Nurses, and the CNA. Related concerns include nurse and homemaker wage disparities, benefits/ recruitment/retention and pay equity. However, the OCSA works with a diverse array of groups on other related issues. The associations meet to develop joint policy positions and papers, and attend joint meetings with representatives of the MOHLTC to discuss issues and concerns related to community health services. A Canadian Palliative Care Coalition has also formed to address issues related to palliative care in the community.

LONG-TERM CARE COALITION

Several groups, including the Ontario Long Term Care Association (OLTCA), the Ontario Association of Nonprofit Homes and Services for Seniors, and the Ontario Health Providers Association (OHPA) work together to develop common positions and joint lobbying efforts. Some of their issues of concern include the *Long Term Care Act*, long-term care funding, occupancy, accountability. The OLTCA and the OHPA have worked together on the *Privacy Act*, the pay equity Bill C-6 (federal), integrated health systems, and human resources recruitment.

MENTAL HEALTH NETWORK

The Ontario Federation of Community Mental Health and Addiction Programs is the largest umbrella organization representing independent service agencies, while the Canadian Mental Health Association is the largest single organization providing community mental health services. The two organizations often advocate policy proposals cooperatively. Physicians are represented by two main groups: the Association of General Hospital Psychiatry Service represents hospital-based psychiatrists, while the Coalition of Ontario Psychiatrists represents community-based psychiatrists and is comprised of the Ontario Medical Association (OMA) section on psychiatry, and the Ontario Psychiatric Association. Consumer associations include the Ontario Council of Alternative Business, and the Ontario Peer Support Initiative. The main family member organization is the Schizophrenia Society of Ontario, while the Mood Disorders Association includes both consumers and family members. The diversity of groups and their conflicting views reflect the silos and competing interests within the mental health policy community, such that tensions exist between the perspective of the medical community, the community services sector, as well as the consumer and family groups.

7

La liberté d'association : réalité juridique évanescente et contrainte

Georges leBel

Dans le climat actuel d'unanimisme et de lutte de « l'empire de l'ordre moral » contre « le mal » où l'on veut supprimer l'espace démocratique et de débat, il peut sembler incongru de se poser la question de la liberté et surtout de la liberté d'association. L'opposition officielle au Canada ne s'insurge-t-elle pas aujourd'hui qu'on ne restreigne pas assez rapidement les libertés de ceux qu'on ne peut désigner et qui risquent d'être parmi les nôtres ?

C'est pourtant dans ces temps qu'il faut se préoccuper des libertés. C'est pourquoi, nous examinerons l'état du droit concernant la liberté d'association au Canada en décembre 2001, au moment où la Cour suprême

---

Ce texte a été écrit antérieurement aux arrêts Advance Cutting (18 octobre 2001) et Dunmore (20 décembre 2001). N'ayant pu en tenir compte nous avons ajouté un post-scriptum explicatif et quelques notes rappelant que si Advance Cutting reprend la jurisprudence antérieure, une innovation importante est introduite dans DUNMORE qui considère que dans certaines circonstances, l'abstention même de l'État pourrait constituer une violation des droits. Dans le discours ésotérique de la Cour, on parle alors d'un « Acte d'abstention » qui permettrait l'examen de la Cour.

s'apprête à rendre sa décision dans Dunmore.[1] Nous espérons que cet exposé permettra de comprendre et d'illustrer le potentiel de changement que comporte cet arrêt.

La Charte canadienne des droits et libertés affirme en son paragraphe 2, d) que « Chacun a les libertés fondamentales suivantes : [...] d) liberté d'association ».

C'est clair, net, simple et semble sans ambiguïté.

Pourtant, l'interprétation juridique qui en a été donnée par la Cour suprême du Canada en fait selon les termes mêmes du juge en chef Dickson[2], alors dissident, une liberté ancillaire « légaliste, parcimonieuse, voire même insipide » dont on n'est pas sûr qu'elle ne se réduise pas à la liberté de ne pas s'associer, au droit à l'isolement.

Nous nous étions posé la question de savoir si les contraintes diverses — juridiques, et administratives — à la liberté d'association pouvaient finir par culminer en une restriction effective de cette liberté. Nous constatons qu'avant d'examiner les contraintes, il nous faudra établir ce qui reste de cette liberté après les restrictions que lui a imposées notre Cour suprême.

La problématique de départ est simple : tant les textes internationaux que les Chartes canadienne et québécoise affirment et garantissent la liberté d'association. Mais la mise en œuvre de cette liberté est restreinte.

La Charte canadienne ne vise qu'à garantir les droits contre l'action du Gouvernement.[3] D'entrée de jeu, on se trouve devant une liberté restreinte, réduite à la non-intervention de l'État. C'est une conception bien étroite de la liberté que de la faire équivaloir à une abstention du pouvoir ; et c'est une vision bien mince du pouvoir que de le réduire à la seule intervention de caractère juridique. Cette interprétation fait de la liberté d'association une liberté négative, comme en creux, qui ne se reconnaîtrait que par l'absence d'action directe de l'État à son encontre.

Pour exister et agir en toute liberté, il nous semble qu'il faille que la loi intervienne pour la protection et la promotion de cette liberté. Or notre Cour suprême a corrélé la liberté et une non-intervention de l'État, comme si la liberté équivalait uniquement à une absence de contrainte et non pas à la possibilité ou la capacité de se réaliser. Il est pourtant simple de constater que l'absence de possibilité équivaut bien à l'absence de liberté.[4]

Mais il y a plus, l'interprétation jurisprudentielle de cette « liberté fondamentale » en a fait surtout un droit individuel. Chaque fois qu'une telle interprétation est énoncée devant une « honnête personne »[5] cela amène un froncement de sourcils interrogatif : Comment les juristes peuvent-ils soutenir sans que le ridicule les foudroie, que le droit de s'associer est une liberté individuelle ? Et le juriste d'expliquer que si c'était simple, on n'aurait pas besoin de juristes.

Cette interprétation restrictive et mesquine repose sur une activité judiciaire réduite ; il y a eu relativement peu de décisions de nos Cours concernant cette liberté.[6] On peut y voir trois raisons : soit la liberté n'y est pas menacée (ce qui serait surprenant)[7] ; soit l'interprétation est telle qu'il y a peu d'espoir à l'invoquer (ce qui n'est pas loin de la réalité) ; soit les recours judiciaires sont tellement onéreux que peu de gens ont la témérité[8] de s'y frotter (ce qui est hautement probable, mais qualifie l'accessibilité à notre justice).

Mais en fait, la Charte n'a pas changé grand-chose, parce que l'activité juridique antérieure à 1982 autour de la liberté d'association était réduite tant du point de vue de la littérature[9] que de la jurisprudence.[10] L'interprétation, alors, était relativement timide, et la venue de la Charte avait permis quelques espoirs. Dans l'affaire Broadway Manor,[11] on reconnaissait que le droit d'association comportait celui de former un syndicat, de négocier et de faire la grève ; et la Cour suprême avait refusé d'entendre l'appel.[12] C'est avec l'affaire Public Service Alliance[13] que la Cour fédérale d'appel, d'abord, puis la Cour suprême saisirent l'occasion de ramener tout le monde à la réalité libérale. Et c'est dans une série de décisions de 1987 que l'on désigne sous le terme de « trilogie, »[14] que la Cour suprême a structuré son interprétation de la « liberté d'association ».
Elle en a finalement donné la définition suivante :[15]

> Après avoir examiné les différents motifs de jugement dans le Renvoi relatif à l'Alberta, j'arrive à la conclusion qu'il se dégage quatre propositions différentes quant à l'étendue de la liberté d'association garantie par l'al. 2, d): premièrement, l'al. 2, d) protège la liberté de *constituer une association*, de la *maintenir* et d'*y appartenir* ; deuxièmement, l'al. 2, d) ne protège pas une activité pour le seul motif que cette *activité* est un objet fondamental ou essentiel d'une association ; troisièmement, l'al. 2, d) protège l'*exercice collectif* des droits et libertés individuels consacrés par la Constitution ; et quatrièmement, l'al. 2, d) protège l'exercice collectif des droits légitimes des individus.[16]

Cette interprétation se résume à dire que l'État peut tout faire en ce qui concerne les associations sauf interdire complètement toute constitution d'association ou le maintien et la participation à toute association. Il peut donc restreindre ou interdire la création, la participation ou le maintien d'une quelconque association particulière. De plus, n'importe quel type d'activités peut être restreint pourvu qu'il reste au moins une activité possible à une hypothétique association, ou que l'activité interdite ne soit pas protégée par la Charte lorsqu'elle est accomplie par un individu. Il suffirait de plus à l'État de déclarer une activité « illégitime »[17] ou contraire à la loi, pour que des individus réunis ne puissent l'accomplir, ce qui équivaut à dire que la liberté existe pourvu qu'elle ne soit pas restreinte par la loi.[18]

La Cour suprême considère donc que la liberté inscrite dans la Charte des droits est une liberté négative, qui protège contre les interférences de l'État,[19] mais pas contre toutes les interférences, parce que, devant une restriction étatique, s'il reste un objet[20] autour duquel on puisse se réunir, (c'est le triste exemple du golf[21]), alors la liberté est considérée comme sauve, même si la loi rend impossible ou inutile de se réunir.[22]

Cette définition de la « liberté d'association » rendait en quelque sorte notre interrogation du départ bien peu pertinente. En effet devant cette interprétation restrictive d'une liberté que certains considèrent comme source de la vie sociale démocratique, l'addition de toutes les contraintes administratives mises à l'exercice de cette liberté étaient bien peu importante et ne changeait pas substantiellement le fond de la question.

La trilogie refuse d'étendre la liberté d'association aux activités de l'association en opposant droits individuels et droits collectifs, alors que les dissidents auraient étendu la protection aux activités licites. Tout ce que garantit l'al. 2,d) selon le juge McIntyre, c'est que le gouvernement ne peut interdire l'exercice collectif d'une activité qui peut être accomplie individuellement ou plus précisément qui ne pourrait être interdite si elle était exercée individuellement.

Pour la Cour suprême, la liberté d'association est une liberté négative qui ne protège que des interventions de l'État contre les seules libertés individuelles déjà garanties. Le droit de ne pas s'associer est presque mieux protégé. Nous attribuerons cette interprétation aux postulats individualistes d'abord et ensuite aux racines corporatistes du droit du travail nord-américain qui a servi de champ principal d'élaboration de cette interprétation.

Devant pareille interprétation, le juriste est confronté à une alternative : soit il essaie de trouver dans le raisonnement des juges de la Cour suprême des failles qui lui permettront de faire valoir un point de vue différent et de faire avancer une liberté qu'ils ont limitée ; soit il constate que les postulats des juges sont tellement emprisonnés dans une idéologie particulière qu'on ne peut que constater l'inadéquation du droit canadien aux exigences de la démocratie.

La première option nous conduirait à essayer de trouver des divergences d'opinion entre différents juges, même si les décisions plus récentes marquent le ralliement des dissidents. Cette option est d'autant plus délicate que les juges se sont abstenus de donner une définition complète de la liberté d'association protégée par la Constitution. Ils se sont contentés de dire que cette liberté ne protège ni les activités ni les fins des associations, et qu'il s'agit d'un droit individuel qui n'a pour effet que de restreindre les possibilités d'action de l'État. Et cette retenue a été exprimée par le juge LeDain, affirmant sa crainte des conséquences qui en résulteraient si on assignait à l'État une tâche positive quant aux conditions nécessaires à mettre en œuvre pour que la liberté existe. Le juge LeDain semble avoir bien compris que cela le conduirait à se distancer des postulats libéraux.

Après avoir en vain trituré les décisions de la Cour suprême, nous nous sommes rendus à l'évidence : la conception libérale individualiste de la Cour ne laisse aucune échappatoire et c'est en vain qu'on cherchera un argument[23] qui permettrait de sortir de l'avenue juridiquement bétonnée par cette idéologie. Pour pouvoir invoquer l'argument démocratique et la participation citoyenne, il faudrait constater d'abord qu'une liberté fondamentale et un droit ont été violés. Or comme la définition donnée ne permet pas de constater qu'il y a violation d'un droit, on ne peut donc aborder l'étape suivante de l'argumentation interprétative que cette violation est incompatible avec le caractère démocratique d'une société libre. Les défenseurs d'une démocratie participative fondée sur le respect du droit d'association ne pourraient prendre appui sur la Charte des Droits telle qu'interprétée par la Cour suprême que pour se défendre mais non pour la promotion de la démocratie. Parvenus à ce cul-de-sac juridique,[24] il ne nous reste plus qu'à exprimer pourquoi une conception de la démocratie exige qu'on s'écarte de cette interprétation mesquine et étroitement libérale.

Partant de ce que la Cour suprême a restreint la liberté d'association à une liberté contre l'État, notre exposé se fera donc en deux temps. Nous verrons d'abord qu'il s'agit bien d'une liberté même si elle est limitée par l'individualisme et son caractère instrumentaire. Nous tenterons ensuite de reprendre l'exercice depuis le début parce que l'apport de l'État est nécessaire pour mettre en œuvre cette liberté. Pour y arriver, nous tenterons d'écarter la perspective corporatiste qui a obscurci le débat sur le syndicalisme pour mettre au centre de notre réflexion les idéaux d'égalité et de démocratie, et donner un peu de place aux rapports sociaux contemporains.

Nous serons alors conduits à accompagner l'ouverture qui est tentée dans l'affaire Dunmore.[25] Nous examinerons donc dans un premier temps les limites mises par la Cour suprême à la reconnaissance de la liberté d'association puis nous essayerons d'expliquer pourquoi et comment elle aurait pu choisir une autre veine interprétative. Nous entreprendrons ce travail non pour exiger une reconnaissance juridique qui nous semble évanescente, mais chercher des moyens pour que la liberté soit réelle, et l'égalité un objectif réaliste.

UNE INTERPRÉTATION INDIVIDUALISANT LA « LIBERTÉ D'ASSOCIATION »

L'individualisme

La Cour suprême a fait de la liberté d'association une liberté individuelle. Dans les termes du juge McIntyre, « les droits et libertés conférés par la Charte sont des droits individuels à part ceux qui y sont spécifiquement énumérés. » Même si la liberté d'association « assure la promotion de nombreux intérêts collectifs, (...) il s'agit néanmoins d'une liberté qui appartient à l'individu et non aux groupes formés grâce à son existence ».[26] Et d'ajouter que la réalisation des droits et des aspirations individuels constitue l'objet central de l'ordre constitutionnel, alors que les groupes ne se voient conférer que des droits spécifiques dont le poids ne peut altérer la nature individualiste intrinsèque de la Charte. Le groupe ne saurait bénéficier d'une garantie constitutionnelle dont l'individu[27] ne jouit pas. La liberté d'association ne fait que protéger l'exercice collectif des droits que possède l'individu. « La liberté d'association s'entend de la liberté de s'associer afin d'exercer des activités qui sont licites lorsqu'elles sont exercées par un seul individu. »[28]

Pourtant la liberté d'association est une des libertés de l'action collective, c'est-à-dire qu'elle est individuelle quant à ses titulaires puisqu'elle appartient à chaque individu, mais son exercice ne peut être que collectif. Un lien est ainsi établi entre l'individuel et le collectif, ce dernier permettant au premier de se réaliser pleinement. Mais nous savons qu'entre les deux peuvent apparaître des tensions et qu'en fait, il faut sans cesse maintenir un équilibre très fragile. L'individuel doit accepter les contraintes du collectif ; le collectif ne doit pas étouffer l'individuel. Ce dernier aspect est certainement l'un des plus délicats (Conseil de l'Europe 1993, 15).

Par ailleurs, si la liberté d'association prévue à la Charte ne confère pas de droits autres que ceux déjà reconnus aux individus, il se peut cependant qu'elle en fasse perdre.[29] Le professeur MacNeil[30] note que lorsqu'il s'agit d'imposer aux associations, et surtout aux syndicats, des obligations et des responsabilités collectives pour des actions individuelles, la Cour n'hésite pas à le faire. Dans les affaires de la trilogie, l'action collective (la grève et la négociation) entreprise par un groupe, est précisément évoquée pour refuser l'application de la Charte, parce qu'il s'agit d'une action collective. Il en résulte donc que le fait d'agir collectivement ne confère pas de droit mais peut cependant créer des obligations.[31]

La cohérence aurait exigé que si la liberté d'association était vraiment une liberté individuelle, alors les juges de la Cour suprême auraient dû unanimement reconnaître le droit de ne pas s'associer ; pourtant, ils ne l'ont pas vraiment fait[32] même s'ils ont en quelque sorte reconnu un droit à l'isolement ; et leurs tergiversations indiquent bien les incohérences de leur position générale. « Il devrait en être de la liberté d'association comme de la liberté de religion qui comporte celle de ne pas en avoir ou la liberté d'expression qui garantit celle de se taire ou de circulation qui garantit le droit de ne pas bouger. Ils reconnaissent que le versement d'une cotisation n'est pas plus un moyen de s'associer qu'un moyen de s'exprimer » (Brun et Tremblay 1997, 1004).

L'incidence de la Charte dans ce domaine fut principalement d'établir une hiérarchie nouvelle entre les différents principes et valeurs qui structurent la légitimité de l'action étatique (Carter 1988, 311). Ainsi, la liberté d'association n'est plus vue seule, mais comme encerclée, enserrée dans un faisceau d'autres principes et de libertés, comme la liberté de pensée, la liberté d'opinion, l'équité procédurale, l'égalité devant la loi ... Plusieurs de ces principes ont reçu une interprétation individualiste telle que les institutions et structures qui ont fait du Canada un pays socialement avancé s'en trouvent mises à mal. Pensons ici au processus interprétatif qui examine une liberté fondamentale en soi et non comme un objectif global dont les conditions nécessaires de réalisation doivent recevoir la protection constitutionnelle. Ainsi, faire de l'individu la pierre de touche de la liberté d'association amène la Cour à négliger que des conditions collectives et restreignant la liberté absolue d'un individu, puissent être nécessaires pour assurer la pleine expression démocratique.

Il est pourtant possible de concevoir le droit d'association dans une perspective autre et comme ayant un statut différent et indépendant des droits individuels (Garet 1983, 1006). Cette conception pourrait prendre en compte que l'existence même de l'individu postule une liaison aux autres souvent par toute une série de groupes variés. La participation des individus, membres du groupe, définit la nature du groupe et l'existence du groupe participe de la définition de l'individu.: « Personhood, communality and sociability are structures of existence, or necessary aspects of human being » (Rhéaume 1988, 1).

Individualisme insoutenable

Dans la trilogie, le juge LeDain commence par caractériser la liberté d'association comme importante pour l'exercice des autres libertés.[33] Cette vision instrumentaire voit la liberté d'association comme une dérivée des droits individuels où seuls les individus sont porteurs de droits.[34] Cette interprétation est curieuse puisque cette liberté est directement affirmée dans la Charte et non pas dérivée d'autres droits.

Cette vision subordonnée et instrumentaire de la liberté d'association vient probablement du fait que la Trilogie s'appuie massivement sur des opinions étatsuniennes. Dans l'affaire du renvoi de l'Alberta (PSERA), qui est l'opinion substantielle, le Juge McIntyre se fonde principalement sur des autorités étatsuniennes.[35] Le professeur Bendel (1986) avait déjà suggéré qu'on interprétât la Charte canadienne à la lumière de l'expérience des États-Unis. L'effet principal de cette référence est surtout de centrer l'ensemble de l'analyse des droits garantis par la Charte canadienne non pas sur les principes démocratiques de l'article premier, mais plutôt sur une interprétation étroitement individualisante et instrumentaire du droit d'association.

La Constitution des États-Unis ne contient pas de disposition qui protège spécifiquement la liberté d'association, mais l'interprétation a déduit son existence comme une exigence inhérente et nécessaire à la pleine réalisation de la liberté de parole et de réunion et statué de ce fait que la liberté d'association ne peut être limitée par le gouvernement, à moins que cette limitation ne serve un intérêt public qui n'est pas lié à la suppression des idées.[36] La liberté d'association devient ici un instrument pour la mise en œuvre des autres libertés.

Cette conception juridique a évolué mais pour les conservateurs américains, la liberté équivaut à un faible niveau de taxation, un gouvernement faible et discret et la possibilité de puiser dans la corne d'abondance des biens dans un marché global déréglementé. Pourtant les luttes sociales américaines sont porteuses de conceptions plus riches de la liberté (Foner 1998).

Certains ont voulu importer cette conception au Canada en l'élargissant. Le juge Dickson, dissident, objecte en se référant « à l'histoire de notre Constitution qui donne un statut spécial aux collectivités et communautés d'intérêts autres que ceux de l'État, du Gouvernement et des partis politiques »[37] (Magnet 1986, 170).

Le professeur Cavalluzzo (1986, 189) prétendait avant la trilogie que la doctrine américaine qui fait de la liberté d'association un droit dérivé, était moins « robuste » que l'affirmation directe canadienne surtout si l'on tenait compte des obligations internationales assumées souverainement par le Canada. Rien n'y fit et la majorité de la Cour suprême balaya ces arguments au détour d'un paragraphe marqué par une adhésion acharnée à l'individualisme libéral quasi-thatchérien.

Le droit civil québécois

Cet individualisme serait infirmé par la disposition expresse du Code civil qui postule la succession perpétuelle de l'association indépendamment du sort de ses initiateurs. S'il s'agissait d'un droit individuel, la société qui n'est pas pourvue de la personnalité juridique distincte, disparaîtrait avec les porteurs de ce droit. C'était le cas d'après le Code civil du Bas-Canada, où la société disparaissait avec la mort d'un des associés ; mais conscient de l'existence de la Charte, le codificateur de 1994 a explicitement statué[38] que la persistance de la société et de l'association ne dépend plus de la vie des initiateurs, mais est maintenue aussi longtemps qu'on a prévu qu'elle existe, que ses objets sont possibles ou que la volonté des participants subsiste pour qu'elle continue d'exister.[39]

C'est un droit individuel curieux qui ne peut s'exercer que collectivement, et dont les conditions administratives d'exercice postulent le dépassement de l'individu. En effet, la responsabilité est générée collectivement, du fait de l'association, même si elle est assumée individuellement. Ce n'est pas comme individu, mais *es qualité* d'« administrateur » que l'article 2274 du Code civil impute la responsabilité car l'article suivant (art. 2275) indique bien que le membre qui n'a pas administré n'est pas tenu aux dettes; seul celui qui a participé à l'action collective y est tenu. Ainsi ce pseudo droit individuel s'exerce collectivement et génère une responsabilité solidaire. (art. 1525) C'est la nature du rapport social qui détermine ici la responsabilité et non pas seulement la preuve du lien entre différentes personnes et la conduite de l'entité collective.[40]

Incohérence

De multiples autres arguments militent contre cette interprétation individualisante du droit d'association. D'abord l'argument de cohérence : comment peut-on restreindre à l'individu la protection de « chacun » à l'art.2, d), alors que cette même expression permet de couvrir d'autres entités lorsqu'il s'agit par exemple de la liberté d'expression ?[41] D'autant plus que dans l'affaire Ford,[42] la Cour avait à interpréter concurremment la Charte québécoise (art 3 et art. 9.1) dont le caractère individualiste semble clair. On a adopté là une interprétation extensive pour couvrir les corporations, mais dans le cas de l'art. 2, d), on impose une interprétation restrictive (Foster 1990, 1150).

Le fait que l'article 2 commence par le mot « CHACUN » (« Everyone ») ne nous semble pas suffisant pour exclure le caractère essentiellement collectif du droit d'association alors que la protection de l'article 8 qui couvre, là aussi, les droits de « chacun », fut étendue aux corporations et autres entités.[43] Au-delà de l'artifice juridique de l'attribution fictive de la personnalité à une somme d'argent structurée en capital-actions, comment ne pas voir que les corporations furent, à l'origine, des regroupements de personnes, des associations, et que s'écarter de cette interprétation reviendrait à accorder des droits de l'Homme au capital ou aux choses ; ce qui n'est pas loin du résultat auquel nous conduit la logique de notre Cour suprême.

Pourtant, lorsqu'il s'agit des sociétés par actions, la Cour n'hésite pas à leur reconnaître des droits à titre de personnes morales. Est-il possible alors que l'exercice de la liberté d'association qualifiée de fondamentale par notre Constitution, puisse dépendre de l'accomplissement d'une formalité juridique discrétionnaire de l'État (le dépôt de la déclaration constitutive) ? Il nous semble qu'il y a là une inversion du raisonnement spécifique de McIntyre puisque le droit individuel est accordé pour protéger l'individu contre l'État et que ce droit ne peut exister dans le cadre de l'association que dans la mesure où ce même État consent à accorder le statut juridique (incorporation) qui conférera cette protection.[44]

Pourquoi nier le caractère collectif du droit d'association alors que la Charte elle-même reconnaît des droits collectifs ? La cohérence interne du texte n'interdisait pas la reconnaissance de libertés collectives dans une Constitution qui reconnaît déjà les écoles confessionnelles (religion), la langue, les autochtones, et surtout l'interdiction fondamentale de toute discrimination fondée sur l'appartenance à un groupe. Il y a là reconnaissance du fondement collectif du droit, puisque sa source négative et comme en creux est l'existence préalable d'un groupe. Il faut que le groupe existe ou soit imputé par le violateur pour que la discrimination existe. L'interdiction de la discrimination (art. 15) repose sur des distinctions juridiquement construites et/ou socialement reconnues (sexe, couleur, âge, religion, langue, l'origine nationale ou ethnique, la race, les déficiences mentales ou physiques) qui postulent toutes l'appartenance à un groupe réel, socialement construit, choisi ou imputé.[45] Il est notable de constater que la liberté fondamentale d'opinion n'est pas mentionnée comme élément de constitution d'un groupe qui pourrait être victime de discrimination, même si le libellé plus général (« notamment ») donne ouverture à pareil argument. Pour nos juges, c'est peut-être qu'une association est nécessairement une entité créée, alors que les catégories qui fondent une interdiction de la discrimination sont des données « naturelles ». Il s'agirait à tout le moins d'une catégorisation contestable.

Certains ont hésité à accepter que cette vision étroitement individuelle des droits « ait complètement fermé la porte à toute protection constitutionnelle du droit de libre association par syndicalisation »[46] d'autant plus que les dispositions contestées avaient pour effet d'empêcher les membres de la GRC de s'associer dans une structure de leur choix, ce qui est en contradiction avec les dispositions du Code du travail et l'art. 22 du Pacte international relatif aux droits civils et politiques.[47] Dans la trilogie, le juge McIntyre semblait ouvrir la porte à la possibilité que certains aspects de l'action collective des syndicats puissent être protégés par la Charte au titre de la liberté d'association : « Toutefois, ma conclusion dans cet arrêt n'écarte pas la possibilité que d'autres aspects de la négociation collective puissent bénéficier de la protection de la Charte en vertu de la garantie de la liberté d'association. »[48] Mais la décision de la Cour suprême dans l'affaire Delisle fermera complètement cette porte affirmant que la Charte ne protégerait que l'exercice collectif des libertés individuelles par ailleurs reconnues et les activités licites permises à l'individu.

Pourtant, lorsque des gens se réunissent pour pratiquer leur religion, cela devient la liberté de culte ; il ne viendrait à personne l'idée de restreindre la liberté de culte parce qu'il s'agit nécessairement d'une action collective qui se distingue de la liberté individuelle ; la liberté de culte n'a aucune signification individuelle. Est-ce que la liberté syndicale ne serait pas une liberté du même type, les personnes se réunissant pour exercer leur liberté contractuelle…? Les juges de la Cour suprême rechignent lorsque les travailleurs tentent d'exercer cette liberté collectivement. Il faut donc se demander depuis quand, pour nos juges libéraux si imbus de la jurisprudence américaine, la liberté de contracter ne jouit pas de la garantie constitutionnelle.[49]

La consécration par notre Cour suprême de la liberté d'association comme liberté individuelle en fait une garantie subordonnée aux autres droits individuels comme la liberté d'expression et à la liberté d'opinion (conscience, religion, pensée). En la réduisant au rôle de moyen et d'instrument de mise en œuvre de droits individuels plus fondamentaux, la Cour suprême rend la mention de la liberté d'association à l'article 2, d) superfétatoire, inutile et redondante. Or c'est un principe simple d'interprétation que le législateur, surtout le constituant, ne parle pas pour ne rien dire et que l'on doit donc accorder un efficace spécifique à chaque mention du texte juridique, ce qu'oublie de faire notre Cour suprême.[50]

Mais il y a probablement une explication contextuelle et historique à cet écart de la Cour. Dans la mesure où l'interprétation de cette disposition a surtout été posée dans le cadre des relations de travail, nous constatons qu'il s'est opéré une sorte de déplacement de la réflexion qui impose peut-être de faire un bref retour sur l'origine de cette liberté d'association et son rapport avec la vie sociale et la démocratie.

UNE INTERPRÉTATION EN PORTE-À-FAUX POUR UNE LIBERTÉ À RECONSTRUIRE

L'individualisme produit par ailleurs des résultats vraiment curieux lorsqu'il est appliqué au domaine du travail et de la négociation collective. Et c'est ce domaine qui a donné la principale production judiciaire et juridique.

Le problème naît de l'incapacité de l'idéologie libérale de concevoir un rôle à la communauté dans la définition et la constitution de l'individu, créant ainsi des barrières artificielles entre l'individu, le groupe et la société. En insistant sur l'importance de l'individu, nos Cours ont tendance à faire l'impasse sur les conditions sociales et historiques d'existence de nos communautés et leur rôle dans la formulation et la promotion des aspirations. C'est vers cela que les pousse la référence aux décisions de nos voisins du Sud.

Pourtant, un retour sur les origines de cette liberté nous apprend qu'elle fut conçue comme une liberté publique et non comme un droit individuel.

Ce sont des choix de ce niveau qui explique d'une part la méfiance de la Révolution française à l'égard des associations et la référence individualiste des constituants américains. La liberté d'association ne figure pas dans la Déclaration de 89 (Révolution française) ni dans la Constitution américaine. En effet, pour le Révolutionnaire français, la liberté de l'individu ne souffre aucun intermédiaire entre elle et l'État qui incarne la Nation.

Jean-Jacques Rousseau écrit dans le *Contrat Social* :

> Mais quand il se fait des brigues, des associations partielles aux dépens de la grande, la volonté de chacune de ces associations devient générale par rapport à ses membres, et particulière par rapport à l'État ; on peut dire qu'il n'y a plus autant de votants que d'hommes, mais seulement autant que d'assocations.(...) Il importe donc pour avoir bien l'énoncé de la volonté

générale qu'il n'y ait pas de société partielle dans l'État et que chaque citoyen n'opine que d'après lui (Rousseau 1972, 66-67).

La menace potentielle ne trouve donc sa résolution que dans deux extrêmes : la négation de toutes les associations, ou leur multiplication à l'infini jusqu'au point où leur prolifération même instaure une régulation par le nombre. La première solution a été mise à l'essai par les révolutionnaires de 89 qui abolirent les corporations, les compagnonnages, les congrégations et même les académies. Lors de l'adoption de la loi qui porte son nom en 1791, Le Chapelier s'exclame : « Il n'y a plus de corporations dans l'État, il n'y a plus que l'intérêt particulier de chaque individu et l'intérêt général » (Fecteau 1990, 97).

Tout le dix-neuvième siècle avec le chartisme, par exemple, est marqué par le combat du pouvoir contre les volontés associatives pour ressusciter les corporations d'abord, et organiser la classe ouvrière naissante ensuite. Madame Anne David résume ainsi l'histoire de cette liberté en France :

> La révolution de 1789, au nom de la liberté individuelle, détruisit les associations existantes et nia le droit d'association sur le terrain professionnel et charitable par volonté de détruire les corps intermédiaires et parce que l'État peut et doit suffire à tout. (…) Le motif principal pour soumettre les associations à des restrictions, était le respect du principe de la libre concurrence, qui condamne les regroupements faits sur une base professionnelle et la peur de la mainmorte, accumulation de biens hors commerce.[51] Les syndicats ouvriers ne seront autorisés qu'en 1884. La crainte était toujours de reconnaître la liberté aux congrégations religieuses, notamment en matière d'enseignement. (1905, loi sur la séparation de l'Église et de l'État) (David 1993, 94-96).

Il faudra donc attendre presque le vingtième siècle pour que soit reconnu en France, par la loi de 1901, le droit de former des associations. Et encore, cette liberté était si délicate à manipuler, qu'on s'est abstenu de la réglementer. Ce n'est que tout récemment que l'utilisation de cette liberté à des fins d'évitement fiscal a remis en cause le traitement qui lui était accordé. Par ailleurs, en Europe comme ici, ce ne sera que très progressivement que la liberté d'association comprendra explicitement la liberté syndicale, probablement parce que cette forme d'association entretenait avec le corporatisme d'antan des rapports suspects.

Ce que la Révolution française a condamné, ce sont les corporations, c'est-à-dire ces associations particulières qui avaient reçu le pouvoir de régir l'entrée, l'exercice, la discipline et l'ordre dans un métier ou une profession donnés. Le Collège des médecins et les différents Barreaux sont de ces reliquats d'Ancien Régime.

Le Corporatisme

On constate qu'une partie du mouvement des travailleurs, lorsqu'il voulut s'organiser, a choisi soit une forme politique d'association, soit la forme corporative appuyée sur des initiatives de secours mutuel ou de coopération. Durant la première moitié du siècle passé, les initiatives organisationnelles des travailleurs étaient devenues si incontournables que les législateurs, probablement dans le dessein de les contrôler, adoptèrent des formes corporatistes d'organisation syndicale. Des sociétés entières, le fascisme italien, le franquisme espagnol et le salazarisme portugais, de même que la dictature bonhomme de Gentulio Vargas au Brésil, entre de nombreux autres, ont été régies selon ce système. Les législateurs nord-américains suivirent ce modèle, aux États-Unis, au Canada de même qu'au Québec.[52] On parle de corporation à partir du moment où un groupe de personnes constitué en organisation se voit confier et assume des fonctions de l'État: « the responsibility for exercising public duties » selon les termes de la Cour européenne.[53] C'est par ignorance de l'Histoire que nos juges confondent maintenant associations et corporations et évaluent les uns et les autres à l'aune de la liberté d'association. Cette liberté, dont une forme importante d'exercice s'est exprimée dans le cadre de l'idéologie corporatiste, fut réinterprétée à partir de 1945 dans les termes de l'idéologie libérale.

Il s'agirait ici de voir le corporatisme pour ce qu'il est et de le traiter comme tel : l'utilisation par l'État des structures associatives pour réaliser des objectifs de politique publique. Si l'on avait placé carrément les syndicats accrédités du côté des politiques publiques, alors la liberté d'association aurait pu prendre son essor, libérée des contraintes que représentent la liaison étroite de l'État et des structures corporatistes du syndicalisme américain. Cela concerne aussi les corporations profession-nelles, le Barreau, le Collège des médecins, et les offices de producteurs agricoles, chacun avec son calibrage de droits et d'obligations spécifiques aux exigences et objectifs de la mission de service public. Cela aurait permis aussi de régler le problème de la liberté négative, c'est-à-dire le droit de ne pas s'associer, le droit à l'isolement.

La Cour Européenne de justice a défini certains groupes de droit public en se fondant, entre autres, sur le fait qu'ils servent l'intérêt public en même temps que les intérêts de leurs membres.[54] Les groupes de ce type ne ressortissent plus à la liberté d'association. En revanche, si le groupe relève, à l'origine, du droit privé et que sa fonction de supervision ne constitue qu'une partie de sa raison d'être du fait qu'il a également pour objet de sauvegarder et de favoriser au regard de la concurrence les intérêts professionnels de ses membres, il remplira les conditions nécessaires pour avoir la qualité d'association privée dont la liberté est garantie. « On a tort d'envisager le droit à la liberté d'association de façon trop abstraite, en comparant une secte religieuse à un syndicat et en tentant d'extraire un unique ensemble de principes, applicables aux partis politiques, des syndicats ou des sectes religieuses. Il y a une différence très nette entre l'obligation de s'affilier à un parti politique et celle d'adhérer à un syndicat » (Conseil de l'Europe 1993, 207).

Lorsque les organisations remplissent des fonctions sociales et publiques vitales, il faut réaliser un équilibre entre l'autonomie de l'association et l'intérêt général. Or c'est cet élément que la Cour suprême a appréhendé vaguement mais n'a pas complètement pris en compte dans l'ensemble de ses jugements sur la liberté d'association dans le domaine du travail.

Pourtant, les syndicats sont des organisations de travailleurs qui se réunissent pour répondre au regroupement ou à l'association qui a déjà été réalisée du côté des employeurs et du capital (MacNeil 1989, 101), avec l'appui de l'État et des législations pertinentes. Leur refuser une considération spéciale, c'est prendre parti pour les uns contre les autres ; alors que le libéralisme postule ici la neutralité de l'État.

Le professeur Leader (Conseil de l'Europe 1993, 187) résume bien le problème que le corporatisme pose à la démocratie lorsque l'on impose l'appartenance obligatoire à une association. À partir d'un certain niveau, naissent des contradictions entre les diverses caractéristiques associatives. On a tendance aujourd'hui à insister sur la participation de ce qu'on nomme la « société civile » à la définition des politiques publiques qui résulterait de la confrontation des intérêts concurrents dans la société. Pour ce faire, on postule que les associations connaissent et représentent effectivement les aspirations et les intérêts de leurs membres, dont elles sont l'expression ; mais aussi qu'elles peuvent exercer les arbitrages nécessaires entre leurs membres pour qu'une fois une position arrêtée, elles puissent agir comme courroie de transmission et mécanisme d'imposition à ses membres des impératifs du bien commun qui peut parfois contraindre les intérêts individuels. Cela va aussi loin que d'exercer un pouvoir de discipline sur les membres qui ne s'y conforment pas.

Suivant cette conception, nous ne pourrions peut-être obtenir les deux premières caractéristiques : — d'une part participation à la définition de politiques publiques des groupes intermédiaires qui connaissent parfaitement les aspirations de ceux qu'ils représentent et d'autre part, imposition du respect de ces politiques par leurs membres — qu'aux dépens de la troisième, c'est-à-dire la liberté d'association.[55] D'autre part, si nous entendons favoriser cette liberté, nous ne devons pas nous étonner qu'elle opère aux dépens des deux premières caractéristiques (courroie et discipline).[56] Nous pouvons obtenir les deux premières (opinion des représentés et conformisme) ou la troisième (libre adhésion), mais pas les obtenir toutes. Cette affirmation ne vaut que lorsque l'action collective s'accompagne de risques ou de coûts substantiels et permet l'action de ceux qui souhaitent que ces groupes fonctionnent à leur profit mais préfèrent ne pas encourir eux-mêmes les risques ou les coûts d'une participation (Conseil de l'Europe 1993, 192 ; Leader 1992).

L'octroi d'un monopole à l'unité de négociation confère aux syndicats une fonction d'institution de caractère quasi-public, et ils deviennent responsables d'assurer non seulement à leurs membres les meilleures conditions, mais aussi et surtout de garantir à l'employeur et à la société en général la « paix sociale ». Le syndicat devient ou acquiert alors une fonction sociale qui en fait un organisme quasi-public, ou plutôt qui lui confère des fonctions de réalisation de l'intérêt général, reconnu par les institutions étatiques et entrant alors dans la catégorie des corporations au même titre que le Barreau ou que le Collège des médecins. Mais il faut comprendre alors que l'on sacrifie au nom du bien commun ou de l'intérêt collectif de la société l'idéal de la liberté d'association. Parce qu'un organisme doté du monopole de la représentation ne peut prétendre représenter tous ses membres ; il n'en représente que la majorité ; et dans ce contexte, il ne peut prétendre respecter le caractère individuel des libertés reconnues par la Cour suprême aux dissidents de cette association. C'est là la contradiction fondamentale : si la liberté d'association est un droit individuel, son exercice ne peut plus représenter une fonction démocratique lorsque l'appartenance devient obligatoire parce que l'adhésion y est forcée et le débat contraint.

La différence entre la liberté d'association libérale et corporatiste, c'est que la libérale accepte le caractère continuellement volontaire de la participation des individus à l'association alors que la corporation rend la participation obligatoire pour pouvoir agir dans la société.[57] Les corporations ne peuvent donc prétendre à une voix démocratique dans la société.

Mais, en combinant un certain anti-syndicalisme à un refus de considérer l'intervention de l'État et en partant de l'individualisme comme centre de gravité de leur raisonnement, les juges'interdisent idéologiquement de voir concrètement la pratique étatique et donc perturbent l'analyse de la liberté d'association de considérations qui n'auraient pas dû y appartenir. M. Le Dain dans la trilogie[58] prétend qu'il n'y a pas de distinction valide entre les différents types d'organisations, et donc que les syndicats doivent être traités comme les autres. Il postule ici que c'est l'octroi de droits égaux qui assure la justice et que l'État est un arbitre neutre entre des parties égales en compétition (Panitch 1980). Cette théorie présume que l'intérêt général n'est pas plus que l'agrégat des intérêts individuels également représentés et capables de prévaloir dans la société et que le processus politique fournit une méthode équitable d'agrégation.

Il est vrai que nous sommes ici en présence d'un *continuum* qui va de l'association totalement collée aux intérêts de ses seuls membres dans un domaine précis (justifiant le départ de ceux-ci si elle s'en écartait) jusqu'à un organisme exerçant des fonctions d'intérêt général en vertu d'une mission qui lui est confiée par l'État et qui peut exiger de ses membres qu'ils se conforment à un certain nombre de règles de comportement (comme un code d'éthique et/ou des exigences de formation ou de mise à jour des connaissances, ou de comptabilité ou de transparence…) et qui en plus occupent dans un champ d'intervention sociale une position monopolistique. Pensons aux infirmières, aux travailleurs sociaux, aux avocats, médecins, etc. Cela se produit lorsque certains droits particuliers sont rattachés à l'appartenance à une association ; par exemple une association de préservation de la nature qui se voit octroyer un monopole de chasse et pêche sur un territoire donné. Se pose alors la question du niveau des obligations juridiques d'ordre public qui doivent être attachées à l'exercice de ce monopole qui signifie exclusion des non-membres de certains avantages ou privilèges. Mais à partir de quel niveau l'octroi d'un privilège public quelconque force-t-il l'organisme privé à respecter les droits des personnes privées en général au-delà du droit à l'égalité ?

La pensée libérale veut que l'État ne doive pas avoir le monopole de prise en charge de l'intérêt général ; mais elle oublie alors que les individus épars ne le peuvent seuls et que regroupés, ils exerceront parfois des fonctions publiques qui impliquent un contrôle public, puisqu'il ne s'agit plus d'une action individuelle. C'est là une autre faille du raisonnement de la Cour Suprême qu'on tente en vain de colmater en ramenant l'action collective à l'expression groupée de l'action individuelle. Cela amène une interprétation négative du critère de l'article premier de la Charte des droits qui réfère pourtant à une société non seulement libre mais aussi démocratique. C'est une interprétation bien maigrichonne de la démocratie que de la réduire à la main invisible, à l'addition concurrente des actions individuelles.

On oublie trop souvent ici que cette liberté est un continuum qui va de la liberté individuelle qui s'exerce pour des intérêts individuels restreints jusqu'à des fonctions sociales nécessaires qu'on appelle démocratie participative et qui visent le bien-être de la communauté. C'est parce qu'ils ne voient pas le caractère corporatiste des syndicats que les juges de la Cour suprême sont incapables de choix tranchés sur le caractère obligatoire de la participation syndicale,[59] alors qu'ils n'ont pas de difficulté à adhérer à l'idéologie corporatiste qui donne son monopole au Barreau ou au Collège des médecins.[60]

C'est ici qu'il faut constater le curieux retour des choses où un argument individualiste libéral vient contrer les structures pré-libérales qui ne reconnaissaient précisément pas le concept d'individu, mais étaient plutôt fondées sur le concept de statut (commerçant, artisan, apprenti, serviteur, paysan, etc.). Cela devient encore plus complexe lorsqu'il s'agit de faire entrer le concept de droit individuel dans un processus d'accréditation d'une unité syndicale.[61] Le juge Sopinka[62] a pensé s'en tirer en affirmant que l'exigence de constitution en personne morale pour se voir octroyer le droit de négocier permettait de dissocier la liberté d'association du droit de négocier.[63] Cela fut sévèrement jugé.

> Peu importe notre interprétation de ce qu'est la négociation collective ou la grève, qu'il s'agisse d'un droit individuel ou collectif ou d'un droit économique ou politique, lorsque la Cour a décidé que la Charte ne protégeait que l'exercice collectif d'activités licites pouvant être exercées individuellement ou l'exercice de droits constitutionnels, elle venait de mettre un sérieux obstacle à la protection de la liberté syndicale (Richard 2000, 235).[64]

On a ici un bel exemple des distorsions qui résultent du passage d'un ordre institutionnel donné à un autre, sans faire les transferts de concepts qui permettent à l'un de se distinguer de l'autre. Le corporatisme n'a jamais été libéral, mais la lecture corporatiste par le droit de l'Amérique du Nord de la volonté organisationnelle des travailleurs, conduit à ces aberrations et entre fatalement en contradiction avec les proclamations libérales de droits. Comment concilier le corporatisme avec la liberté ; c'est précisément l'imbroglio qu'avaient essayé de démêler les juges suprêmes dans l'affaire Lavigne[65] et les commentateurs s'entendent pour dire que l'on ne peut tirer d'opinion claire de ce jugement.

Cette dernière affaire amène la Cour suprême aux conclusions ultimes auxquelles la pousse son raisonnement libéral. En effet, le seul droit que protégerait la Charte canadienne serait celui de ne pas s'associer,[66] mais qui peut s'accompagner de l'obligation d'en assumer les coûts.

Les dispositions du droit international fournissaient pourtant tous les éléments pour résoudre ce problème puisque les principales décisions de la Cour suprême concernent les catégories de travailleurs (militaires, policiers, employés de l'État, services essentiels à la santé) qui peuvent légitimement recevoir un traitement particulier en ce qui concerne la liberté d'association. Théoriquement, c'est aux restrictions à ces seules catégories de personnes que l'on aurait dû appliquer le test de l'article premier qui exige leur compatibilité avec une « société libre et démocratique ». Mais au lieu de traiter de ces situations que le droit considère comme nécessitant des considérations spéciales tenant au caractère essentiel à la collectivité des services fournis par ces travailleurs et travailleuses, on a considéré comme valide la structure américaine actuelle du monopole syndical[67] qui contredit la liberté d'association et se rattache à l'ordre corporatiste de gestion de la société. En ne traitant que des associations qui bénéficiaient de privilèges de droit public issus des anciennes corporations, on a construit une théorie à partir des exceptions et réduit à rien la liberté d'association qui aurait dû appartenir à tous.

La démocratie et l'égalité pour bannière

Pourtant, la promotion et la défense de la qualité du lien social et de la texture démocratique devraient inciter l'État qui s'en réclame à appuyer positivement le phénomène associatif, non pas parce que la réunion des revendications particulières face à l'État constitue la démocratie, mais que cette dernière naît de la multiplication des lieux de gestion collective de tous les aspects de la vie sociale, et non seulement des aspects politiques.[68]

La distinction opérée par nos juges de la Cour suprême entre les droits civils et politiques qui entreraient dans le spectre des droits protégés d'une part et l'univers des droits économiques sociaux et culturels qui y échapperaient, d'autre part, les empêche de voir ici toutes les conséquences de l'article premier de la Charte qui fait de la démocratie le critère de l'action de l'État et de l'égalité son objectif.[69] En effet, ce n'est que si l'on reconnaît qu'un droit a été violé ou qu'une liberté a été restreinte qu'on posera la question de sa compatibilité avec une société libre et démocratique.[70] C'est d'ailleurs parce qu'ils ont fourni une interprétation si étriquée du droit d'association qu'ils n'ont pas vraiment eu à se poser la question de l'idéal démocratique. S'ils avaient reconnu un droit plus large qui aurait été susceptible d'être violé ou restreint par l'État, ils auraient dû alors se poser la question de la démocratie. C'est ici que l'on touche du doigt la conséquence restrictive du processus interprétatif imposé dès les premières affaires invoquant la Charte, où l'on ne se posait la question du respect de la démocratie que si et seulement si on constatait la violation d'un droit individuel.

C'est poser là toute la question de savoir si l'on peut non seulement interdire à l'État de mettre certains obstacles à l'action collective, mais aussi lui imputer une obligation et une responsabilité positive de maintenir les conditions d'exercice de la liberté d'association.

Cette hypothèse a été considérée, mais n'a fait l'objet que de commentaires incidents (obiter dictum), dont le principal est celui du juge

Dickson dans sa dissidence à la trilogie où, dans une remarque qu'il qualifie
« d'observation préalable », il réitère qu'une liberté n'équivaut pas à un
droit,[71]

> car un droit impose à l'autre partie une obligation correspondante de protéger
> le droit en question, alors qu'une liberté impose simplement une absence
> d'intervention ou de contrainte. Cette conception de la nature des « libertés »
> est peut-être trop étroite étant donné qu'elle ne reconnaît pas l'existence de
> certains cas où l'absence d'intervention gouvernementale est effectivement
> susceptible de porter atteinte sensiblement à la jouissance de libertés
> fondamentales (par exemple, une réglementation limitant la monopolisation
> de la presse peut être nécessaire pour assurer la liberté d'expression et de
> presse). Néanmoins, pour les fins de l'espèce, nous n'avons pas à décider si
> une « liberté » peut imposer des obligations de faire à l'État.(…). Nous ne
> sommes pas saisis en l'espèce d'une requête visant à forcer l'État à agir.[72]

Cela implique non seulement que l'État ne peut restreindre indûment le
droit d'association, mais qu'il peut être nécessaire qu'il prenne des dispositions pour promouvoir positivement l'exercice de cette liberté. Or ce sont
les principes de démocratie et d'égalité qui fondent la réflexion sur ce qui
peut être réclamé ici.

Une vision étroitement libérale de la démocratie n'est pas compatible
ici avec l'idéal d'égalité. Pour les libéraux, des intérêts organisés émergent
et se manifestent dans tous les secteurs de nos vies et représentent
adéquatement la plupart de ces secteurs ; ils y surveillent les autres groupes
et cherchent à faire prévaloir leurs exigences envers et contre la société. Le
rôle du Gouvernement est de fournir un accès aux plus efficacement
organisés et de ratifier les ententes et ajustements intervenus entre les
dirigeants en présence. Cela postule faussement une concurrence entre les
groupes qui maintiendraient entre eux une sorte d'équilibre des légitimes
revendications contradictoires,[73] justifiant l'abstention de l'État dont
l'action risquerait de rompre cet équilibre.

Or le professeur MacNeil rappelle que ces ententes et arrangements
entre groupes constituent une force stabilisatrice et conservatrice en face
des revendications pour des changements structurels (Dahl 1982).
L'inégalité des ressources des groupes permet aux plus riches de déterminer
l'ordre du jour du débat public. Il en résulte une exacerbation des inégalités
de richesse et de pouvoir.

Il est crucial de constater ici que, dans certains domaines, il ne pourra pas y avoir d'association parce qu'il n'y a pas d'égalité des parties ; l'inégalité patente exige des structures et des institutions maintenues par l'État. La pensée libérale accepte que des mesures soient prises pour assurer une libre compétition, le fameux « level playing field » que reconnaît la Cour suprême.[74]

Dans ce contexte, l'idéologie libérale n'accorde aucune protection aux groupes qui n'ait été accordée aux individus, en cohérence avec son option individualiste et la distinction entre les sphères politiques et économiques d'action sociale ; et cela parce que l'État prétend ne pas pouvoir choisir entre les différents ordres de valeur existant dans la société. Mais alors le problème naît quand une interdiction (par exemple de faire grève) faite au nom de la protection de l'intérêt général, subordonne l'impératif d'égaliser les forces de négociation des parties en présence à la nécessité de l'ordre ou de la production, violant la règle libérale de la neutralité de l'État entre les intérêts en concurrence MacNeil 1989, p. 108).[75]

Pour le juge Bastarache dans *Delisle*, si le texte et l'esprit du droit à l'égalité emportent parfois une obligation d'inclusion dans un régime législatif, il en va tout autrement des libertés individuelles prévues à l'art. 2, celui-ci n'imposant généralement à l'État qu'une obligation de non-ingérence et ne faisant appel à aucun critère comparatif. En créant un régime législatif non applicable à un groupe d'individus, l'État ne diminue pas la liberté d'association de ces individus. Ainsi, le fait de ne pas pouvoir invoquer la protection d'une loi n'a pas d'incidence sur la liberté d'association dont ces mêmes individus bénéficient en vertu de la Charte.[76] Le droit à l'égalité est ainsi réduit à la seule non-discrimination; et comme la liberté d'association n'est pas prévue ou mentionnée à l'art. 15, ils en déduisent que les obligations qui en découlent sont simplement pour l'État de s'abstenir d'intervenir.

Une des contradictions majeures de la pensée libérale vient de ce que l'État revendique le monopole de l'action juridique. Ce monopole exige donc un double mouvement ; d'abord il faut contrôler par la loi (rule of law) l'imperium de l'État et en limiter le plus possible l'action (l'État minimal), et ensuite refouler dans la sphère privée les manifestations collectives et associatives qui échappent au contrôle de l'État. Le problème en est donc un de frontière entre le public et le privé, le politique et l'individuel.

C'est ce domaine privé que la Cour suprême — les juges McIntyre et LeDain — identifie à l'économique, et que le professeur MacNeil identifie au marché :

> The emphasis on the importance of the private tends to lead to the protection and promotion of the market as the quintessential means of enabling the pursuit of private ends. The role of public institutions is to regulate the private to the minimum extent necessary to ensure efficient ordering (MacNeil 1989, 92).

Le maintien de cette distinction entre le public et le privé résulte d'une vision très limitée des droits à l'égalité : l'égalité devant la loi plutôt qu'une égalité de statut social, politique et économique, peut être garantie constitutionnellement. Une réelle égalité amènerait par ailleurs un effondrement total de la distinction public/privé. Seule une intervention de l'État dans la sphère autrefois jugée privée permettrait de réaliser la nécessaire redistribution (ibid.).

CONCLUSION

Nous pensons que l'interprétation de la Cour suprême n'a pu résister à l'analyse parce qu'elle était trop entachée de ses relations avec l'idéologie ultra-libérale et ses sources corporatistes. Il fallait s'en écarter et l'arrêt Dunmore nous en donne l'espoir. Cependant, nous n'avons que déblayé le terrain pour une réflexion plus large sur ce que devrait être positivement la reconnaissance des exigences des valeurs de démocratie et d'égalité par rapport à la liberté d'association.

Nous pouvons conclure à tout le moins que cela postule et justifie d'abord un examen très critique de toutes les mesures administratives ou réglementaires qui sont imposées aux associations et que cela pourrait justifier un ordre de revendications des associations face à l'État.

L'embêtant, c'est que la Canada s'est engagé au niveau international à reconnaître ce droit, et les actuelles propositions de modification n'en tiennent pas compte, toutes tournées qu'elles sont vers une harmonisation aux législations états-uniennes.

Mais la liberté d'association dépasse de beaucoup le champ de l'action de l'État ; elle occupe un champ plus vaste que ce à quoi le restreint le discours libéral contre l'État. C'est peut-être ce qui explique qu'il y ait si peu de décisions de justice relativement à cette liberté et qu'elles se situent presque toutes dans le domaine du droit du travail ; et plus spécifiquement des problèmes de restrictions des droits syndicaux dans la fonction publique ou para-publique.

La Cour suprême a traité jusqu'ici la liberté d'association comme une menace à la démocratie.

When viewed in light of a judicial fear of collective power in general and union power in particular, a pattern emerges: Adding an expansive definition of the negative component of freedom of association to a narrow definition of the positive component places further limitations on the exercise of collective power. A narrow definition of the positive aspect of freedom of association precludes groups from challenging legislative initiatives that restrict collective action. An expansive definition of the negative aspect of freedom of association precludes legislatures from legislating group solidarity. The combination of the two approaches provides the judiciary with a sturdy constitutional harness to rein in the exercise of collective power (Macklem 1992, 240 et 244).

La charte institue tellement le judiciaire comme entité autonome qu'elle prescrit aux tribunaux d'écarter toute preuve ou élément susceptible de « déconsidérer la justice », ce qui pourrait nous amener à interdire de faire la démonstration devant une cour de justice de ce qui est pourtant une évidence, que les tribunaux canadiens sont un instrument du politique et agissent en conséquence.

Dans la trilogie, les juges refusèrent de placer le droit de négocier et de faire la grève sous la protection de la liberté d'association « sous prétexte que les conventions collectives ne relevaient pas du domaine des droits fondamentaux, mais plutôt de celui de la politique économique. » Pourtant, pareil raisonnement n'a pas été appliqué deux ans plus tard lorsqu'il s'est agi, deux ans plus tard, d'accorder aux sociétés par actions, en vertu de la liberté d'association le droit de faire de la publicité et de fusionner (Mandel 1996).

La vision individualiste de la garantie constitutionnelle est confirmée ; le test est devenu incontournable et par la suite les visions alternatives de la liberté d'association ne furent même pas introduites dans la discussion. N'aurait-il pas été possible d'imaginer que certaines activités essentielles à certains groupes méritent une protection constitutionnelle non seulement contre mais aussi grâce à l'action du Gouvernement simplement à cause de leur centralité et leur importance par rapport à la vie sociale et démocratique ?

Nous nous étions posé la question des limites administratives et techniques imposées à la liberté d'association. Nous avons constaté que cette liberté est réduite pratiquement au rôle d'instrument pour la mise en œuvre des droits individuels et se limite à sa caricature, le droit de ne pas s'associer. Il importe maintenant de nous poser collectivement la question de savoir s'il est nécessaire de restaurer juridiquement la liberté d'association et si oui, comment ?

Notes

Je veux remercier tout spécialement Me François Roch, qui a effectué la recherche documentaire, a passé des jours à photocopier une masse de documents au lieu d'utiliser ses principales qualités de juriste et d'analyste. Ses suggestions et nos trop brèves discussions m'ont été du plus précieux secours, et s'il ne se reconnaissait pas dans mes propos, c'est que les délais de production de ce document et de nouvelles responsabilités administratives nous ont empêché d'en discuter à fond.

[1]Dunmore c. Ontario (Procureur général) 2001 CSC 94. No du greffe : 27216. 20 décembre 2001.

[2]M. le Juge en Chef Dickson, in Re Public Service Employee Relations Act ; [1987] 1 R.C.S. 313. p. 63.

[3]Art 32 de la Charte. Alors que la Charte québécoise couvre l'ensemble des rapports publics et privés, la canadienne ne couvre que l'action des Parlements et des Gouvernements central et des provinces et territoires. C'est ainsi qu'à tous nos arguments sur la liberté d'association, le juge McIntyre répond en quelque sorte : « oui, oui, ce sont des droits ; mais ce ne sont pas des droits garantis constitutionnellement contre l'action de l'État. » Dans l'arrêt Dunmore précité, le Juge Bastarache accepte que l'abstention ou l'omission d'agir de l'État puisse constituer dans certaines circonstances très précises, un « acte » de l'État susceptible de violer les droits protégés. C'est probablement dans le prochain arrêt GOSSELIN, que nous prendrons toute la mesure de la potentielle ouverture ici entrevue.

[4]C'est ici l'exigence minimale posée par les libéraux et que développe Rawls que l'égalité postule au moins l'égalité des chances et des opportunités. Notre Cour suprême ne reconnaît même pas cette exigence libérale minimale, et cela peut équivaloir à dissocier une liberté virtuelle et éthérée de ses conditions concrètes

et matérielles de réalisation. Le Juge Bastarache dans Dunmore semble être prêt à accepter ce postulat libéral.

[5]Qui comme chacun sait a remplacé « l'honnête homme » du siècle des Lumières.

[6]Au moment d'écrire ces lignes, on attendait toujours la décision dans l'affaire Dunmore, concernant les travailleurs agricoles de l'Ontario exclus de la protection des lois du travail et de ce fait incapables d'exercer leur liberté d'association. Nous reviendrons plus loin sur les éléments de cette affaire qui nous semblent importants. *Dunmore v. Ontario (Att Gen) (1997) Can. Cases on Employment Law ; 49 C.C.E.L. (2d) 5 ; affirmed (1999) 49 C.C.E.L. (2d) 29.*

[7]Cela équivaudrait à affirmer que tous les groupes dans la société considèrent que les conditions institutionnelles et juridiques de la démocratie sont pleinement remplies au Canada, ce qui est antinomique d'une conception qui fait de la démocratie un processus continu qui ne peut jamais être achevé ou pleinement accompli. (sauf pour les Hégéliens de droite qui posent la fin de l'histoire comme Fukuyama.)

[8]Rares sont les idéalistes prêts à consacrer le demi-million de dollars qu'il faut minimalement pour porter une cause jusqu'à son terme devant une Cour suprême qui de toute façon, a déjà réduit a peu les chances de gagner. Madame L'Heureux-Dubé, dans une allocution aux étudiants-es de l'Uqam disait que son salaire de juge de la Cour suprême (qui n'est pas négligeable comparativement) ne lui permettrait jamais d'assumer un recours devant celle-ci. Ceux qui ont des problèmes de liberté n'auraient pas accès aux tribunaux, précisément parce qu'il faudrait qu'ils soient organisés, et probablement regroupés en associations, pour avoir les ressources tant financières que techniques pour pouvoir y accéder. Mais on peut aussi considérer comme salutaire de tenir les tribunaux en dehors de la vie associative.

[9]D.A. Schmeiser (1964) n'y consacre que deux petites pages et W.S. Tarnopolsky (1975, 201-209) dix sept ans après l'édiction de la Déclaration, l'associe à la liberté de réunion en quelques maigres pages.

[10]Seulement deux causes à la Cour suprême : Smith & Rhuland Ltd v. R (1953) 2 S.C.R. 95 et Oil, Chemical & Atomic Wks Int. Union v. Imperial Oil Ltd ; (1963) S.C.R. 584 où le juge Martland suggère que les syndicats sont des entités légales qui ne sont pas régies par les mêmes principes que les associations volontaires.

[11]*Re Service Employees' International Union, local 204, and Broadway Manor Nursing Home*, (1984) 4 D.L.R. (4th) 231 à la p. 248 ; commenté dans Beaudouin et Ratushny (1989, 276).

[12]Broadway Manor, (1984) 13 D.L.R. (4th) 220 (Ont. C.A.) La Cour d'appel ne s'étant pas prononcée sur cette question et la permission d'en appeler ayant été refusée (1985) 8 O.A.C. 320 (S.C.C.).

[13]P.S.A.C v. Canada (1984) 11 D.L.R. (4th) 387 (C.A.F.) maintenue à 1987 S.C.R. 424. En se fondant sur une décision du Conseil privé dans une affaire de

Trinidad et Tobago : Collymore v. A.G. Trinidad and Tobago, [1969] 2 All E.R. 1207.(P.C.).

[14]On désigne sous ce nom de « TRILOGIE » les décisions rendues le même jour dans trois affaires similaires : *Renvoi relatif à la Public Service Employee Relations Act (Alb.)*, [1987] 1 R.C.S. 313 : PSERA: Reference Re Public Service Employee Relations Act (Alta) ; *AFPC c. Canada*, [1987] 1 R.C.S. 424 ; *SDGMR c. Saskatchewan*, [1987] 1 R.C.S. 460 (Retail, Wholesale and Department Store Union local 544 et al. V. Saskatchewan). On nous a suggéré de rappeler pour chacune des affaires citées de présenter brièvement les faits, ce que nous ferons dans l'annexe.

[15]Depuis la décision Dunmore (21 décembre 2001) seules les deux premières propositions sont maintenues. Le juge Bastarache au nom de la Cour quasi-unanime écarte explicitement les deux dernières. Voir le post-scriptum.

[16]*Institut professionnel de la fonction publique du Canada c. Territoires du Nord-Ouest (commissaire)*, [1990] 2 R.C.S. 367 à la p. 402 para. 112 opinion du juge Sopinka. En somme, la Cour n'a reconnu que quatre éléments de la liberté d'association : « le droit de constituer des organisations, d'y appartenir, de les maintenir et de participer à leurs activités. » LaForest in Lavigne (p. 323) résumant les conclusions précédentes qui sont reprises intégralement et réaffirmées dans l'affaire *Office canadien de la commercialisation des oeufs c. Richardson*, [1998] 3 R.C.S. 157.

[17]Bien qu'on pourrait tirer argument ici de la distinction entre légalité et légitimité.

[18]C'est la fameuse formule de la Charte québécoise : « sauf dans la mesure prévue par la loi ». Art.6, 10, 24, 44, etc.

[19]Dans les termes du juge Bastarache : « la liberté d'association n'impose au législateur qu'une obligation de non-ingérence. » para.25, dans Delisle c. Canada (sous-procureur général), [1999] 2 R.C.S. 989. p. 1019. Il évoluera…

[20]Nous nous sommes demandé s'il n'y avait pas un lien entre ce refus de reconnaître une forme de protection constitutionnelle à l'objet ou au but pour lequel on se réunit en association et cet autre fait que la législation fédérale, (Loi sur les Corporations commerciales canadiennes, S.C.1974-75-76 c. 33) a remplacé pour ce qui est des corporations commerciales à capital–actions la problématique antérieure des objets corporatifs et la théorie de l'ultra-vires. Sans cet abandon, le refus de reconnaître la protection des objets aurait pu avoir de grandes conséquences sur la gestion du capital. Le fait que cette problématique n'existait plus que pour les corporations sans but lucratif permet de faire l'hypothèse que les juges se sont sentis plus « libres » de rejeter cette problématique de l'objet.

[21]Les exemples du Golf et du club de tir du juge McIntyre dans l'affaire de l'Alberta de la Trilogie ont laissé perplexe quand aux références sociales et à la vie associative de la Cour suprême (Voir Arthurs 1988, 17) « La troisième conception prévoit que toute action qu'un individu peut licitement accomplir à titre d'individu, la liberté d'association lui permet de l'accomplir avec d'autres (…) Il

est vrai bien sûr que, selon cette conception, le champ des activités protégées par la Charte pourrait être réduit par voie de législation. (…) Toutefois, le législateur ne pourrait s'attaquer directement à l'aspect collectif de l'activité, puisqu'il serait constitutionnellement obligé de traiter également groupes et individus. Un exemple simple illustre ce point : le golf est une activité licite qui ne fait l'objet d'aucune garantie constitutionnelle. Selon la troisième conception le législateur pourrait interdire totalement de jouer au golf. Cependant, le législateur ne pourrait pas, de manière constitutionnelle, prévoir que le golf ne pourra être joué par groupes de plus de deux joueurs, car cela enfreindrait la liberté d'association garantie par la Charte. »

[22]Cette opinion est résumée par le juge Bastarache dans l'affaire Delisle de 1999 : « Le refus d'accorder un statut sous le régime d'une loi (ici exclusion des membres de la GRC de la Loi sur les relations de travail dans la fonction publique) ne viole pas la liberté d'association. Une association ne relevant pas de la loi en cause peut exister ou jouir de protections analogues en vertu de l'al. 2d) de la Charte. » (Bastarache, *Delisle*, par. 22) *Delisle* c. *Canada (Sous-procureur général)*, [1999] 2 RCS 989. Autrement dit, ce n'est pas parce que vous n'avez pas accès à la protection particulière d'une loi et de vous constituer en association sous son empire, que vous êtes privés de TOUT droit d'association. Vous pouvez vous réunir pour jouer au golf ou commenter le hockey ; dans cet univers formel, la liberté toute formelle est sauve. C'est aussi cela qui pourra être remis en cause après Dunmore.

[23]Peut-être reste-t-il l'argument reposant sur l'analogie de la liberté du travailleur de contracter qui serait la seule échappatoire juridique à ce cul-de-sac libéral. Nous reviendrons sur cet aspect de la liberté contractuelle.

[24]« Whatever one thinks of the institutional competence of the judiciary in second-guessing policy choices of legislatures, (Weiler) or of the progressive potential of Charter litigation, (Bakan, Petter) the combined effect of the labour trilogy and PIPS is a NATIONAL EMBARRASSMENT. » Macklem (1992, 240). Voir Weiler (1990), Bakan (1991) et Petter (1986).

[25]où la portion suivante de l'opinion du juge Sharpe est portée en appel : « What the applicants seek is to impose upon the province a positive duty to enhance the right of freedom of association by creating in their favour a legislative scheme conducive to the enjoyment of that important right. Certain charter rights assume, and thereby perhaps require, legislation to ensure their exercise. For example, the minority language education rights conferred by s 23 require affirmative government action for their enjoyment. *Freedom of association does not fall into this category.* Rather, it may be seen as essentially a form of negative liberty, precluding the state from violating the protected freedom. » Dunmore vs Ontario (A.G.) (1997) 49 C.C.E.L.(2d) 5 9 déc. 1997 à la p. 17. (1997) 155 D.L.R. (4th) 194. Renversée par la Cour suprême : 2001 CSC 94. No du greffe : 27216. 20 décembre 2001.

[26]*Renvoi relatif à la Public Service Employee Relations Act (Alb.)*, [1987] 1 R.C.S. 313, à la p. 397. C'est précisément ce point qui constitue l'essentiel de la décision Dunmore : Dans certaines circonstances la liberté d'association doit faire l'objet d'une intervention et d'une protection spéciale de l'État pour s'exercer.

[27]Sans entrer dans le débat philosophique, on peut rappeler ici Foucault pour qui le « sujet » est une catégorie sociale laborieusement construite dans une période assez récente et qui aurait pu être remplacée par des forces impersonnelles comme le capital de Marx, l'inconscient de Freud ou la volonté de Nietzsche. Chacune de ces forces porteuses de sens historique a une « généalogie » et une « archéologie ».

[28]idem, p. 409. Le juge Dickson lui fera remarquer en vain qu'il n'y a pas d'exercice individuel du droit de grève, et que cette position équivaut à dire qu'il n'y a pas de droit de grève au Canada. Alors on fera la distinction entre les droits fondamentaux protégés par la Charte, que l'État ne pourrait restreindre qu'en répondant au critère de l'article premier, et les autres droits qui ne sont pas fondamentaux. Le Juge Dickson lance alors un argument vicieux en direction de la droite; le droit de se marier et d'avoir des enfants n'est donc pas protégé par la Charte puisque cela ne peut se faire seul...

[29]Si l'objet poursuivi par l'association n'est pas un fondement pour garantir la liberté, il n'aurait pas dû non plus constituer un fondement pour la restreindre. Voir la remarque de Madame la juge Wilson dans Lavigne, p. 583 : « If the objects of an association cannot be invoked to advance the constitutional claims of unions; then neither, it seems to me, can they be invoked in order to undermine them. » Or LaForest dit clairement que la cotisation obligatoire ne peut être utilisée à des fins « That are beyond the immmediate concerns of the bargaining unit. » Lavigne, p. 624.

[30]Il se réfère alors à l'Affaire International Brotherhood of Teamsters v. Thérien [1960] S.C.R. 265 : « It is ironic that unions have come to be treated as legal persons in key cases where the issue was union liability for acts of individuals. » (MacNeil 1989, 88) Il note que même sans formellement détenir la personnalité juridique, l'imputation massive de droits statutaires et l'imposition de nombreux devoirs aux syndicats finissent par en faire pratiquement des personnes juridiques.

[31]Madame l'Heureux-Dubé est claire sur cette question dans *Institut professionnel de la Fonction publique du Canada* c. *Territoires du Nord-Ouest (Commissaire)*, [1990] 2 R.C.S. 367 : « Selon la majorité dans cet arrêt [Renvoi relatif à la Public Service Employee Relations Act (Alb.), [1987] 1 R.C.S. 313], les *activités* que les individus désirent exercer en commun ne sont pas elles-mêmes protégées par l'al. 2d). Seul le fait de se *joindre à d'autres* est protégé. » Et c'est cette protection qui sans conférer de droit, impose des obligations.

[32]Dans l'affaire Lavigne, seulement quatre des sept juges se prononcent en ce sens ; LaForest appuyé par Sopinka, Gonthier et McLachlin : « La reconnaissance de la liberté de l'individu de ne pas s'associer est la contrepartie nécessaire d'une association constructive conforme aux idéaux démocratiques (...) Il est évident que la liberté d'association qui ne comporterait pas la liberté de ne pas

être forcé de s'associer ne serait pas véritablement une « liberté » au sens de la Charte. Lavigne, pp. 317-318.

[33]*Renvoi relatif à la Public Service Employee Relations Act (Alb.)*, [1987] 1 R.C.S. 313 à la p. 391.

[34]Dans l'arrêt Commercialisation des oeufs, les juges Iacobucci et Bastarache insistent : « Freedom of expression protects only the associational aspect of activities and not the activity itself. » Donc la liberté d'expression n'est pas protégée par 2d., et de plus, la liberté d'expression ici n'est qu'accessoire à la commercialisation des oeufs. *Office canadien de la commercialisation des oeufs c. Richardson, [1998] 3 R.C.S. 157.*

[35]Dans l'affaire du renvoi de l'Alberta (PSERA), le juge McIntyre cite les revues de droit de Harvard, Yale et de l'Université de Pensylvanie : Emerson, (Emerson, Thomas I. Emerson dans « Freedom of Association and Freedom of Expression », 74 Yale L.J. 1 (1964), à la p. 1 : Abernathy : « The Right of Assembly and Association » (1961), à la p. 242 ; Summers, Clyde W. : « Freedom of Association and Compulsory Unionism in Sweden and the United States », 112 U. Pa. L.R. 647, à la p. 647 (1964) : et Raggi, Reena : « An Independent Right to Freedom of Association », 12 Harv. C.R.-C.L. Rev. 1 (1977), et plusieurs affaires dont : Roberts c. United States Jaycees, 468 U.S. 609 (1984), le juge Brennan.

[36]NAACP v. Alabama, Evoquant Cramp v. Board of Public Instruction, Elfbrandt v. Russell, Keyishian v. Board of Regents, et United States v. Robel, le juge Brennan dans l'affaire Communist Party of Indiana v. Whitcomb a associé la liberté d'association à la liberté d'opinion et d'expression. D'où l'étrange problématique de l'imposition du conformisme idéologique qui devient un critère essentiel de la liberté d'association dans l'affaire Lavigne.

[37](Alta Ref. Loc. cit. p. 324).

[38]Bien que le législateur ait connu alors l'effet des décisions de la trilogie et « Institut professionnel » qui sont antérieures à la nouvelle mouture du Code civil du Québec.

[39]Code civil du Québec, art. 2230 pour les sociétés et art. 2277 pour les associations. Est-il inutile d'espérer que notre Cour suprême considère le Code civil non pas comme une loi particulière mais comme porteur de principes pouvant servir, comme le common law, de source générale d'interprétation du droit canadien ? Penser autrement équivaut à interpréter le Code civil à la lumière du Common Law, ce qui constituerait un impérialisme juridique inconstitutionnel. Le Code civil du Québec, à titre de législation particulière d'une province, est soumis à la Charte. Il pourrait en résulter que le Code civil, un élément du caractère distinct du Québec dans les propositions de Meech Lake ou de Charlettown, et dans une loi fédérale, dépende en fait de l'interprétation de la Cour suprême et du Common Law d'Angleterre. Il est cependant peu probable que l'attitude canadienne imbue de la superbe du colonialisme britannique, accepte que l'on puisse jauger ses libertés à l'aune de l'histoire des colonisés. Quoiqu'il en soit, le fait que la Cour suprême ignore ici l'action d'un législateur souverain ne plaide pas dans le

sens de son ouverture d'esprit, et il nous a toujours semblé que l'Assemblée nationale du Québec jouissait d'une légitimité démocratique plus grande que la Cour suprême du Canada.

[40]Nous n'avons pas l'intention de faire ici un exposé sur les dispositions du Code civil spécifiques aux associations, mais il faut savoir qu'indépendamment de ce que l'on dira du caractère individuel du droit, le regroupement de personne même privé de la personnalité juridique, possède quand même la possibilité d'agir en qualité de groupe. La preuve en est que l'art. 2271 du Code civil reconnaît que l'association a des droits et des activités (que le membre individuel ne doit pas indûment entraver art.2273 alinéa 2 C.civ) et qui sont distincts des droits d'agir des autres membres ; qu'elle peut prendre des décisions collectives (art. 2272) qui ne sont pas la simple addition de décisions individuelles, mais résultent de l'application de procédures décidées à la majorité mais qui peuvent ensuite ne pas impliquer la majorité : « sauf stipulation contraire dudit contrat. » (art.2272 alinéa 2 C.c.)

[41]Voir Edmonton Journal v. Alberta (A.G.)1989 2 S.C.R. 1326, qui étend la protection de la liberté d'expression aux corporations « et autres business entities ».

[42]Ford c. Québec; [1988] 2 RCS 712, 764 ; « Alors que le Québec avait conçu ses lois linguistiques pour promouvoir de façon assez explicite les intérêts sociaux, économiques et politiques [et culturels] d'un peuple bien réel qui se définissait entre autres par sa langue, la judiciarisation a transformé la question en une chose assez différente : le droit d'individus abstraits et hypothétiques de choisir l'une ou l'autre langue officielle et de recevoir des services dans cette langue. Ainsi une lutte concrète qui opposait des forces inégales fut transformée en une lutte de droits individuels, c'est-à-dire de droits d'identités abstraites, égales et libres, ce qui n'existe que dans l'esprit des juges » (Mandel 1996, iv).

[43]Hunter v. Southam Inc. [1984] 2 S.C.R. 145. Où l'on confirma la décision du juge de première instance qui avait accordé cette protection « To all human beings and all entities that are capable of enjoying the benefit of security against unreasonable search. » ; Juge CAVANAGH Alta Q.B., Southam Inc. v. Hunter, 1982, 136 D.L.R. (3d) 133, à la p. 141.

[44]C'était précisément la question posée dans l'affaire Institut professionnel où la constitution en corporation, nécessaire à la reconnaissance juridique du syndicat comme seul agent négociateur avait été refusée au groupe d'infirmières des Territoires du Nord-Ouest.

[45]Plutôt que de nous creuser la tête pour trouver une catégorisation univoque selon les mêmes catégories de ces différents sujets, contentons-nous ici de signaler le caractère arbitraire et contestable des catégories « déficiences mentales » et « race ». Ce mode d'interdiction fait reposer sur les motifs erronés de celui qui discrimine la définition de la catégorie ; c'est parce que le discriminateur est raciste qu'on invoque ici le concept de race et non parce que la race correspond à une réalité objective. Nous croyons que la même logique s'applique aussi à l'ethnie,

la nation, la religion et probablement aussi au sexe. Il s'agit d'une sélection par le violateur du droit de caractéristiques qui ne correspondent pas nécessairement à des éléments objectifs.

[46]Baudouin dans Delisle c. Canada (Sous-procureur général) [1997] R.J.Q. 386 ; (C.A. Québec) à la p. 391 et 399.

[47]repris in Richard (2000, 236).

[48]*AFPC c. Canada*, [1987] 1 R.C.S. 424, à la p. 454.

[49]Sans vouloir ergoter, on peut rappeler que la juge McLachlin, maintenant devenue juge en chef, a soutenu que la liberté contractuelle pouvait justifier que soient écartées des dispositions législatives d'ordre public. Voir, Lefebvre c. HOJ Industries et Machtinger c. HOJ Industries ; 14 mai 1992. (1992) 1 R.C.S. 986.

[50]Si la liberté d'association est simplement le droit de poursuivre les autres libertés fondamentales avec d'autres, alors l'énoncé de la Charte est superfétatoire, parce que tous avaient ce droit de toute façon, une liberté fondamentale peut être exercée seule ou avec d'autres. Il n'était pas nécessaire d'en faire mention à la Charte. Si on en a fait un alinéa spécial, distinct du droit de réunion pacifique, il aurait fallu que la Cour suprême lui donne une interprétation autonome. Comme elle ne l'a pas fait, le Constituant aurait bégayé, parlé pour ne rien dire… Hypothèse que les règles d'interprétation nous interdisent de considérer, encore moins d'appuyer. C'est d'ailleurs ce que fait la juge Mclachlin dans l'affaire Lavigne encore (p. 342) lorsqu'elle s'interroge sur le caractère fondamental pourtant affirmé de cette liberté, pour statuer que si l'activité a pour effet d'associer l'individu à des idées et des valeurs auxquelles il ne souscrit pas volontairement, alors les principes de la liberté d'association doivent céder le pas à ceux de la liberté d'opinion … confirmant ainsi le caractère ancillaire et instrumentaire conféré par cette interprétation au droit d'association.

[51]Il est à noter ici que les reliquats de la loi de mainmorte, hérités de la Coutume de Paris, ne disparaîtront du Code civil du Bas-Canada et de la législation québécoise qu'avec la réforme de 1994. Il en reste encore une trace avec l'exigence réglementaire faite aux requérants de lettres patentes en vertu de la troisième partie de la Loi sur les Compagnies du Québec (L.Q. ch C-38) d'indiquer le maximum des biens immeubles que pourra détenir la corporation à naître et certaines exigences concernant la détention d'immeubles par les corporations étrangères.

[52]On sait que la Loi des relations ouvrières du Québec (1944, S.R.Q. 162A) était copiée des lois corporatistes du régime Pétain en France. Mais comme le décret C.P. 1003 promulgé la même année au Canada, cette loi harmonisait aussi la situation syndicale aux dispositions américaines du Wagner Act de 1935, qui mettait en œuvre les mêmes références organisationnelles corporatistes dont la caractéristique est pour l'État de reconnaître des privilèges de réglementation et de discipline d'une secteur donné de la vie sociale à une organisation au nom et à la place de l'État. En Amérique du Nord, on a accordé le monopole de la représentation et des pouvoirs de discipline des travailleurs et même d'exclusion

du travail (close shop) aux associations accréditées par l'État pour négocier collectivement.

[53]dans l'affaire *Sigurdur A. Sigurjónsson v. Iceland* ; (1993) affaire n°24/1992/369/443. 30 juin 1993.

[54]Il en va ainsi de l'Ordre des médecins belge dont les fonctions d'intérêt public ont permis de décréter que l'appartenance obligatoire ne violait pas l'article 11 du Traité sur la libre appartenance à une association, alors que dans le cas d'une association de chauffeurs de taxis, l'appartenance obligatoire constituait une telle violation (affaire : Sigurdur A Sigurjonsson c. Islande (1993) affaire n°24/1992/369/443, par. 35. 30 juin 1993.

[55]J.S. Mills (1904, ch. 11, para. 12) a déjà démontré que les individus qui prennent des risques importants dans leurs organisations pour faire triompher un point de vue qui profitera à l'ensemble du groupe dans la société sont en droit de s'attendre que ceux qui en profiteront soient forcés d'appuyer cette lutte (Voir le cas des luttes syndicales qui profitent même aux jaunes ; et la solution apportée par la formule Rand, qui permet de ne pas être membre, mais ne dispense pas de payer la cotisation) (Voir Olson 1965, 2-55). Leader (in Conseil de l'Europe 1993) démontre que la loi qui confère aux syndiqués le droit absolu de se dissocier de la grève sans crainte de représailles a pour effet de rendre aléatoire la démocratie syndicale parce que ceux qui sont en désaccord ne prendront plus le risque d'aller débattre démocratiquement de leur point de vue sachant qu'ils n'ont que peu à perdre et tout à gagner en restant coi (p. 190). Considérons un groupe de salariés qui n'est pas d'accord avec un autre groupe sur l'opportunité d'une grève : pour peser sur l'issue, il devra participer aux débats et faire connaître son point de vue pour faire changer d'avis certains collègues ; l'expérience de la confrontation pourra se révéler pénible. Supposons maintenant que les adversaires de la grève n'aient rien à craindre d'une décision du groupe du fait qu'ils ne risquent aucune sanction s'ils continuent à travailler ; ils seront alors moins motivés à manifester leur opposition. En conséquence, la décision que pourrait prendre ensuite la majorité en faveur de la grève serait proportionnellement moins représentative des sentiments réels de l'ensemble des salariés. En fait la majorité de ceux qui auront voté la grève pourra fort bien être constituée par un nombre de personnes moins élevé que la majorité effective qui est en fait hostile à la grève, mais qui préférera peut-être éviter de s'imposer les désagréments d'une confrontation avec les collègues plus militants ou même de se donner la peine de voter (Leader in Conseil de l'Europe 1993, 191).

[56]C'est le sens de la remarque du juge Cory dans sa dissidence : « Partout où des personnes travaillent pour gagner leur vie, le droit d'association a une importance énorme. Le salaire et les conditions de travail auront toujours une importance vitale pour un employé. Il s'ensuit que pour un employé, le droit de choisir le groupe ou l'association qui négociera pour son compte ce salaire et ces conditions de travail a une importance fondamentale. L'association jouera un rôle très important dans à peu près tous les aspects de la vie de l'employé dans son lieu de

travail, en faisant fonction de conseiller, de porte-parole dans les négociations et de rempart contre les actes illicites de l'employeur. Pour que les négociations collectives donnent des résultats, les employés doivent avoir confiance en leurs représentants. Cette confiance n'existera pas si l'employé à titre individuel n'est pas en mesure de choisir l'association. » (Cory, dissident, *Institut professionnel de la Fonction publique du Canada* c. *Territoires du Nord-Ouest (Commissaire)*, [1990] 2 R.C.S. 367.

[57]C'est pourquoi le Barreau par exemple ne peut prétendre agir et parler au nom de tous ses membres ; parce que ceux qui sont en désaccord ne peuvent pas supporter les coûts que représente pour le dissident le fait de quitter le Barreau.

[58]Renvoi relatif à la Public Service Employee Relations Act (Alb.), [1987] 1 R.C.S. 313 p. 390.

[59]*Lavigne* c. *Syndicat des employés de la fonction publique de l'Ontario*, [1991] 2 R.C.S. 211.

[60]Ce qui n'a pas semblé poser de problèmes dans l'affaire Black même si la décision reposait plutôt sur le liberté de circulation que sur la liberté d'association. *Black c. Law society of Alberta*, [1989] 1 R.C.S. 591.

[61]Le juge Fish dans l'affaire Delisle refuse d'inclure dans la liberté d'association le droit à l'accréditation parce que ce dernier ne peut pas être un droit individuel. Selon le juge Fish de la Cour d'appel du Québec, (1997) R.J.Q. 386 (p. 399), ce n'est pas le droit individuel d'association qui est ici violé, mais le droit à l'accréditation qui oblige l'employeur à négocier de bonne foi. Ce que les policiers recherchaient, ce n'est pas de s'associer, mais d'obtenir cette accréditation. Or comme l'accréditation n'est pas un droit individuel, il n'est pas couvert par la liberté d'association. Le juge Baudouin dissident considérant que l'interdiction empêchait effectivement la poursuite aussi de tout objectif licite autre que la négociation, (p. 391) suggère que la Trilogie « n'avait pas complètement fermé la porte à toute protection constitutionnelle du droit de libre association par syndicalisation. » La décision Delisle de la Cour suprême viendra fermer plus hermétiquement cette porte où Baudouin avait voulu glisser son pied. La décision Delisle pose donc que l'on n'a pas de droit à une forme particulière d'association ; et que si une seule forme est disponible, alors la liberté d'association est satisfaite. L'efficace de l'association n'est donc pas déterminant pour la réalisation de la liberté. Si pour la réalisation d'un objectif, l'association est nécessairement un moyen, celui-ci sera considéré comme réalisé si une forme quelconque d'association existe, indépendamment du fait que cette forme ne donne pas ouverture à la possibilité d'accomplir le but qu'a pu se fixer cette association.

[62]*Institut professionnel de la fonction publique du Canada* c. *Territoires du Nord-Ouest (commissaire)*, [1990] 2 R.C.S. 367 ; p. 405 ; où la Cour suprême reconnaît valide une loi obligeant d'être constitué en personne morale pour négocier collectivement au nom de ses membres. Il ne s'agirait pas là d'une violation de la liberté d'association. Cette loi « fournit au Gouvernement la possibilité de refuser, pour toutes les fins de la négociation collective, l'existence même à l'association

choisie par les employés pour négocier en leur nom » (p. 381.) et de donner l'exemple d'hockeyeurs qui se verraient autorisés à former une association mais interdire de jouer au hockey. Le droit ne serait pas violé puisqu'il pourrait continuer à parler en association de ce sport et aller voir les autres jouer. Le motif de restriction serait alors que ce sport est dangereux et que contrairement au ridicule, il peut tuer parfois.

[63]On pourrait s'associer à volonté, mais pour négocier, il faudra respecter les conditions posées qui ne violent pas la liberté d'association, mais ouvrent la porte au privilège de la négociation et du monopole de la représentation. Le monopole n'a aucun effet sur l'existence d'une association ou sur la capacité d'une personne d'y adhérer ; il empêche seulement la constitution en personne morale ou l'accréditation. On a donc opéré ici une distinction fondamentale entre l'existence et les activités d'une association. Voir Richard (2000, 240).

[64]Mais cette opinion est largement partagée : « PIPS represents the final curtain on the constitutional garantee of freedom of association in the context of work. Unless there is a major theorical reversal, the combined effect of the labour trilogie and PIPS is to strip the constitutional garantee of freedom of association of any substantive meaning in the context of union power. » Macklem (1992, 238). « The fact that the people who form the association (the union) may still meet together without interference from the state has no meaning if this association cannot be recognized under the relevant labour legislation. » CORY, dissident in PIPS, p. 23. « The whole idea and existence of a union is to foster social solidarity and to establish a collective presence that can overcome workers' vulnerability to the greater power of the employers. Limiting union rights to those that can be exercised by members individually is to subvert the whole raison d'être of unions. » Hutchinson et Petter (1988, 296. Cité par Macklem 1992).

[65]*Lavigne c. Syndicat des employés de la fonction publique de l'Ontario*, [1991] 2 R.C.S. 211.

[66]C'est la mince majorité (quatre sur sept sur ce point) des juges McLachlin, LaForest, Sopinka et Gonthier. C'était la moindre des choses puisque l'article 20(2) de la Déclaration universelle des droits de l'Homme stipule expressément que « Nul ne peut être obligé de faire partie d'une association. »

[67]Le juge Martland avait suggéré en 1963 que les syndicats sont des entités légales qui ne sont pas régies par les mêmes principes que les associations volontaires. Oil, Chemical & Atomic Wks Int. Union v. Imperial Oil Ltd ; (1963) S.C.R. 584.

[68]Etherington note que deux motifs peuvent fonder les libertés de l'article 2 ; soit la défense de l'intégrité de l'individu face à l'État, soit d'autre part la protection du processus politique démocratique. Si la jurisprudence récente insiste sur l'individu, la défense de la démocratie correspond plus à la jurisprudence antérieure à la Charte qui faisait dériver les droits du Préambule du BNA Act 1867, parce qu'ils sont nécessaires au maintien d'un régime parlementaire démocratique :

Ref.Re Alberta Legislation [1938] S.C.R. 10; Saumur v.Ville de Québec : [1953] 2 S.C.R. 299; Switzman v. Elbing [1957] S.C.R. 285.

[69]Ce refus est clairement exprimé par le juge McIntyre dans le Renvoi relatif à l'Alberta : « Cette conclusion est parfaitement compatible avec l'esprit général de la Charte qui confère des droits et des libertés aux individus mais qui, sous réserve de quelques exceptions déjà mentionnées, ne confère pas de droits collectifs. On constatera aussi que la Charte, sauf peut-être l'al.6(2)b) (le droit de gagner sa vie dans toute province) et le par.6(4) ne s'intéresse pas aux droits économiques. »

[70]La démonstration de ce point de vue est faite dans l'arrêt *Office canadien de la commercialisation des oeufs c. Richardson*, [1998] 3 R.C.S. 157 où pour ne pas avoir à se prononcer sur l'aspect démocratique ou politique de la violation d'un droit, il suffit aux juges de considérer que la législation ne viole pas le droit fondamental garanti par la Charte, en considérant tout simplement que la disposition qui écartait les producteurs d'œufs du Nord-Ouest canadien des quotas de production d'œufs ne violait ni la liberté d'établissement et de circulation, ni la liberté d'association. On n'avait plus alors à se demander si cela était raisonnable dans une société libre et démocratique.

[71]Ces différences entre droits et libertés étaient exposées dans Ford, c Québec, [1988] 2 S.C.R 712, pp. 750-754.

[72]M le juge en chef Dickson, appuyé en cela par Madame le juge Wilson, dans le renvoi relatif à l'Alberta de la trilogie [1987] 1 R.C.S. 313. Malheureusement pour nous, ils prendront tous les deux leur retraite après avoir baissé pavillon pour se rallier à la majorité dans l'affaire de l'Institut professionnel [1990] 2 R.C.S. 367 ; où en rendant l'opinion unanime, le Juge LaForest se sent obligé de leur adresser le coup de chapeau en forme de coup de massue suivant : « Cela ne revient pas toutefois à nier l'intérêt collectif que comporte la liberté d'association. Cet intérêt pourrait être celui de la société en général dans les contributions à des causes politiques, économiques, sociales et culturelles qui ne sont rendues possibles que si les *individus* sont libres de travailler de concert. De plus, il est évident qu'il existe un intérêt collectif dans le maintien de la démocratie dont l'un des éléments essentiel est l'activité collective. La question est donc de savoir si la protection de cet intérêt collectif et de *l'intérêt individuel préexistant* exige que la liberté de ne pas être forcé de s'associer soit reconnue en vertu de l'al.2d) de la Charte. »

[73]Cette opinion est magistralement décrite dans l'article de MacNeil (1989, 98).

[74]« L'analyse contextuelle fondée sur la Charte doit également tenir compte de la nécessité traditionnelle de l'intervention gouvernementale pour rendre exécutoires les droits d'association des travailleurs » Madame l'Heureux-Dubé, *Delisle*, par. 6. *Delisle c. Canada (Sous-procureur général)*, [1999] 2 RCS 989.

[75]On peut rappeler ici que le juge LeDain dans la trilogie adopte la version politique libérale où la liberté d'association sert à la réalisation des autres libertés fondamentales. C'est ainsi que l'État en est amené à protéger certaines activités

productives au détriment d'autres (travail) en violation de la neutralité au nom de laquelle il refuse de favoriser l'association. Voir le Renvoi Alberta, p. 391 et sq. dont on peut résumer ainsi la position : Agir dans ce domaine du travail amènerait la Cour dans le champ politique et économique pour lequel elle n'est pas qualifiée. [76]Bastarache déjà cité, in *Delisle*, para. 25 *Delisle c.Canada* , [1999] 2 RCS 989, p. 1019.

Références

Arthurs, H.W. 1988. « The Right to Golf: Reflections on the Future of Workers, Unions and the Rest of Us Under the Charter », *Queen's L.J.* 13 :17.

Bakan, J. 1991. « Constitutional Interpretation and Social Change : You Can't Always Get What You Want (Nor What You Need) », *Can. Bar Rev.* 70 :307.

Beaudouin, G.A. et E. Ratushny. 1989. *Charte canadienne des droits et libertés*, 2e éd. Montréal : Wilson & Lafleur.

Bendel, M. 1986. « La liberté d'association dans l'optique de la Charte canadienne des drois et libertés », in *Perspectives canadiennes et européennes des droits de la personne*, éd. D. Turp et G.A. Beaudouin. Cowansville : Yvon Blais.

Brun, H. et G. Tremblay. 1997. *Droit constitutionnel*, 3e éd. Cowansville : Yvon Blais.

Carter, D.A. 1988. « Canadian Labour Relations Under the Charter: Exploring the Implications », *R.I.* 43 (2) :305.

Cavalluzzo, P.J.J. 1986. « Freedom of Association and the Right to Bargain Collectively », in *Litigating the Values of a Nation: The Canadian Charter of Rights and Freedoms,* éd. J.M. Weiler et R.M. Elliot. Toronto : Carswell.

Conseil de l'Europe. 1993. « Liberté d'Association », Actes d'un séminaire organisé à Reykjavik, Islande, 26-28 août.

Dahl, R.A. 1982. *Dilemmas of Pluralist Democracy: Autonomy vs. Control.* New Haven : Yale University Press.

David, Mme A. 1993. « Liberté d'Association », Actes d'un séminaire organisé à Reykjavik, Islande, 26-28 août 1993.

Fecteau, J.-M. 1990. *L'État, la Révolution française et l'Italie.* « Le pouvoir du nombre » colloque AHHIP, Milan, 1989. Aix-Marseilles : Press Univ.

Foner, E. 1998. *The Story of American Freedom.* New York : W.W. Norton & Co.

Foster, E. 1990. « Corporation and Constitutional Guarantees », *C. de D.* 31 :1125.

Garet, R. 1983. « Communality and Existence: The Rights of Groups », *S.Cal.L.Rev.* 56 :1001.

Hutchinson, A. et A. Petter. 1988. « Private Rights/Public Wrongs: The Liberal Lie of the Charter », *U.T.L.J.* 38 :278. Cité par Macklem 1992.

Leader, S. 1992. *Freedom of Association.* New Haven : Yale University Press.

Lowi, T. 1979. *The End of Liberalism*, 2e éd. New York : W.W. Norton & Co. Cité par MacNeil (1989, p. 101).

Macklem, P.A. 1992. « Developments in Employment Law: The 1990–91 Term », *S.C.L.R.* 3 (2) :227.

MacNeil, M.A. 1989. « Courts and Liberal Ideology: An Analysis of the Application of the Charter to Some Labour Law Issues », *McGill Law Journal* 34 :86.

Magnet, J. 1986. « Collective Rights, Cultural Autonomy and the Canadian State », *McGill Law Journal* 32 :170.

Mandel, M. 1996. *La charte canadienne des droits et libertés et la judiciarisation du politique au Canada.* Traduit de l'anglais. Boréal : Montréal.

Mills, J.S. 1904. *Principles of Political Economy*, Livre V. Londres : Longmans.

Olson, M. 1965. *The Logic of Collective Action.* Cambridge : Harvard University Press.

Panitch, L. 1980. « Recent Theorization of Corporatism: Reflexion on a Growth Industry », *British Journal of Sociology* 31 (2) :159.

Petter, A. 1986. « The Politics of the Charter », *Supreme Court L.R.* 8 :473.

Rhéaume, D. 1988. « Individuals, Groups, and Rights to Public Goods », *U.T.L.J.* 38 :1.

Richard, M.-J. 2000. « La liberté d'association sous l'alinéa 2d) de la Charte canadienne des droits et libertés dans le contexte des relations de travail », *Revue d'études juridiques* 6 :213-251.

Rousseau, J.-J. 1972. *Du contrat social.* Paris : Garnier-Flammarion.

Schmeiser, D.A. 1964. *Civil Liberties in Canada.* London : Oxford University Press.

Tarnopolsky, W.S. 1975. *The Canadian Bill of Rights*, 2e éd. Toronto : MacMillan.

Weiler, J. 1990. « The Charter at Work: Reflexions on the Constitutionalizing of Labour and Employment Law », *U.T.L.J.* 40 :17.

Annexe

NOTE EN FORME DE POST-SCRIPTUM

Cette conclusion a été rédigée avant que la Cour suprême ne rende les deux jugements pendants qui posent encore une fois la question de la liberté d'association.

Ces décisions ont été rendues le 19 octobre et 20 décembre 2001.

Advance Cutting : R. c. Advance Cutting & Coring Ltd.
: 2001 CSC 70. No du greffe : 26664. : 19 octobre 2001.

Cette décision concerne la constitutionnalité de la disposition de la loi québécoise sur l'industrie de la construction exigeant que les travailleurs deviennent membres de l'un des groupes syndicaux énumérés pour obtenir des certificats de compétence leur permettant de travailler.

La décision est ambiguë : quatre juges sont dissidents : pour les McLachlin, Major, Bastarache et Binnie, cette loi viole la liberté négative reconnue à la Charte de ne pas s'associer et n'est pas justifiée dans une société libre et démocratique.

Les cinq autres formant la majorité se divisent sur les motifs. Pour le juge l'Heureux-Dubé, la Charte ne reconnaissant pas la liberté négative de ne pas s'associer, les contraintes ici imposées se justifient. Le juge Iacobucci se rallie à la majorité en notant : « cette loi porte atteinte aux droits à la liberté des appelants. Toutefois, la loi est justifiée en vertu de l'article premier de la Charte. La Loi sur la construction a été adoptée dans un contexte historique unique et complexe et a servi à favoriser des objectifs sociaux et économiques distincts qui étaient, et demeurent, urgents et réels.

Le juge LeBel après s'être livré à un long exposé de l'historique non seulement législatif, mais de la réception sociale de cette loi, écrit les motifs pour les juges Gonthier, Arbour, dans ces termes :

> Il faut laisser au processus politique le soin de régler la question en jeu dans le pourvoi. Une telle solution conserve l'équilibre dans l'application de la

Charte et laisse la gestion légale des relations du travail au Parlement et aux législatures de même qu'aux parties à la convention collective. La gestion des relations du travail exige un exercice délicat de conciliation des valeurs et intérêts divergents. Les considérations politiques, sociales et économiques pertinentes débordent largement du domaine d'expertise des tribunaux. Cette démarche restrictive et prudente en matière d'intervention des tribunaux dans le domaine des relations du travail reflète une bonne compréhension des fonctions des tribunaux et de celles des législatures. Dans l'application de la Charte, elle évite également que tout genre d'action gouvernementale visant la protection des droits de la personne soit considéré, à première vue, comme une violation de la Charte qui doit être justifiée aux termes de l'article premier.

Même si elle avait limité le droit de non-association garanti par l'al. 2d), la loi serait justifiée aux termes de l'article premier de la Charte. Le législateur a droit à un degré de latitude et de retenue important, mais pas absolu, pour régler les questions de politique sociale et économique. Les tribunaux doivent se garder de se substituer, après coup, aux législateurs relativement à leurs choix politiques controversés et complexes. La jurisprudence reconnaît qu'il vaut généralement mieux laisser au processus politique le soin d'élaborer les principes directeurs en matière de législation dans le domaine des relations du travail. Les limites en cause sont prescrites par une loi. La loi porte également sur un objet urgent et réel. L'historique de la loi démontre que l'Assemblée nationale du Québec a tenté de régler des problèmes qui étaient devenus une question sociale et économique urgente, ce qui a donné lieu, pendant des années, à des essais successifs qui se poursuivent d'ailleurs toujours.

En somme, pour quatre des juges, l'obligation d'appartenir à un syndicat, considérée comme le caractère « négatif » de la liberté d'association existe bien dans la Charte, mais des considérations historiques et politiques font que la Cour doit céder le pas pour éviter que ne se reproduisent les violences et problèmes sociaux qui ont marqué les trente dernières années d'expérience de gestion politique de ce secteur du travail et qui présentent actuellement un calme relatif. Pour la Cour, une application stricte de la Charte pourrait dégénérer en de nouveaux troubles sociaux.

Par un processus difficile d'expérimentation législative, le législateur a rétabli dans une certaine mesure la paix et la démocratie syndicale dans l'industrie de la construction du Québec. La Cour est appelée à déterminer la validité d'un régime législatif complexe né d'une succession de tentatives, d'échecs et de déceptions. Au début du présent litige, cette loi représentait l'aboutissement d'environ 30 ans de travail législatif visant à créer un régime approprié de négociation collective dans l'industrie. Il faut faire preuve de beaucoup de retenue envers la législature, compte tenu des difficultés inhérentes à l'art de gouverner dans un environnement traditionnellement aussi conflictuel. L'intervention de la Cour risquerait d'affecter des composantes délicates d'un régime soigneusement équilibré et n'est pas justifiée dans les circonstances de la présente affaire.

Les principes énoncés dans la jurisprudence de la Cour sont donc maintenus, mais on accepte qu'ils sont inapplicables en l'occurrence. Mais c'est surtout l'individualisme libéral qui est ici écarté au profit des exigences politiques de gestion du social.

C'est dans l'affaire Dunmore suivante que la Cour renversera son analyse et posera, avec de multiples précautions et distinguo, les assises d'une nouvelle lecture de la liberté d'association. Cela est d'autant plus important que la décision emporte l'adhésion de tous sauf le juge Major, et l'habituelle décision concurrente de madame L'Heureux-Dubé.

Dunmore c. Ontario (Procureur général)
2001 CSC 94. No du greffe : 27216. 20 décembre 2001.

Cette affaire concerne la suppression par le Gouvernement Harris du droit à la syndicalisation des travailleurs agricoles que leur avait accordé le Gouvernement Rae. Il est à noter que le hasard (!) faisant bien les choses, la Cour a diffusé son jugement attendu depuis septembre après la démission du premier Ministre Harris (annoncée en décembre.)

C'est le Juge Bastarache qui rédige les motifs expliquant pourquoi il abandonne en partie l'analyse qu'il avait si ardemment défendue dans l'affaire Delisle. On reconnait dans ce jugement une certaine obligation de l'État d'agir pour protéger le liberté d'association et que son abstention peut parfois équivaloir à une négation des droits proclamés dans la Charte. Certes, ce revirement est entouré de multiples précautions oratoires; mais l'admission de fait que la position antérieure était devenue intenable n'en est pas moins réelle.

> Généralement, la Charte n'oblige pas l'État à prendre des mesures positives pour préserver et faciliter l'exercice de libertés fondamentales. Il n'existe pas de droit constitutionnel à la protection légale comme tel. Toutefois

l'histoire a montré, et les législateurs canadiens ont reconnu, qu'une attitude de retenue de la part du gouvernement dans le domaine des relations de travail expose la plupart des travailleurs non seulement à diverses pratiques déloyales de travail, mais peut aussi engager leur responsabilité juridique en common law pour coalition ou restriction du commerce. Dans ce contexte très particulier, pour que la liberté syndicale ait un sens, l'al. 2d) de **la Charte peut imposer à l'État l'obligation positive d'étendre la protection légale à des groupes non protégés.** La distinction entre obligations positives et négatives de l'État doit être nuancée dans le contexte des relations de travail, en ce sens que *l'exclusion des travailleurs agricoles de l'application d'un régime de protection contribue substantiellement à la violation de libertés protégées.*

Le pas est considérable et le revirement significatif. La porte est maintenant ouverte à l'élaboration d'une véritable liberté d'association au Canada. Ce n'est pas cette décision qui accomplit cette tâche, mais la Cour qui s'était mise hors-jeu par son interprétation individualiste et corporatiste, vient de redevenir un lieu où de nouvelles batailles pourront faire progresser la liberté.

Des quatre éléments qui constituaient le test issu de la trilogie, le juge Bastarache n'en retient plus que deux. Pour bien comprendre, reprenons le texte du paragraphe 14 du jugement Bastarache qui reprend : … Le résumé du juge Sopinka dans cet extrait souvent cité de la décision « IPFPC », [1990] 2 R.C.S. 367 (), p. 401-402 :

> Après avoir examiné les différents motifs de jugement dans le Renvoi relatif à l'Alberta, j'arrive à la conclusion qu'il se dégage quatre propositions différentes quant à l'étendue de la liberté d'association garantie par l'al. 2d) : premièrement, l'al. 2d) protège la liberté de constituer une association, de la maintenir et d'y appartenir; deuxièmement, l'al. 2d) ne protège pas une activité pour le seul motif que cette activité est un objet fondamental ou essentiel d'une association; troisièmement, l'al. 2d) protège l'exercice collectif des droits et libertés individuels consacrés par la Constitution; et quatrièmement, l'al. 2d) protège l'exercice collectif des droits légitimes des individus.

Le troisième et le quatrième de ces principes ont remporté un appui moindre de la part des juges que les deux autres, n'étant confirmés expressément que par trois des six juges dans le Renvoi relatif à l'Alberta et deux des sept juges dans IPFPC. En outre, ces composantes de l'al. 2d) n'ont pas été d'une grande utilité à notre Cour dans Office canadien de commercilisation des oeufs c. Richardson, [1998] 3 R.C.S. 157 (« OCCO »), où il était clair que l'activité en cause ne pouvait pas être accomplie par une seule personne. Plus récemment, dans Delisle, précité, notre Cour n'a pas eu à statuer sur la validité du cadre existant puisque toutes les activités visées s'y inséraient. Notre Cour a précisé dans cet arrêt que l'al. 2d) ne garantit pas l'accès à un régime particulier de relations de travail lorsque les demandeurs peuvent exercer de manière indépendante les droits que leur confère l'al. 2d).

Plus loin, (para. 16)

À mon avis, même si le critère à quatre volets applicable à la liberté d'association clarifie cette notion, il ne rend pas compte de toute la gamme d'activités protégées par l'al. 2d). En particulier, il y a des cas *où une activité* **n'est pas visée** *par les troisième et quatrième règles* énoncées par le juge Sopinka dans IPFPC, précité, mais où l'État l'interdit néanmoins en raison seulement de sa nature associative. Il s'agit d'activités 1) qui ne sont pas protégées par une autre liberté constitutionnelle, et 2) qui ne peuvent, pour une raison ou une autre, être considérées comme des activité licites d'un individu. (…) J'estime que limiter l'application de l'al. 2d) aux activités qui peuvent être accomplies individuellement viderait de leur sens ces actes fondamentaux.

et para. 17

À mon avis, la notion même d' « association » reconnaît les différences qualitatives entre individu et collectivité…. Dans tous les cas, la collectivité a une existence propre et ses besoins et priorités diffèrent de ceux de ses membres individuels.

C'est ce qu'on appelle un revirement jurisprudentiel. Le juge Bastarache tout en insistant sur la spécificité de l'affaire, s'est distancé de l'individualisme de la trilogie et a abandonné la règle limitant la protection constitutionnelle aux seules associations défendant les droits par ailleurs garantis par la Charte. Il accepte de plus de faire référence aux textes internationaux beaucoup plus généreux et qui lient le Canada.

Permettez-moi d'ajouter que je me réjouis que cette dernière décision rende dépassée une partie du travail soumis dans la mesure où un espace nouveau de lutte pour la liberté d'association vient de s'ouvrir au Canada.

Georges leBel, 21 décembre 2001

SOURCES

Table de la jurisprudence analysée pour le présent travail

Décision de la Cour suprême du Canada * voir un résumé des faits in fine.

AFPC c. Canada, [1987] 1 R.C.S. 424 *

Augustus c. Gosset, [1996] 3 R.C.S. 268

Black c. Law society of Alberta, [1989] 1 R.C.S. 591 *

Delisle c. Canada (sous-procureur général), [1999] 2 R.C.S. 989 *

***Institut professionnel de la fonction publique du Canada c. T N-O (commissaire)*,** [1990] 2 R.C.S. 367 *

Lavigne c. Syndicat des employés de la fonction publique de l'Ontario, [1991] 2 R.C.S. 211 *

Libman c. Québec (Procureur Général), [1997] 3 R.C.S. 569

Oil, Chemical & Atomic Wks Int. Union v. Imperial Oil Ltd; (1963) S.C.R. 584

Office canadien de la commercialisation des oeufs c. Richardson, [1998] 3 R.C.S. 157 (CEMA) *

R. c. Skinner, [1990] 1 R.C.S. 1235

Renvoi relatif à la Public Service Employee Relations Act (Alb.), [1987] 1 R.C.S. 313 *

SDGMR c. Dolphin delivery ltd., [1986] 2 R.C.S. 573

SDGMR c. Saskatchewan, [1987] 1 R.C.S. 460 *

Smith & Rhuland Ltd v.R (1953) 2 S.C.R. 95

Décisions d'autres niveaux

Alex Couture inc. Canada (PG), [1990] R.J.Q. 2668 (C.S.)

Al Yamani c. Canada (solliciteur général), [1996] 1 C.F. 174

Archibald c. Canada, [1997] 3 C.F. 335

Banque canadienne impériale de commerce c. Rifou, [1986] 3 C.F. 486

Barry's ltd. c. Fisherman Food and Allied Workers union, (1995) 413 A.P.R. 156 (C.A. Nfld)

Beck c. Edmonton (City), [1993] 17 M.P.L.R. (2nd) 1 (B.R. Alta); 12 Alta L.R. (3rd) 272 (B.R. Alta)

Black c. Law society of Alberta, (1986) 27 D.L.R. (4th) 527 (C.A. Alta)

Canada (PG) c. Alex Couture inc., [1991] R.J.Q. 2534 (C.A.)

Catholic C.A.S. of Metro Toronto c. S.(T.), (1989) 60 D.L.R. (4th) 397 (C.A. Ont.)

Citizens Against Amalgation Committee et al. c. New Brunswick), [1998] 510 A.P.R. 184 (C.A. N.-B.)

Comité paritaire du Bois-ouvré c. 2536-8283 Québec inc., [1995] R.J.Q. 993 (C.Q.)

Commission de la Construction du Québec c. Bâtiment Fafard international inc., [1998] R.J.Q. 589 (C.Q.)

Costco Wholesale Canada c. B.-C. (Board of examinees in optometry), (1998) 157 D.L.R. (4th) 725

Delisle c. Canada (sous-procureur général), [1997] R.J.Q. 386. C.A. Qué.

Dion c. Régie intermunicipale d'assainissement des eaux de Ste-Thérèse et Balinville, [1998] R.J.Q. 2731 (C.S.)

Dolphin Delivery ltd. c. Retail Wholesale and dpt Store Union, local 580, (1984) 10 D.L.R.(4th) 198 (C.A.C.-B.)

Droit de la famille 1741, [1993] R.J.Q. 647 (C.A.)

East York (Borough) c. Ontario (AG), [1997] 4 O.R. (3rd) 789 (O.C. (G.D.))

East York (Borough) c. Ontario, [1997] 36 O.R. (3rd) 733 (C.A. Ont.) ; 47 C.R.R. (2nd) 232

Feldhaus c. B.C. (Registrar of companies), (1994) 114 D.L.R. (4th) 334 (C.A. C.-B.)

Gaylor c. Couture, [1988] R.J.Q. 1205 (C.A.)

Hélie c. Tourigny, [1989] JE 89-439 (C.S.)

Jones c. Ontario (AG), (1992) 89 D.L.R. (4th) 11 (C.A. Ont)

Lavigne c. OPSEU, (1989) 56 D.L.R. (4th) 474 (C.A. Ont.)

MacPhee c. Nova Scotia (Pulpwood Marketing Board), (1989) 56 D.L.R. (4th) 582 (C.A. N.É.)

Martin c. British Columbia (Attorney General), (1989) 53 D.L.R. (4th) 198 (C.S. C.-B.)

Merry c. Man., [1989] 2 W.W.R. 526 (B.R. Man.)

Metro, Stores (MTS) ltd. c. Man Food & Commercial Wkrs, loc. 832, [1988] 5 W.W.R. 544 (B.R. Man.)

M.K.S. and J.D. c. Nova Soctia (minister of community services), [1989] 225 A.P.R. 418 (N.S.R)

Montréal (Communauté urbaine de) c. Policière de la CUM inc., [1995] R.J.Q. 2549 (C.A.)

Moumdjian c. Canada, [1999] 4 C.F. 624 (C.A.)

OPSEU c. National Citizen Coalition, (1989) 35 C.R.R. 184 (H.C. Ont.); (conf. C.A. Ont)

Parti Union nationale c. Côté, [1989] R.J.Q. 2502 (C.S.)

Patry c. Barreau du Québec, [1991] R.J.Q. 2366 (C.S)

Port Moody, Dist. 43, Police Union c. Police Bd. (Port Moody), [1991] 54 B.C.L.R. (2nd) 26 (C.A.C.-B.)

Québec (PG) c. Perrault, [1992] R.J.Q. 993 (C.Q.)

R. c. A.T., [1997] 472 A.P.R. 397 (C.A. N.-B.)

R. c. S. (M.), [1996] 40 C.R.R. (2nd) 216 (C.A. C.-B.)

RBC DS Financial Services inc. c. Life insurance council, [1998] 10 W.W.R. 748 (B.R. Sask)

Re Service Employees'Intern'al Union, local 204, and Broadway Manor Nursing Home, (1984) 4 D.L.R.(4th) 231

Re SEIU, local 204, and Broadway Manor Nursing Home, (1985) 13 D.L.R. (4th) 220 (C.A. Ont)

Re Pruden Building ltd. and construction union, local 92, (1985) 13 D.L.R. (4th) 584 (B.R. Alta)

Strickland c. Ermel, [1994] 1 W.W.R. 417 (C.A. Sask.)

Syndicat des infirmières de la Nouvelles-Ecosse, section locale DEVCO c. Canada (CRO), [1990] 3 C.F. 652 (C.A.)

Syndicat intern'al des débardeurs et magasiniers-Canada, section locale 500 c. Canada, [1992] 3 C.F. 758 (C.A.)

Thériault c. R., [1998] R.J.Q. 911 (C.S.)

Yuun c. Canada (Minister of Citizenship and Immigration), [1999] 63 C.R.R. (2nd) 332 (C.F.)

Décisions québécoises (Charte québécoise)

Association des professeurs de Lignery (A.P.L.), syndicat affilié à la C.E.Q. et autres c. Florence Alvetta-Comeau et autres, [1990] R.J.Q. 130 (C.A.)

Claude Perreault et autres c. Syndicat des salariés de Blanchard-Ness Ltée, [1986] T.T. 171

Corporation municipale de Lanoraie D'autray c. le juge Céline Pelletier et P.G. du Québec, [1986] D.L.Q. 386

Dufour c. Syndicat des employés de Pierre-Joseph Triest (C.S.N.), [1999] R.J.Q. 2674 (C.S.)

Fraternité des policiers de St-Bruno de Montarville inc. c. St-Bruno (ville de), (1985) JE 85-756 (C.S.)

Fraternité des policiers de St-Bruno-de- Montarville inc. c. Ville de St-Bruno [1989] R.J.Q. 485 (C.A.)

Hogan c. Association de l'industrie et du commerce, local 614 (A.T.T.I.C.), [1991] R.J.Q. 805 (C.S.)

Lefort c. Syndicat canadien de la Fonction publique, section locale 3247, [1993] T.T. 346

Malcolm de Sousa et al. c. Syndicat des ouvriers unis de l'électricité, section locale 568, [1986] T.T. 17

Ouellette c. Association des propriétaires des domaines joyeux de Granby inc., (1988) JE 88-1060 (C.A.)

Union des employés de service, section locale 298 (F.T.Q.) et armée du Salut, [1986] D.L.Q. 363

West island Teachers' association et autres c. Madeleine Nantel et autres, [1988] R.J.Q. 1569 (C.A.)

Décisions relatives à l'association non-personnifiée

Camo Bearhonstok c. MSA Gestion conseil inc., (25 mai 2000) Montréal 500-22-043875-007 (C.Q.).

Claude Beaudoin. c. Syndicat des t. en charcuterie (18 mai 2000) Saint-François 450-05-001914-973 C.S.

F. Smith Jr. c. Bruce A. Bishop et South Branch Conservation Ltd., St-François 450-32-001508-969 (C.Q.)

Jean-Paul Lavoie et al. c. Teamsters union local 230 et al., (27 juin 1997) Hull 550-05-001756-934 (C.S.)

Hélène Lauzier inc. c. Michel Nadeau, (24 février 1998) Québec 200-02-014974-960 (C.Q.).

Le club juridique c. Gérald Lafrenière, (6 octobre 1999) Montréal 500-09-008164-998 (C.A.).

Léon Mathieu c. Claudette Jean, (26 novembre 1997) Québec 200-32-012376-975 (C.Q.)

Service Barbara-Rouke c. Sous-Ministre du Revenu du Québec, (30 nov 1999) Québec 200-02-020823-987 (C.Q.)

Syndicat des employés de production c. Bergeron Montréal 500-05-016424-960, D.T.E. 96T-696, (C.S.)

Urbain Lévesque et al. c. MFQ VIE, (le 6 mai 1996) Québec 200-05-004086-968, (C.S.)

Yeshivah of Montreal c.Donald Myron Abramovitch (7 mai 1997), Montréal 500-14-005850-979, (C.S.)

Cour européenne de Justice

Young, J. et Webster, du 13 août 1981 (série A n°44 p. 21 et 22) , (rapport de la commission du 14-12-79, par. 167, Cour Eur. DH, série B n° 39, p 47 ; Young, James et Webster c. Royaume-Unis, 1981, IRLR 408, par. 86.)

Sigurdur A Sigurjonsson c. Islande (1993) affaire n°24/1992/369/443, par. 35. 30 juin 1993 :

Chassagnou et al. v. France, judgment of 29 April 1999, appl. nos. 25088/94, 28331/95, 28443/95)

RÉFÉRENCES

Charte canadienne des droits et libertés, L.R.C. (1985), App. II, no 44, ann. B, Partie I.

Charte des droits et libertés de la personne, L.R.Q., c. C-12.

Universal Declaration of Human Rights, G.A. Res.217A(III), U.N. GAOR, 3d Sess., pt. 1, at 71, U.N. Doc. A/810 (1948) (art. 20(1) ; art. 23(4)).

International Covenant on Civil and Political Rights, Dec. 16, 1966, 999 U.N.T.S. 171 (art. 22).

International Covenant on Economic, Social and Cultural Rights, Dec. 16, 1966, 993 U.N.T.S. 3 (art. 8).

American Declaration of the Rights and Duties of Man, 1948, in Final Act, Ninth International Conference of American States, Bogota, Colombia, Articles 21, 22. « American » here refers to the Americas, including North, Central and South America and the Caribbean region.

American Convention on Human Rights, OAS Official Records, OEA/Ser.A/16 (English), T.S. No. 36 (Nov. 7-22, 1969), Article 16.

European Convention for the Protection of Human Rights and Fundamental Freedoms, Nov. 4, 1950, E.T.S. No. 5 (entered into force, Sept. 3, 1953), Article 11.

European Union, Community Charter of Fundamental Social Rights of Workers, in Roger Blanpain and Chris Engels, eds., European Labour Law (The Hague, Kluwer Law International, 1998), Articles 11-13.

ILO Convention No. 87, Articles 2, 11.

North American Agreement on Labor Cooperation, Annex 1, Labor Principles 1-3.

Broadbent report came out in early February, delayed many believe, until the Supreme Court came down with the Vancouver decision. This report, entitled Building on Strength: Improving Governance in Canada's Voluntary Sector was the final report of the group and was based on cross-country hearing and submissions which were stimulated by its earlier discussion paper, Helping Canadians Help Canadians: Improving Governance and Accountability in the Voluntary Sector. The Panel on Accountability and Governance in the Voluntary Sector (PAGVS) was established in October 1997 by the Voluntary Sector Roundtable. The Panel (known as the Broadbent group after its Chair)

Les articles cités par le juge McIntyre dans le Renvoi de l'Alberta, mais non vérifiés :

Thomas I. Emerson « Freedom of Association and Freedom of Expression », 74 Yale L.J. 1 (1964), p. 1:

Abernathy le fait observer dans son ouvrage intitulé The Right of Assembly and Association (1961), p. 242:

Clyde W. Summers affirme, dans « Freedom of Association and Compulsory Unionism in Sweden and the United States », 112 U. Pa. L.R. 647, à la p. 647 (1964):

Reena Raggi, dans son article intitulé « An Independent Right to Freedom of Association », 12 Harv. C.R.-C.L. Rev. 1 (1977), expose la situation clairement, aux pp. 15 et 16.

Roberts c. United States Jaycees, 468 U.S. 609 (1984), le juge Brennan, cité par McIntyre.

Même s'il est toujours réducteur de résumer les faits d'une affaire, nous indiquerons à la suite dans quel domaine et quelle question principale était soulevée par les faits dans les grandes affaires relatives à la liberté d'association décidées par la Cour Suprême du Canada et ici commentées.

On désigne sous ce nom de « TRILOGIE » les décisions rendues le même jour dans trois affaires similaires :

Renvoi relatif à la Public Service Employee Relations Act (Alb.), [1987] 1 R.C.S. 313 : PSERA : Reference Re Public Service Employee Relations Act (Alta) ;

Les dispositions de cette loi qui interdisent aux employés de la fonction publique, pompiers, policiers, et employés d'hopitaux, le recours à la grève et imposent l'arbitrage obligatoire pour résoudre les impasses dans les négociations collectives sont-elles incompatibles avec la Charte ? Réponse : NON ; la Charte ne garantit ni le droit à la négociation collective, ni le droit de grève.

AFPC c. Canada, [1987] 1 R.C.S. 424 ; (PSAC v. Canada). Alliance de la Fonction publique du Canada : Une loi spéciale sur les restrictions salariales du secteur public suspend les négociations dans la fonction publique, interdit la grève (sans prévoir d'arbitrage) et proroge la convention collective pour quatre ans et fixe unilatéralement les salaires de tous ces employés. Il fut décidé que cela ne portait pas atteinte à la liberté d'association.

SDGMR c. Saskatchewan, [1987] 1 R.C.S. 460 (RWDSU et al. v. Saskatchewan). Syndicats des détaillants, grossistes et magasins à rayons, section locale 544, 496, 635 et 955 contre Saskatchewan : Au cours de négociations dans le domaine de l'approvisionnement en lait du Manitoba, les employeurs décrètent un lock-out; et la province adopte une loi spéciale interdisant la grève et le lock-out. Cette loi n'est pas considérée comme violant la liberté d'association qui ne comporte pas le droit de faire la grève.

Black c. Law society of Alberta, [1989] 1 R.C.S. 591. Des avocats albertains s'associent à un cabinet d'avocats de l'Ontario. Le Barreau de l'Alberta adopte un règlement interdisant aux avocats d'appartenir à plus d'un cabinet d'avocats. Ce règlement est contesté au titre de la restriction à la liberté d'association. La décision reposa plutôt sur le liberté de circulation qui se serait trouvée injustement restreinte par ce règlement. — Cela est clairement exprimé par le juge McIntyre « On constatera aussi que la Charte, sauf peut-être l'al.6(2)b) (le droit de gagner sa vie dans toute province) et le par.6(4) (programmes de discrimination positive) ne s'intéresse pas aux droits économiques. »

Institut professionnel de la fonction publique du Canada c. Territoires du Nord-Ouest), [1990] 2 R.C.S. 367
Dans cette affaire, une trentaine d'infirmières qui étaient à l'emploi du Ministère fédéral canadien des Affaires indiennes et du Grand-Nord canadien, passent à l'emploi d'une nouvelle administration avec l'érection

en entité administrative autonome des Territoires du Nord-Ouest canadien. Ces infirmières autrefois syndiquées à la fonction publique canadienne, demandent leur reconnaissance à la nouvelle autorité territoriale qui la leur refuse au motif que leur association aurait dû préalablement être constituée en corporation en vertu des nouvelles dispositions territoriales ce qui leur est impossible, puisque la loi qui leur aurait permis de la faire n'a pas encore été adoptée. Cette exigence et ce refus sont contestés par les infirmières. La Cour suprême reconnaît valide la loi obligeant d'être constitué en personne morale pour négocier collectivement au nom de ses membres. Il ne s'agirait pas là d'une violation de la liberté d'association. Cette loi « fournit au Gouvernement la possibilité de refuser, pour toutes les fins de la négociation collective, l'existence même à l'association choisie par les employés pour négocier en leur nom » (p. 381.) et de donner l'exemple d'hockeyeurs qui se verraient autorisés à former une association mais interdire de jouer au hockey. Le droit d'association ne serait pas violé puisqu'il pourrait continuer à parler en association de ce sport et aller voir les autres jouer. Un motif valable de restriction pourrait être alors que ce sport est dangereux et que contrairement au ridicule, il peut tuer parfois.

Lavigne c. Syndicat des employés de la fonction publique de l'Ontario, [1991] 2 R.C.S. 211.

Le professeur Lavigne est soumis à l'application de la formule Rand qui prévoit la perception obligatoire de la cotisation syndicale qui est par ailleurs utilisée à des fins politiques avec lesquelles il est en désaccord, invoquant ainsi sa liberté individuelle d'association. Les juges majoritaires constatent la violation du droit négatif de ne pas s'associer, (et non de la liberté d'opinion), mais la considèrent justifiée dans une société libre et démocratique.

Office canadien de la commercialisation des oeufs c. Richardson, [1998] 3 R.C.S. 157.(Cema v. Richardson).

L'Office canadien de commercialisation des oeufs exige un permis des producteurs d'oeufs pour produire et impose des quotas pour vendre sur le marché inter-provincial ou international. Or les Territoires du Nord-Ouest ne se sont pas vu attribuer de quota de production, et les demandeurs sont donc privés de permis. La disposition qui écartait les producteurs d'œufs du Nord-Ouest canadien des quotas de production d'œufs ne violait ni la liberté d'établissement et de circulation, ni la liberté d'association. Le fait de ne pas être inclus dans le régime de commercialisation des oeufs ne viole pas la liberté d'association, qui ne s'étend pas au droit d'être associé à un commerce.

Delisle c. Canada (sous-procureur général), [1999] 2 R.C.S. 989.
Dans cette affaire, les policiers de la Gendarmerie royale du Canada qui œuvrent au Québec contestent l'interdiction qui leur est faite de se faire accréditer pour négocier collectivement leurs conditions de travail. Le juge Fish de la Cour d'Appel du Québec (1997) R.J.Q. 386.(p. 399), refuse d'inclure dans la liberté d'association le droit à l'accréditation parce que ce dernier ne peut pas être un droit individuel. Ce ne serait pas le droit individuel d'association qui est ici violé, mais le droit à l'accréditation qui oblige l'employeur à négocier de bonne foi. Ce que les policiers recherchaient, ce n'est pas de s'associer, mais d'obtenir cette accréditation. Or comme l'accréditation n'est pas un droit individuel, il n'est pas couvert par la liberté d'association. La Cour suprême confirme.

Advance Cutting : R. c. Advance Cutting & Coring Ltd. : 2001 CSC 70.No : 26664. : 19 octobre 2001.
Cette décision concerne la constitutionnalité de la disposition de la loi québécoise sur l'industrie de la construction exigeant que les travailleurs deviennent membres de l'un des groupes syndicaux énumérés pour obtenir des certificats de compétence leur permettant de travailler. La Cour suprême décide que cette limitation à la liberté individuelle et négative de ne pas s'associer viole effectivement le liberté garantie, mais est justifiable dans une société démocratique. Les principes énoncés dans la jurisprudence de la Cour sont maintenus, mais on accepte qu'ils soient inapplicables en l'occurrence. Mais c'est surtout l'individualisme libéral qui est ici écarté au profit des exigences politiques de gestion du social.

C'est dans l'affaire Dunmore suivante que la Cour renversera son analyse et posera, avec de multiples précautions et distinguo, les assises d'une nouvelle lecture de la liberté d'association. Cela est d'autant plus important que la décision emporte l'adhésion de tous sauf le juge Major, et l'habituelle décision concurrente de madame L'Heureux-Dubé.

Dunmore c. Ontario (Procureur général) 2001 CSC 94. No du greffe : 27216. 20 décembre 2001.

Cette affaire concerne la suppression par le Gouvernement Harris du droit à la syndicalisation des travailleurs agricoles que leur avait accordé le Gouvernement Rae. Le Juge Bastarache, pour une cour quasi-unanime, abandonne en partie l'analyse qu'il avait si ardemment défendue dans l'affaire Delisle et reconnait une certaine obligation de l'État d'agir pour protéger la liberté d'association et que son abstention peut parfois équivaloir à une négation des droits proclamés dans la Charte. Certes, ce revirement est entouré de multiples précautions oratoires; mais l'admission de fait que la position antérieure était devenue intenable n'en est pas moins réelle. Des quatre éléments qui constituaient le test issu de la trilogie,le juge Bastarache n'en retient plus que deux. Pour bien comprendre, reprenons le texte du paragraphe 14 du jugement Bastarache : « J'estime que limiter l'application de l'al. 2d) aux activités qui peuvent être accomplies individuellement viderait de leur sens ces actes fondamentaux. » et para. 17 « À mon avis, la notion même d'' association ' reconnaît les différences qualitatives entre individu et collectivité…. Dans tous les cas, la collectivité a une existence propre et ses besoins et priorités diffèrent de ceux de ses membres individuels. »

8

The Third Sector Meets the National Security State: The Anti-Globalization Movement in Canada after 9/11

Ann Capling and Kim Richard Nossal

INTRODUCTION

The rise of the third sector has been as pronounced in global politics as it has in domestic politics. Much of the commentary on the impact of the third sector on international relations fixes on what Lester M. Salamon has called the "associational revolution" of the 1980s and 1990s (Salamon 1994; Salamon *et al.* 1999) — the way in which non-governmental organizations (NGOs) have become increasingly embedded in the processes of world politics (Mathews 1997; Spiro 1995; Lynch 1998; Keck and Sikkink 1998; O'Brien *et al.* 2000; Smith, Chatfield and Pagnucco 1997). While we have seen the rise of transnational global social movements in all spheres of world politics, their impact has certainly been most pronounced in the area of globalization, global governance, and global trade negotiations. Beginning in the mid-1990s, and particularly after the large demonstrations at the ministerial meetings of the World Trade Organization (WTO) in Seattle in November and December 1999, international organizations and sovereign governments have been consistently confronted by demands for greater input into the process of policy-making by civil society organizations. Whenever and wherever governments gathered for large-scale summit meetings, large-scale street demonstrations and public protests consistently sought either to close the meetings down completely or at minimum to cause as much disruption as possible.

The growing strength of the global social movements against globalization in the late 1990s prompted the rise of a widespread view that the third sector has indeed become a "third force" in contemporary global politics, to use the title of a recent volume edited by Ann M. Florini (2000). In this view, the civil society organizations (CSOs) of the third sector have become deeply entrenched in the processes of global governance, and able to exert influence on the behaviour of sovereign states and firms in the global marketplace. Indeed, at least one NGO activist, Jody Williams, the International Campaign to Ban Landmines, claimed that the role of NGOs in the land-mines case demonstrated that global civil society had become "a new superpower" in global politics (Williams and Goose 1998, 47).

Such positive views of the role of CSOs in the policy process have certainly found an echo in the context of the making of Canadian foreign policy. Alison Van Rooy (1999), for example, has argued that civil society organizations have had an increasing impact on the evolution of foreign policy. For his part, Maxwell Cameron (1999) has examined the land-mines issue to demonstrate empirically the way in which CSOs were involved in some Canadian foreign policy issues in the 1990s. And Canada's minister of foreign affairs in the late 1990s, Lloyd Axworthy, has acknowledged the degree to which he sought to make NGOs part of the policy-making process: "one can no longer relegate NGOs to simple advisory or advocacy roles in this [policy-making] process. They are now part of the way decisions have to be made." Axworthy made no secret of his view that this was a welcome development: as he put it in 1998, "civil society has earned a place at the table" (1998, 2).

In this chapter we examine the anti-globalization social movement in Canada and offer a somewhat different conclusion about the impact of civil society organizations on Canadian foreign policy. First, we examine the rise of the third sector as a third force in Canadian foreign policy, and

Canadian trade policy in particular, demonstrating the degree to which the rise of civil society groups and transnational social movement organizations in contemporary international politics was deeply related to shifts in present-day politics and we explore the degree to which the broader trends in global politics have been mirrored in Canada. We then look at the challenges for the anti-globalization movement created by the attacks on the United States that occurred on 11 September 2001 (9/11), and argue that the decision by the United States government and its allies such as Australia and Canada to begin to engage in open warfare with one transnational social movement, radical Islamism, will have a profound impact on the operations of another group of transnational social movements, the anti-globalization movements, as they meet the re-emergent national security state.

We conclude that since the protests at the World Trade Organization ministerial meeting in Seattle in November and December 1999, the impact of civil society organizations on the making of Canada's foreign policy has been overstated. More importantly, however, much of the analysis of the centrality of CSOs in the policy-making process in Canada was rendered before 9/11. To what extent did those events — and the war that was unleashed in their aftermath — change the role of civil society organizations in the shaping of Canada's international negotiations on trade policy, and the processes of globalization and global governance more generally? The purpose of this chapter is to offer an assessment of the degree to which the assumptions and conclusions about the role of CSOs in the politics of policy-making in Canada on global economic issues have been altered by the transformation of world politics on and after 11 September 2001. Our speculations focus in the first instance on the quite sudden resurrection of the national security state in the wake of 9/11 — a political environment in which state officials organize and concentrate the power of the state apparatus to try to ensure the security of the citizenry and employ the concept of "national security" to trump all other concerns. The reappearance of the national security state has, not surprisingly, been most marked in the United States, but it has also occurred in Canada, which shares a border with the United States. The re-emergence of the national security state has considerable implications for the involvement of the third sector in international policy-making, as we will show.

THE "THIRD FORCE" IN CANADIAN FOREIGN POLICY

Over the last generation there has been a radical shift in relations between state and society. In most liberal democracies, there has been a sustained assault on what John Ruggie (1982) has described as the "embedded liberalism" of the period immediately after the Second World War, when the Keynesian welfare state and its essentially *national* economic decision-making sat uneasily with a multilateral economic system designed to avoid a repeat of the collapse of global trade during the 1930s. With the collapse of the Bretton Woods system in the early 1970s, however, these organizing ideas lost much of their prominence. First, the idea of the welfare state and its commitment to active government involvement in national economic planning, the redistribution of wealth, and the provision of a range of services by state agencies gave way to the idea that the state should in essence withdraw from certain activities, and allow private actors to deliver many public services. Second, the protective state and its commitment to the development of a distinctly *national* economy behind the protective barriers gave way to the related ideas of economic liberalization *within* political communities, and the freer movement of all of the factors of production except labour *between* political communities. In this transformation, the watchwords everywhere have been downsizing, streamlining, re-engineering, rationalizing, outsourcing, privatizing, and liberalizing.

Paradoxically, this political transformation was only made possible by the very citizens who benefited from the policies of the welfare state and the protective state, but who voted for those political parties which espoused the ideas of the new emerging neo-liberal consensus. While some of these votes might have been initially cast simply with the intention of voting a governing party out, it is clear that in many instances voters returned again and again to the parties which in power pursued policies designed to implement key planks of the neo-liberal platform. Indeed, in some countries, political parties were quick to recognize this broad shift in voter preferences, and sought to "rebrand" themselves, in the process abandoning the "old" ideas that had won them elections in the past, and embracing instead "new" ideas that allowed them to catch the wave. Certainly "new" Labour in Britain, the Liberals in Canada, and the Australian Labor Party all demonstrated not only the capacity of political parties to rebrand themselves, but also to attract votes after having done so. By contrast, those parties that tried to continue carrying the banner of the welfare state or the protective state, for example, the New Democratic Party in Canada, were simply marginalized by the voters.

At the same time, however, this change produced a paradoxical situation. The more the state downsized, rationalized, privatized, and liberalized, the more the politics of community in western countries changed. Michael Walzer has argued that associational life in the West was increasingly at risk as a result of "a steady attenuation of everyday cooperation and civic friendship"(1995, 8). A fuller exploration of this phenomenon has been articulated by Robert Putnam, whose exploration of life in contemporary America revealed a distinct decline in "social capital," in other words, the "features of social organization such as networks, norms, and social trust that facilitate coordination and cooperation for mutual benefit" (Putnam 1995, 66). While "social capital" can take many forms, Putnam was particularly concerned about civic engagement, or connections to community, and argued that there was a decline in civic engagement — hence the notion of "bowling alone."

In addition, citizens increasingly became, in Kathy Brock's words, "disillusioned by the impotence and unwillingness of their own governments to address certain needs or problems"; and increasingly they turned to non-governmental organizations "to defend their interests, promote their rights and deliver needed services." In response, governments, "besieged and belittled," sought to assuage the rising tide of demands by both citizens and non-governmental organizations by establishing more institutionalized links with the third sector (Brock 2000).

In a range of policy sectors, these emerging patterns of state-societal relations basically "worked," not in the sense that there were no problems or flaws in the new arrangements, but rather in the broader sense that the state was able to come to a more or less workable accommodation with the voluntary sector to deliver a range of services, as, for example, the chapter by Mary Wiktorowicz, Miriam Lapp, Ian Brodie and Donald Abelson shows. Moreover, we have seen a willingness on the part of the Canadian government to try to institutionalize the creation and maintenance of partnerships with the voluntary sector in a formal and programmatic way via the Voluntary Sector Initiative inaugurated in 1999–2000 (Brock 2001).

While these new and emerging arrangements are not without their problems — as, for example, the chapter by Ken Rasmussen and David Malloy on the deep ethical divide between the third sector and the state makes quite clear — there is little doubt that harnessing the enthusiasm and community reach of the voluntary sector has had a mitigating impact on service delivery, and thus, one assumes, also on citizen concerns.

In at least one area, however, the emerging relationship between the third sector and the state has not managed to assuage the concerns of the citizenry. As the chapter by Elizabeth Smyth and Peter J. Smith above demonstrates, increasing concerns about globalization and its impacts generated a politics of opposition the likes of which have not been seen in western countries since the peace movements of the early 1980s or the student, anti-Vietnam war, and civil rights protest movements of the late 1960s. Much of the anti-globalization movement of the 1990s focused on the apparent loss of local autonomy as a consequence of the processes of globalization, the seeming impossibility of national decision-making, and the increasing prominence of the institutions of global governance such as the G7/8, the International Monetary Fund, and the WTO. The opposition manifested itself in a variety of ways, most commonly in the rise of global social movements (O'Brien *et al.* 2000), Internet-based campaigns against such emblematic attempts at global governance as the Multilateral Agreement on Investment (MAI)[1] or the Free Trade Area of the Americas, (Ayres forthcoming) and mass street protests against such institutions as the WTO, the World Bank, the Summit of the Americas, and the G7/8.

Moreover, in this sector, there was considerable resistance to the efforts of the state (and indeed international institutions themselves) to try to manage CSO/NGO opposition by pursuing the same strategies followed in other sectors — notably by seeking to bring the voluntary sector into the process of policy-making. On the contrary: many of those in the anti-globalization social movement sought to remain resolutely outside the embrace of the state; others participated in state-led efforts to "bring the NGOs in," but nonetheless remained deeply opposed to the processes of globalization.[2]

Canadian experience reflected these broader global trends. In the 1990s, the Liberal government of Jean Chrétien made a conscious effort to involve CSOs in the policy-making process. Indeed, in opposition, the Liberals had criticized the foreign policy-making of the Progressive Conservative government of Brian Mulroney as élitist and anti-democratic, and promised that a Liberal government would pursue a more "democratic" foreign policy. Once in power, the Chrétien government embarked on a sustained effort to involve the third sector in foreign policy to an unprecedented degree, and indeed even sought to entrench such involvement in bureaucratic practice: consultation was one of the objectives of Public Service 2000 initiated by the Privy Council Office. While it can be questioned whether the increased involvement of these groups in the foreign policy process constitutes greater democracy, there can be little doubt that non-governmental organizations played a greater role in making foreign policy in Canada since 1993 (Nossal 1993, 1995; see also Cameron 1998; Riddell-Dixon 2001, esp. 6-7).

For example, as Elizabeth Riddell-Dixon's examination of Canadian participation in the UN Conference on Women in Beijing demonstrates, NGOs were already deeply entrenched in the policy-making process in Canada by the mid-1990s (Riddell-Dixon 2001). And under Lloyd Axworthy, the minister of foreign affairs from 1996 to 2000, that process intensified. As minister, Axworthy ensured that civil society organizations enjoyed a privileged position in the making of Canadian foreign policy. He brought these groups deeply into the initiative to ban anti-personnel land mines, indeed working with them without the knowledge of other governments to put pressure on those governments to join the Canadian initiative. Likewise, he extended and deepened the existing commitment of the Canadian government to ensure that Canadian voices at global United Nations conferences were as pluralistic as possible, even when, as occurred in the case of the World Conference against Racism, Racial Discrimination, Xenophobia and Related Intolerances, held in Durban, South Africa, from 31 August to 7 September 2001, the Canadian government provided travel funds to a large number of delegates attending the NGO forum, but was nonetheless denounced at the forum as "racist" by some of the very delegates who had had their way to Durban paid by the government in Ottawa (*National Post*, 31 August 2001).

For some, this increased involvement in foreign policy was normatively welcome. For example, examining the role of non-governmental organizations in the Beijing conference on women in 1995, Riddell-Dixon concludes that NGO influence on policy-making has been, on the whole, a positive development. She accepts that third sector groups are less representative of the electorate than members of Parliament are, and that they may be quite self-interested actors. On the other hand, she points out that CSOs can be a valuable part of the policy process because they facilitate two-way communication between governments and NGO members; they provide a mechanism by which people can articulate shared interests and positions to government; they act as channels for governments to communicate information to attentive publics; they monitor both the development and implementation of policy; they can provide new ways of conceptualizing problems and solutions; they can contribute expertise and experience to policy discussions; and they often play important roles in program delivery (Riddell-Dixon 2001, 7-8; Capling 2001, 207).

While the Chrétien government's commitment to the democratization of foreign policy clearly created space for greater NGO participation in trade negotiations in the 1990s, we should sound some "cautionary notes" about the limits of this democratization process.

First, it should be noted that in a Westminster parliamentary system, whatever "democratization" of foreign policy there may be will always be heavily dependent on the government of the day. Because of the hierarchical organization of political authority in a Westminster system, there are none of the institutional sources of "openness" that one finds, for example, in the United States, where the separation of powers ensures that the policy-making process is inherently open to a wide variety of societal inputs. By contrast, in a Westminster system, it matters who is in power, and the attitudes toward state-society relations that ministers of the Crown have.

Thus we can find clear differences *between* governments: the Australian government of John Howard, for example, treated third sector groups very differently than the government in Ottawa. Canadian third sector groups were accorded, relatively speaking, far greater access to the development of trade policy than Australian groups were by the government in Canberra.[3] We can also see differences *within* the same country: for example, there were considerable differences in the way in which civil society was involved in the foreign policy process between the Progressive Conservatives under Brian Mulroney and the Liberals under Jean Chrétien (see e.g., Nossal 2001). And even within the same government we can see differences: Axworthy's departure changed the tenor, and many of the practices, of multi-stakeholder politics on trade issues.

Second, even in those countries where governments and particular ministers are inclined to bring CSOs into the process of developing policy on international economic policy, we must conclude that such "democratization" is still occurring at a fairly shallow level. Civil society organizations and the voluntary sector were generally not as deeply involved as "producer" groups — from manufacturing, extraction, agricultural/fishing, and service industries. Those groups representing interests that have a concrete impact on the economy simply tend to be treated more seriously by the state than not-for-profits and others in the voluntary/CSO sector. And protest groups, whether relatively institutionalized groups like the Council for Canadians or groups that are simply deemed too radical for inclusion in policy development, such as Direct Action Is So Yummy, tend to be conspicuous by their absence from the "real world" of policy development, at least as it defined by state officials.

One measure of the level of democratization is to look at the pattern of involvement by different groups in activities related to international nego tiations on trade. As Table 1 shows, the Canadian groups active at the WTO ministerial meeting in Seattle in November and December 1999 were predominantly economic groups, representing the interests of producers, manufacturers, and others in the economy. Civil society and not-for-profit organizations were active at Seattle, but their numbers were small relative to the economic groups.

Another measure is to look at the degree of institutionalization in the groups involved by the state in the process of consultation. Institutionalization reflects not only certain capabilities not enjoyed by a wide range of groups but the degree of exclusion necessary for stakeholder politics to work smoothly. This pattern was certainly evident in the "multi-stakeholder consultations" conducted by the Department of Foreign Affairs and International Trade in the run-up to the Summit of the Americas in April 2001. Table 2 lists groups that were conspicuous by their absence from the process of consultation or formal activity at international trade meetings. By contrast, Table 3 shows the degree to which the stakeholders involved in the one-day information exchange session in Ottawa were overwhelmingly institutionalized groups.

Table 1: Canadian Non-Governmental Organizations Attending the Third WTO Ministerial Conference, Seattle, 30 November–3 December 1999

Agri-Industry Trade Group
Alberta Economic Development Authority
Alliance of Manufacturers and Exporters Canada
Asia Pacific Foundation of Canada
Brewers Association of Canada
Business Council on National Issues
Canada-ASEAN Business Council
Canada-Korea Business Council
Canadian Alliance of Agri-Food Exporters
Canadian Association of Broadcasters
Canadian Broiler Hatching Egg Marketing Agency
Canadian Cattlemen's Association
Canadian Centre for Policy Alternatives
Canadian Chemical Producers' Association
Canadian Conference of the Arts
Canadian Council for International Business
Canadian Egg Marketing Agency
Canadian Electricity Association
Canadian Environmental Law Association
Canadian Feminist Alliance for International Action
Canadian Foodgrains Bank
Canadian Labour Congress
Canadian Library Association
Canadian Oilseed Processors' Association
Canadian Pork Council
Canadian Pulp and Paper Association
Canadian Restaurant and Foodservices Association
Canadian Steel Producers Association
Canadian Sugar Beet Producers' Association
Canadian Sugar Institute
Canadian Wheat Board
Canadian Wine Institute
Centre for Asia-Pacific Initiatives

Centre for Trade Policy and Law
Chicken Farmers of Canada
Coopérative Fédérée de Québec
Dairy Farmers of Canada
EKOS 707
FOCAL – Canadian Foundation for the Americas
Food and Consumer Products Manufacturers of Canada
Information Technology Association of Canada
Institute for Media Policy and Civil Society
International Centre for Human Rights and Democratic Development
International Council on Metals and the Environment
International Institute for Sustainable Development
National Dairy Council of Canada
National Farmers' Union
National Union of Public and General Employees
OXFAM Canada
Polaris Institute
Potato Growers of Alberta
Public Interest Advocacy Centre
Sierra Club of Canada
Sierra Youth Coalition
The Canadian Bar Association
The Canadian Chamber of Commerce
The Canadian Federation of Agriculture
The Council of Canadians
The Mining Association of Canada
Transparency International Canada
Union des Producteurs Agricoles
Western Canadian Wheat Growers Association
World Federalists of Canada

Table 2: Canadian Non-Governmental Organizations Not Present at Multi-Stakeholder Consultations or Members of Canadian Delegations

APEC Alert	Mobilisation for Global Justice (MobGlob)
Canadian Action Party	No to APEC
Citizens Concerned About Free Trade	Northeastern Federation of Anarcho-
Common Frontiers	Communists (Sécrétariat francophone)
Communist Party of Canada (Marxist-Leninist)	Ontario Northumberland against the FTAA
Convergence des Luttes anti-capitaliste	Opération Québec printemps
Cross-Canada WTO Caravan	Parkland Institute
Democracy Street	Peacewire
Direct Action Is So Yummy (DAISY)	People's Action Network Edmonton
Ecumenical Coalition for Economic Justice	Radical Cheerleaders Canada
Green Party	Raging Grannies
Groupe Main noire	Rebuilding the Left
Independent Media Centers (Calgary, Hamilton, Montreal, Ontario, Vancouver, Windsor)	Réseau québécois sur l'intégration continentale
Industrial Workers of the World (Canada)	Stop the FTAA
Maquila Solidarity Network	TransFAIR Canada
	WTO Action

Moreover, the shallowness occurs on yet another dimension. The vast majority of the NGOs and CSOs invited by the Canadian state to participate in multi-stakeholder consultations are only able to come because the government has chosen to fund them. Unlike producer groups, whose members sustain them so that they can maintain their independence from the state, most CSOs are only able to support themselves because they receive core funding from the state. This creates a deep dependence, for there is always the threat that if the CSO does not behave in ways deemed appropriate by state officials, funding can be swiftly brought to an end (though, as noted above, government officials in Canada have demonstrated a fascinating tolerance for continuing to fund groups that delight in roundly criticizing the Canadian state).

In short, while we have seen the growth of third sector *activity* in the development of Canadian government policy as it relates to international

Table 3: Canadian Non-Governmental Organizations Attending the Summit of the Americas Multi-Stakeholder Information Exchange Session, Ottawa, 28 March 2001

Association of Canadian Community Colleges
Association of Consulting Engineers of Canada
Association of Universities and Colleges of Canada
Association québécoise des organisms de cooperation internationale
Business Council on National Issues
Canadian Association for Community Living
Canadian Bankers Association
Canadian Chamber of Commerce
Canadian Conference of Catholic Bishops
Canadian Council for the Americas
Canadian Council for International Business
Canadian Council for International Cooperation
Canadian Environmental Law Association
Canadian Federation of Agriculture
Canadian Federation of Students
Canadian Human Rights Commission
Canadian Institute for Environmental Law and Policy
Canadian Labour Congress
Canadian Manufacturers and Exporters
Canadian Society for International Health
Canadian Teachers Federation
Canadian Wheat Board
Centre for Innovation in Corporate Responsibility
Coalition for Cultural Diversity
Conference Board of Canada
Confédération des Syndicats nationaux
Congress of Aboriginal Peoples
Conseil du Patronat du Québec

Consumers' Association of Canada
Dalhousie University
Development and Peace
Fédération des travailleuses et travailleurs du Québec
Federation of Canadian Municipalities
FOCAL—Fondation canadienne pour les Amériques
Forest Products Association of Canada
Grey, Clark, Shih and Associates
Human Rights Internet
Human Rights Research and Education Centre
International Council for Social Welfare
Inuit Tapirisat of Canada
Manufacturiers et exportateurs du Québec
Métis National Council
Métis National Council of Women
National Council of Women of Canada
North-South Institute
Option Consommateurs
Oxfam-Québec
Polaris Institute
Public Interest Advocacy Centre
Rights and Democracy
Symposium hémisphérique sur le commerce et l'environnement
Transparency International Canada
Union des producteurs agricoles
University of Calgary
Université McGill, Faculté de droit
World Federalists of Canada
World Vision Canada
World Wildlife Fund Canada

Source: http://www.dfait-maeci.gc.ca/tna-nac/summit-lop.asp.

economic activity and globalization, it falls rather short of being a third *force*. Moreover, as we will argue below, what gains that third sector groups may have made in access to policy-making in Canada over the course of the 1990s will likely be challenged by the aftermath of the events of 11 September 2001.

AFTER 9/11: PROSPECTS AND CHALLENGES FOR CSOs

What effects have the attacks on the United States on 11 September 2001 and the pursuit of a "war on terrorism" by the US and a number of its allies had on the anti-globalization movements in Canada? We suggest that there have been two major impacts.

Rolling Up the Sidewalks

First, the attacks on 9/11 affected how government leaders conduct global diplomacy, accelerating a trend that was already noticeable in the wake of the "Battle of Seattle" in November and December 1999. While a physical venue has never been a necessary condition for the global anti-globalization movement (as the protests against the MAI clearly demonstrated), there can be little doubt that the anti-globalization movement relied on the frequent summit meetings of world leaders and the tendency of international organizations to conduct international negotiations at major conferences. In other words, the anti-globalization protests of the mid- and late 1990s that germinated in Geneva and blossomed at Seattle heavily depended on *place* for their success. The protestors depended on the tendency of those leaders, and particularly the host, to want those summits to be glitzy showpieces. Moreover, summit diplomacy, as it was practised in the last quarter of the twentieth century, grew to the point where summit meetings between a small number of government leaders became massive undertakings, routinely involving a supporting cast of thousands of staffers, gofers, and media dispatched to cover the meetings.[4] And the very size of contemporary summitry meant that meetings tended to be held in those locales that could accommodate the sudden influx of several thousand people. Summit sites were invariably in downtown conference centres (or, in the case of Melbourne, in a casino located in the central business district), with national delegations and the international press concentrated in the five-star hotels normally clustered around such venues. And, in turn, those locales provided protestors with an excellent venue for their own political street theatre: conference centres or casinos proved a ready magnet, relatively easy to surround and disrupt traffic flows. Central business districts, being central, made convergence from different locales easy. Moreover, downtowns had the additional attraction of being littered with businesses emblematic of globalization, ripe for symbolic trashing.

Even before 9/11, the nature of summitry was in the process of being changed. Local authorities, in consultation with central governments, were beginning to change the security arrangements as a means of avoiding the mounting costs of playing host to an international meeting. For example, the 2000 G7/8 summit was held on the sprawling United States air base at Kadena in Okinawa, with some 30,000 protestors kept well outside the perimeter. The Summit of the Americas in Quebec City in April 2001 featured efforts to physically isolate the core of the old city, where the summit was to be held, from the rest of the city by a fence. Genoa, site of the G7/8 in July 2001, was divided into a red maximum security zone that was separated from a larger yellow zone surrounding it by a large fence; all protests were supposed to be conducted outside the yellow zone in officially sanctioned protest areas. Likewise, in their choices of summits for the 2001–02 season, organizers appeared to favour locales where the security apparatus was in full control (meetings of the Asia-Pacific Economic Cooperation forum in Shanghai in October 2001); or that were expensive to get to (the WTO ministerial meeting in Doha in November 2001), or were remote (Kananaskis). Summit organizers and local police forces also changed their tactics in actually dealing with protestors, involving protest group leaders in planning, but at the same time promising that violence would bring harsh reactions. Certainly in Quebec City in April 2001 the police responded forcefully to maintain the integrity of the fence.

After 9/11, all of these trends deepened. Summit meetings themselves became less frequent than in the past as security considerations prompted leaders to be more selective about their international travels. Certainly in the immediate aftermath of 9/11 the 2001 Commonwealth Heads of Government Meetings in Brisbane were cancelled, as were the IMF and World

Bank meetings. The G20 meetings were relocated from India to Ottawa at the last moment, and the World Economic Forum was moved from its traditional venue in Davos, Switzerland to Whistler, BC. Moreover, national governments playing host to international summits tightened their border controls to limit the influx of protestors, making it more difficult to get to meetings. For example, relatively few Canadian NGOs attended the WTO ministerial meeting in Doha in 2001, as Table 4 shows, largely because of security concerns. Likewise, would-be protestors discovered in June 2002 that because of instructions to officials of the Canada Customs and Revenue Agency to deny entry to those who appeared to want to enter Canada from the United States for the purpose of protesting the G7/8, the Canadian border was much less permeable in the run-up to Kananaskis. And, after 9/11, there was also a sharper response by the security forces in dealing

Table 4: Canadian Non-Governmental Organizations Registered to Attend WTO Ministerial Meeting, Doha, November 2001

Alberta Economic Development Authority	Coopérative Fédérée du Québec
Canada-Korea Business Council	Council of Canadians
Canadian Agri-Food Trade Alliance	Dairy Farmers of Canada
Canadian Bar Association	Fédération des producteurs du lait du Québec
Canadian Centre for Policy Alternatives	Federation of Law Societies of Canada
Canadian Chamber of Commerce	Fraser Institute
Canadian Council for International Cooperation	Greenpeace Canada
Canadian Environmental Law Association	International Centre for Human Rights and Democratic Development
Canadian Federation of Agriculture	International Institute for Sustainable Development
Canadian Foodgrains Bank	
Canadian Manufacturers and Exporters	International Network for Cultural Diversity
Canadian Restaurant and Food Services Association	National Farmers' Union
	National Union of Public and General Employees
Centre for International Sustainable Development Law	Oxfam-Canada
Centre for Trade Policy and Law	Oxfam-Québec
Chicken Farmers of Canada	Polaris Institute
Coalition for Cultural Diversity	Union des producteurs agricoles
Confédération des Syndicats nationaux	

with protestors: in the G7/8 planning meeting in Halifax in June 2002, and in both Kananaskis and Calgary, the police were accused of overreacting to protestors who tried to break police lines or break through the secure cordon around Kananaskis.

In short, in the years since Seattle, but particularly since 11 September 2001, governments have tried to deny anti-globalization protestors space to conduct the street theatre so vital for political mobilization against globalization. By rolling up the sidewalks and holding their meetings in remote locales that are relatively difficult to reach, relatively easy to make secure, and where there are no Starbucks to trash, governments have ensured that anti-globalization protestors are left on the margins. And the more remote from the centre of the "action," the less magnetic street protests will be, as the relatively thin turnout in Calgary demonstrated (somewhat down from the 200,000 protestors who gathered in Genoa the year before).

Return of the National Security State

A second major effect of 9/11 on the anti-globalization movement has been that the attacks on the United States prompted the reappearance of security as a primary focus of foreign policy, not only in the United States, but in other countries, including Canada. The involvement of Canadians in the US-led "war against terrorism" served to reduce, and even sideline, CSO input into the foreign policy process, including policy on economic issues. After 9/11, the foreign policy apparatus in Canada began operating in what one senior official has termed "unabashed crisis mode," with much of the "ordinary" or routine business of many units in the Department of Foreign Affairs and International Trade and other departments with international mandates simply subordinated to the demands of the war, or simply suspended altogether.

In such a climate, the claims of third sector groups for a continuation of "business-as-usual" consultations (much less an intensification of earlier processes) tended not to carry a great deal of weight with a state apparatus preoccupied with war and security. One small but telling measure was the abrupt abandonment, in early 2002, of Axworthy's policy of careful nurturing of the CSO/NGO community in the run-up to Kananaskis. Indeed, it could be argued that some of these trends were in effect anyway with the retirement of Axworthy from politics prior to the November 2000 general elections. With Axworthy's departure, the foreign affairs portfolio passed to John Manley, the minister of industry. As foreign minister, and then as deputy prime minister with responsibility for the Canadian-American relations portfolio, Manley never demonstrated the kind of unbridled enthusiasm that Axworthy clearly had for engaging the third sector directly in policy-making. And while the Department of Foreign Affairs and International Trade continues to devote a great deal of time and resources consulting with civil society organizations, the process has not enjoyed the same status as it did during Axworthy's years as foreign minister.

This diminished concern for the CSO community, moreover, fitted well with shifts in public opinion on the issue of trade and globalization. As Matthew Mendelsohn and Robert Wolfe (2001) have demonstrated, one needs to draw conclusions about public opinion on globalization and international trade with some care. Nonetheless, it can be argued that public opinion polls suggest that tolerance and sympathy for mass protests have diminished dramatically since 9/11, particularly in cases where there is violence that involves confrontation between police and protestors. Not only have the police themselves shown less tolerance toward protestors engaging in violence, as we noted above, but it would appear from public opinion polls that after 9/11 there was considerable public support for a harder police line against violent protestors: a poll in November 2001, for example, revealed that 44 percent of the respondents approved of the use of all necessary force to control protestors, even if it involved the loss of life (Kirton 2001/02).

The re-emergence of national security as a dominant focus of foreign policy suggests that it is possible to see some shifts in the underlying construction of identity, which in turn will have an impact on the anti-globalization movement. Hilary Cunningham (2000) has argued that transnational social activism was intrinsically linked to the "deterritorialized" identity of those involved in transnational social movements. By territorialized identity, Cunningham is not referring to the irrelevance of national borders, but rather, an identity politics that renounces the state (in her case study, the US state) as a central source of authority. It could be argued that the events of 9/11, and the resurgence of national security issues, the tightening of borders, both material and cultural, and the extraordinary resurgence of patriotism and nationalism, particularly in the United States, have contributed to a "reconstruction" of territorialized identities, which has set back the cause of transnational social activism, and has had an impact on the "fields of action" in which NGOs might operate. Indeed, Jeffrey Ayres and Sidney Tarrow (2002) argue that in the wake of 9/11, NGO activity should focus more sharply on the state as the most appropriate target for activism.

The re-emergence of security also may have a longer term impact. It is possible that the US-led counterattacks on terrorism after 9/11 could re-kindle citizens' trust in governments, at least with respect to transnational activities and the need for governments to protect citizens against some transnational movements (such as terrorism). And if citizen distrust for, or at least frustration with, governments does wane, we hypothesize that there could be associated, and potentially quite negative, implications for third sector activities.

If citizens do regain some trust in government, it is possible that NGOs, particularly transnational NGOs, could face a corresponding decrease in public confidence. Even prior to 11 September 2001, NGO claims to moral authority were being openly questioned (Diebert 2000). For example, Greenpeace lost a great deal of its authority as a result of its successful campaign to prevent Royal Dutch/Shell from disposing of the oil rig Brent Spar by sinking it, even when it was shown that the environmental damage would be insignificant (Simmons 1998). Likewise, Care Australia was highly embarrassed by allegations that two Care Australia aid workers arrested by Serbian forces in 1999 were in fact engaged in spying activities for Australian, British, and US intelligence — just as the Serbs had claimed.

Moreover, it is possible that the claims of NGOs to be representative of a broader global interest, so commonly asserted in the 1990s, may be subjected to increased scepticism. Already NGOs have been the target of considerable criticism. Some have noted the class bias of NGO membership (Scholte 1999). For their part, southern NGOs have expressed concern over the tendency of NGOs in the developed capitalist world to clothe their parochial northern interests using the rhetoric of the "global interest." In the north itself, some critics have noted the often undemocratic and unaccountable practices of NGOs. Given this, it is entirely possible that if the events of 9/11 lead to the "re-discovery" of the state as a more positive force in community life, there will be even greater demands for increased transparency and accountability from the third sector.

CONCLUSION

In this chapter we have sought to assess some of the possible consequences for third sector activism of the sudden and dramatic re-emergence of the national security state in Canada in the wake of the terrorist attacks of 11 September 2001. We have argued that third sector mobilization against the forces of globalization and the institutions of global governance has become more difficult in the immediate term, as security concerns trumped other arguments, perspectives, and policy prescriptions. We have also suggested that in Canada the pace of multi-stakeholder consultation and "democratization" of the foreign policy process on the issues of global economic policy has slowed, and not only because the unabashed champion of bringing civil society organizations into the policy process, Lloyd Axworthy, retired.

Finally, our analysis of the re-emergence of the national security state also suggests one other possibility, somewhat longer term, and somewhat broader in scope. We suggest that among the longer term effects of the events of 9/11 may be a change in how the state is regarded in Canada. While we are not suggesting that there will be a full and widespread restoration of citizen confidence in the state as a result of the events of 9/11, or an end to the malaise in community spirit identified by Walzer or Putnam, we suggest that the rediscovery of the importance of national security after 9/11 *will* have an impact on public perceptions of the proper role of the state, particularly in the "provision" of security for the community — and the evident difficulty of involving the third sector in this sphere of state activities.

Notes

We would like to thank the Nonprofit Sector Research Initiative at the School of Policy Studies, Queen's University, and the Kahanoff Foundation, for a grant which made the research for this project possible, and Al Roberts for his helpful comments on a first draft.

[1]There is a large literature on the anti-MAI campaign: see Kobrin (1998); Smith and Smythe (1999); Barlow and Clarke (2001); and Goodman and Ranald (2000).

[2]For an exploration of the different orientations of civil society organizations toward the WTO, see Scholte, O'Brien and Williams (1999).

[3]For the role of the third sector in the development of Australian trade policy, see Capling and Nossal (2001*a* and *b*). For a discussion of the Canadian approach to the involvement of the third sector in trade policy development, see Stairs (2000); also Curtis and Wolfe (2000, 330-32).

[4]For a good survey of the evolution of the G7/8 summit, see Bayne (2000).

References

Ayres, J. Forthcoming. "Transnational Activism in the Americas: The Internet and Mobilizing against the FTAA," *Research on Social Movements, Conflict and Change.*

Ayres, J. and S. Tarrow. 2002. "The Shifting Grounds for Transnational Civic Activity," in Social Science Research Council, *After September 11: Essays,* available at <http://www.ssrc.org/sept11/essays/ayres.htm>.

Axworthy, L. 1998. "Lessons from the Ottawa Process," *Canadian Foreign Policy* 5 (3):1-2.

Barlow, M. and T. Clarke. 2001. *Global Showdown: How the New Activists are Fighting Global Corporate Rule.* Toronto: Stoddart.

Bayne, N. 2000. *Hanging in There: The G7 and G8 Summit in Maturity and Renewal.* Aldershot, UK: Ashgate.

Brock, K.L. 2000. "Was Seattle Significant? The Emerging Interest in the Third Sector," *CPSA Bulletin* (March).

_____ 2001. "State, Society and the Third Sector: Changing to Meet New Challenges," *Journal of Canadian Studies* 35 (4):203-20.

Cameron, M.A. 1998. "Democratization of Foreign Policy: The Ottawa Process as a Model," *Canadian Foreign Policy* 5 (3):147-65.

_____ 1999. "Global Civil Society and the Ottawa Process: Lessons from the Movement to Ban Anti-Personnel Mines," *Canadian Foreign Policy* 7 (1):85-102.

Capling, A. 2001. *Australia and the Global Trade System: From Havana to Seattle.* Cambridge: Cambridge University Press.

Capling, A. and K.R. Nossal. 2001*a*. "Death of Distance or Tyranny of Distance? The Internet, Deterritorialization, and the Anti-Globalization Movement in Australia," *Pacific Review* 14:2.

_____ 2001*b*. "Square Pegs and Round Holes: Australia's Multilateral Economic Diplomacy and the Joint Standing Committee on Treaties." Paper presented to the International Studies Association, Chicago, 21 February.

Cunningham, H. 2000. "The Ethnography of Transnational Social Activism: Understanding the Global as Local Practice," *American Ethnologist* 26 (3):583-604.

Curtis, J.M. and R. Wolfe. 2000. "The WTO in the Aftermyth of the Battles in Seattle," in *Canada Among Nations 2000: Vanishing Borders.* Toronto: Oxford University Press.

Diebert, R.J. 2000. "International Plug 'n Play? Citizen Activism, the Internet, and Global Public Policy," *International Studies Perspectives* 1:255-72.

Florini, A.M. ed. 2000. *The Third Force: The Rise of Transnational Civil Society.* Washington, DC: Carnegie Endowment.

Goodman, J. and P. Ranald, eds. 2000. *Stopping the Juggernaut: Public Interest versus the Agreement on Investment.* Annandale NSW: Pluto Press.

Keck, M.E. and K. Sikkink 1998. *Activists Beyond Border: Advocacy Networks in International Politics.* Ithaca: Cornell University Press.

Kirton, J.J. (2001/02). "Guess Who Is Coming to Kananaskis? Civil Society and the G8 in Canada's Year as Host," *International Journal* 57 (Winter):100-110.

Kobrin, S.J. 1998. "The MAI and the Clash of Globalizations," *Foreign Policy* 112 (Fall):97-110.

Lynch, C. 1998. "Social Movements and the Problem of Globalization," *Alternatives* 23 (?)·149-73.

Mathews, J. 1997. "Power Shift," *Foreign Affairs* 76 (January/February):162-77.

Mendelsohn, M. and R. Wolfe. 2001. "Probing the Aftermyth of Seattle: Canadian Public Opinion on International Trade, 1980-2000," *International Journal* 56 (Spring):234-60.

Nossal, K.R. 1993. "The Democratization of Canadian Foreign Policy?" *Canadian Foreign Policy* 1 (Fall):95-104.

_____ 1995. "The Democratization of Canadian Foreign Policy: The Elusive Ideal," in *Canada Among Nations, 1995: Democracy and Foreign Policy*, ed. M.A. Cameron and M.A. Molot. Ottawa: Carleton University Press.

_____ 2001. "Opening Up the Policy Process: Does Party Make a Difference?" in *Diplomatic Departures: The Conservative Era in Canadian Foreign Policy, 1984-93*, ed. N. Michaud and K.R. Nossal. Vancouver: UBC Press.

O'Brien, R., A.M. Goetz, J.A. Scholte and M. Williams. 2000. *Contesting Global Governance: Multilateral Economic Institutions and Global Social Movements.* Cambridge: Cambridge University Press.

Putnam, R. 1995. "Bowling Alone: America's Declining Social Capital," *Journal of Democracy* 6:65-78.

Riddell-Dixon, E. 2001. *Canada and the Beijing Conference on Women: Governmental Politics and NGO Participation.* Vancouver: UBC Press.

Ruggie, J.G. 1982. "International Regimes, Transactions and Change: Embedded Liberalism in the Postwar Economic Order," *International Organization* 36

(Spring), reprinted in *Constructing the World Polity*. London: Routledge, 1998, pp. 62-84.

Salamon, L.M. 1994. "The Rise of the Nonprofit Sector," *Foreign Affairs* 73 (4):109-22.

Salamon *et al.* 1999. *Global Civil Society*. Manchester: Manchester University Press.

Scholte, J.A. 1999. "Global Civil Society: Changing the World?" (May). Available at: <http://www.warwick.ac.uk/fac/soc/CSGR/wpapers/wp3199.pdf>.

Scholte, J.A., R. O'Brien and M. Williams. 1999. "The World Trade Organization and Civil Society," in *Trade Politics: International Domestic and Regional Perspectives*, ed. B. Hocking and S. McGuire. London: Routledge, pp. 162-178.

Simmons, P.J. 1998. "Learning to Live with NGOs," *Foreign Policy* 112 (Fall):82-96.

Smith, J., C. Chatfield and R. Pagnucco, eds. 1997. *Transnational Social Movements and Global Politics: Solidarity Beyond the State*. Syracuse: Syracuse University Press.

Smith, P.J. and E. Smythe. 1999. "Globalization, Citizenship and Technology: The MAI Meets the Internet," *Canadian Foreign Policy* 7 (2):83-106.

Spiro, P.J. 1995. "The Role of Non-Governmental Organizations in International Decision-Making Institutions," *Washington Quarterly* 18 (Winter):45-56

Stairs, D. 2000. "Foreign Policy Consultations in a Globalizing World: The Case of Canada, the WTO, and the Shenanigans in Seattle," *Policy Matters* 1:8.

Van Rooy, A. 1999. "How Ambassadors (Should) Deal with Civil Society Organizations: A New Diplomacy?" *Canadian Foreign Policy* 7 (1):147-57.

Walzer, M. 1995. "The Concept of Civil Society," in *Toward a Global Civil Society*, ed. M. Walzer. Providence: Berghahn Books.

Williams, J. and S. Goose. 1998. "The International Campaign to Ban Landmines," in *To Walk Without Fear: The Global Movement to Ban Landmines*, ed. M.A. Cameron, R. Lawson and B.W. Tomlin. Toronto: Oxford University Press.

9

NGOs, Technology and the Changing Face of Trade Politics

Elizabeth Smythe and Peter J. Smith

INTRODUCTION

This chapter examines the development of transnational networks of non-governmental organizations (NGOs) in challenging economic globalization and various international trade and investment agreements and the significant role that information and communication technologies (ICTs), especially the Internet, have played in that process. As such it builds on research that recognizes the importance of NGOs as a means of shaping political discourse and collective political activity and increasingly challenges a more state-centric orientation in particular in international relations (IR). Traditionally, many IR scholars emphasized the nation-state as the primary unit of analysis in a political universe composed of sovereign states — specific territorial units with their own population and exclusive jurisdiction within their borders (Krasner 1999). However, a number of scholars in the discipline have recently questioned the notion that NGOs and social movements were marginal actors in the drama played out between states (Wapner 2001, 1).

While a state-centric view of IR was never completely accurate (Kilby 2000; Florini 2000; Smith 2001*a*), it has only been recently that the international role of NGOs has become impossible to ignore, partly because of their impressive growth. According to Salamon *et al.,* "a veritable 'global associational revolution' appears to be underway, a massive upsurge of organized private, voluntary activity in literally every corner of the world" (1999, 4). Moreover, thanks in part to the Internet, the activities of these organizations are extending beyond national borders, forming coalitions and networks of like-minded organizations which are inserting themselves into decision-making processes at the national and global levels. Rare is the transnational issue that does not attract the attention of transnational NGOs.

Much of this research on transnational networks has focused on what Keck and Sikkink (1998) have called "advocacy networks" dealing with issues such as human rights, environmental agreements or land mines (Scott 2001; Cameron1998). This chapter instead focuses on the efforts by national and transnational NGOs to organize, mobilize, and influence the outcome of negotiations of multilateral economic institutions, in particular the World Trade Organization (WTO) and its General Agreement on Trade in Services (GATS) negotiations. We build on previous research that examined how activists have used ICTs to organize and mobilize the Multilateral Agreement on Investment (MAI) and attempts to launch a new round of international trade negotiations in Seattle (Smith and Smythe 1999). Here we analyze how NGOs, acting as a part of a transnational campaign, attempted to inform and educate the public as well as influence the position of their respective governments on international trade and investment negotiations. Our argument, in essence, is that ICTs have played an important role in facilitating links between the local and the global and thus had an important impact on both the development of these transnational networks and the trade-policy processes themselves at both the national (or regional) and the global level. The processes have not replaced what might be called the traditional politics of trade policy, but rather have emerged alongside them and created a process that, it could be argued, is more transparent, inclusive, contentious, and ultimately less coherent.

Whether they have had an impact on substantive policy outcomes is much harder to assess. However, we will argue that they have brought new issues onto the agenda, raised public awareness of the impact of trade and investment agreements on daily lives, and altered the discourse surrounding globalization. Moreover, many NGOs have come to recognize a need to link to broader global networks in order to achieve their goals at the domestic level.

Our evidence is drawn from a number of sources and a variety of methodologies, including the analysis of Web sites and the gathering of basic data on 77 non-governmental organizations active on these issues. In addition, evidence is drawn from three case studies comparing the activities of NGOs in Canada, Australia, and the European Union, and the response on the part of negotiators in each case to these concerted NGO campaigns. Data have been gathered via a series of interviews with both NGO representatives and negotiators in 2000 and 2001.

The chapter begins with a discussion of NGOs as civil society organizations, their relationship to democracy and politics, and the reasons for their growth, accentuating the role that new information technologies, in particular the Internet, have played in associational revolution and organizational life. We then examine in detail how networks of NGOs using ICTs have attempted to influence trade policy in the three cases.

NGOs AS CIVIL SOCIETY ORGANIZATIONS

While NGOs are now beginning to receive the attention they deserve, they are hardly new political phenomena. NGOs, defined most broadly as voluntary organizations, have virtually co-existed with modernity as non-state instantiations of the contested term, "civil society." Beginning primarily with Tocqueville, voluntary organizations have been acknowledged to play important societal roles whether as safety valves — as a means of giving voice beyond the electoral process — or, as safety nets: providing needed services by charitable organizations to those most adversely affected by the vicissitudes of the market economy (Bach 2001).

These functions of organizing political expression and dissent within civil society, acting as advocacy organizations, and as a means of delivering services not provided by government, remain key activities of NGOs today. These functions are also reflective of two competing visions of civil society. The first is the civic republican vision espoused by Tocqueville who viewed civil society as a wide variety of voluntary associations that were free schools of democracy preparing citizens for participation in public life. Central to Tocqueville's analysis is a vision of politics and democracy that is state-decentred and grounded in civil society, a vision of politics that has taken root in contemporary social movements and NGOs. Today, as Robert Cox notes, civil society has a Tocquevillean interpretation, as a "mobilized participant citizenry juxtaposed to dominant economic and state power" (1999, 6) This should be contrasted with another equally prominent view in the nineteenth century of civil society as liberal, that is, as an apolitical or pre-political, space organized around the market economy (Taylor 1990). Today, this interpretation is embodied in neo-liberal globalization. These two interpretations of civil society and NGOs clash with one another, as they did in the nineteenth century, with some viewing NGOs primarily as advocacy organizations protesting, for example, against economic globalization while others, in particular donors such as the World Bank, viewing NGOs as non-political privatized delivery systems for services such as welfare, education, health care, clean water, and so on (Jordan and van Tujil 1998). In reality, many NGOs act as both advocacy and supply-side organizations reflecting the tensions of civil society itself.

The meaning of NGOs is often contested. What all NGOs share is their name, *non-governmental organizations*, which identifies them in a negative sense, in terms of the other, that is, what they are not. Other definitions, such as that of the United Nations Economic and Social Council, stress elements that many NGOs might question, for example, that they be oriented toward the rule of law. Indeed, many organizations, such as Greenpeace, reflect a growing emphasis on contentious politics and frequently break the law in pursuit of their objectives. Unlike the Mafia, however, these organizations do not have criminal goals and generally try to work within the rule of law (Hobe 1998). This chapter adopts the approach of Salamon and Anheier (1999) who de-emphasize legal criteria and employ a more inclusive definition of voluntary organizations. Accordingly, nonprofit, or non-governmental organizations, share common characteristics. That is, they are:

- "Organizations, i.e., they have an institutional presence and structure;
- Private; i.e., they are institutionally separate from the state;

- Not-profit distributing; i.e., they do not return profits to their managers or to a set of 'owners';

- Self-governing, i.e., they are fundamentally in control of their own affairs; and

- Voluntary, i.e., membership in them is not legally required and they attract some level of voluntary contribution of time or money" (Salamon and Anheier 1999, 3-4).

While the above definition has the virtue of being inclusive it is necessary to point out that the word "private" can be misleading, as it embodies a contested notion of what is public and political. Here it means that the organization is not part of the government apparatus and public administration nor is it dominated by public officials (Anheier and Salamon 1998). However, NGOs should not be construed as non- or apolitical since their activities have an impact on power relations within a society. For example, according to Jordan and Van Tuijl, "Even the smallest bread and butter intervention by an NGO at a local level will affect power relations. Digging a well, for example, will increase the availability of water and will affect patterns of ownership, distribution, income and social culture intercourse in a village" (1999, 6).

THE RISE OF NGOs

The number of NGOs has been rising exponentially, whether they are national or transnational. According to Michael Edwards, in 1909 there were 176 "international" NGOs, a figure that had risen to 28,900 in 1993 with over 20,000 transnational NGO networks active worldwide, virtually all have been formed during the last 30 years (Edwards 2000, 9). The story is much the same, with the exception of those countries with repressive regimes, in both developed and developing countries.

To a considerable extent the growth of NGOs is attributable to "the crisis of the state." For over two decades there has been a widespread perception of state failure, fed by an era of massive state deficits, financial crises, and economic restructuring. Ideologically, neo-liberal economics replaced Keynesian economics signaling a sharp shift in ideas on how governments should conduct their affairs. Government was to be restructured along the lines of a corporatist market model, emphasizing private delivery of services because of perceived efficiency and cost-effectiveness. Increasingly, governments withdrew from certain fields of endeavour to be replaced by NGOs that were seen by governments and citizens as credible alternatives to the state. The bias here clearly is on the supply or operational side.

Others, however, questioned the "neo-liberal consensus," viewing NGOs far differently, not as "simply instruments to pick up the pieces of state and market failure ... but a force for transformation in global politics and economics" (Edwards 2000, 6) In brief, power and domination from above were encountering resistance and politics from below. According to this view, NGOs had a different purpose, to serve as a means of democratization, of giving voice to citizens, and to serving as a counterweight to state and economic power.

The belief that NGOs had a responsibility to act as alternative vehicles of citizen participation held at both the national and transnational levels of governance. Many issues of concern to citizens — pollution, human rights, the economy — increasingly transcend state borders. Indeed, just as states have mobilized to create multilateral instruments of global governance to address many of these issues, civil society-based non-state actors, NGOs, and social movements have demonstrated a remarkable ability to organize and network on a transnational basis. This is particularly evident with respect to the growing civil society opposition to economic globalization and efforts to challenge global institutional agendas, including the MAI, the WTO meetings, the Free Trade Area of the Americas (FTAA), and G8 and other similar meetings.

Facilitating the associational revolution of NGOs, transnational nongovernmental organizations (TNGOs), and Transnational social movements is the communications revolution. Just as new communication technologies have facilitated the growth of a global informational economy and the restructuring of capitalism, equally so they have facilitated the ability of NGOs to exchange ideas, organize, and network on both national and transnational bases. Indeed, we argue that the informational revolution, particularly the use of the Internet, is a key to understanding the associational revolution and that new communications technologies have enhanced the capacity of organizations to operate outside the gaze of the state and network on a global basis. ICTs are restructuring organizational life away from its traditional emphasis on centralized hierarchies to more horizontally linked networked organizations.

Communications analysts have long noted a close relationship between forms of communication, political power, and organizational means of social control. The Canadian historian and social scientist, Harold Innis, argued that each communications medium had a bias which had significant societal implications. Some forms of communication favour time over space while others have the opposite effect. Oral communication and writing on clay tablets, for example, helped create a sense of continuity with the past (Babe 2000). Other forms of communication, however, had a space bias, that is, they favoured "administrative institutions and techniques that are required for managing and governing a given territory" (Zerker in Seigel 1996, 31). Papyrus, for example, was instrumental to the coordination and administration of the Roman Empire. Space-biased media, Innis maintained, tended to erode local cultures and promote cultural homogenization. As Robert Babe notes, "by favouring one-way communication and centralized control, they contribute to … a decline in democracy" (2000, 76). Innis's ideas are particularly applicable to the relationship between print, the creation of modern bureaucracies with their emphasis on logical, rational, linear thought, and the rise of sovereign nation-states with common senses of national identity and culture. Andrew Calabrese's analysis echoes that of Innis.

> For better or worse, the legitimacy of sovereignty depends at least in part on a common sense of national identity. In an emerging European system of sovereign states, the printed word played a great part in shaping such identities (Calabrese 1999, 316).

More recently, the advent of radio and television accentuated the one-way, centralized bias of previous space-biased media. According to Hans Geser, "since the inception of the printing press in the sixteenth century, only the 'one-to-many' media have made significant technological progress: culminating in the highly centralized modern mass media systems (press, radio, TV, and cinema) which are largely dominating the public sphere" (2000, 3). Geser's analysis implicitly reinforces that of Innis. Geser argues that:

> The deficient technological support for bottom-up and multilateral commu-
> nication may explain why all major societal developments of the last five
> centuries have predominantly been shaped by rather authoritarian types of
> organizations (bureaucracies, business corporations, etc.), while associational
> organizations (co-operatives, parties, unions, etc.) have played a more mod-
> est role (Geser 2000, 3).

All these organizations, it must said, tended to be organized along
territorially, segmented lines. The Internet, claims Geser, represents a significant departure from previous media in that it permits horizontal
bi-directional and multilateral communications, a boon to associational
activity.

Similar to Geser, Manuel Castells contends that the rise of a new global
informational economy is accelerating a "shift from vertical bureaucracies
to the horizontal corporation" (1996, 164). Moreover, this transformation
of organizational structures is penetrating all aspects of life. According to
Castells,

> our exploration of emergent social structures across domains of human ac-
> tivity and experience leads to an overarching conclusion: as a historic trend,
> dominant functions and processes in the information age are increasingly
> organized around networks. Networks constitute the new social morphol-
> ogy of our societies, and the diffusion of networking logic substantially
> modifies the operation and outcomes in processes of production, experi-
> ence, power, and culture. While the networking form of social organization
> has existed in other times and spaces, the new information technology para-
> digm provides the material basis for its pervasive expansion throughout the
> entire social structure (Castells 1996, 469).

One result, maintains James Rosenau, is that new technologies have created a relational revolution with profound implications for voluntary
associations, NGOs, and civil society. These organizations have not only
increased in number but also have the ability to act upon a global stage.
"Clearly, then," Rosenau insists, "the availability of information technologies facilitates the exercise of human agency" (2001, 3). The ability of
NGOs to operate outside state control and beyond national borders poses a
critical challenge to the notion that politics and democracy can only be
state-centred. How can this increasingly transnational or deterritorialized
democracy best be theorized? As Tocqueville argued, politics need not be
centred around the activities of the state. Befitting an era where the nation-

state and national media have lost control of publicity, Tocqueville conceived of political space as being plural rather than singular. Moreover, Tocqueville viewed politics as agonistic, an interpretation consistent with NGOs and transnational social movements contesting economic globalization. "In the world of politics," Tocqueville wrote, "everything is in turmoil, contested, and uncertain" (1835, 47). Written more than a century and a half ago these words are more appropriate than ever.

GLOBALIZATION AND THE DEVELOPMENT OF NETWORKS OF RESISTANCE

This section both argues that the processes of globalization have generated networks of resistance and examines why particular organizations like the WTO and trade and investment agreements have become a target of these networks. Economic globalization can be defined as a set of globally-inte grated processes of production of goods and services, characterized by a transnational division of labour crossing state boundaries, yet organized within a single or linked set of corporations. The capacity to organize production in this manner in the postwar period has been facilitated by three trends. First, the declining costs and rising speed of transportation have allowed larger quantities and lower cost movements of goods, capital, and services. Second, communications technologies have lowered costs and increased the speed of the movement of ever larger amounts of information, data, and ideas. Third, states lowered, either unilaterally or through bilateral and multilateral agreements, barriers to the movement of goods, capital, and, more recently, services.

The size, scope, speed, and intensity of these movements of goods and capital and information are seen to have major implications for states and thus ultimately, citizens (Held 1999). Critics of the process of globalization also point out that it is a highly uneven process which has produced many winners and losers in the global economy. The growth in inequality has resulted, in part, from the domestic policies in many, including the most industrialized, countries, which have included the shrinking of state regulation and social programs that were designed to redistribute wealth. This change is often justified domestically in the name of deficit reduction, the unsustainability of high taxes given capital mobility, and the need to create a positive economic climate designed to lure or retain new private investment. The mantra of globalization was often used to defuse or discredit political opposition. The ideological hegemony of neo-liberalism, however, was never complete, and coupled with the result for a number of citizens of a rising level of economic uncertainty and instability, provides some of the seeds of domestic opposition to globalization.

A second aspect of the later postwar period relevant to our understanding of networks of resistance to globalization and the targets they have chosen was the creation of the set of international governmental organizations (IGO) after the Second World War under American hegemony, some of which were intended to address questions of international peace and security while others were to move countries to re-open their economies to the freer movement of goods and capital. These institutions became the key venues for periodic negotiation and institutionalization of international norms and economic rules.

In conjunction with and parallel to the increase in the number of intergovernmental organizations came the increase in non-governmental organizations discussed above. Many of these groups gained specific formal standing or recognition within certain organizations almost from the start, as in the case of the United Nations Economic and Social Council, thus gaining both access to resources and legitimacy. These more NGO-friendly organizations and institutions provided venues and opportunities for groups to meet, interact, network, and articulate values that, in some cases, challenged those of market-based economic globalization. In particular, world conferences (often under United Nations auspices) on issues such as social development (Copenhagen), women's issues (Beijing), and the environment (Rio) afforded groups some influence over agreements which often had a limited binding authority or inadequate resources for implementation.

In contrast, economic IGOs have became important venues to develop and enforce a set of binding rules through interstate negotiation which were designed, by and large, as neo-liberal ideologies took hold, to liberalize national economic policies by limiting state policy discretion. Regional and multilateral trade and investment agreements became a means to insulate policies from popular influence in many countries, thus providing more certainty to foreign investors and exporters. The states most affected were those most dependent on the resources that the most influential economic actors controlled, be they pools of capital or market access. These organizations were by and large ones where, with the exception of a few business-based or economic stakeholder NGOs, most other non-governmental actors had little or no voice or influence. In the case of the World Bank, however, an effective campaign of opposition in the 1980s ultimately forced open the doors to recognition and consultative status for a select group of developmental and environmental NGOs (Foster 1999), providing once again, the resources and opportunities for groups to inter-act and connect internationally.

The fact that many states were increasingly in competition for mobile capital and market access facilitated the development of international economic rules within NGO unfriendly organizations. Thus, interstate negotiations covered an expanding agenda, well beyond that of trade in goods which reached deeply into areas of traditional domestic state regulation. With its coverage of investment, services and intellectual property, the Uruguay Round of trade negotiations exemplified this trend. Often these rules were developed first at the regional (North American Free Trade Agreement, NAFTA) or bilateral level (bilateral investment and trade treaties).

These international economic rule-making organizations were constituted as multilateral clubs (Keohane and Nye 2000a), venues where powerful state actors hammer out agreements and deals which other members then ultimately join. In some cases, such as the International Monetary Fund and the World Bank, state influence is directly reflected in weighted voting. In the case of the General Agreement on Tariffs and Trade (GATT) and the WTO the façade of consensus merely obscured a situation where, in reality, the organization was dominated by the largest economic actors including the United States, the European Union, and Japan.

The broadening scope of the agenda and the ability for these rules to be enforced by sanctions has raised major questions about legitimacy and democracy (Krajewski 2001; Keohane and Nye 2000a). State bureaucrats, usually under a mandate and delegated authority from elected political executives, crafted agreements and deals which were then presented to legislative bodies in national capitals as a *fait accompli* to be duly ratified. In many instances, elected legislatures played only a marginal role and public debates of these agreements were few and far between. As the content of these agreements penetrated more and more into domestic laws and regulations and, as Keohane and Nye (2000*a*) point out, the length of the chain of political accountability lengthened to a point where the legitimacy of this process and ultimately democracy came to be questioned by a number of organizations and concerned citizens.

A final factor in the proliferation of non-governmental organizations is also as a result of the retrenchment of the state sector, leading states to encourage voluntary associations to take over, at least in part, the role of governments in delivering services both within local communities and internationally (especially in the case of development assistance). In the post-Cold-War rhetoric of democratization, the growth of "civil society," especially in Central and Eastern Europe and the post-Soviet republics, was seen as a hallmark and key building block of democracy.

Thus, as we have indicated here, economic globalization and the strengthening of international rules and norms of economic liberalization through the negotiation of regional and international agreements facilitated the rise of NGO networks. The stage was set for the development of transnational networks challenging globalization. But the way in which these networks emerged and the capacity of national organizations to insert into them was greatly facilitated by information and communication technologies, themselves often promoted and encouraged by government support.

THE INTERNET, NGOs AND GLOBALIZATION: THE MAI AND SEATTLE EXPERIENCE

Networks have been defined as "forms of organization characterized by voluntary, reciprocal and horizontal patterns of exchange" (Keck and Sikkink 1998, 8). They precede the development of the Internet. However, a number of analysts have pointed to the Internet in accelerating the development of recent networks where "activists are forming into open, all channel, multi-hub designs whose strength depends on free-flowing discussion and information sharing" (Arquilla and Ronfeldt 2001, 326). As such, they do not have a headquarters or bureaucracy. Groups often work fairly independently, but they are in constant communication and coordinate with counterparts elsewhere, a process that the Internet facilitates. At the same time, the development of organizations and the conferences and meetings they have spawned, also means many of the key individuals in-volved have personal relationships of trust. These characteristics describe the groups that came together to challenge global trade and investment agreements in the 1990s.

Drawing on the two cases of the campaign of opposition to the MAI from 1997–98 and the organization of opposition and protest against a new round of WTO trade negotiations in Seattle in 1999 (Smith and Smythe 1999; Smythe and Smith 2002), along with additional research studies (Warkentin 2001), this section examines some of the ways in which NGOs have used new technology and how ICTs have facilitated the development and transformation of international networks, allowing the linking of the local and the global. Further insights are provided from data we have gath-ered on 77 organizations active in these campaigns and the broader efforts to challenge globalization.

These two cases are important and closely linked as many of those groups involved in attempts to influence negotiations at the WTO came together as part of the opposition to the MAI. Second, for many of these groups, one of the key lessons from that campaign was the importance of the Internet. The MAI case also represented a learning experience for govern-ments, including Canada's, on the limitations of trade policy-making and the existing consultation processes along with the need for governments to better use the new technology to get its message out.

It is clear from these cases and other studies that many of the advantages of the Internet relate to several characteristics of it as a medium of commu-nication, namely the fact that it is an interactive, unmediated, one-to-many, low-cost and high-speed means of moving large amounts of information. There are five advantages of the Internet for NGOs that we and others (Warkentin 2001, 35) have identified.

- *Facilitation of Internal Communication and Provision of Services to Members*

For many of the NGOs we have interviewed and studied, the Internet, es-pecially e-mail, listservs, and Web sites, have provided an inexpensive method of internal communications and lowered the cost and increased the speed of distribution of material such as newsletters. Strategy discus-sions and input of members at a distance are all made easier. In some cases, such as that of the south-based network of women's organizations, Development Alternatives with Women for a New Era (DAWN), access to the Internet in 1997 enabled them to strengthen their network by facilitating consultation even as they were able to decentralize and rotate their secretariat to far-flung places such as Fiji (Bunch *et al.* 2001, 25).

• *Shaping Public Perception and Framing Policy Debates*

This was brought home most vividly in the case of the MAI. Despite the launching of negotiations at the Organisation for Economic Co-operation and Development (OECD) in May 1995, virtually no mainstream media paid any attention to the negotiations, and government officials in many OECD countries treated the negotiators as largely technical matters. Only with the leaking of the draft text and its publication on North American NGO Web sites in February 1997, and the subsequent portrayal of secret and substantive negotiations ongoing in Paris did mainstream media pay attention in a number of countries.[1] By that time the NGOs had been successful in framing the debate. Both governments and business organizations, by their own admission, were slower to see the potential of the technology and much later in getting their side of the negotiations out to the broader public.

• *Dissemination and Sharing of Large Amounts of Information*

This is one of the most important aspects of the role of ICTs. The Internet facilitates the sharing and moving of large amounts of complex information easily and quickly. This is not a trivial matter. Trade and investment negotiations involve very complex and highly technical matters. Many resource-poor activist NGOs cannot or do not wish to put the significant kinds of resources into research that credible entry into the policy debates would require, and they are often marginalized as a result (Harper 2001). Now they are able, via the Internet, to quickly and easily access research done by the organizations that do have these resources and, moreover, can freely revise and tailor it to suit local needs. In the case of the MAI, larger environmental, trade union, and other organizations like the Council of Canadians and Public Citizen in the United States were able to share very detailed analysis with these groups. In turn, these organizations could reach thousands of activists worldwide with their research at very low cost.

Second, the speed of the Internet allowed for the strategic sharing of information on the state of play of negotiations, country positions, and statements, which countered the traditional bureaucratic control of information that characterized interstate negotiations. Groups could counter misleading, or selective information of their own state bureaucrats.

- *Encouraging and Facilitating Public Participation and Mobilization*

While in the case of the MAI much of the use of the technology was to raise awareness and knowledge of the agreement and to facilitate groups trying to influence their own governments, in the case of the WTO ministerial meeting, the Internet played another role as part of a process of organizing and mobilizing opposition to the launching of a new round of negotiations at the meeting venue itself in Seattle. The organization of activities including caravans, teach-ins, protests, street theatre, and civil disobedience were all facilitated by the Internet along with the interaction and connection of activists who could share and access practical information on everything from transportation to housing at protest sites (Smith and Smythe 1999). Most NGO sites also provided quick and easy means for citizens to contact officials, sign petitions, and download kits for local actions and events, thus also facilitating what might be seen as traditional political activity.

- *Providing and Opening New Public Space*

Our analysis of the campaign opposing the launch of a new round of negotiations in Seattle (Smythe and Smith 2002) traced a huge increase in both the number of Web sites worldwide and their regional distribution. As well, we noted the appearance of organizations such as One World, Corporate Watch, the Institute for Global Communications, and Webnet which initially began as Internet service providers for nonprofit, progressive NGOs lacking the hardware and expertise to create their own Web sites. As small NGOs have become even more adept in this area, these organizations have moved on and, along with Indymedia, have become Web-based broadcasting systems which contained thousands of print, but also audio and video files and news stories submitted by and from the perspective of activists from around the world. Sites like Indymedia were able to provide their own audio and video clips after the meetings to counter and provide an alternative interpretation of events to that of mainstream media.

COMPARING NGOs

In order to probe a bit further into the nature of the NGOs involved in challenging organizations like the WTO, we created a database of 77 organizations which have been active on WTO trade issues at various points.[2] While the emphasis is on Canadian organizations, a variety of groups based in different regions of the world are included. For comparative purposes, a number of business organizations were also included. The data compare the financial resources, funding sources, goals and purposes, tactics, and structures of accountability.

What is clear from the data is that there is a significant variation across groups on a number of dimensions. Among those who have challenged globalization and the WTO are some of the largest environmental and developmental organizations with, as in the case of Oxfam, budgets in excess of US$16 million, Greenpeace (US$120 million). Others included midsized advocacy organizations such as the Council of Canadians (CDN$4 million), and smaller research organizations such as Focus on the Global South (US$500,000). Others are tiny organizations such as Citizen on the Web, which is funded by a single individual out of his Web business, and has the equivalent of one half-time person. Business organizations, in contrast, can often rely on the staffs and resources of their large corporate members, and while it is difficult to obtain data on budgets, the fact that the International Chamber of Commerce has a staff of 80 suggests substantial resources.

All of these organizations have access to e-mail and in almost all cases a Web site. A number now also have extensive and searchable databases and archives and some, such as Oxfam, have consciously made their Web sites user-friendly to journalists. The most intensive users of this technology, however, tend to be the smaller organizations with the least resources. These tend to be of two types, those such as Direct Action Network and People's Global Action which are very decentralized activist networks or Web-based organizations which provide space for other groups and activists. In contrast, the business organizations, despite having major resources, were slow to use the Internet as part of their advocacy and generally saw it as a way to communicate with members. This pattern would appear to support the arguments that the Internet is a preferred medium for alternative groups and organizations and decentralized networks.

There is a discernable pattern in the tactics used by groups. Most groups fell into two categories: first, what we would call traditional forms of advocacy, including public education, lobbying, and petitions; and second, what we have labelled "performance politics," including activities such as protests, civil disobedience, and street theatre. All of the business organizations fell under the first category only, while 11 of the non-business organizations included both traditional advocacy and performance politics in their tactics. Among the latter group were a number of trade unions.

In the case of accountability, groups often identified two types: downward to members or clients and upward to governing boards or committees. This was the case for all of the business organizations. A large proportion of non-business organizations, however, saw themselves as accountable to a broader public, and of these, another 17 were part of broader networks, coalitions or partnerships to which they also felt accountable.

Along with our interviews of NGOs the data do suggest that the new forms of activity do not replace or displace the traditional range of actions by which civil society groups and individuals sought to influence government. Organized lobbying, meetings, letters, and calls to officials and ministers continue to occur. Rather, the rich variety of new activities and networks exist alongside them. In fact, many organizations and networks engage in traditional lobbying even as they are part of more contentious activities such as protests, demonstrations, and civil disobedience.

Second, these activities occur at all levels, the national state still being *a*, but not *the*, focus. Local, regional, transnational, and cyber-based activities are also part of the process. Third, these activities occur in many instances, apart from and outside, the partisan political processes for a number of reasons. As indicated below the traditional partisan processes have not proved capable of addressing these issues and many comparative studies indicate that although support for values of democracy remain strong, citizens are increasingly sceptical and distrustful of government (Inglehart 1999).

How have the activities of NGOs influenced trade policy-making? We turn now to the example of Canada.

NGOs, NETWORKS AND THE CONTENTIOUS POLITICS OF CANADIAN TRADE POLICY-MAKING

Overall in the late 1990s it could be argued that Canadian opponents of further trade and investment liberalization have been able to use a transnational campaign of opposition to help reconfigure the domestic trade-policy process and re-politicize the trade debate in Canada. That Canadian non-governmental organizations have been organized and quickly join campaigns at the global level should be no surprise given the access to information and communications technology, and the deep roots of many groups and individuals in the battle over continental integration. To understand, however, the link between the transnational and domestic processes we need to begin with an overview of how trade and investment negotiations have been conducted in the past.

Trade policy-making has reflected Canada's parliamentary and federal constitution, making it executive-dominated but also with some voice for the provinces. Much of trade negotiations in the postwar period involved tariffs and issues related to market access for goods and centred around consulting the provinces and sectoral industry or producer representatives most directly affected by these tariff changes. By 1986 this had evolved into a set of committees, including an overarching international trade advisory committee (ITAC), and a series of sectoral industry advisory (SAGIT) committees with representatives invited to sit on the committee by the trade minister. Provincial input came via periodic meetings of trade officials or ministers and their provincial counterparts. This process was in play for the GATT, Canada-United States Free Trade Agreement (CUFTA), and NAFTA negotiations. It had, however, several limitations which became increasingly apparent in the late 1990s.

First, the initial model presumed that negotiations centred on traditional trade issues involving tariffs on goods and the impact of changes to levels of protection on producers. Even by the time of the CUFTA and the Uruguay Round in 1986 this was clearly no longer the case. The issues of culture, access for goods produced in low-wage economies where workers did not enjoy minimum standards of protection (labour standards) and concerns about the downward pressure on environmental protection posed by footloose investment had emerged as part of the NAFTA debate. Gradually a broader range of representatives were added to advisory committees.[3]

Second, the model also assumed that any national debate on these issues, if it occurred at all, would come through the partisan electoral process which gives governments a broad mandate. The Cabinet would authorize officials to negotiate a deal and then ultimately approve it. Governments would presumably be held accountable for a bad deal in ensuing elections. No real role exists for Parliament in debating negotiating mandates or ratifying trade and investment agreements beyond passing implementing laws or amending national legislation once a deal had been made.

Our electoral process and the strong majorities it often produces based on a minority of public support, coupled with very tight party discipline imposed on elected representatives, and the marginal role of backbenchers in trade policy means that any real ongoing public voice for the majority of citizens is muted. As the agenda of trade and investment negotiations expanded to include investment and services the partisan political process and the limited existing consultation process proved inadequate.

A third problem with the earlier model of trade policy-making is that consultation was also geared toward discrete and episodic periods of interstate negotiation, however, trade and investment rules were increasingly being interpreted and reinterpreted. Thus, trade rules are re-made on an ongoing basis in a way that has had a major impact on public policies and the lives of many Canadians. These dispute processes and procedures are deliberately designed to distance and isolate those interpreting the rules from outside national "political interference." While heralded as creating a rules-based system which ensures that the strong do not dominate, the process raises real concerns about accountability in a democracy.

Networking in Canada: From the National to the Transnational

While large coalitions of NGOs in Canada have their roots in the battle over free trade, subsequent campaigns against NAFTA, Asia-Pacific Economic Council (APEC), and the Free Trade Area of the Americas (FTAA) have broadened these networks to include the rest of North America, Asia, and Latin America. For some groups, such as the Council of Canadians, however, it was the experience of the MAI campaign which brought home the lesson that even what had traditionally been a nationalist organization would need to be part of a broader international network to stop the development of further trade and investment agreements like the MAI or the FTAA. Many of these campaigns also brought together labour, environmental groups (not traditional allies), along with groups in both the north and the south, and, despite divisions on tactics and specific issues, groups have been able to unite around the articulation of a range of concerns about the impact of globalization. In contrast to previous producer-based opposition to free trade these movements are not solely about protecting the domestic market but are value-based.

A range of Canadian NGOs, including environmental, labour, and cultural organizations participated in a variety of alternative activities as part of the campaign to stop a new trade round being launched in Seattle. Groups like the Council of Canadians are part of the International Forum on Globalization, another network whose other members include groups from the south such as Third World Network. Many of the representatives of these organizations meet and strategize at various international events and IGO meetings. Because of the proximity of Seattle, thousands of Canadians traveled to the city and were part of the demonstrations, protests, and civil disobedience. Canadian groups acted both inside the convention centre and outside in the streets.

The failure of the Seattle ministerial meeting, however, did not mean the end of trade negotiations. As a result of the "built-in agenda" of unfinished business from the Uruguay Round, negotiations were going forward at the WTO in both services and agriculture. In addition, Canada was simultaneously and actively involved in the negotiations of the FTAA where the issues of investment protection (similar to chapter 11 of NAFTA and the MAI) and services would also be addressed. Thus, for the NGOs opposed to the continued attempts to launch a new round of WTO negotiations and services negotiations, activity in a number of international and regional networks continued of necessity.

The campaign regarding the WTO focused on two main areas. The first was the opposition to a new round of trade negotiations which, with the failure of Seattle, would be addressed by the ministerial meeting due to take place in the fall of 2001. The extent of success of NGOs in mobilizing global networks of opposition to the WTO was reflected in the fact that, as one WTO official recently admitted, "we are bad news" to any city. No country, by the spring of 2001, with the exception of the small state of Qatar was willing to host the ministerial meeting. Holding the meetings in Doha immediately limited the possibility of mounting the kind of demonstrations and street protests seen in Seattle in 1999 and Geneva in May 1998. Distant and isolated, with a government more willing to repress dissent, Doha's lack of space limited NGO representation to less than one-third of the number in Seattle.[4] NGOs did, however, strategize extensively via e-mails, online chat groups and various closed and open listservs on how to organize opposition and protests. Protests were organized in a number of cities to coincide with the meetings and raise public awareness. In Canada, the Common Front Against the WTO[5] established a Web site (wtoaction.org) and a listserv and began coordinating efforts that included a cross-Canada WTO "Quebec to Qatar" Caravan in October 2001, designed to raise awareness and mobilize opposition as it visited different cities, similar to that undertaken for the Seattle WTO ministerial meeting. Again, the Internet also played a role in linking groups internationally, permitting the sharing of strategy and intelligence about the efforts at the WTO to build support for a new round and sharing ideas and strategy through international listservs such as the Stop WTO Round, regular contact with a network of groups such as Public Citizen in the US and Third World Network in Asia and periodic meetings. Canadian groups also signed onto the international NGO statement " Our World is not for Sale WTO: Shrink or Sink."

The second key area of concern for a number of Canadian NGOs was the continued services negotiations. Services has been one of the most complicated and controversial new areas where the WTO seeks to impose discipline on states in the kind of restrictions that can be placed on the delivery of services. Because services, unlike goods, can be delivered in a variety of ways (four modes in WTO jargon), including the right of foreign firms to establish (i.e., foreign investment) and the movement of natural persons, rules on services reach deeply into many areas of domestic regulation. Negotiations aroused the concern of Canadian NGOs to the question of health and educational services and the fear that these publicly provided services will be opened to foreign competition and backdoor privatization. Here too, Canadian NGOs have joined a broader group of over 500 organizations internationally united around the statement, "Stop the GATS Attack."

Groups are also working to increase public awareness of the implications of the GATS for public services and the effort has included a public education campaign using the Internet and the publication of accessible and downloadable explanations and guides to the negotiations such as Scott Sinclair's *GATS: How the World Trade Organization's New "Services" Negotiations Threaten Democracy* (2000). Even more successful has been a campaign of opposition at the local level. Through the distribution of information kits which take the complicated issues of the international GATS negotiations and translate their impact to the local level, raising the spectre of services obligations reaching deep into the regulatory purview of municipalities, along with vigorous lobbying of city councils, groups have been successful in passing council resolutions. This culminated in a resolution presented at the annual meeting of the Federation of Canadian Municipalities in June 2001 which called on the Canadian government to exclude subnational governments and local governments from the GATS obligations.

The Impact

What impact have these efforts had? We can look for evidence in three areas: process, public awareness and attitudes toward these agreements, and changes to government policies and negotiating positions regarding the WTO.

The clearest impact since the MAI has been on the policy process. The MAI had been a cautionary tale for trade officials on how not to develop policy; and it was decided in early 1999 that the Department of Foreign Affairs and International Trade (DFAIT) would consult widely pre-Seattle and go beyond the earlier ITAC-SAGIT model.[6] The resulting process was multi-faceted but rather ad hoc. In 1999, DFAIT organized a series of cross-

Canada roundtable meetings to deal with various issues. The groups included representatives from business, labour, environmental, human rights and development organizations. Two multi-stakeholder meetings were held in Ottawa in May and November 1999. Along with these meetings, DFAIT established the Division of Trade Policy Consultation and Liaison in October. However, with a staff of three, and a broad mandate to facilitate consultations and train officers in DFAIT, resources devoted to consultations are still fairly limited.

For the public at large, DFAIT launched a new Web site in May dedicated to trade negotiations and agreements where a number of issue papers were published and public comment and response were called for. Prior to that, in September 1998, the minister of trade had called on the House Standing Committee to hold hearings on Canada's priorities in any future Millennium Round of negotiations. The committee traveled across Canada in the winter and spring of 1999, heard from over 400 groups and individuals and was able to submit its report well in advance of the November Seattle meeting.

At the WTO itself Canada also had been pushing for more transparency via the faster release of documents to the public. Canada included members of various business, labour, and environmental organizations as advisors to the delegation, a practice which the United States, the European Union, and other countries have also used, along with provincial ministers and officials and members of Parliament.[7] These delegates had access to extra briefings and contact with the negotiators but were not present at the table. Canadian officials held nightly briefings in Seattle for NGO representatives.[8]

In the case of services the department undertook a major round of cross-Canada consultations on the GATS between 23 June and 11 October 2000 involving over 300 groups. In addition, the department solicited comments and sent out e-questionnaires to over 100,000 businesses via the interdepartmental WinExport/Strategis Web site. Canada's basic negotiating proposals in each of the service sectors have also been posted along with the names, contact numbers, and e-mail addresses of negotiators — a further attempt to show transparency in the negotiation process. While the e-mail response has been modest, the extent to which the Web site has become an important source of information for Canadians is reflected in the statistics on hits on the Web site, which doubled from January 2000–January 2001, averaging over one million per month.[9]

The efforts at consultation have not necessarily satisfied NGOs who are critical of the government's position. Some critics question the process, given the government's commitment to liberalization and are thus sceptical that it is anything more than an elaborate public relations exercise and are wary of being co-opted.[10]

On the other hand, DFAIT officials claim that they are not in a position to engage in dialogue or debate about the government's position given that their direction must come from the political executive.[11] However, they argue that the process of consultations has been useful. The NGOs, in their view, are increasingly knowledgeable and more able to provide substantive input than has been the case in the past. They also claim that the extensive concern regarding health, education, and public services in the GATS negotiations has, if anything, reinforced the need to safeguard the domestic right to regulate in this area. The depth of the concern of Canadians expressed through the Web site strengthens their negotiating position. They also point out, however, that other groups and organizations, including universities, have identified interests in opening up other countries' educational services markets to Canadian exports. Civil society, they point out, does not speak with one voice on the services issues.

There is some evidence that the campaign has had an impact on public awareness of trade issues, especially since Seattle. The extent to which it has altered public attitudes is less clear. A survey undertaken by Ekos research and commissioned by DFAIT in 2001 (Ekos Research 2001) reflects this. Over 60 percent of Canadians were aware of media reports on trade issues. While they believe that trade agreements primarily benefit big business, they also associated increased trade with access to technology and more jobs. Over half thought that protestors had raised valid concerns about trade agreements. Protecting social services, they indicated as well, should be government's top priority. These data suggest that some of the messages of the NGOs are getting through, but it does not suggest a groundswell of opposition to negotiations. Increasingly aware and supportive but sceptical would seem to best describe the public attitude toward trade negotiations.

AUSTRALIA AND THE EMERGING POLITICS OF TRADE POLICY

Australian NGOs, in contrast to Canadians, have not had as extensive networks organized around trade issues prior to the MAI. Still, Australian NGOs tend to be well-connected and active on trade and investment issues. The Internet clearly played a role in facilitating the rapid organization of a network and its insertion into the global anti-MAI campaign.

In terms of its process of trade policy-making, there are broad similarities to Canada in its parliamentary and federal constitution and the dominant role of the executive in trade negotiations. As a so-called middle power, Australia, like Canada, has a trade-dependent economy. However, it also provides a number of contrasts to Canada in terms of its regional location, its relationship to its trading partners, and in the nature of its parliamentary institutions — especially its elected upper house and the role of Parliament in trade agreements. Like Canada, Australia is highly dependent on exports, but more diverse in its trading partners, with 20 percent of exports going to its most important market, Japan, (Capling 2001,1) in contrast to Canada's extreme dependence on the US as a market for over 80 percent of exports. Because it is a relatively small player in terms of the size of its economy and market it has, like Canada, vigorously supported the strengthening of rules in multilateral organizations like the WTO, particularly as they relate to non-discrimination.

The experience of the MAI has been frequently cited by both trade officials and non-business NGOs in Australia as one of the key turning points in the recent trade-policy process.[12] The other turning point was the passage in 1996 of a statute requiring a national interest analysis of all international treaties and their review by a Joint Standing Committee (of the Senate and House) on Treaties (JSCOT). Passed as a result of a range of concerns about various treaty obligations that Australia had undertaken in areas such as human rights and the environment with little public consultation, the statute calls for a public interest assessment for each treaty prior to approval. Most important is that it mandates that the committee assess the adequacy of the public consultations undertaken by government. The committee has provided an opening for NGOs in giving them an opportunity to appear before it to challenge or critique government policy in negotiations. This proved to be very important in the case of the MAI and also enabled NGOs to insist upon consultations in relation to the WTO.

The international campaign against the MAI became mobilized as a result of the leak of the text of a draft agreement on the Internet in March 1997. The Internet also facilitated the rapid development of an international network of over 600 organizations which worked to stop the agreement. MAI negotiations had been undertaken by the Treasury Department with few internal or external consultations, except with a few large business organizations such as the Business Council of Australia and the Australian Chamber of Commerce. With the assistance of transnational links providing information on the draft text and detailed analysis, a group of NGOs were able, in January of 1998, to form a broad Stop-MAI coalition in Australia. (Goodman 2000). In March 1998, as a result of growing public concern, the JSCOT initiated an inquiry on the MAI despite the fact that negotiations were not completed. As a result, over 900 submissions were made to the committee, the vast majority critical of the agreement. In March 1999, after negotiations had ceased at the OECD, the committee issued a final report rejecting the agreement and strongly criticizing the Treasury Department's conduct of the negotiations.

Recognizing the continued push for investment rules to be negotiated at the WTO would continue even with the failure of the MAI negotiations and the collapse of the Seattle WTO ministerial meeting in the fall of 1999, NGOs in Australia continued to coordinate their efforts; and in February 2000 these groups created the Australian Fair Trade and Investment Network (AFTINET). The network includes a broad range of over 50 organizations (many of them peak associations or networks themselves) and another one hundred individuals. Members include trade unions, environmental, developmental and advocacy organizations, as well as faith groups such as the Uniting Church. AFTINET itself maintains regular contact through Public Citizen in the United States, with a range of international groups and networks, including those in Canada discussed above.

The network, however, is not linked directly to political parties. The Australian Labor Party, in power during the negotiations of the MAI, and a proponent in the 1980s of "economic rationalism" (the Australian term for neo-liberalism) has had, for example, an ambiguous relationship to the critics of globalization. This is best reflected in the case of the Australian Manufacturing Workers Union (AMWU), which has increasingly focused on the link between the global and the local, especially since Seattle, and has pushed the Labor Party to adopt a policy of "fair trade not free trade" which was rejected at the party conference in Hobart in 2000. The union has increasingly distanced itself from the party and worked more closely with broad networks such as AFTINET in recognition that many of the union's concerns in Australia are tied to globalization.

Like Canadian NGOs, Australian NGOs have increasingly focused on opposition to a new trade negotiating round and to the services negotiations. Like Canadian groups, they have not been reluctant to engage in direct action, even as groups continue with the traditional processes of lobbying, meeting with officials, and making submissions to parliamentary committees. Perhaps most controversial were the series of demonstrations and blockades which occurred in September 2000 when the World Economic Forum held its Asia-Pacific Economic Summit in Melbourne just prior to the Sydney Olympics. Demonstrators using civil disobedience were able to block some participants from entering the meeting. This action was accompanied by confrontations with the police, arrests and some property damage. While these confrontational tactics have raised some concerns, most NGOs recognize the need to accommodate a range of tactics within the movement. Protests, sponsored by a broad coalition of groups, were also organized to coincide with the final day of the Doha meetings and a major meeting of an international union federation (13 November 2001) in Sydney. In the case of services, many NGOs have been involved in a broad public education campaign, providing input into departmental consultations and participating in hearings before JSCOT.

Australian NGOs believe that they have made some progress in moving critiques of globalization out of the margins as reflected by an increase in mainstream media coverage, a major achievement given the high concentration of corporate media and the dominance of "economic rationalism." The battle not to be marginalized is constant, however, given that, unlike Canada, the extreme right-wing nationalist party, One Nation, has been part of the opposition to both the MAI and globalization. NGOs are careful to point out that their critique is of a particular version of corporate globalization. Groups have largely eschewed the partisan process because both the governing coalition and the Labor opposition have embraced trade and investment liberalization even though Labor has come out more strongly for exempting education and health services from the GATS negotiations.

What role has technology played in the development of these NGO networks and in their activities? Many of the NGOs we interviewed saw ICTs as a critical tool in their work. First, the technology allows for the maintenance of links with other groups and networks both globally and within Australia. Much of the work of groups such as AFTINET is conducted by e-mail and listervs because of the lower costs and speed. In addition, groups have used Web sites to disseminate large amounts of information on WTO negotiations quickly and cheaply via newsletters and bulletins. Listservs provide fast and inexpensive ways to alert network members of new developments and to share strategy. Some concerns do remain about the digital divide, both generational and regional, especially in areas outside the cities which are not well served with high-speed Internet connections. In the traditional activities of lobbying and submitting briefs, the technology has facilitated collaboration by allowing small numbers of staff (AFTINET has, for example, only one policy person and a half-time support position) to produce and manage large amounts of information. The technology allows many organizations with fairly limited resources to undertake and coordinate activities more easily. For a number of organizations and faith-based groups such as the Uniting Church (an AFTINET member) the Internet has facilitated closer connections with other networks of churches and women's organizations in Asia allowing groups to build a southern perspective and critique into their work on globalization.

Impact

What has been the impact on the trade-policy process? The trade-policy consultation process in Australia prior to the MAI and Seattle looked very much like the Canadian process, although perhaps even more closed and restricted. It consisted mainly of a Trade Policy Advisory Committee (much like ITAC) composed of appointed business and industry sector representatives. Consultations with states and territories took place once a year at the ministerial level and twice a year at the official level. Environmental and labour concerns received little hearing well into the late 1990s as reflected in Treasury's vigorous opposition to addressing these issues in even the most minimal way at the MAI negotiations and the exclusion of organizational representatives from Australia's delegation to Seattle.

Since that time, however, there has been an increase in efforts to consult more broadly, although the impact of these consultations on trade policy remains open to question. Two sets of consultations were initiated in 2001. Early in the year, the JSCOT began an inquiry into Australia's relations with the WTO with fairly broad terms of reference. These consultations included public hearings, panel discussions, and a call for submissions.

The Department of Foreign Affairs and Trade (DFAT) also launched consultations on the question of Australia's approach to Doha and on the services negotiations. The trade minister, Mark Vaile, announced the creation of a new WTO Advisory Panel to provide input on the upcoming ministerial meeting. At the urging of groups like AFTINET the department decided to hold meetings with groups in Sydney and Melbourne in June and July 2001. A Doha Web site was also established by the department and an electronic newsletter for about 400 interested groups was created. The parliamentary and departmental consultations are not seen in competition with one another. This contrasts to Canada where parliamentarians remain wary of officials consulting civil society. DFAT officials see the requirement for them to consult flowing out of the statute and the committee on treaties.

How effective have these consultations been? NGOs remain sceptical. While they concede that there has been a change in departmental attitudes from that of outright dismissal of their concerns to a polite hearing, they are sceptical that policy will change and point to the composition of the new WTO advisory committee — largely business representatives and a few academics. They do, however, avail themselves of every opportunity to raise their concerns.

A similar attitude is taken to the work of JSCOT where they recognize that while it provides an opportunity to air their concerns in public, the reality is that both the governing coalition and the opposition Australian Labor Party are strongly supportive of further liberalization through the WTO. Nothing could have more clearly illustrated this support than the submission to JSCOT by Peter Cook, Labor's shadow trade critic. He criticized the committee's terms of reference and the "globophobic" NGOs and pointed to "the great good that the WTO has done"(Cook 2000). For many NGOs, the hearings provide one more opportunity to drive home the extent of both their and the public's concerns, which then become easily accessible to the public on the parliamentary Web site.

DFAT officials view the consultations slightly more positively, and claim that the process has been useful in increasing their awareness of the sensitivity of service issues and concerns about protesting the domestic right to regulate. NGO input, they claim, moderates their natural bias to liberalization and provides the minister with a range of views informing the context of the negotiations. They are wary, however, of how much weight to give groups, even if they make a lot of noise, when it is not clear whom they represent. Officials also view consultations, like the Web site, as a way to get their message out and educate the public.

Consultations have not gone as far, or been as extensive in Australia as they have been in Canada despite the presence of JSCOT. Australian consultations, however, it could be argued, are on a firmer legislative footing in contrast to Canadian consultations which remain much at the discretion of, and in control of, the government of the day. For many NGOs in both countries the broader goal is a long-term one of raising public awareness and changing broader attitudes. A critical part of this effort is the sharing of information and the exposure of negotiations and rule-making at the WTO to the light of day — a process that the Internet greatly facilitates.

THE EUROPEAN UNION

The complex dynamic between globally articulated local networks challenging globalization and the national trade-policy processes of Canada and Australia are paralleled within the European Union. The EU provides an interesting dimension for two reasons. It is one of the most important players in multilateral trade negotiations and is a strong advocate of the WTO. In 1998, as the world's largest trading bloc, the EU accounted for 21 percent of global merchandise exports (Wood and Yesilada 2002, 181). Second, the EU, unlike Australia and Canada, lacks a recognizable government. As Richardson notes "European governance, rather than government, is clearly the appropriate label for a system of policy-making which displays a considerable diffusion of power" (2001, 97). However, while the EU lacks a party-based government "the familiar institutional paraphernalia of the modern state have emerged" (ibid., 97) These new policy-making institutions have provided new opportunity structures for networked NGOs that have attempted to fill the advocacy void left by the absence of party government (Warleigh 2000). The Internet has played an important role in facilitating this process. Moreover, the EU, in need of democratic legitimacy, is encouraging this relationship with civil society organizations. In fact, the dialogue between civil society organizations and the EU in the area of trade-policy negotiations is emblematic of the growing symbiosis between the EU and European civil society organizations in general.

This trade-policy process is very different from Canada and Australia. Article 113 [133] of the Treaty of Rome (1958) establishing the European Community granted exclusive competence to the Community (Union) in the management of external trade (Bretherton and Vogler 1999, 46), while in the area of services, intellectual property, and investment, member states retain internal competence. The European Commission, as the executive body of the EU acting through its Directorate General (DG) Trade, conducts the actual negotiations but does not formulate its own mandate. Rather, the Commission proposes and the Council of Ministers, an intergovernmental body of ministers of state (in this instance, of foreign ministers), approves the mandate. When it comes to any particular WTO ministerial meeting, the Commission in the form of DG Trade and its commissioner represents the position of the WTO. It is at this time that trade ministers meet at the Council "where they are able to adjust the Commission's negotiating mandate 'on the spot'" (ibid., 51). Critical to understanding at this point is that under Article 113 [133] the European Parliament has no competence, no recognized legal role in the negotiation or conclusion of trade agreements.

The weakness of the European Parliament in the overall process poses special problems for the Commission. Lacking democratic legitimacy, the Commission must mobilize political support for its actions. This provides a special opportunity for NGOs to represent the sectoral concerns of citizens regarding trade negotiations and a link between the citizen at the local, regional, and nation-state levels, and the European level. Indeed, the weakness of representative institutions in Europe, including the European Parliament and political parties presents a severe problem of democracy and agency. According to Eric Dacheux "Plus l'Europe devient concrète, moin le processus politique d'unification rencontre de soutien. Paradox qui, dans une démocratie ne peut se maintenir durablement" (2001, 168).

Increasingly, Dacheux argues, associational networks are filling the void in terms of advocacy, agency, and citizen participation. According to Dacheux these associational networks, assisted by informational technologies, are playing a fundamental role in the construction of Europe. Networks of European associations are articulating concerns of citizens between the local and national levels and the wider European political community. The involvement of interest groups also contributes to the shift in sovereignty from the nation-state to the Union (Richardson 2001, 106). The EU, Richardson maintains, is increasingly proving to be an attractive venue for all interest groups — whether they are big firms or groups with less resources such as women's organizations (ibid.).[13] In turn, as the EU intervenes more in the life of Europeans but continues to lack democratic legitimacy "elles cherchent maintenant à instaurer un 'dialogue civil'" (Dacheux 2001, 179).

Prior to 1998 there was little of what came to be called a civil society dialogue on trade policy. Until 1998 DG Trade officials, not unlike their Canadian and Australian counterparts, were able to carry on trade negotiations insulated from civil society within the traditional hierarchical bureaucratic model of trade specialists. At the WTO ministerial conference in Singapore in 1996 few European NGOs were represented and no dialogue with civil society took place prior to the conference (Raphael 2001). The only voice for Europe was the Commission. More NGOs were represented in Geneva at the Second Ministerial Conference in 1998.

The defeat of the MAI in 1998 signaled a change in the relationship between the Commission and European civil society organizations. By September 1998, aware that it had a civil society problem, the Commission managed to convince the Council of Ministers that both a process of engaging civil society organizations along with a dedicated office were needed. Consultation with civil society organizations began on an ad hoc basis under Commissioner Sir Leon Brittain in late 1998 and, prior to the Seattle ministerial two more meetings took place under the direction of Brittain's replacement, Pascal Lamy, who became commissioner, DG Trade in September 1999.

The year 1999 was one of adaptation for both DG Trade and European NGOs. By then Commission officials had realized that a dialogue with civil society was required. DG Trade opted for a definition of civil society that included business organizations, a decision that has rankled non-business NGOs. Following their inability to influence events in Geneva in 1998, non-business NGOs began to organize and strategize utilizing already existing networks and the Internet, e-mail, and listservs, to coordinate their activities. Most importantly for the civil society dialogue that followed, NGOs began to cluster with similar NGOs in a series of networks that collaborated to formulate positions on issues of globalization of particular interest to them — all of this facilitated by ICTs.

What has emerged is a clustering of four large functional networks in the areas of the environment, social affairs, development, and human rights that operate at different levels of governance in Europe to influence EU decision-making. For example, the Green G8 is a federation of the eight largest environmental organizations and networks in Europe with a total membership of 20 million people, 5 percent of the population of the EU. Within the Green G8 are such organizations as Friends of the Earth Europe which, in turn, is not only a network of organizations in Europe but is also integrated into global environmental networks. Within each network are independent groups with thousands of local groups.[14] The Green G8 coordinates its activities with other networks such as the Social Platform, which includes almost all European social NGOs, 1,700 organizations and associations in all, at the local, national, regional, and European levels (Platform of European Social NGOs 2001a). For the Social Platform, the process of banding together in large groupings had already begun in 1995. By 2001 it was, in effect, a network of 37 networks in Europe. It includes such prominent organizations as SOLIDAR, an alliance of NGOs linked to independent trade unions emphasizing labour and social rights. These large networks coordinate their activities through contact persons in key NGOs.

In Seattle, while a number of these NGOs had representatives on the official EU delegation, a price they had to accept was the decision of the Commission to include business representatives as civil society representatives. In addition to the Commission, 9 of the 15 member states of the EU also had NGO representatives. While the process of institutionalizing the civil society dialogue had begun in Seattle it was informal, and it was not until after Seattle that the civil society dialogue on trade began to take a more formal and coherent form.

Seattle represented a turning point for the Commission, if not for the non-business NGOs. Pascal Lamy, for example, recognized that he had a "civil society problem," that the process of negotiating trade had to be more transparent and inclusive of civil society, and that the concerns of developing countries had to be recognized (European Commission. DG Trade 2001*a*). After Seattle, the DG Trade initiated a "civil society dialogue" which included dedicating resources and personnel.

The dialogue process is highly structured (ibid., 2001*b*). Acting as intermediary between DG Trade and civil society organizations is the Contact Group composed of both business and non-business NGOs. The members of the Contact Group are selected by their constituencies and they help with the circulation of information to their respective organizations. Together with DG Trade, the Contact Group ensures coordination in the running of issue groups which include such topics as trade in services, access to health, and WTO reform and transparency. Groups meet in Brussels, up to six times a year. Some participants are reimbursed by DG Trade for their travel expenses. In 2000, discussion concluded on the first series of issue groups and in 2001, a new series focusing on the fourth ministerial meeting in Doha, Qatar began. Meetings of the issue groups are complemented by two general meetings a year which are chaired by Lamy, where organizations discuss reports of the issue groups meetings, the organization of the dialogue itself, and future topics. Issue groups and general meetings are further complemented by Internet dialogues, "chats" organized on a regular basis to facilitate a wider debate with European citizens. DG Trade also provides information on the dialogue on an extensive and detailed Web site. For their part, NGOs attempted to strengthen their voices in the dialogue by forming a steering group and selecting representatives to influence the EU on a variety of issues, including development, the environment, and social affairs. Many NGOs have prepared and submitted papers on topics such as WTO reform as part of their input into the formation of the official EU position on the topic.

Impact

Assessment of the dialogue process is mixed. In general DG Trade is given high marks for its efforts to inform and consult with civil society, for emphasizing development issues, and for its support of access for NGOs and civil society at the ministerial meeting in Doha (SOLIDAR 2001). Beyond this, however, many non-business NGOs have expressed frustration with the dialogue process and are critical of the large number of business groups participating. They argue that the dialogue was nothing more than an exercise in public relations. In an open letter to Pascal Lamy, the "Seattle to Brussels Network" complained that "many members of organizations ... are of the opinion that participation in these consultations is pointless and even counterproductive" (Seattle to Brussels Network 2001). As a result, they claimed, many NGOs were dropping out of the dialogue process. The Commission has acknowledged a "dialogue fatigue" and that attendance at issue groups is not as high as anticipated. The Commission also admits that it is hard to pinpoint the impact of NGOs on the positions the Commission takes on the WTO (Interview, DG Trade, November 2001).

Yet the Commission argues that there have been positive changes. For example, the mindset of DG Trade officials has changed and they acknowledge that trade negotiations are more than a state-to-state affair. The Commission also has its doubts about the dialogue. They question the democratic credentials of groups and how representative of civil society many participants in the dialogue are. They point out that it has been difficult to get NGOs outside Brussels to attend meetings even with reimbursement of costs. DG Trade officials question NGO knowledge of trade matters, seeing it more as a critique than a substantive understanding. Finally, DG Trade expressed frustration that the diversity of opinion among NGOs make it difficult for NGOs to take ownership of the dialogue process (ibid.).

Both civil society organizations and DG Trade noted the limitations of the Internet in relation to the trade-policy process. Both use the Internet extensively for disseminating information and clearly it has been indispensable for facilitating the activities of the four large functional networks of NGOs. Many NGOs and officials also acknowledge that they are suffering from information overload, particularly as a result of increases in e-mail and the expectations of rapid turnaround. The inefficiency and ineffectiveness of e-mail was leading FOE Europe, for example, to place greater emphasis on telephone conferencing.

While the dialogue will continue it is clear that this process has its limitations, in particular, an inability to bestow democratic legitimacy and accountability. Both the Commission and NGOs have expressed a desire for the European Parliament to have competency over trade. The Commission argues that the European Parliament should have a co-decision-making role in trade. Lamy has acknowledged the problem, stating that "What people overlook is the democratic deficit in the European trade policy, the fact that the European Parliament is excluded from trade policy. That democratic deficit is unacceptable" (Lamy 2000). For both the Commission and NGOs, the European Parliament having greater competency over trade policy would have a number of advantages. For the Commission, it would provide a counterweight to the Council of Ministers representing individual states and would, perhaps, over time mean that the Commission would only have to work with the Parliament on trade policy. For NGOs, European Parliament involvement could provide more effective oversight of the trade-policy process than they have been able to provide themselves and would represent an improvement of the oversight provided by individual states.

Clearly in the case of the EU, networking has been an integral part of the process of dialogue with civil society mirroring the institutional structure of the EU and the Commission's perception, post-Seattle, of a need to bring legitimacy to the process via a more inclusive and open dialogue with NGOs. NGOs wishing to influence trade policy have no choice but to be part of the broader European networks described above. ICTs have played a key role in this process, reflecting both the availability of the technology (37.7 percent of households as of 2001 were connected to the Internet[15]) and the size and scale of the groups involved. Although the trade-policy process has changed and may change further if a greater role for the European Parliament is achieved, the question remains as to how much of a substantive difference it will make to policy itself.

CONCLUSION

Our argument at the outset of this chapter was that ICTs play a major role in the development of transational networks linking the global and the local, allowing a wide array of NGOs an increased capacity to challenge globalization and attempt to influence trade and investment agreements. The three cases we have examined — Canada, Australia, and the EU — illustrate the extent to which this is so.

In the case of Canada, groups were able to build on existing national networks growing out of the battle over continental integration and with the MAI placing those campaigns into a broader global context where linking, strategizing with other NGOs, and sharing information proved to be critical. In the case of Australia, technology allowed groups less networked to move quickly in the case of the MAI to form a national network linked to the global campaign which has continued to develop a critique of Australian trade and investment policy. In the case of the EU, ICTs have been integral to the development of huge functional networks of NGOs across Europe.

ICTs have played a key role, particularly in facilitating the movement and sharing of large amounts of detailed technical information and have improved the ability of groups to coordinate and strategize, often in rapid response to international developments. This technology has also been a key part of the creation of open, horizontal, and decentralized networks and thus facilitated the rapid moblization of a wide array of groups using a variety of tactics.

Groups functioned both globally and locally, becoming increasingly hybrid organizations. For many groups it is only by inserting themselves into transnational networks that they feel they are effective locally. By facilitating the sharing of information on negotiations, often very technical and complicated, ICTs have gone some way toward levelling the playing field for NGOs in terms of their capacity to access and use information within the policy process. However, it would be naïve to suggest that information alone can transform imbalances of power and influence. What it has done, however, is provide part of the means by which networks of NGOs have been able to challenge the prevailing discourse of trade liberalization and globalization.

The efforts of NGOs have developed alongside traditional trade policy even as NGOs have played a role in re-shaping that policy process to make it somewhat more inclusive and transparent. The Canadian and Australian governments and the EU Commission have responded to what they clearly see as a challenge to the legitimacy of trade policy by engaging in dialogue, increasingly using the Internet to disseminate information on the negotiations. In all three cases, moreover, representative institutions, historically marginalized in the trade policy-making process, have been turned to as well as a way of addressing legitimacy.

The result, however, has not been, at least to date, a substantive shift in the content of trade policy. The EU, Australia, and Canada continue to zealously support further trade liberalization in areas such as services and the new round of WTO negotiations. However, they have recognized that the relentless criticism from NGOs has increased public awareness and required at least some effort to consult more widely to address legitimacy questions. Moreover, the determined attitude of many developing countries required a shift, at least in rhetoric, to one of stressing the economic development benefits to the south of the new round of trade negotiations. NGOs, however, have viewed all these efforts somewhat sceptically. The increased transparency and the opening of a dialogue have not diminished criticisms of policy or the willingness of many activists to continue to engage in contentious politics around trade issues even as they engage with officials in the consultation process.

Notes

We wish to acknowledge the funding assistance of the Kahanoff Foundation via the Nonprofit Sector Research Initiative of the School of Policy Studies at Queen's University and the research assistance of Janet Ilin Mou.

[1] The first major article in a Canadian newspaper dates from April 1997, and is a direct result of the leak and Web publication of the draft.

[2] A core group of organizations was created by cross-referencing a number of sources, including the lists of NGOs officially registered for the Seattle WTO meeting, participants in major alternative events such as teach-ins, those organization most frequently listed as links on Web sites and organizations listed by those we interviewed as key participants in campaigns. The list includes broad advocacy organizations (10), business organizations (8), trade unions (7) environmental and sustainability groups (13) human rights and development (7), educational, research or training institutes (15) and farmer/peasant organizations (3).

[3] An environmental SAGIT was also added which includes representatives from organizations such as the International Institute for Sustainable Development and the Sierra Club, alongside the BCNI, and Proctor and Gamble. How this relates to the mining and forest products SAGIT is somewhat unclear.

[4] As of October the total number of registered groups was just over 550. With only one delegate each permitted this is significantly less than the over 2,000 delegates (to a maximum of four per NGO)permitted in Seattle.

[5] Initially the members of the CFWTO included the Canadian Labour Congress, the Council of Canadians, the Sierra Club of Canada, West Coast Environmental Law Association, the Canadian Environmental Law Association and the Polaris Institute.

[6]Based on interviews with officials in Ottawa in February and May 2001.

[7]The two environmental representatives were David Runnalls of the International Institute for Sustainable Development and Elizabeth May of the Sierra Club of Canada.

[8]Dennis Stairs has included these meetings as examples of trade consultations in a monograph on foreign policy consultations. However, having attended these meetings, which were edited descriptions of the day's events, followed by a question and answer session, the notion that they provided any real opportunity for groups to have input is questionable. They more accurately reflected a desire of Canadian ministers and officials to show a willingness to share information, a laudable effort nonetheless.

[9]DFAIT, Statistics on Web site hits, provided to the authors in April 2001.

[10]Based on interviews with a number of NGOs in Ottawa, February 2001.

[11]Based on interviews with DFAIT officials involved in the services public consultations in April 2001.

[12]The following section is based on a series of interviews with NGO representatives, trade officials and parliamentarians in Sydney, Canberra, and Melbourne in August 2001.

[13]Interest groups, not NGOs, is the term preferred by Richardson.

[14]This section draws on interviews with FOE Europe and SOLIDAR in November 2001.

[15]Figures are from the e-Europe Benchmarking Report as cited in Giles Scott-Smith 2002). While below the Canadian levels, this represents a huge increase from 18 percent in 2000.

References

Anheier, H.K. and L.M. Salamon, eds. 1998. *The Nonprofit Sector in the Developing World.* Manchester, UK: Manchester University Press.

Arquilla, J. and D. Ronfeldt, eds. 2001. *Networks and Netwars: The Future of Terror, Crime and Militancy.* Santa Monica, CA: The Rand Corporation.

Australia. Department of Foreign Affairs and Trade. 2000. *Australia's Relationship to the WTO.* Submission to the Joint Standing Committee on Treaties.

Babe, R.E. 2000. *Canadian Communications Thought: Ten Foundational Writers.* Toronto: University of Toronto Press.

Bach, J. 2001. "Technologies of Civil Society: NGOs and Interactive Technology in Postsocialist East Central Europe." Paper for International Studies Association Conference, Chicago, Illinois, February.

Bretherton, C. and J. Vogler. 1999. *The European Union as a Global Actor.* London: Routledge.

Bunch, C. *et al.* 2001. "International Networking for Women's Human Rights," in *Global Citizen Action*, ed. Edwards and Gaventa, pp. 217-30.

Cameron, M. 1998. *To Walk Without Fear.* Toronto: Oxford University Press.

Calabrese, A. 1999. "Communication and the End of Sovereignty?" *The Journal of Policy, Regulation and Strategy for Telecommunications Information and Media* 1 (4):313-26.

Capling, A. 2001. *Australia and the Global Trade System.* Oakleigh: Cambridge Press.

Castells, M. 1996. *The Information Age: Economy, Society and Culture*, Volume I: *The Rise of Network Society.* Oxford: Blackwell Publishers.

_____ 1997. *The Information Age: Economy, Society and Culture*, Volume II: *The Power of Identity.* Oxford: Blackwell Publishers.

Civil Society Declaration. 2001. *Our World is Not for Sale WTO: Sink or Shrink.* Available at <www.canadians.org>.

Cook, P. 2000. Letter to Grant Harbison, Joint Standing Committee on Treaties, Australia, 28 August.

Cox, R. 1999. "Civil Society at the Turn of the Millennium: Prospects for an Alternative World Order," *Review of International Studies* 25 (1):3-28.

Dacheux, E. 2001. "Les association dans l'espace européen" in *Association, démocratie, et société civile*, ed. J.-L. Laville *et al.* Paris: Éditions La Découverte, pp. 165-82.

Edwards, M. 2000. *NGO Rights and Responsibilities.* London: The Foreign Policy Centre.

Edwards, M. and J. Gaventa, eds. 2001. *Global Citizen Action.* Boulder: Lynne Reinner.

Ekos Research Associates. 2001. *Canadian Attitudes Toward International Trade.* Ottawa: Ekos Research.

European Commission. DG Trade. 2001*a*. "The Commercial Policy of the European Union," June. At <http://europa.eu.int/comm/trade>.

_____ 2001*b*. "Towards Sustainable Trade," January. At <http://europa.eu.int/comm/trade>.

Florini, A.M., ed. 2000. *The Third Force: The Rise of Transnational Civil Society.* Washington DC: Carnegie Endowment for International Peace.

Foster, J. 1999. *Whose World Is it Anyway? Civil Society, the United Nations and the Multilateral Future.* Ottawa: The United Nations Association of Canada.

Geser, H. 2000. "On the Function and Consequences of the Internet for Social Movements and Voluntary Associations," *Sociology in Switzerland.* Online publications Social Movements, Pressure Groups and Political Parties, April.

Goodman, J. 2000. "Stopping the Juggernaut: The Anti-MAI Campaign," in *Stopping the Juggernaut: Public Interest versus the Multilateral Agreement on Investment*, ed. J. Goodman and P. Ranald. Annandale, NSW: Pluto Books of Australia.

Harper, C. 2001. "Do Facts Matter? NGOs, Research and International Advocacy," in *Global Citizen Action*, ed. Edwards and Goventa, pp. 247-58.

Held, D. 1999. *Global Transformation*. Stanford: Stanford University Press.

Hobe, S. 1998. "Global Challenges to Statehood: The Increasingly Important Role of Nongovernmental Organizations," at <http://www.globalpolicy.org/ngos/role/intro/def/2000/chaleng.htm>.

Inglehart, R. 1999. "Postmodernization Erodes Respect for Authority but Increases Support for Democracy," in *Critical Citizens: Global Support for Democratic Governance*, ed. P. Norris. Oxford: Oxford University Press.

Jordan, L. and P. van Tuijl. 1998. "Political Responsibility in NGO Advocacy: Exploring Emerging Shapes of Global Democracy," Euforic Page, One World Online. At <http://www.oneworld.org/euforic/novib/novib1.htm>.

Keck, M.E. and K. Sikkink. 1998. *Activists Beyond Borders: Advocacy Networks in International Politics*. Ithaca: Cornell University Press.

Keohane, R. and J. Nye. 2000a. "The Club Model of Ministerial Cooperation and Problems of Democratic Legitimacy." Paper presented at the American Political Science Association Convention, Washington, DC, September.

_____ 2000b. "Globalization: What's New? What's Not (And So What?) *Foreign Policy* (Spring):104-19.

_____, eds. 2000c. *Governance in a Globalizing World*. Washington, DC: The Brookings Institution.

Kilby, C. 2000. "Sovereignty and NGOs," in *Global Institutions and Local Empowerment*, ed. K. Stiles. New York: St. Martin's Press, pp. 48-65.

Krajewski, M. 2001. "Democratic Legitimacy and Constitutional Perspectives on WTO Law," *Journal of World Trade Law* 35 (1):167-86.

Krasner, S. 1999. *Sovereignty: Organized Hypocrisy*. Princeton: University Press.

Lamy, P. 2000. "NGO Dialogue: Introductory Remarks," Brussels, 23 November. Available at <http://www.europa.eu.int/comm/trade/speeches_articles/spla39_eu.htm>.

Platform of European Social NGOs. 2001a. "About Us." At <http://www.socialplatform.org/AboutUs.asp?SectionID=6>.

_____ 2001b. "NGO Report of DG Trade Contact Group Meeting." At <http://www.socialplatform.org>.

Raphael, M. 2001. "Civil Society's Influence on the European Union's Position Toward the World Trade Organization." Available from <www.solidar.org>.

Richardson, J. 2001. "Policy-Making in the EU: Familiar Ambitions in Unfamiliar Settings," in *From the Nation State to Europe*, ed. A. Hanon and V. Wright. New York: Oxford University Press, pp. 97-117.

Rosenau, J. 2001. "Three Overlapping Revolutions: One Neutral, All Powerful." Paper presented at the annual meeting of the International Studies Association," Chicago, February.

Salamon, L.M. and H. Anheier. 1999. *Global Civil Society: Dimensions of the Non-Profit Sector.* Baltimore, MD: Johns Hopkins Center for Civil Society Studies.

Salamon, L.M., *et al.* 1999. *Global Civil Society.* Manchester, UK: Manchester University Press.

Scott, M. 2001. "Danger----Landmines! NGO-Government Collaboration in the Ottawa Process," in *Global Citizen Action*, ed. Edwards and Gaventa, pp. 121-34.

Scott-Smith, G. 2002. "European Citizenship, Social Cohesion and Network Society." Paper presented at the annual meeting of the International Studies Association, New Orleans, March.

Seattle to Brussels Network. 2001. "Open letter to Trade Commissioner Lamy Concerning the European Commission's 'Civil Society' Dialogues on the WTO," May. At <http://www.foeeurope.org/trade/wto/Open_letter_to_Lamy.htm>.

Seigel, A. 1996. *Politics and the Media in Canada.* Toronto: McGraw-Hill Ryerson.

Sinclair, S. 2000. *GATS: How the World Trade Organization's New "Services" Negotiations Threaten Democracy.* Ottawa: Canadian Centre for Policy Alternatives.

Smith, J. 2001a. "Global Civil Society: Transnational Social Movement Organizations and Social Capital," in *Beyond Tocqueville: Civil Society and Social Capital in Comparative Perspective*, ed. R. Edwards, M. Foley and M. Diani. Hanover: NH: University Press of New England.

_____ 2001b. "Globalizing Resistance: The Battle of Seattle and the Future of Social Movements," *Mobilization* 6 (1):1-20.

Smith, P.J and E. Smythe. 1999. "Globalization, Citizenship and Technology: The MAI Meets the Internet," *Canadian Foreign Policy* 7 (2):83-106.

Smythe, E. and P.J. Smith. 2002. "New Technologies and Networks of Resistance," in *Cyber-Diplomacy*, ed. E. Potter. Montreal and Kingston: McGill-Queen's University Press, pp. 48-82.

SOLIDAR. 2001. "EU Back NGO Concerns Over NGO Access at Qatar WTO Meeting," February. Available at <www.solidar.org>.

Taylor, C. 1990. "Modes of Civil Society," *Public Culture* 3 (1):95-118.

Tocqueville, A. de. 1835. *Democracy in America*, Vol. 1, ed. J.P. Mayer. New York: Anchor Books, Doubleday and Co. (1969 edition).

Wapner, P. 2001. "Horizontal Politics: Transcendental Environmental Activism and Global Cultural Change." Paper presented at the annual meeting of the International Studies Association, Chicago, February.

Warkentin, C. 2001. *Reshaping World Politics: NGOs, the Internet and Global Civil Society.* Lanham, MD: Rowman and Littlefield.

Warleigh, A. 2000. "The Hustle: Citizenship Practice, NGOs and 'Policy Coalitions' in the European Union—The Cases of Auto Oil, Drinking Water and Unit Pricing," *Journal of European Public Policy* 7 (2):229-43.

Wood, D.M and B.A. Yesilada. 2002. *The Emerging European Union*, 2d ed. New York: Addison-Wesley.

Contributors

Donald Abelson, Professor, Department of Political Science, University of Western Ontario

James Agarwal, Associate Professor, Haskayne School of Business, University of Calgary

Kathy L. Brock, Associate Professor and Head of Public Policy and the Third Sector, School of Policy Studies, Queen's University

Ian Brodie, Associate Professor, Department of Political Science, University of Western Ontario

Ann Capling, Department of Political Science, University of Melbourne

Miriam Lapp, Assistant Professor, Department of Political Science, University of Western Ontario

Georges leBel, Professeur et avocat, Université du Québec à Montréal

Heidi MacDonald, Assistant Professor, Department of History, University of Lethbridge

David Malloy, Professor, Faculty of Kinesiology and Health Studies, University of Regina

Kim Richard Nossal, Professor and Head, Department of Political Studies, Queen's University

Susan D. Phillips, Professor, School of Public Policy and Administration and Director, Centre for Voluntary Sector Research and Development, Carleton University

A. Paul Pross, Professor Emeritus, School of Public Administration, Dalhousie University

Ken Rasmussen, Professor, Faculty of Administration, University of Regina

Peter J. Smith, Professor, Department of Political Science, Athabasca University

Elizabeth Smythe, Associate Professor, Department of Political Science, Concordia University College of Alberta

Kernaghan R. Webb, Adjunct Professor, Department of Law and School of Public Policy and Administration, Carleton University

Mary E. Wiktorowicz, Assistant Professor, School of Health Policy and Management, Atkinson Faculty of Liberal and Professional Studies, York University

Queen's Policy Studies
Recent Publications

The Queen's Policy Studies Series is dedicated to the exploration of major policy issues that confront governments in Canada and other western nations. McGill-Queen's University Press is the exclusive world representative and distributor of books in the series.

School of Policy Studies

Beyond the National Divide: Regional Dimensions of Industrial Relations, Mark Thompson, Joseph B. Rose and Anthony E. Smith (eds.), 2003
Paper ISBN 0-88911-963-5 Cloth ISBN 0-88911-965-1

The Nonprofit Sector in Interesting Times: Case Studies in a Changing Sector, Kathy L. Brock and Keith G. Banting (eds.), 2003
Paper ISBN 0-88911-941-4 Cloth ISBN 0-88911-943-0

Clusters Old and New: The Transition to a Knowledge Economy in Canada's Regions, David A. Wolfe (ed.), 2003 Paper ISBN 0-88911-959-7 Cloth ISBN 0-88911-961-9

Knowledge, Clusters and Regional Innovation: Economic Development in Canada, 1 Adam Holbrook and David A. Wolfe (eds.), 2002
Paper ISBN 0-88911-919-8 Cloth ISBN 0-88911-917-1

Lessons of Everyday Law/Le droit du quotidien, Roderick Alexander Macdonald, 2002
Paper ISBN 0-88911-915-5 Cloth ISBN 0-88911-913-9

Improving Connections Between Governments and Nonprofit and Voluntary Organizations: Public Policy and the Third Sector, Kathy L. Brock (ed.), 2002
Paper ISBN 0-88911-899-X Cloth ISBN 0-88911-907-4

Governing Food: Science, Safety and Trade, Peter W.B. Phillips and Robert Wolfe (eds.), 2001 Paper ISBN 0-88911-897-3 Cloth ISBN 0-88911-903-1

The Nonprofit Sector and Government in a New Century, Kathy L. Brock and Keith G. Banting (eds.), 2001 Paper ISBN 0-88911-901-5 Cloth ISBN 0-88911-905-8

The Dynamics of Decentralization: Canadian Federalism and British Devolution, Trevor C. Salmon and Michael Keating (eds.), 2001 ISBN 0-88911-895-7

Institute of Intergovernmental Relations

Canada: The State of the Federation 2001, vol. 15, *Canadian Political Culture(s) in Transition,* Hamish Telford and Harvey Lazar (eds.), 2002
Paper ISBN 0-88911-863-9 Cloth ISBN 0-88911-851-5

Federalism, Democracy and Disability Policy in Canada, Alan Puttee (ed.), 2002
Paper ISBN 0-88911-855-8 Cloth ISBN 1-55339-001-6, ISBN 0-88911-845-0 (set)

Comparaison des régimes fédéraux, 2ᵉ éd., Ronald L. Watts, 2002
ISBN 1-55339-005-9

Health Policy and Federalism: A Comparative Perspective on Multi-Level Governance,
Keith G. Banting and Stan Corbett (eds.), 2001
Paper ISBN 0-88911-859-0 Cloth ISBN 1-55339-000-8, ISBN 0-88911-845-0 (set)

Disability and Federalism: Comparing Different Approaches to Full Participation,
David Cameron and Fraser Valentine (eds.), 2001
Paper ISBN 0-88911-857-4 Cloth ISBN 0-88911-867-1, ISBN 0-88911-845-0 (set)

Federalism, Democracy and Health Policy in Canada, Duane Adams (ed.), 2001
Paper ISBN 0-88911-853-1 Cloth ISBN 0-88911-865-5, ISBN 0-88911-845-0 (set)

John Deutsch Institute for the Study of Economic Policy

Framing Financial Structure in an Information Environment, Thomas J. Courchene and
Edwin H. Neave (eds.), Policy Forum Series no. 38, 2003
Paper ISBN 0-88911-950-3 Cloth ISBN 0-88922-948-1

*Towards Evidence-Based Policy for Canadian Education/Vers des politiques canadiennes
d'éducation fondées sur la recherche,* Patrice de Broucker and/et Arthur Sweetman (eds./dirs.),
2002 Paper ISBN 0-88911-946-5 Cloth ISBN 0-88911-944-9

*Money, Markets and Mobility: Celebrating the Ideas of Robert A. Mundell, Nobel Laureate
in Economic Sciences,* Thomas J. Courchene (ed.), 2002
Paper ISBN 0-88911-820-5 Cloth ISBN 0-88911-818-3

The State of Economics in Canada: Festschrift in Honour of David Slater,
Patrick Grady and Andrew Sharpe (eds.), 2001
Paper ISBN 0-88911-942-2 Cloth ISBN 0-88911-940-6

The 2000 Federal Budget: Retrospect and Prospect, Paul A.R. Hobson and
Thomas A. Wilson (eds.), Policy Forum Series no. 37, 2001
Paper ISBN 0-88911-816-7 Cloth ISBN 0-88911-814-0

Available from: McGill-Queen's University Press
c/o Georgetown Terminal Warehouses
34 Armstrong Avenue
Georgetown, Ontario L7G 4R9
Tel: (877) 864-8477
Fax: (877) 864-4272
E-mail: orders@gtwcanada.com